Advances in Written Text Analysis

Advances in Written Text Analysis provides an overview of a wide range of exciting and compatible approaches to written text analysis. The collection has all the advantages of coming from a single 'school of thought' – it consists solely of papers by present and past Birmingham staff and students, plus three 'honorary' colleagues M.A.K. Halliday, Peter Fries and Greg Myers, frequent and highly stimulating visitors. Lying behind the articles in this collection are several shared assumptions: that text analysis is best located within a Systematic view of language; that written text is essentially interactive; that it is imperative when analysing texts to be aware of the purpose and the process of creation; that any given text is just one of a series of possible textualizations and for that reason gains part of its meaning from what has *not* been said.

The book includes both classic and specially commissioned papers and the focus of the individual papers ranges from single words and individual expressions through the patterning of clauses to the organization of paragraphs, sections and complete texts. The examples are selected from a wide variety of subject areas, texts and text-types: pure and social science, academic and popular journals, newspapers and weekly magazines, literary and non-literary narratives.

Although each of the papers is concerned with fundamental research and can be read without reference to any of the others, the collection has been organized so that the first seven papers can be used as the basis of a course on written text analysis for advanced undergraduate and postgraduate students.

Advances in Written Text Analysis

Edited by Malcolm Coulthard

London and New York

First published 1994
by Routledge
11 New Fetter Lane, London EC4P 4EE

Simultaneously published in the USA and Canada
by Routledge
29 West 35th Street, New York, NY 10001

Reprinted 1998

Typeset in Times by
Ponting-Green Publishing Services, Chesham, Bucks

Printed and bound in Great Britain by
TJ International Ltd, Padstow, Cornwall

Printed on acid-free paper

British Library Cataloguing in Publication Data
A catalogue record for this book is available from the British
Library

Library of Congress Cataloging in Publication Data
A catalogue record for this book is available from the Library of Congress

ISBN 0–415–09520–4   0–415–09519–0 (pbk)

Contents

About the authors   vii

Preface   xi

Acknowledgements   xiii

1 **On analysing and evaluating written text**   1
Malcolm Coulthard

2 **Trust the text**   12
John McH. Sinclair

3 **Signalling in discourse: a functional analysis of a common discourse pattern in written and spoken English**   26
Michael Hoey

4 **Clause relations as information structure: two basic text structures in English**   46
Eugene Winter

5 **Predictive categories in expository text**   69
Angele Tadros

6 **Labelling discourse: an aspect of nominal-group lexical cohesion**   83
Gill Francis

7 **The text and its message**   102
Tim Johns

8 **The analysis of fixed expressions in text**   117
Rosamund Moon

9 **The construction of knowledge and value in the grammar of scientific discourse, with reference to Charles Darwin's *The Origin of Species***   136
M. A. K. Halliday

10 **Frames of reference: contextual monitoring and the interpretation of narrative discourse**   157
Catherine Emmott

11 **Inferences in discourse comprehension**   167
    Martha Shiro

12 **Narratives of science and nature in popularizing molecular
    genetics**   179
    Greg Myers

13 **Evaluation and organization in a sample of written academic
    discourse**   191
    Susan Hunston

14 **Genre analysis: an approach to text analysis for ESP**   219
    Tony Dudley-Evans

15 **On Theme, Rheme and discourse goals**   229
    Peter H. Fries

16 **Negatives in written text**   250
    Adriana Pagano

17 ***It, this* and *that***   266
    Michael McCarthy

18 **The structure of newspaper editorials**   276
    Adriana Bolívar

19 **On reporting reporting: the representation of speech in
    factual and factional narratives**   295
    Carmen Rosa Caldas-Coulthard

    References   309

About the authors

Adriana Bolívar is Senior Lecturer in English Language and Discourse Analysis at the Central University of Venezuela in Caracas. Her recent publications include 'The analysis of political discourse, with particular reference to Venezuelan political dialogue', *ESP Journal*, 1992 and, in Spanish, 'El encuentro de dos mundos a través del discurso' in *Homenaje a los quinientos años del descubrimiento*, 1993.

Carmen Rosa Caldas-Coulthard is Professor of English in the Graduate School of English at the Federal University of Santa Catarina, Brazil. Her most recent publications are the edited collection of articles on translation, *Tradução: teoria e prática*, 1991 and 'From discourse analysis to Critical Discourse Analysis', in *Techniques of Description*, 1993. An edited collection of articles entitled *Critical Discourse Analysis* is in preparation.

Malcolm Coulthard is Professor of English Language and Linguistics at the University of Birmingham. His recent publications include three edited collections, *Talking about Text*, 1986, *Discussing Discourse*, 1987, *Advances in Spoken Discourse Analysis*, 1992, and, in Portuguese, *Linguagem e sexo* and *Tradução: teoria e prática*, both published in 1991.

Tony Dudley-Evans is Senior Lecturer and Director of the English for Overseas Students Unit at the University of Birmingham. Among his recent publications are the edited collections, *Genre Analysis and ESP*, 1987; with W. Henderson, *The Language of Economics: the Analysis of Economics Discourse*, 1990; and with W. Henderson and R. Backhouse *Economics and Language*, 1992. He is currently co-editor of the journal *ESP*.

Catherine Emmott is Lecturer in English Language at the University of Glasgow. She has recently published 'Splitting the referent: an introduction to narrative enactors', in *Advances in Systemic Linguistics*, 1992. A book, *Mind Reading: Cognitive Modelling and Narrative Discourse*, is currently in preparation.

Gill Francis is a Senior Researcher working with the Cobuild project at the University of Birmingham on a corpus-based grammar. Among her recent publications are *Anaphoric Nouns*, 1987, 'Aspects of nominal group lexical cohesion', *Interface*, 1989, 'Noun group heads and clause structure', *Word*, 1991 and, with A. Kramer-Dahl 'Grammaticalising the medical case history', *Essays in Contextual Stylistics*, 1993.

Peter H. Fries is Professor of English and Linguistics at Central Michigan University. His major publications are *Tagmeme Sequences in the English Noun Phrase, On the Status of Theme in English: Arguments from Discourse, Towards an Understanding of Language: C. C. Fries in Perspective*, and *Lexico-Grammatical Patterns and the Interpretation of Texts*.

M. A. K. Halliday is Emeritus Professor of Linguistics at the University of Sydney. His major work has been in systemic functional grammar and its use in language description, text analysis and language education. Among his recent publications are *An Introduction to Functional Grammar*, 1985, *Spoken and Written Language*, 1989, and (with J. R. Martin) *Writing Science: Literacy and Discursive Power*, 1993.

Michael Hoey is Baines Professor of English Language at the University of Liverpool. His major publications are *Signalling in Discourse*, 1979, *On the Surface of Discourse*, 1983/91, *Patterns of Lexis in Text*, 1991, which was awarded the English Speaking Union's prize for the best book in Applied Linguistics in 1991, and the edited collection, *Data Description, Discourse*, 1993.

Susan Hunston is a Senior Researcher working with the Cobuild project at the University of Birmingham on a corpus-based grammar. Her 'Text in world and world in text' was published in the *Nottingham Linguistic Circular* in 1985 and 'Evaluation and ideology in scientific English' in *Register Analysis: Theory and Practice*, 1993.

Tim Johns is Lecturer in English Language in the English for Overseas Students Unit at the University of Birmingham. He is currently best known for his work on computer-assisted language learning and computational linguistics. He published *Computers and Language Learning* with J. Higgins in 1984, edited with P. King a special issue of the *ELRJ*, *Classroom Concordancing* in 1991 and a version of his concordancing programme, *Microconcordancer*, developed with M. Scott, appeared in 1993.

Michael McCarthy is Senior Lecturer in English Studies and Director of the Centre for English Language Education at the University of Nottingham. His recent publications include *Vocabulary*, 1990, *Discourse Analysis for Language Teachers*, 1991, and with R. Carter, *Vocabulary and Language Teaching*, 1988, and *Language as Discourse: Perspectives for Language Teaching*, 1993.

Rosamund Moon is an editorial manager of the Cobuild Project at the University of Birmingham. In addition to lexicographical work with both

HarperCollins and Oxford University Press, she has published several papers on meaning in dictionaries and on fixed expressions. She is currently carrying out research into the distribution and textual behaviour of fixed expressions in English.

Greg Myers is Lecturer in Linguistics and Modern English Language at the University of Lancaster. He is best known for his work on scientific writing. Among his recent publications are 'Every picture tells a story: illustrations in E. O. Wilson's *Sociobiology*', 1988, *Writing Biology: Texts in the Social Construction of Scientific Knowledge*, 1990 and *Words in Ads*, 1994.

Adriana Pagano teaches English and translation in the Department of Modern Languages at Faculdades Integradas Newton Paiva. She holds an MA in English Language and Literature from the Federal University of Santa Catarina and is currently working towards her PhD at the Federal University of Minas Gerais in Belo Horizonte, Brazil.

Martha Shiro is a Lecturer at the Central University of Venezuela in Caracas. She holds an MA in Applied Linguistics from the University of Birmingham. She has taught EFL courses, discourse analysis, grammar and psycholinguistics at postgraduate and undergraduate levels. Her research areas are language comprehension, grammar and discourse, areas in which she has published several articles.

John Sinclair is Professor of Modern English Language at the University of Birmingham and Editor-in-Chief of Cobuild Publications. His most recent books are *The Structure of Teacher Talk*, 1990, *Corpus Concordance, Collocation*, 1991, and the edited collections *Looking Up*, 1987 and, with M. Hoey and G. Fox, *Techniques of Description*, 1993. The Cobuild team produced *The BBC Dictionary* under his editorship in 1992.

Angele Tadros is Lecturer in English at the King Saud University in Riad. She is best known for her work on the analysis of expository text and in particular economics text. Her monograph *Prediction in Text* was published in 1985. For many years she was editor of the journal *ESPMENA*.

Eugene Winter is Honorary Research Fellow in the School of English at the University of Birmingham. His major publications are 'A clause relational approach to English texts', in *Instructional Science*, 1977, *Towards a Contextual Grammar of English*, 1982, and 'The notion of Unspecific versus Specific as one way of analysing a fund-raising letter', in *Diverse Analyses of a Fund-raising Letter*, 1992.

Preface

In putting together this collection of papers, *Advances in Written Text Analysis*, I have been very conscious of the fact that there is still no satisfactory single-author work, like *An Introduction to Discourse Analysis*, which can serve both as a student text-book and as a starting point for academic research. To date, teachers planning courses on text analysis have, of necessity, been forced to produce reading lists of difficult-to-find articles and any researchers looking for new approaches to analyse their chosen texts were forced to scour the journal indexes. For both these audiences this collection represents a major advance, although the decisions that I have taken quite deliberately and advisedly mean that the collection has all the advantages and disadvantages of coming from a single 'school of thought' – it consists solely of papers by present and past Birmingham staff and students, plus three 'honorary' colleagues, Michael Halliday, Peter Fries and Greg Myers, who have been frequent and much valued visitors and whose work has proved, over the years, to be a major stimulus.

Although English Language Research at the University of Birmingham is widely known for its work on the analysis of spoken discourse, it has rarely been recognized as a centre for work on written text, despite the fact that, paradoxically, during the 1980s much more staff and research student effort went into analysing written than spoken texts. I suspect this lack of recognition is due, in large part, to the fact that no comprehensive *method* of analysis emerged to parallel that in the area of spoken discourse, which other researchers could then either adopt or react against. There is, however, by now a substantial body of published research and analysis to which this collection gives easy access for the first time and which offers a series of exciting and compatible approaches to examining the creation, the structure and the nature of written text.

Lying behind the articles in the collection are several shared assumptions: that text analysis is best located within a Systemic view of language; that written text is essentially interactive; that it is imperative, when analysing texts, to be aware of both the purpose and the process of creation; and that any given text is just one of a series of possible textualizations which gains for that reason part of its meaning from what has not been said.

The volume has not been organized into sections simply because there seemed to be no obvious major classificatory boundaries; however, the papers have been sequenced carefully and deliberately to create topical coherence and progression for the reader who begins at the beginning and works systematically through to the end of the collection.

The first seven papers report approaches which have for several years formed the basis of Birmingham text analysis courses both at home and abroad: in themselves they constitute an excellent introduction to text analysis. All of these papers, except that by Johns, have been specifically written or rewritten and updated for this collection. The only major omissions from these introductory papers are discussions of lexical patterning and collocation analysis, because between the planning of the volume and its publication there appeared Michael Hoey's *Patterns of Lexis in Text* and John Sinclair's *Corpus Concordance Collocation*, to which the reader is referred.

The remaining twelve papers are more specialized analyses and applications. In text analysis courses we would refer our students selectively to this research after they had absorbed the initial framework and methodology.

The examples chosen by all the authors reflect, inevitably, their own interests and the types of text for which and from which they developed their descriptions, but none of the papers is text-bound – all the approaches to description reported here are appropriate to other types of text; indeed, the strength of the volume is that it offers so many different approaches, almost all of which can be applied to any chosen text.

Together these papers constitute an exciting, varied and stimulating collection and they will be read with great interest by anyone who has a commitment to the analysis of written text.

Malcolm Coulthard
Birmingham
March 1993

Acknowledgements

Chapter 1, 'On analysing and evaluating written text', is a substantially revised version of 'Evaluative text analysis', first published in R. Steele and T. Threadgold (eds), *Language Topics, Essays in Honour of Michael Halliday*, Amsterdam: Benjamins, 1987, 181–90.

Chapter 2, 'Trust the text', first appeared in M. Davies and L. J. Ravelli (eds), *Advances in Systematic Linguistics: Recent Theory and Practice*, London: Planter, 1992, 5–19.

Chapter 3, 'Signalling in discourse . . .', is a substantially shortened version of the monograph *Signalling in Discourse*, Birmingham: University of Birmingham, 1979.

Chapter 4, 'Clause relations as information structure . . .', is a revised version of an article of the same name which appeared in R. M. Coulthard (ed.), *Talking about Text*, Birmingham: University of Birmingham, 1986.

Chapter 5, 'Predictive categories in expository text', is a substantially shortened version of the monograph *Prediction in Text*, Birmingham: University of Birmingham, 1985.

Chapter 6, 'Labelling discourse: an aspect of nominal group lexical cohesion', is a substantially revised and shortened version of *Anaphoric Nouns*, Birmingham: University of Birmingham, 1985.

Chapter 7, 'The text and its message', first appeared as 'The text and its message: an approach to the teaching of reading strategies for students of Development Administration' in H. von Faber (ed.), *Leserverstehen im Fremdensprachenunterricht*, Munich: Goethe Institut, 1980, 147–70.

Chapter 9, 'The construction of knowledge . . .', was first published in the conference proceedings, ed. C. de Stasio, M. Gotti and R. Bonadei, *La Rappresentazione verbale e iconica: valori estetici e funzionali, Atti dell' XI Congresso nazionale dell' A.I.A., Begamo 24 e 25 ottobre 1988*, de Stasio C, M Gotti and R Bonadei (eds), Milan: Guerini Studio, 1990, 57–80.

All the other chapters were written specially for this volume.

1 On analysing and evaluating written text

Malcolm Coulthard

The higher level of achievement is a contribution to the evaluation of the text.

(Halliday 1985: xv)

INTRODUCTION

All branches of linguistics are first and foremost descriptive and thus it is no surprise that text linguistics confines itself to describing what *is*, in other words to (selections from) already existing and usually published texts. The past thirty years have seen fascinating and lively debate about the nature and boundaries of linguistics, but one tenet has remained unchallenged: that linguistics is concerned solely with making descriptive and not prescriptive statements. While it is universally agreed that evaluating alternative grammars is a proper concern of linguistics, evaluating the comparative communicative success of two alternative sentences generated by any given grammar is not – despite the fact that both pure and applied linguists, in their role as teachers, are daily involved in telling students how to improve their linguistic skills.

There were, of course, in the late 1960s and early 1970s, important sociolinguistic reasons for emphasizing the validity of difference and denying the inherent inferiority of minority dialects. However, this battle has long since been won, following research into West-Indian English in Birmingham by Wight and Sinclair and into Black English in New York by Labov. Now the advances in descriptive linguistics of the last generation should give us the confidence to re-introduce evaluation, to admit what we have always secretly acknowledged, that some texts and some writers are better than others, and to try to account not simply for difference and for how existing texts mean, but also for quality and for why one textualization might mean more or better than another.

It is for this reason that I prefer to see any given text as just one of an indefinite number of possible texts, or rather **possible textualizations**, of the writer's message – parts of this chapter, for instance, have passed through more than a dozen drafts, sometimes undergoing minor and sometimes major changes and, of course, not always changing for the better. It is evident that as writers we have no hesitation in evaluating our own texts, although as professional linguists we shy away from evaluating the texts of others – even in the field of translation studies, where alternative translations of major literary works are quite common, House (1977) is almost alone in investigating evaluation.

In this chapter I want to suggest that an investigation of the writer–reader communication process can enable us to derive some principles for evaluating texts and for preferring some textualizations over others.

One productive way forward is to focus on problematic texts – just as studies of aphasia and slips of the tongue have provided fruitful evidence for hypotheses about how language is organized in the brain, so a study of badly written text, or **inadequate textualizations**, may help us to understand better the nature of successful textualization.

I propose to use, for exemplificatory purposes, a short extract from an eight-page pamphlet entitled *Holidays and Travel for Diabetics*, published by the British Diabetic Association in 1977 and brought to me several years ago by a nurse who worked in a clinic for diabetics, with the complaint 'our patients can't understand this', and the request 'can you help me to re-write it?' I propose to examine the first thirteen sentences of the text, up to the end of the first section entitled *Food*, but I have included the next section on *Drink* in order to show how the text continues.

Holidays and travel for diabetics
(1) The well-controlled diabetic can enjoy travelling and holidays abroad as much as anyone else, but he must go well prepared.
Food
(2) Most diabetics think that food will be a problem when travelling. (3) However, food in any country consists of the same basic ingredients. (4) Potatoes, rice and other starchy vegetables or cereals, and products containing flour and/or sugar, are the main source of carbohydrates. (5) Bread, in whatever form, has 15 grams of carbohydrate to the ounce. (6) Rice and pasta (macaroni, spaghetti, ravioli, etc.) are used instead of potatoes in many countries. (7) Before travelling you should buy the 10 gram Exchange List, available from the British Diabetic Association. (8) 10 gram portions of unfamiliar foods can then be weighed until you learn to judge them at a glance. (9) Protein foods are easily recognisable (meat, fish, eggs and poultry), and fats consist of butter, margarine, cooking fats and olive oil. (10) Overweight diabetics should cut fats to a minimum as they are very high in Calories or Joules. (11) A basic knowledge of cooking helps you to assess any dish so it is always worthwhile to study a cookery book. (12) Sweets and puddings should be avoided, but fresh fruit and plain ice cream or cheese and biscuits are easily calculated substitutes. (13) As 'starters' tomato juice, hors d'oeuvres and clear soup are all low in carbohydrates and Calories or Joules.

Drink

(14) All spirits are free of sugar and dry wine or sherry contains so little sugar that moderate amounts can be taken. (15) All beers, sweet cider, sweet wines and liqueurs (except diabetic preparations) contain some sugar. (16) Alcohol should be avoided by the overweight diabetic as it is high in Calories or Joules. (17) Fruit drinks and minerals usually contain high quantities of sugar, but Coca Cola is known to have 20 grams carbohydrate to the 6-ounce (150 ml) bottle – a useful form of topping up when swimming, dancing, etc. (18) Four ounces (100 ml) of fresh orange juice contains 10 grams carbohydrate. (19) Tea and coffee are, of course, free, but avoid Turkish coffee which is often served ready sweetened.

I have presented this text to many groups of professional and student linguists all over the world and the vast majority found it difficult to discover exactly what is intended or meant, although all agreed that the main effect is one of discouraging rather than encouraging foreign travel. In other words, the published textualization seems to fail on both the ideational and the inter-personal levels.

We have long been accustomed to thinking of **ideational** in terms of clauses but have no real way of approaching the ideational content of a whole text, except as a collection of the ideational contents of the constituent clauses. This, however, is not useful or even possible for my purposes, because what I am interested in exploring is the *possible* textualizations of the ideational, of which the one we have here is merely one sample realization. Looking at the communication process from the composer/writer's point of view, we can see the ideational as *pre*-textual, although, unless one focuses on oneself, which is a flattering redefinition of the label 'ideal speaker', the only access one has to a writer's ideational is through his/her text(ualization).

Thus, at this stage it is heuristically very useful to begin from an actual text, attempt to derive the ideational and then propose alternative and preferable textualizations. My task here, while not easy, is considerably simplified because the text is a mere 21-line extract from a much longer text, a justifiable isolable unit, because the lines comprise a section marked as such by the writer.

We have no automatic, standard or even agreed procedures for going from text to ideational content, but I must stress that the general points I am trying to make do not, in fact, depend on the correctness of my ideational analysis. What we need initially is a summary of the ideational content and I suggest that the message this author wants to put across and the message the diabetic/reader wants to read is:

I assure you that: (1) Food abroad need not be a problem for the well-controlled diabetic.

For reasons we will now consider, (1) could not on its own be a possible textualization of the message.

IMAGINED READERS AND REAL READERS

Discussions of written communication are often presented in terms of a Writer communicating directly with his/her Readers by means of a written Text. In this model the text carries, transparently, the writer's ideational content and any problems readers have with the text tend to be seen as deficiencies in the reader, deficiencies which are obviously compounded if the reader is not a native reader of the language of the text.

However, it is in fact an unhelpful formulation to see a writer as creating his/her text for *those who actually read it*. As I create this text I have no way of knowing anything about you, my current reader, nor of when or where you will read my text. Thus, I cannot create my text with you in mind, I cannot take into account what you already know and what you do not know, what you believe and what disbelieve.

The only strategy open to me, therefore, is to *imagine* a Reader, and to create my text for that imagined reader. Only in this way can I decide what I need to say and what I can assume, what parts of my argument must be spelled out in detail and what can be passed over quickly or omitted completely – a writer cannot begin at the beginning of everything. For example I work and write within a Hallidayan framework and thus I wrote above, without a second thought (and therefore without any overt reference to Halliday or any of his published works), about a textualization failing 'on both the *ideational* and the *interpersonal* levels'. This would cause no problems for my Imagined Reader, to whom I have attributed a basic knowledge of Halliday; however, once my text is finished and published, it will be processed by Real Readers, like yourself, some of whom will be very familiar with Halliday and some of whom will know only the name. More generally, some of my Real Readers will be very similar, in terms of knowledge and background, to my Imagined Reader, while some will be very different. If you happen to know less about my topic than my Imagined Reader, you may find my text difficult, if you know more, you may find I have nothing new or of interest to say.

Significantly, it is the creation of the Imagined Reader which allows us as writers to keep the ideational within manageable limits – without a clear sense of audience, it is impossible to make the right decisions about what of the ideational to textualize. (It is, of course, an irony that we frequently complain about the quality of students' writing but still all too often put them in the impossible situation of having to write essays and examination answers aimed at not a real known person but an imagined construct, the Ideal Marker, who is intelligent and generally well informed, but at the same time fortuitously ignorant of the central topic of the piece of work to be assessed.)

Since Halliday and Hasan's *Cohesion in English* (1976), we have been very conscious of the many ways in which texts are organized by means of, and analysable into, 'given' and 'new'. However, what is less recognized is that any writer is faced with two major ideational/interpersonal decisions: first, what can s/he assume his/her intended audience (should) know and second, what of what they do know is it still useful or necessary to textualize. Thus, not only is there textually 'given' and 'new', there is also ideationally 'given' and 'new'. Indeed, one of the significant contributions of Brazil (1985) was to demonstrate that speakers have available, in the intonation system through the proclaiming/referring tone choice, an option for marking items as ideationally given or new. There is no comparable generalized option for the writer, but this is not to say that s/he cannot lexicalize the distinction. In fact, I have just noticed that my two phrases 'we have been very conscious' and 'less recognized' at the beginning of this paragraph are markers respectively of the ideational given and new.

Because texts are designed for a specific audience, once they exist, they define that audience; indeed, as no writer can create even a single sentence without a target Imagined Reader, almost every sentence provides some clue(s) about this Reader which allows any Real Reader to build up cumulatively a picture of his/her Imagined counterpart.

However, some texts create confusion, or worse, because the author has failed to maintain a consistent Imagined Reader from sentence to sentence or paragraph to paragraph. This is clearly true of the Diabetics text. It is supposedly addressed to 'diabetics who want to go on holiday'; however, an examination of the first thirteen sentences of the pamphlet presented above is sufficient to show that the writer has no clear picture of the Imagined Reader – for example, sentence (1) appears to be addressed to those who live with diabetics: 'but he (i.e. not "*you* the diabetic") must go well prepared'; sentence (10) to 'overweight diabetics' alone; sentences (3) and (4) to those diabetics who have not grasped the dietary basis of their problem; and sentences (10) and (13) to the very small group of British diabetics who actually know what a 'Joule' is.

When we begin to contemplate how we might improve this short text, the first step is to define more clearly a single Imagined Reader, whom we could perhaps best conceptualize as 'a *well-controlled* (male) *diabetic* who is interested in the problems of foreign travel'. We could then be reasonably confident about what such an Imagined Reader would already know, what he would want to learn from reading the text and what he would there-fore need to be told. This would enable us to see more clearly both the irrelevance of some of the ideational information included in the original, for example that addressed to overweight diabetics, and the need for some information which is missing from the original, for example a definition or explanation of 'Joules'.

WHO IS AVERRING?

All non-fictional authors must concern themselves with, though not neces-sarily be responsible for, the truth of what is contained in their texts. As Sinclair (1986) points out, one of the things factual texts do is to **aver**, that is to 'assert that something is the case'. Averrals contrast with facts as follows:

It is a fact that my left foot is slightly larger than my right foot. It is an averral when I say in a shoe shop 'My left foot is slightly larger than my right foot'.

(Sinclair ibid.: 44)

The responsibility for the truth of what is averred lies with the averrer, who may or may not be the writer of the text, because all writers have the option, which I myself exercised above, of transferring the role of averrer by quoting another writer (or speaker). Indeed, some students seem to feel that their job when writing essays and term papers is merely to sew together a series of averrals from experts with no intervening text of their own. However, even when quoting, the author cannot escape his/her responsibility as the **evaluator** of the truth value of what is presented in the text – ultimately you are reading my text to know what *I* think, even if, at times, I use other voices to help me to express my views. It is for this very reason that I overtly associated myself with Sinclair's opinion above by saying '*As* Sinclair (1986) points out'.

It is incumbent on writers to make clear at all times who is averring and, if it is not them, what is their personal evaluation of the averral. Indeed, so powerful is this obligation that Tadros (1985) claims that if a writer quotes another without immediately evaluating s/he has an obligation to the reader to evaluate at a later point in the text, although there are, of course, occasions when a lack of overt evaluation is taken as indicative of positive evaluation.

In reporting another's averral the writer can choose to jointly assert, to withhold judgement on, or to contradict the proposition(s) s/he reports, by choosing what Leech (1983) classifies as respectively **factive**, **non-factive** and **counter-factive** reporting verbs:

(a) Most diabetics *know* that food will be a problem when travelling.
    (food *will* be a problem)
(b) Most diabetics *think* that food will be a problem when travelling.
    (food *may or may not* be a problem)
(c) Most diabetics *pretend* that food will be a problem when travelling.
    (food *will not* be a problem)

Difficulties can arise for readers when writers, having chosen the second option, delay the evaluation or fail to realize it in part or *in toto*. We can see such an example of potential confusion in the Diabetics text. Sentence (2) reads 'Most diabetics *think* that food will be a problem . . .'. Some readers misread this sentence and see the writer as averring that 'food *will* be a problem when travelling', but even those who read it correctly as a non-factive report of someone's else's averral look in vain for an explicit positive or negative evaluation. Only on rereading do most readers realize that sentence (2) is in fact the first part in a three-part **Assertion–Denial–Justification** structure from which the Denial has been omitted, leaving as the only clue to interpretation the 'however' at the beginning of sentence (3).

SIGNALLING

The discussion above highlights another of the writer's responsibilities: it is not sufficient for him/her to organize the material into a textual form, the writer must also indicate or **signal** (see Hoey, this volume) to the reader the status and/or discourse function of individual parts of the text. We have noted already the signalling use of factive, non-factive and counter-factive verbs and commented on the failure to signal Denial and Justification in sentences (2, 3) of the text under consideration. A clearly signalled version might have had a warning 'although' in sentence (2) to preface the Assertion and thus prevent any ambiguity arising from the non-factual 'think', plus an explicit evaluative item, like 'wrong' to signal the Denial and a 'because' to signal the Justification. Thus the whole could have read something like:

> *Although* most diabetics think that food will be a problem when travelling they are *wrong*, *because* food in all countries . . .

RHETORICAL STRUCTURES

Knowledge is not linear, but text is. Thus every writer is faced with the problem of how to organize and present his/her non-linear message in a comprehensible linear form. There are several popular rhetorical patterns; I will focus on two, **General/Particular** and **Problem–Solution** (Hoey, 1983; Winter, 1986).

The General/Particular pattern

One of the ways in which we frequently group words together for lexical analysis is in terms of general and particular or, more familiarly, **superordinate** and **hyponym**, for instance *family*: *parent/child*; *parent*: *mother/father*. What is less well recognized is that (parts of) texts can be and often are organized in terms of general/particular as well. For example, several of the sentences of the Diabetics text, (4, 5, 6, 9), are concerned with providing, firstly, the hyponyms of the superordinate 'ingredients', that is 'carbohydrates', 'fats' and 'proteins' and then in turn the hyponyms of these hyponyms – in the case of 'fats', 'butter, margarine, cooking fats and olive oil' and in the case of 'protein foods', 'meat, fish, eggs and poultry'.

There are two major signals of the General/Particular relation, **enumerables** (Tadros, 1985) and **matching relations** (Hoey, 1983; Winter, 1986). Tadros points out that undefined sub-technical nouns typically predict a subsequent particularization. Thus in sentence (3) 'consists of the same basic ingredients' leads the reader to expect a specification of the word 'ingredients'. Interestingly, the signal of the realization of hyponyms in text is often a matching relation, that is the partial repetition of a piece of text where a combination of repeated **constant** and new **variable** forces the reader to see items not otherwise overtly linked as comparable. Thus:

> Once upon a time there were *three bears*   (enumerable/general)
> *father* bear, *mother* bear and *baby* bear   (matched particulars)

One of the difficulties with the Diabetics text under discussion is that it is not at all clear, on a first reading, what the hyponyms of 'ingredients' are. First, superordinates are typically followed closely in texts by their hyponyms, so in this text it is quite natural to assume that 'ingredients' is being used as a superordinate for the items at the beginning of sentence (4) – 'potatoes, rice and other starchy vegetables . . .' – particularly as these items are compatible with the dictionary definition of 'ingredient'. Second, the text does not signal the actual co-hyponyms as clearly as it could: 'carbohydrates' occurs as the grammatical element **Complement** almost hidden at the end of a long sentence, while in the case of 'proteins' and 'fats', even though both occur in **Subject** position in their respective clauses, they are not presented in a paralleled matching relation structure. A 'classic' version would be

> (3) However, food in any country consists of the same basic ingredients: carbohydrates, proteins and fats. (4) The main source of carbohydrates is . . . ; the main source of proteins is . . . ; and that of fats is . . .

The Problem–Solution pattern

A second option open to writers is to organize what they have to say as *solutions* to *problems* in terms of the four-part structure Situation–Problem–Solution–Evaluation, a structure exemplified by Winter's (1976) short invented example reproduced below:

> I was on sentry duty   Situation
> I saw the enemy approaching   Problem
> I opened fire   Solution (to the Problem)
> The enemy retreated   Evaluation (of the Solution)

This is a deceptively simple example, though a moment's reflection allows us to see that the macro-organization of a typical research thesis can be analysed in the same terms: *Situation*: review of the literature; *Problem*: the question(s) the researcher has chosen to address; *Solution*: the researcher's answers/proposals; *Evaluation*: a concluding section commenting on what has been achieved and what remains to be done. It is not by chance that I have chosen to present my ideas on text creation within a framework of improving a problematic text.

The basic four-part structure can be complicated in several ways – for instance by embedding a complete four-part structure inside one of the components of another structure – but by far the most common complication is when the Evaluation of a Solution is negative, as it would be, for instance, in Winter's example above if the enemy had kept on advancing despite the fact that the 'I' of the text 'opened fire'. In such circumstances the same or a slightly modified problem is often reinstated and an alternative solution tested; this creates a potentially indefinitely recursive structure:

```
                  Situation
                  Problem
                  Solution
   Negative  →    Evaluation =  Problem
                                Solution
                  Negative  →   Evaluation =  Problem
                                              Solution
                                              Evaluation
```

That is, in fact, a very frequently used expository structure and once we realize that the Diabetic text is concerned with solutions to a series of linked problems we can restructure it explicitly in terms of Problem–Solution. In other words, we can present the same content as contained in the original text as a progression from larger to smaller problems:

Problem or Question		*Solution or Answer*
1 Will food be a problem?		No, because food is essentially the same in all countries.
	but	Recognition might be a problem.
2 How will I recognize food?		Ordinary food will be recognizable just like food at home.
	but	There may be problems with unfamiliar dishes and with quantities.
3 How can I cope?		(i) A cookery book will give you an idea of what local dishes contain (ii) the 10 Gram Exchange List will help you with quantities.
4 And if I still have problems?		You can use the avoidance strategies that you already use to choose reliable/ safe food.
Evaluation		Therefore food will not be a problem when travelling.

A textualization of this underlying structure would be much more accessible than the published text.

TEXTUAL DEFINITION OF WORDS

Ultimately a text is a string of words and a writer has to encode the ideational meaning into, and the reader to decode that meaning from, words. Problems arise because word meanings are not fully fixed; rather, words derive some of their meaning from the context in which they appear. Indeed, it is one of the fascinating features of texts that they can alter quite significantly the accepted (i.e. dictionary definition) meanings of words. It is not simply that texts create contextual synonymy from words that have similar dictionary definitions – we are all familiar with sequences like:

This procedure has several *drawbacks* . . .
    the first *problem* . . . ;
    the second *difficulty* . . . ;
    the third *disadvantage* . . .

it is rather that words are sometimes used in meanings not even recognized in any dictionary – a nice confirmation of the Caterpillar's assertion in *Alice in Wonderland* that if you are strong enough you can do anything you like with words.

Let us take the word 'ingredients' again as an example. On a first reading all readers seem to assume that it means something like: 'things that are used to make something, for example all the different foods you use when you are cooking a particular dish' (Cobuild Dictionary definition), that is, very like the list which occurs at the beginning of sentence (4) – 'potatoes, rice and other starchy vegetables or cereals'; only later, if at all, do readers realize that in this text the word 'ingredients' is being used to mean, and only to mean, 'carbohydrates, fats and proteins'. In a similar way, only after several readings does the reader perceive that the word 'dish' is being used as a technical term.

Given that the writer has so much lexical power, it is incumbent on him/her to signal when s/he is being 'creative'; technical terms, for example, can be signalled by *italic*, less usual usages by single quotes and nonce usages like that of 'ingredients' above by providing immediately afterwards textual definitions, for example, '. . . consists of the same basic *ingredients*: carbohydrates, fats and proteins'.

CONCLUDING REMARKS

I have deliberately discussed only a few of the approaches to the analysis of text structure which are useful in a consideration of the composition and evaluation of written texts. I hope, however, that I have done enough to allow readers to apply and amplify the methodology.

To conclude, I offer an alternative textualization, which, while simultaneously using as much as possible of the original wording, attempts to take account of a single Imagined Reader, to present him (i.e. not *her*) with the necessary information in a clear sequence and to signal the textual relations. Signalling items are marked in bold, other additions in italic:

Holidays and travel for diabetics
If you are a well-controlled diabetic *you* can enjoy travelling and holidays abroad as much as anyone else.
Food
Although most diabetics think that food will be a **problem** when travelling, *they are* **mistaken**, **because** food in any country consists of the same basic ingredients: *carbohydrates, proteins and fats*. **As you know** the main source of carbohydrates *is* potatoes, rice and other starchy vegetables or

cereals, and products containing flour and/or sugar; **the main** protein foods are easily recognizable (meat, fish, eggs and poultry), and **the main** fats *are* butter, margarine, cooking fats and olive oil.

Occasionally, you may be unsure about the nature and quantity of ingredients, but this should not be a major **problem**. Before travelling you should buy the 10 Gram Exchange List, available from the British Diabetic Association. **Then** 10 gram portions of unfamiliar foods can be weighed until you learn to judge them at a glance. Bread, **for instance**, in whatever form, has 15 grams of carbohydrate to the ounce.

Of course, *you are likely to find dishes which do not occur on the Exchange List. To* **prepare** *for this, you could* study *in advance* a cookery book *from the countries you intend to visit or alternatively you can use* **avoidance strategies**. *Remember that* as 'starters' tomato juice, hors d'oeuvres and clear soups are all low in carbohydrates and Calories *and that while* sweets and puddings should be avoided, fresh fruit and plain ice cream or cheese and biscuits are easily calculated substitutes.

Finally, 'Joule' *is used as a unit of measurement in some countries instead of Calory; make sure you know how to convert.*

2 Trust the text

John McH. Sinclair

By way of a sub-title to this chapter, I should like to quote a short sentence from a recent article in *The European*, by Randolph Quirk:

The implications are daunting.

I shall refer to the discourse function of this sentence from time to time, but at present I would like to draw attention to its ominous tone. The implications of trusting the text are for me extremely daunting, but also very exciting and thought-provoking.

The argument that I would like to put forward is that linguistics has been formed and shaped on inadequate evidence and, in a famous phrase, 'degenerate data'. There has been a distinct shortage of information and evidence available to linguists, and this gives rise to a particular balance between speculation and fact in the way in which we talk about our subject. In linguistics up till now we have been relying very heavily on speculation.

This is not a criticism; it is a fact of life. The physical facts of language are notoriously difficult to remember. Some of you will remember the days before tape recorders and will agree that it is extremely difficult to remember details of speech that has just been uttered. Now that there is so much language available on record, particularly written language in electronic form, but also substantial quantities of spoken language, our theory and descriptions should be re-examined to make sure they are appropriate. We have not only experienced a quantitative change in the amount of language data available for study, but a consequent qualitative change in the relation between data and hypothesis. In the first part of the chapter I hope to raise a point about description based on the appreciation of this fairly fundamental appraisal.

Apart from the strong tradition of instrumental phonetics, we have only

This chapter is edited from the transcript of a talk I gave to the seventeenth International Systemics Congress at Stirling in July 1990. I would like to thank Kay Baldwin for her excellent transcript.

This version has greatly benefited from the plenary and informal discussions at Stirling, and from the comments of two colleagues, Michael Hoey and Louise Ravelli, who kindly read the first written version and made extensive comments.

recently devised even the most rudimentary techniques for making and managing the recording of language, and even less for the analysis of it. In particular we should be suspicious of projecting techniques that are suitable for some areas of language patterning on to others.

This is my first point. Until recently linguistics has been able to develop fairly steadily. Each new position in the major schools has arisen fairly naturally out of the previous one. However, the change in the availability of information which we now enjoy makes it prudent for us to be less confident about re-using accepted techniques.

My second main point is that we should strive to be open to the patterns observable in language in quantity as we now have it. The growing evidence that we have suggests that there is to be found a wealth of meaningful patterns that, with current perspectives, we are not led to expect. We must gratefully adjust to this new situation and rebuild a picture of language and meaning which is not only consistent with the evidence but exploits it to the full. This will take some time, and the first stage should be an attempt to inspect the data with as little attention as possible to theory.

It is impossible to study patterned data without some theory, however primitive. The advantage of a robust and popular theory is that it is well tried against previous evidence and offers a quick route to sophisticated observation and insight. The main disadvantage is that, by prioritizing some patterns, it obscures others. I believe that linguists should consciously strive to reduce this effect, until the situation stabilizes.

The first of my points takes us into the present state of the analysis of discourse which is now twenty years old and worth an overhaul; the second plunges us into corpus linguistics, which, although even more venerable, has been rather furtively studied until becoming suddenly popular quite recently. They might seem to have very little in common, but for me they are the twin pillars of language research.

What unites them is:

(a) They both encourage the formulation of radically new hypotheses. Although they can be got to fit existing models, that is only because of our limited vision at present.
(b) The dimensions of pattern that they deal with are, on the whole, larger than linguistics is accustomed to. Both to manage the evidence required, and even to find some of it in the first place, there is a need to harness the power of modern computers.

The most important development in linguistic description in my generation has been the attempt from many different quarters to describe structures above the sentence and to incorporate the descriptions in linguistic models. The study of text, of discourse, including speech acts and pragmatics is now central in linguistics. Since the early 1950s a number of approaches have been devised that attempt to account for larger patterns of language. Although large-scale patterns are clearly affected by, for example, sociological variables, they still lie firmly within the orbit of linguistic behaviour for as long as linguistic techniques can be used as the basis of their description.

No doubt we quite often begin a new study by projecting upwards the proven techniques of well-described areas of language. To give you an example of this, consider distributional techniques of description which began in phonology. These led in the early 1950s to attempts by, for example, Zellig Harris, to describe written text using essentially the same methods, by looking for repeated words and phrases which would form a basis for classifying the words and phrases that occur next to them. This is just the way in which phonemes were identified and distinguished from allophones; the basis of the famous 'complementary distribution'. Now there is only a relatively small number of phonemes in any language, numbered in tens, and there is a relatively large number of words, numbered in tens of thousands. The circumstances are quite different, and in the pre-computer era this kind of research faced very serious problems. The unlikelihood of finding exactly repeated phrases led Harris to the idea that stretches of language which, though physically different, were systematically related, could be regarded as essentially the same. This was articulated as grammatical transformation. It is an object lesson in what can go wrong if you project your techniques upwards into other areas without careful monitoring and adaptation. In the event, transformations provided the key feature with which Chomsky (1957) launched a wave of cognitive, non-textual linguistics.

Discourse study took off when speech acts (Austin 1962) were identified in philosophy. It took a development in a discipline outside linguistics to offer a reconceptualization of the function of the larger units of language. However, much of the description of discourse since then has been the upward projection of models, worked out originally for areas like grammar and phonology. I cheerfully admit '*mea culpa*' here, in having projected upwards a scale and category model in an attempt to show the structure of spoken interaction (Sinclair *et al.* 1972). It has been a serviceable model, and it is still developing, along lines which are now suitable for capturing the general structure of interactive discourse. Recent work on conversation by Amy Tsui (1986), on topic by Hazadiah Mohd Dahan (1991) and by others incorporating the relations between spoken and written language are continuing within the broad umbrella of that model while making it more convenient as a vehicle for explaining the nature of interaction in language.

Louise Ravelli's study of dynamic grammar (forthcoming) is an interesting exercise in turning the new insights of a theoretical development back on to familiar ground. It is in effect a projection downwards from the insights of discourse into some aspects of language form.

While using familiar tools is a reasonable tactic for getting started, we should also work towards a model of discourse which is special to discourse and which is not based upon the upward projection of descriptive techniques, no matter how similar we perceive the patterns to be. In this case, for the description of discourse, we should build a model which emphasizes the distinctive features of discourse. A special model for discourse will offer an explanation of those features of discourse that are unique to it, or characteristic of it, or prominent in discourse but not elsewhere.

Many of the structural features of discourse are large scale and highly variable. As the units of language description get larger, the identification of meaningful units becomes more problematic. The computer is now available to help in this work.

However, we should not use the computer merely to demonstrate patterns which we predict from other areas of language study. It will labour mightily and apparently with success, but it may also labour in vain. Mechanizations of existing descriptive systems are present in abundance. Many teams of scholars have made excellent, but limited, use of the computer to model a premechanized description of part of language form, and tested the model against data. The computer will expose errors and suggest corrections; it will apply rules indefatigably, and it will continue to tell us largely what we already know.

Instead I would like to suggest that we might devise new hypotheses about the nature of text and discourse and use the computer to test whether they actually work. Computers have not been much used in this way so far in language work; their main role has been checking on detail. Gradually, computers are becoming capable of quite complex analysis of language. They are able to apply sophisticated models to indefinitely large stretches of text and they are getting better and better at it. As always in computer studies, the pace is accelerating, and this will soon be commonplace.

I would like to put forward one hypothesis, or perhaps a small set of related hypotheses, which should simplify and strengthen the description of discourse. It is a stronger hypothesis than one normally encounters in discourse, and it is one where the computer can be used in a testing role. It is explicit enough to identify a large number of cases automatically. Where it fails, the cases will be interesting to the analyst, because in such cases the hypothesis is either wrong or not properly stated, or the evidence is too vague or idiosyncratic to be covered by general statement.

This hypothesis draws on something by which I set very great store: the prospective features of spoken discourse. For me the study of discourse began in earnest when I classified initiations in exchanges according to how they preclassify what follows (Sinclair 1966, quoted in Sinclair and Coulthard, 1975: 151: see also p. 133). This approach broadened into the view that a major central function of language is that it constantly prospects ahead. It cannot determine in most cases what actually will happen, especially not in spoken interaction, but it does mean that whatever does happen has a value that is already established by the discourse at that point. So the scene is set for each next utterance by the utterance that is going on at the moment. Over the years, the more that attention has been focused on the prospective qualities of discourse the more accurate and powerful the description has become.

In contrast much of the analysis of written language as text has concerned retrospective pattern. Patterns of cohesion, of repetition, reference, replacement and so on. Complex patterns emerge, linking parts of a text to each other. Some become very complex indeed, and sample texts have many lines drawn from one part of the text to another to indicate ties, links, chains, etc. I accept, as I am sure most scholars do, that written and spoken language are different in many particulars, but are they as different as the styles of analysis suggest? Is it really true that we mainly find prospection in the spoken language and retrospection in the written language? That would suggest that they are very different indeed.

Of course there are backward references in conversation. But why are they not apparently as important to the analyst as they are in the written language? *Vice versa*, there are prospections that can be identified in the written language, as Winter (1977a) and Tadros (1985) have shown.

People do not remember the spoken language exactly and so they cannot refer back to it in quite the simple way that they can with the written language. Because we have written text in front of us to check on, it is apparently easy to rely on retrospective reference. But do we really in the normal course of reading actually check back pronominal reference and so on? I doubt it. The point could no doubt be checked by doing studies of eye movements but I doubt if many researchers would consider it worth checking.

Informal experiments which colleagues and I did many years ago supported the common-sense view, which is that in general people forget the actual language but remember the message. And so the question that I would like to ask is 'Do we actually need all the linguistic detail of backward reference that we find in text description?' Text is often described as a long string of sentences, and this encourages the practice of drawing links from one bit of the text to another. I would like to suggest, as an alternative, that the most important thing is what is happening in the current sentence. The meaning of any word is got from the state of the discourse and not from where it came from. A word of reference like a pronoun should be interpreted exactly like a proper name or a noun phrase. The reader should find a value for it in the immediate state of the text, and not have to retrieve it from the previous text unless the text is problematic at that point.

The state of the discourse is identified with the sentence which is currently being processed. No other sentence is presumed to be available. The previous text is part of the immediately previous experience of the reader or listener, and is no different from any other, non-linguistic, experience. It will normally have lost the features which were used to organize the meaning and to shape the text into a unique communicative instrument.

From this perspective, there is no advantage to be gained in tracing the references back in the text. The information thus gleaned will not be relevant to the current state of the discourse because previous states of the text are of no interest to the present state of the text; nor is it important how the present state of the text was arrived at.

I reiterate this point because, although it is straightforward, it is not an orthodox position and yet it is central to my argument. There are minor qualifications to be made, but nothing should disturb the main point. The conceptual difficulty arises, I believe, from the fact that the previous text is always present and available to the analyst, and the temptation to make use of it is too strong.

The notion of 'primed frames' in Emmott (this volume) is promising. Some form of mental representation of the text so far, the state of the text, must be building up in the mind of a competent reader, and must be available for interpreting the text at any particular point. It would be a digression in this argument to discuss positions concerning mental representations, because my concern is to explain how the text operates *discoursally* – while someone is experiencing its meaning. Very roughly we can understand it as the previous sentence minus its interactive elements – whatever enabled it to be an interaction at a previous stage in the text – plus the inferences that have been used in order to interpret the text at this particular point.

Let us take as a starting position the view that 'the text' is the sentence that is being processed at any time and only that. The text *is* the sentence that is in front of us when an act of reading is in progress. Each sentence then is a new beginning to the text. Each sentence organizes language and the world for that particular location in the text, not dependent on anything else. (No wonder, by the way, that we have had such problems in the past about the definition of a sentence, if it is indeed synonymous with the definition of a text. The paradox of the structure which represents a 'complete thought', but which is often verbalized in a form that is clearly part of a larger organization, is resolved.)

The relation between a sentence and the previous text is as follows: each sentence contains one connection with other states of the text preceding it. That is to say it contains a single act of reference which encapsulates the whole of the previous text and simultaneously removes its interactive potential. The occurrence of the next sentence pensions off the previous one, replaces it and becomes the text. The whole text is present in each sentence. The meaning of each previous sentence is represented simply as part of the shared knowledge that one is bringing to bear in the interpretation of a text at any point.

My position, then, is that the previous states of the text up to the one that is being processed, are present in the current sentence in so far as they are needed. Previous sentences are not available in their textual form, but in a coherent text there is no need to have them. The same interpretive mechanism that we use to identify proper names, or other references from the text into our experience of the world, is suitable for processing that part of our experience which has been produced by previous text.

If this view is accepted, the way is then clear to concentrate in description on the communicative function of each sentence and not to worry about what its textual antecedents might have been.

I now return to my original text, 'The implications are daunting'. This text is obviously an act of reference to the whole of the preceding sentence, because the phrase 'the implications' does not carry within itself a clear indication of what it refers to. The word 'the' says that the reference of the noun group is knowable, and 'implications' need to be implications of something. We may assume that the whole of the preceding sentence is whatever has implications. The preceding sentence reads like this:

> The Japanese use western languages not merely to market their goods but to improve their products by studying those of their rivals.

The act of reference works if readers are satisfied that the two sentences can be interpreted in this way.

This sentence also prospects forward to the sentences that we have not yet read. This is one of the Advanced Labelling structures that Tadros (1985) has described in detail. If you mention 'implications' in this way, you have to go on to list them; so we may assume that the next sentence or sentences will be understandable as implications. The quoted sentence tells us in advance that what follows are implications. Here is what follows:

> Not merely must the business have personnel with skills in different languages but the particular languages and the degree of skill may vary from person to person according to his or her job within the business. They may also vary from decade to decade as new markets open up in different countries.

These are the implications. So the hypothesis that I am putting forward is that the text at any particular time carries with it everything that a competent reader needs in order to understand the current state of the text. It encapsulates what has gone before in a single act of reference, so that the previous text has exactly the same status as any other piece of shared knowledge. In many cases it also prospects forward and sets the scene for what follows.

The sentence that follows 'The implications are daunting', quoted above, does not contain an act of reference, and so it constitutes a counterexample straight away. The reason is that this sentence is fully prospected by its predecessor. If you think for a moment of spoken discourse, you find that an answer, which is prospected by a question, does not contain an act of reference that encapsulates the question. It would be bizarre if this were the case: the occurrence of the answer is made understandable by the prospection of the question, and yet the answer would encapsulate the question and so cancel its discourse function.

A question can indeed be followed by an utterance that encapsulates it; for example *That's an interesting question*. Such utterances are called **challenges** (Burton 1980) just because they encapsulate the previous utterance and cancel its interactive force.

We therefore conclude that the prospection of a sentence remains pertinent until fulfilled or challenged, although the sentence itself is no longer available in the normal business of talking or writing. Prospected sentences do not contain an act of reference, though they may, of course, themselves prospect. Prospection thus provides a simple variation in text structure. If a sentence is not prospected by its predecessor, it encapsulates it, and by so doing becomes the text.

In this chapter it is only possible to give the very broadest outline of this set of hypotheses. There is a lot of detail and a number of qualifications, and it will become much more elaborate as ways are developed of coping with dubious examples. But the basic idea is simple, and probably testable by present techniques. Most acts of reference can be identified by currently available software. The proposal is much simpler than many other models of text because it selects the features of sentence reference and prospection as being particularly important in structure. If it turns out to be adequate for a starting description of text then it should commend itself because of its simplicity. It also simplifies the business of understanding text structure, in that it points out that each successive sentence is, for a moment, the whole text. This could lead eventually to a really operational definition of a sentence.

So my first main point is a double-edged one. I put forward some proposals for text structure as illustrations of strong and testable hypotheses. I suggest we should use the ability that we now have to perceive the higher structures of language and the powerful computing tools that we now have and that we should find out how reliable and how useful our hypotheses are.

Much of the description of the higher organization of language has remained at the stage of patterns and labels. Little has been done to describe restrictions or to explain the reasons for the patterns, that is, to make a proper structural description. Similarly, many investigations in language, particularly in areas like stylistics, have remained at a relatively modest level of achievement for a very long time, simply because of the technical problems involved in validating statements. Very detailed and careful analysis is required in stylistics, and it is still usually done by hand (though see the *Journal of Literary and Linguistic Computing, passim*). We are now in a position to be bold, to look for testable hypotheses which may simplify and clarify the nature of text and discourse. It is not enough that a particular description of language can actually provide a set of boxes into which text can be apportioned. We must look for models which help the text to reveal itself to us.

If we are going to take advantage of the computer's ability to test hypotheses over large stretches of text, there is a price to pay, but the opportunity is worth paying for. The price is the requirement of precision of statement, which will add pressure to move linguistics towards scientific rigour; the opportunity is the freedom to speculate and get fairly quick feedback from the computers about the accuracy and potential of the speculations. Far from restricting the theorist, computers will actually encourage hunch-playing and speculation at the creative stage. The wealth of data and the ease of access will, however, encourage the compilation of statements which are firmly compatible with the data.

The relationship between the student of language and the data is thus changing. My other point is that we as linguists should train ourselves specifically to be open to the evidence of long text. This is quite different from using the computer to be our servant in trying out our ideas; it is making good use of some essential differences between computers and people. A computer has a relatively crude and simple ability to search and retrieve exhaustively from text any patterns which can be precisely stated in its terms. Now of course we cannot look with totally unbiased eyes at these patterns, but I believe that we have to cultivate a new relationship between the ideas we have and the evidence that is in front of us. We are so used to interpreting very scant evidence that we are not in a good mental state to appreciate the opposite situation. With the new evidence the main difficulty is controlling and organizing it rather than getting it. There is likely to be too much rather than too little and there is a danger that we find only what we are looking for.

I would like to summarize the kind of observations which are already emerging from such studies, the kinds of studies that have been done in Cobuild and elsewhere. Sometimes they cast doubt on some fairly well established areas of conventional language description.

I shall begin at the lowest level of abstraction, the first step up from the string of characters, where word forms are distinguished by spaces. It has been known for some time that the different forms of a lemma may have very different frequencies. (The forms of a lemma differ from each other only by inflections.) We generally assume that all the forms of a lemma share the same meanings, but we are now beginning to discover that in some cases, if they did not share similar spelling, we might not wish to regard them as being instances of the same lemma. For example, take the lemma *move*. The forms *moving* and *moved* share some meanings with *move*, but each form has a very distinctive pattern of meaning. Some of the meanings found elsewhere in the lemma will be realized, and some will not. In the word *moving*, for example, there is the meaning of emotional affection which is quite prominent.

This kind of observation makes us realize that lemmatization is not a simple operation; it is in fact a procedure which a computer has great difficulty with. Of course with evidence like this it is quite difficult to persuade the computer that lemmatization is a sensible activity. The difference between *move* and *movement* is not noticeably more extreme; yet *movement*, being a derived form, would be expected to constitute a different lemma from *move*.

Such complexities have also been found in several other European languages in a project sponsored by the Council of Europe. When you think of a language like Italian, blessed with a multiplicity of verb forms, and the prospect that in principle each of those could be a different semantic unit, and also that there is evidence in many cases that this is so, then you can see the kind of problem that lies ahead. Bilingual dictionaries may soon grow in size substantially as the blithe assumption of a stable lemma is challenged.

Second, a word which can be used in more than one word class is likely to have meanings associated specifically with each word class. Just to give one example, the word *combat* as a noun is concerned with the physical side of combat, and as a verb is concerned with the social side. There is an exception: in the phrase *locked in combat*, *combat* is used in the social meaning although it is a noun. The exception draws attention to another useful point: that the correlations of meaning and word class break down when the words form part of some idiomatic phrase or technical term.

We have not yet made estimates of the proportion of the vocabulary which is subject to this phenomenon, but in the compiling of the *Cobuild Dictionary* (Sinclair *et al.* 1987) we tried to identify the predominant word class of each meaning of each word. We were pretty flexible in judgement and kept the detail to a minimum – even so, if you look at a few pages of that dictionary you will get the strong impression that meaning correlates with word class.

Third, a word may have special privileges of occurrence or restrictions in group structures. For example, there is a class of nouns whose members occur characteristically as prepositional objects, and not as subjects or objects of clauses; *lap* as a part of the body is one such. There is a large class of nouns whose members do not occur alone as a group or with only an article; they have to be modified or qualified in some way. I shall not develop this point here because Gillian Francis (forthcoming) gives an excellent account of the phenomenon as applied to nouns. This work is a close relation of valency grammar, which is likely to see an upsurge of interest in the next few years.

Fourth, traditional categories, even major parts of speech, are not as solidly founded as they might appear to be. A recent computational study (Sinclair 1991) of the word *of* revealed that it is misleading to consider it as a preposition. Only occasionally, and in specific collocations with, for example, *remind* does it perform a prepositional role. Normally it enables a noun group to extend its pre-head structure, or provide a second head word. In due course the grammatical words of the language will be thoroughly studied, and a new organizational picture is likely to emerge. We must not take for granted the lexical word classes either.

A fifth type of pattern occurs when a word or a phrase carries with it an aura of meaning that is subliminal, in that we only become aware of it when we see a large number of typical instances all together, as when we make a selective concordance. With an innocent verb like *happen*, for example, if we select the most characteristic examples of it, we find that it is nearly always something nasty that has happened or is going to happen. Similarly with the phrasal verb *set in* – it is nasty things like bad weather that set in. This feature associates the item and the environment in a subtle and serious way, that is not explained by the mechanism of established models.

As a corollary to this, I must emphasize that a grammar is a grammar of meanings and not of words. Grammars which make statements about un-differentiated words and phrases leave the user with the problem of deciding which of the meanings of the words or phrases are appropriate to the grammatical statement. Most dictionaries give us very little help, and since distinctions in meaning are arrived at without any systematic consideration of grammar (apart from the Cobuild dictionaries) they cannot be used as evidence in this case. Each grammatical feature will probably correlate with just one meaning, unless it is a very common word, or a word of very multifarious meaning, in which case the same grammar may apply to two or three meanings. But the coincidence of distinct environmental patterns with the shades of meaning of a word is remarkable, and is confirmed all the more as we examine the detail in more and more instances.

Sixth and last, and for me the most interesting result of this research concerns the area of shared meaning between words and between phrases; the results of collocation. Put fairly bluntly, it seems that words in English do not normally constitute independent selections. I cannot speak with much confidence yet about other languages, with different principles of word construction, except to say that the underlying principle, that of collocation, is certainly to be found operating in languages like German and Italian, and on that basis one can predict with fair confidence that shared meaning will be a feature.

One way of describing collocation is to say that the choice of one word conditions the choice of the next, and of the next again. The item and the environment are ultimately not separable, or certainly not separable by present techniques. Although at this point I risk my own censure about the upward projection of methodology, I find myself more and more drawn to Firth's notion of prosody in phonology to apply to the kind of distribution of meaning that is observed in text when there is a large quantity of organized evidence. Successive meanings can be discerned in the text, and you can associate a meaning or a component of meaning or a shade of meaning with this or that word or phrase that is present in the text. But it is often impossible in the present state of our knowledge to say precisely where the realization of that meaning starts and stops, or exactly which pattern of morphemes is responsible for it. This may be simply an unfortunate stage in the development of the description, but I do not think so. I think that there probably is in language an interesting indeterminacy. Once you accept that in many or most cases of meaningful choice in English the words are not independent selections, but the meanings are shared, then you are in an area of indeterminacy from which I cannot at the moment see any exit. It is no longer possible to imagine a sharp division between one type of patterning which behaves itself and conforms to broadly stateable rules, and another which is a long list of individual variations, and then to insist that they both create meaning at the same time.

Now a model which does not take into account this point is going to represent the language as carrying more information (in the technical sense of information theory) than it actually does. The patterns which are marginalized by our current attitudes include everything from collocation of all kinds, through Firth's colligations, to the conditioned probability of grammatical choices. This is a huge area of syntagmatic prospection. If a model claims to include all such features but does not explain their effect on conventional grammar and semantics, it will exaggerate the meaning that is given by the choices. That is a fairly serious misrepresentation if the grammar creates more meaning in a set of choices than is mathematically possible.

In the way in which we currently see language text, it is not obvious how each small unit of form prospects the next one. We identify structures like compounds, where the assumption is of a single choice, or idioms, although the precise identification of these is by no means clear cut. The likelihood is of there being a continuum between occasional quite independent choices and choices which are so heavily dependent on each other that they cannot be separated, and so constitute in practice a single choice.

At present what we detect is a common purpose in the overlapping selection of word on word as if these are the results of choices predetermined at a higher level of abstraction. The choices of conventional grammar and semantics are therefore the realizations of higher-level choices. Phrasal verbs are quite an interesting case in point, recently documented in a dictionary that Cobuild has published. Phrasal verbs are difficult to enumerate or identify because there are so many grades and types of co-selection that the relevant criteria are difficult to state and even more difficult to apply. But contrary to what is often claimed, each word of a phrasal verb does contribute something semantically recognizable to the meaning of the whole. In some cases, it is mainly the verb, and in other cases it is mainly the particle.

For instance, the Particles Index in the *Cobuild Dictionary of Phrasal Verbs* shows that the particle can often guide you to the meaning through a semantic analysis of the phrasal verb. A particle like *along*, for example, combines with common verbs such as *get* and *come* to make a range of linked meanings. From a basic sense of 'travel' there is the related meaning 'progress' in literal or figurative terms. In parallel to this is the meaning of 'accompany', as found in *tag along* among others. This develops into the notion of 'accept', and collocation with *with* is strong. We can make a diagram:

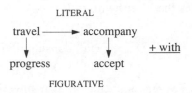

The phrasal verbs are semantically ordered in this analysis.

The meaning of words chosen together is different from their independent meanings. They are at least partly delexicalized. This is the necessary correlate of co-selection. If you know that selections are not independent, and that one selection depends on another, then there must be a result and effect on the meaning which in each individual choice is a delexicalization of one kind or another. It will not have its independent meaning in full if it is only part of a choice involving one or more words. A good deal of the above evidence leads us to conclude that there is a strong tendency to delexicalization in the normal phraseology of modern English.

Let me try to demonstrate this by looking at the selection of adjectives with nouns. We are given to understand in grammar that adjectives add something to the noun, or restrict the noun or add some features to it. That is no doubt true in some cases, but in the everyday use of adjectives, there is often evidence rather of co-selection and shared meaning with the noun. Here are some examples, using recent data from *The Times*, with grateful acknowledgement to the editor and publishers. Classifying adjectives are more prone to show this, but it is common also in qualitative adjectives.

Here are some nouns that are modified by *physical*:

physical assault   physical confrontation
physical attack   physical damage
physical attributes   physical proximity
physical bodies

In these cases the meaning associated with *physical* is duplicated in one facet of the way we would normally understand the noun. The adjective may focus the meaning by mentioning it, but the first meaning of *assault* is surely physical assault. It is not suggested that of all the different kinds of assault this is identified as one particular kind, namely physical assault. This co-selection of noun and adjective does not make a fixed phrase, nor necessarily a significant collocation; this is just one of the ordinary ways in which adjectives and nouns are selected. The selections are not independent; they overlap.

Here are some nouns that occur with *scientific*:

scientific assessment   scientific analysis
scientific advances   scientific study
scientific experiment

Here *scientific* is fairly seriously delexicalized; all it is doing is dignifying the following word slightly.

Here are some nouns that occur with *full*:

full enquiry   full range
full account   full consultation
full capacity   full circle

These are mainly types of reassurance more than anything else. We would be unlikely to have an announcement of a partial enquiry.

Here are some nouns that occur with *general*:

general trend   general perception
general drift   general opinion
general consent

In all of these cases if the adjective is removed there is no difficulty whatsoever in interpreting the meaning of the noun in exactly the way it was intended. The adjective is not adding any distinct and clear unit of meaning, but is simply underlining part of the meaning of the noun.

In such ways we can see that many of the word-by-word choices in language are connected mainly syntagmatically; the paradigmatic element of their meaning is reduced to the superficial. The same phenomenon occurs with qualitative adjectives such as *dry* in *dry land, dry bones, dry weight* (which is perhaps slightly technical), or *loud* in such combinations as *loud applause, loud bangs, loud cheers*.

The co-selection of adjective and noun is a simple and obvious example. There are many others: for example, there are in English many phrases which behave something like idioms; they are built round a slightly specialized meaning of a word that goes with a specific grammatical environment.

Take, for example, the framework *an* ... *of* one of the commonest collocations in the language. Consider the words that go in between those two words, in collocation with the word that immediately follows. There may be quite a small range, for example, with *an accident of* there is *an accident of birth, an accident of nature, an accident of society*. The whole phrase *an accident of* seems to have an idiomatic quality (Renouf and Sinclair, forthcoming).

These are subliminal idioms which were heralded many years ago (Sinclair, Jones and Daley 1972). They do not appear in most accounts of the language and yet they are clearly found in texts. We understand them as centring on a slightly specialized meaning of a word in a common grammatical environment and in a regular collocation. This alignment of grammar and lexis is typical of co-selection.

The sub-title of this chapter is 'The implications are daunting'. Relating this sentence to the points I have made, clearly 'daunting' is a member of an odd lemma. There are no finite forms *I daunt, you daunt*, etc. Further, *daunting* is obviously co-selected with *implications*. I do not know what other things can be daunting, but the collocation of *implications* and *daunting*, with those inflections, and either in an attributive or predicative syntax, illustrates the shared meaning in that phrase. So the sentence also does duty as an example of co-selection.

In summary, I am advocating that we should trust the text. We should be open to what it may tell us. We should not impose our ideas on it, except perhaps just to get started. We should only apply loose and flexible frameworks until we see what the preliminary results are in order to accommodate the new information that will come from the text. We should expect that we will encounter unusual phenomena; we should accept that a large part of our linguistic behaviour is subliminal, and therefore we may find a lot of surprises. We should search for models that are specially appropriate to the study of texts and discourse.

The study of language is moving into a new era in which the exploitation of modern computers will be at the centre of progress. The machines can be harnessed in order to test our hypotheses; they can show us things that we may not already have known and even things which shake our faith quite a bit in established models, and which may cause us to revise our ideas very substantially. In all of this my plea is to *trust the text*.

3 Signalling in discourse: a functional analysis of a common discourse pattern in written and spoken English

Michael Hoey

THE PURPOSE OF THE CHAPTER

This chapter is a much reduced version of a monograph first published in 1979. Although I find myself in the fortunate position of not disagreeing with what I said all those years ago, there was inevitably much in the original monograph that has little relevance to the present day. Rather than engage in substantial rewriting, I have largely confined my revising role to cutting what is no longer of interest and have altered the wording in only minor ways. With the solitary exception of an additional reference to a book by Michael Jordan, I have made no attempt to update the bibliography, though I have removed most of the referencing that the monograph contained. If a survey of the relevant literature of the period is desired, the reader is invited to consult the original monograph. I hope, though, that those readers familiar with the monograph will feel that I have retained the essence of what it had to offer and that the much larger body of readers who have never read or heard of it will feel that it was worth the archaeological effort to bring it to light again after all these years. The original monograph was dedicated to Eugene Winter. Articles are not normally dedicated to anyone but my debt to Eugene Winter will be apparent throughout.

The chapter attempts to examine the way in which monologue structures are efficiently signalled to listeners or readers. It concentrates specifically on the way in which a particular English discourse structure – the Problem–Solution structure – is signalled by the means of questions and vocabulary items of a particular type. The chapter does not, however, pretend to present a complete explanation of the complexities of monologues nor of their signalling systems; it should be taken rather as a first exploration which exposes as many questions as it answers.

PREVIOUS WORK ON THE PROBLEM–SOLUTION STRUCTURE

The structure for which I shall attempt to demonstrate the signalling mechanisms is one that has been sporadically identified as important for over forty years, and is commonly referred to as the **Problem–Solution** structure.

Although Beardsley (1950) appears to have been the first to identify the structure, its recognition by linguists seems to date from the late 1960s. In Young, Becker and Pike (1970), following work by Becker (1965) and Young and Becker (1965), the structure is offered as a 'generalised plot' common in discourse and worthy of heuristic use. Labov (1972) and Longacre (1974, 1976) identify structures for narrative that may not be the same as the Problem–Solution structure but are clearly related. Van Dijk (1977) notes the existence for narrative of the structure Setting–Complication–Resolution–Evaluation–Moral, and for scientific discourse of the structure Introduction–Problem–Solution–Conclusion, noting that 'it is the task of a general theory of discourse to classify and define such categories, rules and their specific textual functions' (p.155).

Grimes (1975) also recognizes the Problem–Solution structure. He comments (p. 211) 'Both the plots of fairy tales and the writings of scientists are built on a response pattern. The first part gives a problem and the second its solution. The solution has to be a solution to the problem that was stated, not some other; and the problem is stated only to be solved.' He adds: 'How to express this interlocking seems to be beyond us . . . but that is the shape of the relation.'

Although they are aware of its existence, none of these linguists discusses the Problem–Solution structure in any detail. A more crucial role and a fuller description are, however, assigned to it in two papers by Hutchins (1977a, b) which discuss the structure as it applies to scientific texts and relate it to other posited structures. Hutchins' description is more delicate than that of Longacre, Van Dijk or Grimes, but still leaves some important questions unanswered. Perhaps the most crucial of these is the one alluded to earlier: how are the structure and its component parts identified by the reader/listener? In other words, is the Problem–Solution structure reflected in the language used, or can its existence only be intuited?

In 1969, in a mimeographed but otherwise unpublished paper, Winter attempted to provide a partial answer to the above problem by using a question technique. In 1976, in a similarly mimeographed paper, he further developed this and other techniques for revealing the Problem–Solution structure. His only published reference to the structure has been in *Instructional Science* (1977a), and that was only a passing reference. Nevertheless, all of what follows builds on his work. Both his notion of the structure and the names he gave to the elements of that structure are essentially those used here. My part has been to bring together the various threads in such a way as to systematize them and thus provide a clearer picture of how the structure is signalled to the reader/listener.

A MINIMUM STRUCTURE

We begin by looking at a brief artificial discourse originally invented by Eugene Winter for teaching purposes.

If we take the four separate sentences listed as example 1, we find that one sequence seems more natural than any other, namely:

1 I was on sentry duty. I saw the enemy approaching. I opened fire. I beat off the enemy attack.

There are twenty-four possible sequences, but this is the only one that can be read without special intonation and make perfect sense. Others, however, need not be nonsense. If read with a parenthetical intonation on the second sentence, sequence 2 (among others) also makes good sense:

2 I saw the enemy approaching. (I was on sentry duty.) I opened fire. I beat off the enemy attack.

Other sequences seem never to be acceptable, for example:

3 I opened fire. I was on sentry duty. I beat off the enemy attack. I saw the enemy approaching.

The fact that out of twenty-four possible sequences only one is acceptable without special intonation and with equal emphasis on all sentences, very few are acceptable even *with* special intonation and most are never acceptable, leads us to suggest that we can divide sentence sequences into three categories – unmarked sequences, marked sequences and incoherent sequences, matching closely the notions of unmarked, marked and ungrammatical when applied to sentences.

The unmarked sequence is the one in normal time sequence, and this is sufficient to explain the preferability of version 1 over the others. But it is not just the sequence of the sentences that is important, it is also their presence. None of the four sentences can be omitted (unless certain information is presupposed) without threatening the text's clarity or completeness. What this suggests is that each of the four sentences is essential to the structure. Were time sequence the only factor to consider, the first three sentences of sequence 1 would form a complete text. Since they do not, we must assume that each sentence in the sequence has its place in an overall structure. That structure we can tentatively identify as the Problem–Solution structure, with the following elements

Situation	I was on sentry duty.
Problem	I saw the enemy approaching.
Response	I opened fire.
Evaluation	I beat off the enemy attack.

The question then arises: how does the reader/listener identify this structure in the discourse? We shall consider two possible answers to this question, which can be briefly indicated as (a) projection into dialogue, and (b) the identification of lexical signals.

PROJECTION INTO DIALOGUE

A monologue, written or spoken, may be regarded as a dialogue in which the reader/listener's questions or comments have not been explicitly included but which retains clear indications of the assumed replies of the reader.

Winter (1974) shows how the use of questions helps to explain the relations that hold between a sentence and its context. The same idea is pursued, though in less detail, in Winter (1977a), where he discusses questions as the most marked form of connection between sentences. It is, however, in an unpublished paper by Winter, mimeographed by the Hatfield Polytechnic in 1976, that he has most fully pursued the use of the question technique at a level greater than the immediate context of the sentence. In this paper he draws attention to the characteristic questions answered by scientific texts, basing his prescriptive advice on the detailed study of large numbers of short scientific/technical reports. These characteristic questions are discussed in modified form below.

The projection of monologue into dialogue must be done with the greatest caution. To begin with, we must introduce into the interviewer's 'speech' as little extraneous material as is compatible with explaining the sentences in the monologue. Second, for every sentence a number of questions may be provided that are capable of eliciting it. Let us look, for example, at the final sentence, in the following extract from an Eden Vale advertisement:

4 Sometimes we don't do a thing to Cottage Cheese, down at Eden Vale. We simply leave it plain. At other times, though, we do add things to it. Like pineapple, chives or onion and peppers.

    But plain or fancy, the cheese itself is still stirred carefully, by hand, until it reaches exactly the right consistency.

A number of questions are capable of eliciting the last sentence in this context (ignoring the conjunction *but*). Among them are:

How are the Eden Vale Cheeses prepared?
How much care is taken in the preparation of Eden Vale Cheeses?
What feature do all Eden Vale Cheeses share?

The fact that more than one question may elicit the same answer does not reflect a weakness in the dialogue-projection technique but reflects instead the considerable complexity of monologue. We need to select the form of the question that is most revealing or manifests most clearly a common pattern. The three questions given above, for example, all recur in innumerable other contexts in the more general forms:

How is/was x done/made?
How well is/was x done/made? (= evaluation of action)
What features do/did A and B share, whatever their differences?

The tense and modality of the verb forms used in the questions vary according to the context in which the discourse is being produced and according to the type of discourse produced. So, for example, a procedural discourse (e.g. a series of instructions on how to rustproof your car) might include the answer to the question *How might x be done?* or an interview might include the question *How will x be done?*

Our four-sentence artificial text can now be projected into dialogue. As a consequence of selecting an artificial example, the last sentence involves the conflation of two questions, both of which are given below:

5   A: What was the situation?
    B: I was on sentry duty.
    A: What was the problem?
    B: I saw the enemy approaching.
    A: What was your solution?
    B: I opened fire.
    A: What was the result?
    and
        How successful was this?
    B: I beat off the enemy attack.

The questions used here need some refinement. *What was the problem?* is a reasonably natural form of the more precise question *What aspect of the situation required a response?* As we shall see, there are other good reasons for defining *problem* as *an aspect of situation requiring a response*; these will become apparent below.

The question *What was the solution?* also requires qualification. As it stands, it is the natural form of the much less likely question *What was your response* (to the aspect of the situation requiring a response)? Although it is convenient most of the time to talk about Problem–Solution structures, it is important to notice that the word *solution* contains within it an evaluation of a particular response as successful. Since we shall want to be able to account for texts which describe unsuccessful responses, it is worth keeping the more artificial question as our more precise test of the existence of that part of the 'Problem–Solution' structure.

The final pair of questions in our dialogue version of the 'sentry' text also require discussion. We have seen, of course, that one sentence may answer more than one question. What we must now note is that these questions need not suggest exactly the same communicative function for the sentence that answers them. For example, in our artificial text, the first question, *What was the result?*, can be answered by a statement of non-evaluated detail, for example:

6   A: What was the result?
    B: The result was that two hundred men died;

which is relatively neutral as to the speaker's attitude. The second question can be answered by a statement of evaluation, for example:

7 A: How successful was this?
   B: This proved a successful move;

which is relatively unspecific and evaluative.

It is doubtful, moreover, whether the questions and answers can be satisfactorily exchanged. Even allowing for the fact that we are playing with artificial examples, 8 and 9 seem highly contrived.

8 A: What was the result?
   B: It proved a successful move.

9 A: How successful was this?
   B: The result was that 200 men died.

It is reasonable therefore to assume that the fourth sentence of our artificial text serves two functions, one, that of *result*, the other, that of *evaluation*, which can be fused but need not be. More strictly, we might argue that the fourth sentence has *result* as a primary function and *evaluation* only as a secondary function. The reason for this analysis is that it answers the question *What is the result?* directly:

10 A: What was the result?
   B: (The result was that) I beat off the enemy attack.

It does not, however, answer the question *How successful was this?* quite so directly:

11 A: How successful was this?
   B: It was very successful.
   A: What is your basis for saying so?
   B: I beat off the enemy attack.

Our final structure for our minimum text is then as follows:

Situation[1] . . . Problem . . . Response . . . (Result/Evaluation).[2]

The coherence of this structure is better shown if the fuller labels are used:

Situation
Aspect of Situation requiring a Response
Response to Aspect of Situation requiring a Response
Result of Response to Aspect of Situation requiring a Response
Evaluation of Result of Response to Aspect of Situation requiring a Response

This looks neat; the truth is slightly less so. To begin with, *Evaluation* may and often does precede *Result*. So we might have had:

12 I was on sentry duty. I saw the enemy approaching. I opened fire. This
   did the trick. I beat off the enemy attack.

In this order, the last sentence serves as the *basis* for the *evaluation* at the
clause relational level. The structure would then be *Situation–Problem–
Response–Evaluation* with the last two sentences supplying the *Evaluation*.

LEVELS OF DETAIL

This leads us to an important modification to our case as stated so far. For the
sake of simplicity of presentation, an artificial text has been used with a one-
to-one correspondence between sentence and structural element. No such
correspondence exists in real texts; if it did, no text would be longer than a
handful of sentences. So we could have, for example,

13 A: What was the situation?
   B: It was six o'clock in the evening. I was on sentry duty.
   A: What was the aspect of the situation that required a response?
   B: I saw the enemy approaching. There were five hundred of them in all.
   A: What was your response?
   B: I sent a message for reinforcements. At the same time I opened fire
      with a machine-gun.
   A: How successful was this? *and*
      What was the result?
   B: At first they kept on coming. In the end, however, I beat off the enemy
      attack.

where each of the structural elements is taken up by two sentences. It should
be noticed that in this expanded version of the artificial text, the new
sentences answer typical questions such as *What else did you do?* and *How
many?*; these do not alter the structure of the text but ask that additional detail
be supplied.

   A diagrammatic representation of the structure of our text now looks like
this:

$$A \quad\text{---}\quad B \quad\text{---}\quad C \quad\text{---}\quad D$$
$$a \uparrow b \qquad a \uparrow b \qquad a \uparrow b \qquad a \uparrow b$$
$$t_1 \qquad\qquad t_2 \qquad\qquad t_3 \qquad\qquad t_4$$

where the upper-case letters ABCD represent the sentences' functions in the
overall structure, the lower-case letters a and b represent the sentences'
relations with their neighbours and the lower-case letters t_1, t_2, t_3, t_4, represent
chronological sequence.[3] It should be noted that this diagram merely represents levels of detail of analysis; it does not carry the implication that each
level is a different 'rank' from the one above and below it in Halliday's sense
(1961), though it does carry the implication that structural links only occur at
one level at a time. It should also be noted that the diagram carries with it the

possibility of recursiveness, so it is possible to have one complete structure inside an element of another complete structure.

PROBLEM–SOLUTION: LANGUAGE OR LIFE

The projection of monologue into question-and-answer dialogue form is an important test of the structure of a discourse. Examples of its operation on real discourses will be given shortly. But it might be argued that the possibility of such projection is the consequence of describing not the language but the reality which the language encodes.

Consider the following extract from an advertisement for cold wax strips:

14 The other day my teenage daughter asked me about hair removal for the first time. Apparently, her new boyfriend has passed a comment about her legs being hairy, and she wanted to do something about it before a party on Friday night.
(from 'Carol Francis Talks about Unwanted Hair Removal', an advertisement current in the 1980s)

You do not have to accept the writer's claim that hairy legs are a problem to recognize that the writer is reporting them as a problem; indeed many readers would claim that the writer is wrong in identifying hair as the problem and would suggest that the real problem was the boyfriend's attitude. In other words, a linguistic 'problem' need not be seen as a real-world problem by the reader, nor need the reader accept a linguistic 'solution' as a real-world solution. How then does the reader identify the writer's problem and solution? Presumably it is because they have been presented as such in the language itself. It is no counterargument to point out that they are presumably realities to the writer; the writer's realities in this case and in most others are only accessible through the language he or she uses. Put simply, it is normally the structure that tells us of the reality, not the reality that helps us create the structure. In the next few sections, we shall look at several aspects of signalling in a discourse of a Problem–Solution structure.

VOCABULARY 3

In a detailed study of the metalanguage of English, Winter (1977a) shows that relationships between clauses can be signalled in one of three ways: by subordination, which he terms Vocabulary 1; by sentence connectors, which include conjuncts, and which he terms Vocabulary 2; and by lexical items, which he terms Vocabulary 3. He notes that items from all three vocabularies can frequently be used to paraphrase each other. So for example *by ing*, *thus* and *instrumental* may all be used to indicate the logical sequence relation of instrument:

15 *By* appeal*ing* to scientists and technologists to support his party, Mr
Wilson won many middle-class votes in the election.

16 Mr Wilson appealed to scientists and technologists to support his party.
He *thus* won many middle-class votes in the election.

17 Mr Wilson's appeals to scientists and technologists to support his party
were *instrumental* in winning many middle-class votes in the election.

(all three examples from Winter 1977a)

He points out that the differences between these possibilities lie not in the
relations they represent but in the contexts in which they would most
naturally appear. Since Vocabularies 1 and 2 are closed-system, their
Vocabulary 3 paraphrases must, he suggests, share some of their closed-
system features. He goes on to show how these closed-system Vocabulary 3
items with the grammatical appearance of open-system lexis operate and how
they may be identified.

The notion of Vocabulary 3 is crucial to our understanding of how a
discourse signals to its reader/listener what structure it has. Although Winter's
main concern is to show the operation of lexical signalling at the level of the
paragraph or below, he makes mention of its operation at a larger level.

I have included the following five items which represent a larger clause-
relation in English. My reason for doing so is that these relations may
sometimes exist as clause relations within the unit of the *paragraph*. The
items are *situation*, *problem*, *solution*, *observation*, and *evaluation*.

(Winter 1977a:19)

It is this extension of the notion of Vocabulary 3 to cover whole discourses
which enables us to demonstrate the ways in which discourses signal their
structure.

LEXICAL SIGNALLING AND THE 'SENTRY DUTY' DISCOURSE

We can now see that one of the features that contributes to the unreality of our
'sentry duty' example as a discourse is the total absence of any lexical
signalling.

A more natural telling of the same story might have been the following:

18 I was on sentry duty. I saw the enemy approaching. To prevent them
coming closer, I opened fire. This way I beat off the enemy attack.

In this version the purpose clause in the third sentence is a two-way signal. It
indicates that what follows is Response and that what precedes it is Problem;
this is achieved by the item *prevent* and grammar of purpose, *to x*. *This way*
is also a two-way signal, indicating that what follows it is Result and what
precedes it is Response. Thus Response is signalled twice in this version
before we begin to use the question tests.

THE EVALUATIVE NATURE OF LEXICAL SIGNALLING

There is one more point that needs to be made about lexical signalling before we move on to the examination of a complete real text. Vocabulary 3 signalling is essentially evaluative, whether in signalling sentences, clauses or phrases, though not at the level of the overall structure. So:

19 A: I saw the enemy approaching.
   B: How did you evaluate this?
      or
      What did you feel about this?
   A: It (This) was a problem.

If we accept this, it follows that our structures and relations themselves are also evaluative, for example:

20 A: I opened fire. I beat off the enemy attack.
   B: What is your evaluation of these two facts?
   A: I feel they are related in a solution-result way (or, on a different level, an instrument-achievement way).

This would mean that a fuller representation of the Problem–Solution structure would be as follows:

Situation	——	Evaluation of Situation
Situation	——	Evaluation of Situation as *Problem*
Situation	——	Evaluation of Situation as *Response* or *Solution*
Evaluation		

The italicized elements represent the structural elements of the text.

It follows from the essentially evaluative nature of the discourse structure that its parts can be signalled by purely evaluative means. So, for instance, in the following extract the Problem is signalled initially by the negative evaluation *poor*:

21 If thyristors are used to control the motor of an electric car, the vehicle moves smoothly but with *poor* efficiency at low speeds.
                    (from Technology Review, *New Scientist*, 1970)

THE SIGNALLING OF THE PROBLEM–SOLUTION STRUCTURE IN REAL DISCOURSES

We are now in a position to examine how the discourse structure we have been describing operates in a complete discourse. The discourse we have chosen is drawn from the Technology Review, in the *New Scientist*; each sentence is numbered for convenience of reference.

22 Balloons and Air Cushion the Fall
(1)(a) Helicopters are very convenient for dropping freight by parachute
(b) but this system has its problems. (2) Somehow the landing impact has
to be cushioned to give a soft landing. (3) The movement to be absorbed
depends on the weight and the speed at which the charge falls. (4)
Unfortunately most normal spring systems bounce the load as it lands,
sometimes turning it over.

(5) (a) To avoid this, Bertin, developer of the aerotrain, has come up
with an air-cushion system (b) which assures a safe and soft landing. (6)
It comprises a platform on which the freight is loaded with, underneath, a
series of 'balloons' supported by air cushions. (7) These are fed from
compressed air cylinders equipped with an altimeter valve which opens
when the load is just over six feet from the ground. (8) The platform then
becomes a hovercraft, with the balloons reducing the deceleration as it
touches down.

(9) Trials have been carried out with freight-dropping at rates of from 19
feet to 42 feet per second in winds of 49 feet per second. (10) The charge
weighed about one and a half tons, but the system can handle up to eight
tons. (11) At low altitudes freight can be dropped without a parachute.

(from Technology Review, *New Scientist*, 1970)

This text has the following basic structure:

The first half of sentence (1) (1a)	Situation
Sentences (1b)–(4)	Problem
Sentences (5)–(8) (excluding 5b)	Response
Sentences (5b) and (9)–(11)	Evaluation

The following sections seek to provide an account of the signalling of this
structure (and in so doing a justification for identifying such a structure).

SITUATION AND EVALUATION

Example 22 begins with a very short Situation clause which is couched in
evaluative terms. By this we mean that the first half of sentence (1) (1a) is
an example of the possibility described on page 35, namely, Situation–
Evaluation of Situation. This can be shown if it is paraphrased into two
separate sentences thus:

23 Helicopters are used for dropping freight by parachute. They are very
convenient for this.

where the first sentence is Situation and the second is Evaluation of Situation.
It is not uncommon to have an evaluative element within a Situation. Another
example of a Situation with such an element was 21, repeated for convenience below:

24 If thyristors are used to control the motor car, the vehicle moves smoothly

where *smoothly* evaluates positively the control of the motor car, in preparation for the negative evaluation to follow – *but with poor efficiency at low speeds*. As we shall see, much the same contrast of 'good' and 'bad' evaluations is present in our main text. The function of a 'good' evaluative element within the Situation is to put the Problem – which is a 'bad' aspect of the Situation – into the larger context of 'good' aspects of the Situation. (Else why 'solve' the Problem at all?[4])

THE SIGNALLING OF SITUATION IN THE SAMPLE DISCOURSE

The function of (1a) can be identified as Situation in the following ways.

(a) *Verb tense*: One reason for treating sentence (1a) as Situation is that the verb is in the simple non-past form. Context by its nature does not normally involve a moment in time, unless it is a summary of events or a recapitulation. We would *a priori* expect therefore that the verb form for Situation would be one that indicated a period of time rather than a point in time. When the Situation is part of either a narrative or is itself a recapitulation of past events, the verbs are, however, normally of the simple past type.

(b) *Lexical signalling*:[5] A second reason for identifying sentence (1a) as situation is that sentence (1b) (i.e. *but this system has its problems*) contains an anaphoric reference to (1a) in the phrase *this system*. *System* is an item which can be used to signal either Situation or Response, and in this case retrospectively indicates that sentence (1a) is to be regarded as Situational.

(c) *Position*: The position of (1a) is that of first clause in the discourse. The expectation of the first sentence of any discourse is that it will provide a context for subsequent sentences. It is, of course, quite possible to thwart this expectation, and position by itself cannot be allowed to carry too much weight.

THE SIGNALLING OF PROBLEM IN THE SAMPLE DISCOURSE

Sentences (1b)–(4) can be identified as constituting the *problem*. A number of features signal this as their function; most of these are sufficient by themselves to serve as an adequate indication of the three sentences' function within the discourse. All are instances of lexical signalling.

(a) *'but this system has its problems'*: The first and perhaps the most obvious signal of Problem is the signalling clause *but this system has its problems*. As a general statement, such a clause will normally be followed by particulars. In the absence of any evidence for a contrary reading, therefore, sentences (2)–(4) will be read as providing the particulars to the general statement about the existence of Problems.

Sometimes the signalling item Problem precedes even the Situation. In the following example, the item Problem requires further specification.

25 I doubt that many of the readers suffer from my problem. I am expecting our second baby but unlike most women who go off things like tea and coffee, I have completely gone off wine!

(from the letter column of *The Winemaker* February 1975)

(b) *Need:* A second signal of Problem in our main text is the verb phrase *has to* in sentence (2). This indicates a need. Indeed it is possible to paraphrase the sentence using *need to* in place of *have to*, viz.:

26 Somehow the landing impact needs to be cushioned to give a soft landing.

One definition of *need* might be *an aspect of situation requiring a response*, which we used as our alternative formulation of Problem on page 30.

(c) *'Somehow'*: A third signal of Problem in our main discourse is the use of *somehow* in sentence (2). The use of the indefinite adjunct of instrument *somehow* indicates that we have an unfulfilled Instrument–Purpose relationship. This can be shown by the following informal dialogue:

27 A: The landing impact has to be cushioned to give a soft landing.
    B: How?
    A: Somehow.
    B: Yes, but how?

Somehow is the signal of a needed and missing Response. It should be noted that even if no mention were made of Problems in the signalling clause, the missing instrument would still be sufficient to signal Problem:

28 Helicopters are very convenient for dropping freight by parachute, but somehow the landing impact has to be cushioned to give a soft landing.

The *but* left over from the signalling clause has a part to play in this; it indicates that the following clause (formerly sentence (3)) contains material that is incompatible with the positive evaluation of sentence (1a).

(d) *Negative evaluation*: In sentence (4), the item *unfortunately* indicates a negative evaluation in contrast to the positive one of sentence (1a). As a disjunct, however, it does not convert the whole sentence into an Evaluation, but remains a comment on the information carried in the clause to which it is attached. It can be paraphrased thus:

29 Most normal spring systems bounce the load as it lands, sometimes turning it over. This is unfortunate.

When an aspect of Situation is negatively evaluated, it is likely to involve the identification of *an aspect of situation requiring a response* especially in the context of a signalling clause such as (1b). Even without the signalling clause, though, we would still have an acceptable Situation–Problem pair:

30 Helicopters are very convenient for dropping freight by parachute. Unfortunately most normal spring systems bounce the load as it lands.

Another instance of the use of *unfortunately* to signal Problem is the following:

31 *Unfortunately*, it's only too human for a messenger (or a manager, come to that) to stop and chat about football. (Or simply to wait till enough paperwork has piled up before he thinks it's worth doing his rounds.)
(from an advertisement for D. D. Lamson current in 1978)

As was remarked on page 35, negative evaluation is a common signal of Problem.

(e) *'Avoid'*: In sentence (5), the signalling clause *to avoid this* refers anaphorically to sentence (4) and retrospectively categorizes it as 'something to avoid'. *Avoid* is an item that may serve as a two-armed signpost, pointing to both Problem and Response, where what is to be avoided is categorized as Problem and what is to be adopted as the means of avoidance is categorized as Response. Another example of *avoid* being used in this way is:

32 Plaque is a sticky film that clings to teeth, causing decay and the unhealthy gum condition that dentists call gingivitis. To *avoid* this condition, use Inter-Dens Gum Massage Sticks regularly.
(from an advertisement for Inter-Dens Gum Massage Sticks current in 1978)

Other items that function similarly to *avoid* are *prevent* and *stop*, for instance:

33 What is required is something that can be brought into action very quickly to *prevent* flooding . . .
(from *New Scientist*, Note on the News, August 1967)

34 I have a small rug which is on a polished wood floor. It slides dangerously every time anyone steps on it, and I'm afraid someone will slip and hurt themselves. Can you tell me how to *stop* the rug from sliding?
(from *Living*, 'The Oracle', July 1978)

THE SIGNALLING OF SOLUTION (OR RESPONSE)

Sentences (5)–(8) comprise our next main functional element within the text, that of Solution (or Response). Some of the reasons for regarding these sentences as Solution also serve to provide further evidence for treating sentences (2)–(4) as Problem; that they are handled here rather than above should not be allowed to obscure that fact. We exclude from our analysis at this stage the subordinate clause in sentence (5); the reasons for this will become apparent shortly.

The main features that identify sentences (5)–(8) as Response are as follows:

(a) *Lexical signalling*: The phrase *to avoid this* explicitly signals the Response to a Problem, as has already been noted. The phrasal verb *come up with* is a Vocabulary 3 item signalling a Response to a Problem (normally), though perhaps more frequent in journalism than in technical writing. It is commonly used in phrases such as *come up with a solution*, *come up with an answer* and *come up with an idea*. A more common lexical item for signalling Solution (or Response) is *develop*. Examples of the use of *develop* in a similar context to that of *come up with* in our chosen discourse are as follows:

35 This is why the Vichy laboratories *have developed* Equalia.
　　　　　　　　　　　　(from an advertisement for *Equalia* current in 1978)
36 The North Holland Provincial Water Authority *has developed* an ingenious solution, in the form of an inflatable dam made of steel sheets and rubber-nylon fabric.
　　　　　　　　　　　　(from the *New Scientist*, Notes on the News, August 1967)

(b) *Verb form*: The change of verb form that occurs in sentence (5) indicates the beginning of a new functional unit. The verb of sentence (5) is the form traditionally known as the present perfect, that is, *have -ed*. This verb form is used to describe happenings that either began or took place wholly in the past but that continue or have consequences of interest in the present. As such it is the natural tense for the description of Response since responses normally occur at a definable time in the past and by their nature have consequences for the present. Once, however, the general nature of the response has been described, the verb form reverts to the simple non-past since the method of response continues to be valid over a period of time extended beyond the present. This is totally compatible with the Responses being regarded as providing New Situation.[6] In scientific reportage the pattern of *have -ed* followed by simple non-past is a very common one for Response.

Further examples can be found in 35 and 36 just quoted, where *develop* combines with the *have -ed* form.

THE SIGNALLING OF EVALUATION IN THE SAMPLE DISCOURSE

In the above analysis we omitted the subordinate clause in sentence (5). This is because its function is that of Evaluation. The lexical item *assures* is used to express Evaluation; assurance can never be a matter of fact, only of assessment.[7] The evaluative clause appears where it does because it serves to provide an incentive to read on. By evaluating Bertin's solution as successful, the writer encourages the reader to find out more about it. This is quite common in popular scientific texts, particularly those reporting someone else's work. Winter (1976) refers to it as the previewing function.

　　Another example of a Solution being immediately evaluated is:

37 The North Holland Provincial Authority has developed an *ingenious* solution . . .

The evaluation need not be positive, in which case the Solution is better termed a Response, for example:

38 So he went all over the world looking for one. But every time there was *something the matter.*
(from Hans Andersen's *The Princess on the Pea*, trans. by Reginald Spink (1960) Everyman Library, J M Dent)

As we have already seen, a negative evaluation may signal a Problem. In such circumstances a recursive structure may occur where the Evaluation of Response is New Problem, thus:

```
                Situation
                Problem
                Response
(negative)      Evaluation =    Problem
                                Response
          (negative)      Evaluation =    Problem
                                          etc.
```

The beginning of the Hans Andersen story just quoted manifests in a simple form such a recursive structure.

Sentences (9)–(11) of our *New Scientist* text combine with the evaluative clause in sentence (5) to form the Evaluation of the discourse. Sentences (9) and (10a) are not in themselves evaluative but provide the Basis for the evaluative clause in sentence (5). What this means is that we have a clause relation at paragraph level which we can term Evaluation Basis, which in turn comprises (part of) the evaluation at discourse level:

Situation – Problem – Response – Evaluation

Evaluation   Basis[8]

The most important evidence for such an analysis comes from the question test. Nevertheless two features are present which help to signal the functions of sentences (9) and (10a).

(1) There is a change in verb form from simple non-past in sentences (6), (7) and (8) to present perfect in sentence (9) and simple past in sentence (10a). As has elsewhere been remarked, a change of verb form is frequently a signal of structural change.

(2) The term *trials* is one of a set also including *test* and *experiment* used to indicate Basis for Evaluation. These are frequently collocated with the verb *carry out.*

Sentences (10b) and (11) are also part of the Evaluation, but unlike sentences

(9) and (10a), they are evaluative in themselves. This is in part signalled by:

(a) the change of tense to simple non-past;
(b) the use of *can*. *Can* is an evaluative item used to assess possibilities. *Can he do it?* asks for an evaluation of a man's capability, and the reply *Yes, he can* is taken as such.

THE USE OF THE DIALOGUE TEST

In the previous five sections we have described the signalling system of the discourse under discussion. In this section, we briefly demonstrate the applicability of the question test outlined on pages 29–31. There are two reasons for such an order of presentation. First, in one sense the signalling system is prior to and more important than the implicit question–answer system of the discourse in that the signals are already there as a physical part of the discourse, whereas questions involve the introduction into the discourse of what is not explicit. Second, since the question test does involve the introduction into the discourse of artificially regulated signals, it is necessary at times for the signals already present in the discourse to be removed if a superfluity of signals is not to result. The discourse can be projected into dialogue form as follows:

39 A: What is the situation (for which helicopters are suited)?
   B: Helicopters are very convenient for dropping freight by parachute.
   A: What aspect of this situation requires a response?
       or
       What is the problem?
   B: Somehow the landing impact has to be cushioned to give a soft landing. The movement to be absorbed depends on the weight and the speed at which the charge falls. Unfortunately, most normal spring systems bounce the load as it lands, sometimes turning it over.
   A: What response has there been?
       or
       What solution has been proposed?
       or
       Who has proposed a solution?[9]
   B: Bertin, developer of the aerotrain, has come up with an air-cushion system.
   A: How successful is it?
   B: It assures a safe and soft landing.
   A: What are the details of this solution?
   B: It comprises a platform on which the freight is loaded with, underneath, a series of 'balloons' supported by air cushions. These are fed from compressed air cylinders equipped with an altimeter valve which opens when the load is just over six feet from the ground. The platform

then becomes a hovercraft, with the balloons reducing the deceleration as it touches down.

A: What evidence have you for saying it is successful?

B: Trials have been carried out with freight dropping rates of from 19 feet to 42 feet per second in winds of 49 feet per second. The charge weighed about one and a half tons.

A: What is it capable of?

B: The system can handle up to eight tons. At low altitudes freight can be dropped without a parachute.

POINTS OF INTEREST

Several points of interest arise out of the analysis of this text. First, it will be noticed that there is a crude approximation between the functional units Situation, Problem, Solution (Response) and Evaluation and the orthographic unit of the paragraph. Similar (and closer) approximations can be found in many other texts.

Second, it is also worthy of note that a reasonable skeleton summary of the text can be achieved by the simple expedient of taking the first full sentence of each functional unit, as long as we (1) exclude the signalling clauses *but this system has its problems* and *to avoid this*, and (2) either exclude the evaluative element of sentence (1a) or include the conjunction *but* that follows it. This gives us 40 and 41:[10]

40 Helicopters are used for dropping freight by parachute. Somehow the landing impact has to be cushioned to give a soft landing. Bertin, developer of the aerotrain, has come up with an air-cushion system which assures a safe and soft landing. Trials have been carried out with freight-dropping at rates from 19 feet to 42 feet per second in winds of 49 feet per second.

41 Helicopters are very convenient for dropping freight by parachute but somehow the landing impact has to be cushioned to give a soft landing. Bertin, developer of the aerotrain, has come up with an air-cushion system which assures a safe and soft landing. Trials have been carried out with freight-dropping at rates of from 19 feet to 42 feet per second in winds of 49 feet per second.

DISCUSSION AND CONCLUSIONS

The following claims have been made in this chapter:

(1) There are three types of sentence sequence: unmarked, marked and incoherent.

(2) Each sentence in a complete text has a function in the structure as a whole either in itself or as part of a larger unit, and not just in relation to the preceding sentence.

(3) All structural functions can be defined only in terms of each other and the whole.
(4) Normally each structural function is overtly signalled linguistically.
(5) Some clauses and sentences have as their main function the clarification of the structure of the discourse to which they belong.
(6) Each structural function can be isolated by means of the projection of the discourse into question–answer dialogue or by the insertion of appropriate lexical signals.
(7) One common discourse structure in English (though not the only one) is that of Situation–Problem–Solution (or Response)–Result–Evaluation.

The discourse structure outlined in this chapter is not confined to the types of discourse illustrated. It can be applied effectively, for example, to discourses as disparate as fairytales (see Grimes 1975) and interviews. The signalling system, however, varies in detail somewhat from discourse type to discourse type, though not in underlying nature.

In general terms, what this chapter has attempted to do has been to show how the English language indicates to the reader/listener the functions of a particular discourse's constituent sentences. Lack of space has prevented the examination of discourses whose use of the language's signalling facilities is 'faulty'. Nevertheless such discourses do exist and problems of comprehension can be shown to arise from 'faulty' or missing signalling. If this is accepted, important practical consequences can be glimpsed for the field of rhetoric. In particular, the thorny question of how to improve the communicative skills of student scientists and technologists might in part be answered by demonstrating to them not only the typical Problem–Solution structure but also the signalling system available to make clear the structure of whatever they write.

NOTES

1 As will be seen below, Situation is definable both in terms of its relationship with the other elements of the structure and in terms of its typical signals. Although it has some features in common with Setting as used by Gleason (1968) and Grimes (1975), it differs from that category in being wider (including events at times) and in being defined structurally as well as internally.
2 The parentheses indicate fusion of elements of the structure.
3 Chronological sequence underpins the whole structure. Sentences (2) and (3) can both be seen as answering the question 'What happened (next)?' Interestingly, another question that could elicit *I beat off the enemy attack* is 'How did it all end?' (I am indebted to Eugene Winter for this point.)
4 This analysis is oversimplified in fact. It is possible to analyse these sentences in terms of Problem–Solution–Evaluation. The Evaluation is of the use of helicopters (Solution) to meet the need (Problem) of dropping freight by parachute.
5 Here and elsewhere the signals discussed should in no way be considered exhaustive. Situation, for example, is often signalled by the items *occasion*, *place*, *background* and, of course, *situation*, none of which appear in the discourse under discussion. Further discussion of the signals of Problem–Solution can be found in

Hoey (1983); Jordan (1984) also contains detailed discussion of the pattern and its signalling.

6 A Response or Solution is a change in situation; when the details are given, they are often couched in situational form, reflecting their status as New Situation.

7 *Assures* is not a paraphrase of *yields* but of *makes certain*.

8 The Basis can itself be further analysed into component parts relating to the structure of the trial.

9 Each question presupposes a slightly different emphasis in the answer.

10 That is, the first sentence of the Situation, Problem, Solution and Evaluation. The first sentence of Basis is also given.

4 Clause relations as information structure: two basic text structures in English

Eugene Winter

INTRODUCTION TO CLAUSE RELATIONS

This chapter describes two basic discourse structures in English within their linguistic contexts, noting that the study of written discourse should include the following perspectives of language use:

(a) A study of the grammar of the clause in the sentence. This includes such connective devices as conjunctions and their lexical paraphrases (lexical metalanguage), other adverbials, substitutes of various kinds and repetition, which includes the *replacement of the clause* (see examples 1–5 for this on pp. 51 and 52), tense, modality, aspect etc., all of which signal the place of the clause in its sentence with respect to clauses in adjoining sentences.

> *Preview of some repetition and replacement*
> (The *repetition structure* is shown in italics, with the remainder of the clause as *replacement change*)
> 1 'What we have still not forgiven him for', she says, 'is that he [Mozart] *reasoned*.' Miss Brophy, whose spiritual home is the eighteenth century enlightenment, also *reasons*.
> 2 The symbols *seem easy to the point of glibness. So does* the scepticism that repeatedly informs them.
> 3 No Russian *wants to conquer the world*. Some Americans *do*, on the best crusading grounds.
> 4 'Little boys don't *play with dolls*, girls *play with dolls*.'
> 5 '*The bee* didn't *get* tired – *it got* dead.'

(b) A study of the **basic clause relations**. These are the *sequential relations* between clauses, both inside the grammatical domain of their sentences and immediately outside this domain – the significant sequence of grouped sentences whose sequence may be further signalled by the connective devices mentioned in (a).

(c) A study of the two **basic discourse structures** in English whose meanings may organize significant sequences of sentences as part of their wholes as '**messages**'. We could regard them as **vehicles** of the basic clause relations.

Three assumptions about the clause

We begin with three assumptions upon which our theoretical approach to the clause in context is based.

The first assumption

We start with the assumption of a limited communication, and ask ourselves what the clauses in our sentences are doing in the kind of discourse structure we accept as some kind of complete message. A commonplace in communication studies is that all communication is, by definition, imperfect, though we rarely get statements of *why* it is imperfect. As linguists, this question directly concerns us if we wish to account for how language works in a manner that can be practically applied. This is where the notion of relevance is central. We will start with the grammar of the clause in the sentence.

Taking up the communication idea again, communication is imperfect if only because *we cannot say everything about anything at any time*. Quite apart from the physical fact that neither we nor our listeners have unlimited energy, time and patience, very powerful forces prevent this perfection. We are forced to settle for saying less than everything by the need to produce *unique sentences* whose selected content has been in some way *predetermined* by that of its immediately preceding sentences or by the previous history of its larger message structure. The central discipline acting upon our production of sentences in a discourse structure is the need for relevance.

What does relevance imply linguistically? To the decoder, relevance implies the relevance of the topic and its development in the sense of being told something s/he does not know in terms of something s/he does know, and this implies a *unique message* transmitted for *a particular purpose* in *a particular context* at *a particular time*. To the encoder, relevance means being compelled to choose words lexically as permitted by the grammar of their lexical patterns for each of the sentences in turn of the above message, significant clusters of words which not only represent a knowledge of the world which s/he shares with his/her decoder, but which also have to be judged as relevant to the particular purpose of the unique message. This implies the encoder's assumption of the uniqueness of his/her message.

In the process of settling for saying much less than everything, the clause, not the sentence, is the device of relevance; that is, their lexical and hence the grammatical choices permitted by this lexical choice are guided by *their perceived relevance to the unique message*. The clause imposes a very powerful constraint on what we select from the large whole of our knowledge of the world of the immediate situation which we are communicating. In a word, the clause is strictly a partial linguistic representation of the larger linguistic and non-linguistic context of the knowledge of the encoder who is doing the communicating. As such, the study of verbal interaction should be a study of how we use grammar and lexis to settle for saying less than everything.

In any sequenced utterance, the signals of lexis and grammar and of the grammatical status of the clause are crucial to the *understanding and interpretation of the message*, and any discourse analysis which skips the surface grammar of the clause in these early days does so at its peril.

To demonstrate that we are very sensitive to the grammar of the final grammatical status of the clause, imagine a situation where you are desperate to find out something for the purpose of taking decisive action, and the information you want is contained in a text sixty sentences long which is available in two versions. Text A has no emphasis; everything is unmarked. Text B has the normal emphasis most writers would place: that is, we have both the unmarked (the so-called scientific objectivity) and the marked clause structure. Now which would you choose, the poker-faced text A which betrays no emotions, or the more human appropriately emphasized text B?

Why would you choose text B? The lay reply would be that it is more interesting to read. The linguist's reply must be that, by using the marked grammar of elements of the clause, the writer is drawing our attention to particular clauses in particular sentences as being more important at that point in the context. These emphases represent *his/her personal evaluation of what s/he is saying*. In this sense, then, the emphases are subjective.

Whatever it is, the emphases guide us to what the writer feels or how s/he sees or interprets what s/he is saying. In text A, we would have to work out for ourselves what might be important in each sentence we read unless the writer actually *says* something is important, such as *This is most important . . . it is vital that . . .* A crude parallel in spoken texts is the difference between a monotone delivery and normal intonation. This suffices to illustrate the crucial nature of the signalling by the lexical grammar of the clause.

The second assumption

As we have already noted above, the clause is the significant semantic unit of sentence function, so that a sentence can consist of one or more clauses. For this, the traditional notions of simple sentence for the one-clause sentence (independent clause) and complex and compound sentences suffice. Whatever it is, we as discourse analysts have to account for every clause in every sentence since every clause ultimately matters to the message, if we assume efficient expert purposeful communication. The significance of 'clause' will become more apparent in the discussion of clause relations below.

The third assumption

Whatever theory we might have about clause relations as such, we have got to assume that the relations between the clause in its sentence and its adjoining sentences cannot be random or haphazard, and extending this beyond the sentence, the meaning of every sentence is a function of its adjoining sentences, particularly those which immediately precede it. What this means is that if you think of the clause as a grammatical device which constrains lexical selection, then the relevance of its lexical selections are also in some way constrained by the relevance of those in its adjoining clauses. Here we enter into the realm of clause relations.

Clause relations

How can we approach clause relations in the simplest possible manner? Let us for the moment ignore the two facts of grammar: on the one hand, where we have connection within the domain of sentence, that is, apposition, co-ordination and subordination; and on the other hand, where the clause may be part of the grammar of a larger clause such as subject, object, complement, adjunct, etc. The moment you put together any two sentences for a purpose, your listener or reader looks for a sensible connection between their topics, and if they make sense to him/her, it will be because s/he can *relate the two sentences* in the same way as they relate the constituents of the clause in *expected ways*. The important fact in these utterances is the fact of *sequence*. It is not generally recognized even now that our shared consensus about the interpretation of sequence is analogous to that of the grammar of the clause. It is not merely the putting together of two clauses that affects sequence meaning but also the sequence in which they are put together, as example 11 on page 56 below demonstrates.

Preview of sentence sequence of newspaper hoarding in example 11

(a)	(b)	(c)	(d)	(e)	(f)
Enjoy it	Buy it	Read it	Enjoy it	Buy it	Read it
Buy it	Enjoy it	Enjoy it	Read it	Read it	Buy it
Read it	Read it	Buy it	Buy it	Enjoy it	Enjoy it

My latest definition of clause relations takes the clause as the largest unit of meaning in the sentence, so that relations between sentences are really the synthesized sum of the relations between their constituent clauses. It is as follows:

> A Clause Relation is the shared cognitive process whereby we interpret the meaning of a Clause or group of clauses in the light of their adjoining clauses or group of clauses. Where the clauses are independent, we speak of 'sentence relations'. (This revises Winter 1971, 1974, 1977a, 1979, and 1982.) It is in no way incompatible with Hoey (1983: 19) quoted here:

> A clause relation is also the cognitive process whereby the choices we make from the Grammar, Lexis and intonation in the creation of a sentence or group of sentences made in the light of its adjoining sentence or group of sentences.

(See also the early work of Beekman and Callow (1974) and Longacre (1972) for descriptions of propositions between sentences.)

In this chapter, I am concerned with the notion of clause which is subsumed as part of the sentence in Hoey's definition.

I divide clause relations into two main kinds of relation between a membership of clauses or sentences in which the one (**basic clause relations**) can be found within the structure of membership of the other (**basic text structure**). Basic clause relations are our *stock relations between any two clauses or sentences* the moment they are put together. Basic text structures are the *basic message structures* which act as particular linguistic contexts or vehicles for basic clause relations. Like basic clause relations, basic text structures can form complete structures whose membership can consist of as little as two one-clause sentences. Where there is more than a two one-clause membership for basic text structure, we enter into the domain of internal detail of the text, that of basic clause relations.

At its most simple, basic clause relations can either be **matching** or **logical sequence**, or a composite or multiple relation in which the semantics of both matching and logical sequence relate the same two members. This last is called a **multiple** or **mixed relation**. Similarly, basic text structures can be one of two kinds: **Situation** and **Evaluation** and **hypothetical** and **real**, or they can be a combination of structure of both sets of text relations.

I will now briefly describe basic clause relations and then concentrate more on basic text structures and their text relations. In describing basic clause relations, we take the matching relation first for convenience, then follow this with logical sequence and multiple clause relations.

BASIC CLAUSE RELATIONS 1: THE MATCHING RELATION

The matching relation is the term I have given to the larger semantic field which is characterized by a high degree of systematic repetition between its clauses, and by the semantics of compatibility or incompatibility. Within compatibility, we have comparisons, alternatives and the crucial unspecific–specific relation, which includes general and particular and appositions; within incompatibility, we have contrasts and contradictions which includes **Denial** and **Correction**. (See Winter (1974: 103) for the notion of denial and correction. This relation was first described by Poutsma (1926–9: 157) as Substitutive Adversative Co-ordination.)

Taking comparisons, which can be compatible and incompatible, we note that a matching relation is where we compare or match one attribute, person, action, event, thing, etc. in respect of their similarities and differences. The notable thing about this relation, apart from the likelihood of a very high degree of repetition, is that its **unspecific matching semantics** can be expressed as: 'What is true of X is true of Y in respect of Z feature' (= compatibility or comparative Affirmation (Winter 1974: 387; 1977a: 54)).

The important function of repetition structure (systematic repetition) which is still largely overlooked is that its primary function is to focus upon the **replacement** or change within the repetition structure. This replacement dominates the meaning of the second member of its clause relation. We see this in examples 1 and 2 below, where the predication structure is repeated (the constant) and only the subjects are replaced (the variables). These two terms were used by H.W. Fowler (1926: 517) to describe the mechanics of the current fashion of avoiding repetition at all costs.

1 'What we have still not forgiven him for', she says, 'is that he [Mozart] *reasoned.*' Miss Brophy, whose spiritual home is the eighteenth century enlightenment, also *reasons.*

2 The symbols *seem easy to the point of glibness. So does* the scepticism that repeatedly informs them.

We will now take up the notion of relevance as a function of lexical choice mentioned earlier. In the above matching relations, the repetition structure of the matched members signals that two sets of subjects are matched as alike in respect of their **unique predication**; that is, the lexical choice of subject is *varied* while those of their predication structure are *held constant*. What this means is that, *as presented* or *as signalled*, the relevance of, say, the subject 'he' in the first member of example 1 is matched with the equally relevant choice of subject 'Miss Brophy' in the second member.

In example 2, however, instead of repetition structure, we have the *So-*substitute inversion as proxy repetition structure for the unique predicate signalling a compatible replacement of the subject. We can get a glimpse of the equality of the relevance of subjects by considering the question version of the above substitute paraphrase. Taking its subject 'the scepticism that repeatedly informs them' as the new information of the match, we note that it is roughly congruent with the answer to the question: 'What else seems easy to the point of glibness (besides the symbols)?'

We turn now from compatibility to incompatibility of the match. We will illustrate this with *Contrast* in example 3 and *Denial* and *Correction* in example 4.

The unspecific semantics of matching Contrast can be expressed as: 'What is true of X is *not* true of Y in respect of A feature' (= the difference/contrast/incompatibility or comparative denial). Again in example 3, we see the predication structure is held constant while the compared subjects are replaced:

3 No Russian *wants to conquer the world.* Some Americans *do*, on the best crusading grounds.

Notice the contrastive replacement of the subject 'No Russian' of the first member with 'Some Americans'; and notice too the repetition of the predication 'wants to conquer the world' by the substitute verb 'do' in this second member. In terms of the relevance of subjects discussed above for examples 1 and 2, notice that the relations between the members signal that the choice of *No* in 'No Russians' is not relevant for *all* Americans but only for *some* Americans.

We can see the contrast in relevance by considering the question which would account for the second member as an answer on the first member: 'Is this true of (all) Americans?' Answer: 'No, it is (only) true of some Americans.' However, what marks the clause of the second member is the **replacement by addition** of the new information of the adverbial phrase of purpose: 'on the best crusading grounds' (see Winter 1979: 105).

Finally, in example 4, we have yet another example of the predication held constant while the subjects are replaced. Now instead of the relation of Contrast we had in example 3, we have a relation of *Denial* and *Correction*. In this particular repetition relation, the second clause exactly repeats the first denied clause except for the replacement or change of the subjects, which is taken as the Correction. Here the subject 'little boys' is denied and replaced by 'girls' as what is true.

4   'Little boys *don't play with dolls*, girls *play with dolls*.'

This is a remark attributed to a working-class mother who is scolding her son for his interest in dolls. Here the subject 'little boys' is replaced by the new subject 'girls'. Incidentally, Denial and Correction is one of the earliest clause relations in child language development, as in the child of three years correcting a parental euphemism for a dead bee:

5   '*The bee* didn't *get* tired – *it got* dead.'

More importantly, Denial and Correction are an integral part of the text structure **real** in **hypothetical** and **real**, which is discussed later, a funda-mental part of the rhetoric of argument, where you offer what is true for what you are denying as true.

Examples 1–4 illustrate the replacement of subject; example 5 illustrates the replacement of complement, in which the adjective 'tired' is replaced by the adjective 'dead', which corrects it. Needless to add, any element of grammar in the clause can be replaced in some way.

BASIC CLAUSE RELATIONS 2: THE LOGICAL SEQUENCE RELATION

The logical sequence relation should be seen as being in contrast with the matching relation. It is not concerned with the compatibility or otherwise of the grammar of the lexical choice of matched clauses, but with the other meanings that go to make up the basic clause relations. The two relations should be seen as complementary parts of a larger semantic whole in which we may see the one requiring the other.

At its simplest, the logical sequence relation is concerned with representing selective changes in a time/space continuum from simple time/space change to deductive or causal sequence which is modelled on real-world time/

change. These relations can be expressed by such purely chronological event questions such as: 'What happened next?' for the next significant event, and 'What happened before that?' for the preceding significant event. They can be expressed by deductive questions such as: 'What did that lead to?', 'What caused that to happen?', 'What do you conclude from that?', etc.

Of the deductive questions, an important one belonging to the real member of hypothetical and real relation is that of Basis/Reason. This is the question: 'How do you know that it is true?' For an Evaluation clause, this could be: 'How do you know that you are correct in your opinion?' Basis belongs to Reason or answers the *why*-question but differs from Reason in requiring facts of evidence. But an Evaluation clause can prompt the *why*-question too: He is angry with her. Why is he angry with her? Answer: she let him down.

We now consider some instances of the logical sequence relation which are signalled by such conjuncts 'thereafter' 'then' and 'thereby' in examples 5 and 6 below. We ignore instances of 'weak logical sequence', where there are no signals by conjunct, subordinator or lexical paraphrases of the relation (e.g. *The consequence was...*). We require powerful criteria to argue for the intuitive analysis of a clause pair such as 'means' and 'result', and this is not the place for such a discussion. (See Beekman and Callow 1974: 301–2.)

In example 6 below, we have a matching Contrast between two sets of co-ordinated clause pairs whose memberships are signalled separately as logical sequence by the conjuncts 'thereafter' and 'then' respectively.

6   After 10 moves or so, the men chose cooperation and *thereafter* rarely changed course. *Not so* the women, who would cooperate for a while and *then* revert to independence.

In each membership, we have the answer to the same question: 'How did the men/women behave after (choosing) cooperation?' The informal grammar of 'Not so the women' signals that the second sentence here is a *no*-answer to the question on the first sentence: 'Was that so with the women too?' Thus we have a larger clause relation of matching Contrast whose two members contain a logical sequence relation.

Next, in example 7, the use of the conjunct 'thereby' signals that the second co-ordinated clause is an **achievement** for which the first clause is its **instrument**:

7   Once on this page I announced 'I am no warped spinster waving the feminist flag', and *thereby* gravely offended some spinster readers.

Notice the paraphrase of this clause relation as expressed in the question which could elicit the verb of the second clause as new information: 'What kind of effect did you have on some spinster readers by announcing "I am no warped spinster waving the feminist flag?"'

We now consider instances of the multiple clause relation, which contains both matching and logical sequence, not as separate relations but as composite relations.

BASIC CLAUSE RELATION 3: THE MULTIPLE CLAUSE RELATION

As mentioned above, we can have a multiple relation where both the relations of matching and of logical sequence are present *in the same clause pair*. This is easier to see where you have subordination and significant repetition structure. In example 8(a) below, we have the logical sequence *if*-clause signalling a **negative condition**, or hypothesis, for which the main clause is the *deduced* **positive consequence**.

8(a) *If* the Russians *were not to blame*, then the Americans *must be*.

Notice the repetition structure (partly concealed by deletion) of Denial and Correction which signals matching, but notice too the asymmetry introduced into the repetition structure by the presence of the modal verb 'must'. Compare this with the meaning of the independent clause pair which has the symmetrical repetition structure of pure matching in example 8(b) below (see Winter 1979: 103–4). To show the repetition structure I will restore the deletion of the *to*-infinitive clause:

8(b) The Russians *were* not *to blame*; the Americans *were* [*to blame*].

We now lack the deductive matching of example 8(a), which is a function both of the *if*-clause and the asymmetrical addition of the modal 'must'. In example 9 below, we have two independent clauses, again, in deductive matching relation.

9   *Perspiration offends* others. *It* should *offend* you, too.

Here the asymmetry by the modal verb 'should' in the second member introduces a deductive hypothesis into the matching. This is a hypothesis whose signalled real is a Denial clause: perspiration does not offend you. In other words, we use the modal verb 'should' to hypothesize about a reality which does not exist.

   Next, we have in example 10 a pattern of clause relations beginning with a *denial clause* in sentence 1. This clause becomes the basis for the conclusion drawn by sentence 2: a deductive replacement which reformulates the Denial clause of sentence 1. The third and fourth sentences provide a *basis* for this evaluation of the Denial clause of sentence 1. Here only the replacement is shown in italic:

10 [The destruction of the European Jews by Hitler was not the calculated extermination of human beings, ordered and carried out in cold blood. It *could* not be.] Cold blood and massive mechanical murder do not go together, even in Nazi Germany. Those who had the strength of nerve to carry it out needed a messianic conviction. And they had it ...

The second sentence exactly repeats the first sentence except for the addition of the modal verb 'could'. The pronoun 'It' repeats the subject 'the destruction of European Jews by Hitler', the denial by negator 'not', and the complement 'the calculated extermination of human beings etc.' which is repeated by deletion. The focus of the matching relation is upon the replacement by addition of the modal verb 'could' which deductively evaluates the Denial in the first sentence as 'not possible'. This example prepares us for Evaluation and Basis for Evaluation which follow as part of the text structure Situation and Evaluation.

The well-known concessive relation is a case of matching semantics operating within the deductive reasoning of logical sequence. Take Quirk's (1954: 8) discussion of the two different logical sequence relations, in which concession is signalled by the conjunct *yet*, and the purely deductive reasoning of logical sequence is signalled by the conjunct *therefore*, as in his example below:

I'm not rich and *yet* I am happy (concession) I'm rich and *therefore* I am happy (cause).

Quirk noted that the 'cause and concession are obviously connected'. If we rewrite his 'therefore' example, as 'I'm *not* rich and therefore I'm *not* happy' – where one Denial leads logically to another Denial – we see that the conjunct 'yet' denies that the Conclusion 'I'm *not* happy' follows its Basis 'I'm *not* rich'. We can paraphrase the conjunct 'yet' here as: 'I'm not rich. *It does not follow from this that I am not happy* – I am happy, very happy indeed.' This is an example of matching Denial between the consequent unexpressed (*therefore*) clause 'I'm not happy' and the actual concessive (*yet*) 'I'm happy'.

This suffices to illustrate some of the characteristic features of matching with logical sequence, but it is only one aspect of multiple meaning clause relations. The reader is referred to Jordan's (1978: 41–7) discussion of the wider phenomena of simultaneous, joint and combined clause relations, where he notes that these occur when two or more questions are answered about the same input by the same clause.

We now turn to basic text relations which are the communicative vehicle for the basic clause relations so far described.

INTRODUCTION TO BASIC TEXT STRUCTURE

So far we have had what I see as a fairly non-controversial description of basic clause relations. Earlier I said we cannot say everything about anything and noted the role of the clause as a device of selection whose relevance constrains us in what we say within the sentence, and that basic clause relations in turn constrain us to have a related relevance. What is true of basic clause relations is equally true of basic text structure: as a vehicle for systematically settling for saying less than everything on a strict relevance principle. We have a mutually expected text structuring or **linguistic consensus** about the beginning and the end of the structures with which we *all* comply when communicating with others.

Here is an example which illustrates the role of sequence and an awareness of its meaningful units in the structuring of a basic text or **message**. To appreciate this point in example 11 below, you are asked to choose one sequence only in answer to the question: 'Which one of the six patterns shown below represents the actual sequence observed on a street poster which was advertising *The Harpenden Weekly News*?'

11 (a)	(b)	(c)	(d)	(e)	(f)
Enjoy it	Buy it	Read it	Enjoy it	Buy it	Read it
Buy it	Enjoy it	Enjoy it	Read it	Read it	Buy it
Read it	Read it	Buy it	Buy it	Enjoy it	Enjoy it

In Britain (and in Japan) at this time, we would all choose the fifth sequence, (e), because it corresponds with our cultural expectations about the time sequence in which we habitually buy and read a newspaper. We can justify the sense which sequence (e) makes to us by paraphrasing the relations holding for us between the three imperative clauses as follows: 'You have to buy the newspaper *before* you can read it, and you have to read it *before* you can enjoy it.' In the analysis, note the following three points:

(1) In a three-element structure like this, the first is potentially the 'beginning' and the last is potentially the 'end'.
(2) The culturally familiar **Situation** of obtaining newspapers is compressed into the actions of the first two clauses, and their **Evaluation** is expressed by the last clause.
(3) The three imperative clauses are in a relation of 'weak logical sequence' of simple narrative time with each other, where each event is assumed to follow the other in time.

This is just one example of the **Consensus Principle**; you are invited to test it out on others, asking them to justify their choice of sequence from the above six assumed possibilities.

What we are talking about here is a consensus about typical message structure or texts which take the following three common forms:

(1) *Situation* and *Evaluation*, which is illustrated by examples 11, 12, 13 and 14.
(2) *Hypothetical* and *Real*, which is illustrated by examples 15, 16 and 17.
(3) *Combinations* of both text structures (1) and (2) above, which is illustrated by example 18.

We begin with the basic text structure of Situation and Evaluation.

BASIC TEXT STRUCTURE 1: SITUATION AND EVALUATION

Fundamentally, this text structure is the old commonplace of *saying what you know about something* (the facts = the Situation for an identified X) and then *saying what you think or feel about it* (the interpretation of the facts =

Evaluation of Situation for X, or the Evaluation of X in this Situation). Linguistically, it means expectedly presenting the Situation in one or more sentences, and expectedly presenting your Evaluation in one or more sentences. In this way, we can have a minimal written structure of a *mere two clauses*, one representing the Situation and the other representing the Evaluation element. We communicate in terms of the notion of Situation as a meaningful linguistic context which we may interpret for the decoder.

The important thing to grasp here is that Evaluation itself has as part of its consensus structure the expectation of the basic clause relations of Reason/ Basis, so that we could symbolize a common form of this text structure as an expected trio of **Situation–Evaluation–Basis/Reason for Evaluation** which is illustrated below in example 12.

I might add that the most fully developed form of this text structure could have the addition of the elements of *Problem–Solution*, each with their own *Evaluation* elements as an aspect of the Situation element in the simplified four-part structure of *Situation–Problem–Solution–Evaluation*. We will largely ignore this fuller structure here. Readers are referred to a detailed description of basic clause relations and basic text relations in English texts by Hoey (1983), and to the description of basic text relations, particularly as they apply to very short texts in English in Jordan (1980, 1981, 1984). We concentrate on the characteristic features of text structure *Situation–Evaluation–Basis/Reason* here.

For purposes of illustration, we can take the element Situation to represent a question which the encoder asks of him/herself: 'What/who am I talking about (in this Situation)?'; the element Evaluation as 'What do I think about it?', 'How do I feel about it?' and 'How do I see/interpret it?', and the element Basis/Reason: 'How do I know (I am right)? Why do I think this/I am right?'

The *what/who* element in the question 'What I am talking about?' does not merely require the encoder to identify the Situation but, more importantly, to identify the participants and the topic likely to be developed by the next sentence, whether it is a basic clause relation or the larger clause relation which I am calling basic text structure.

The very important educational and philosophical aspect to note about Evaluation is that it often works by matching other related Situations from previous experience or knowledge with the present Situation being reported. That is to say, its Situation may be presented in a matching relation with another Situation. It is well known that we 'judge by making comparisons' and also that we might object to an unfavourable Evaluation (criticism) as 'making unfair comparisons' especially where no Basis or Reason has been offered in support. The quality of an Evaluation may depend on the quality of the Basis/Reason offered for it.

The basic information structure of Situation and Evaluation (Basis/Reason) is most conveniently illustrated by its use in picture-postcard writing. The picture represents the Situation being observed, and the back of the postcard can carry the Evaluation or Comment, and with it, a likely Basis/Reason. In the continuum of detail given by texts, postcards contrast sharply with articles and books. In postcards *you can say the least to fulfil your text structure* – a mere clause or sentence per element perhaps; in articles or books, you can say the most to fulfil text structure, using as many sentences as you please.

The postcard structure

Example 12 is a postcard written by an Australian man from Queensland who is touring the beaches of France. It is commenting on a colour photograph of one of the French beaches he has just visited. The picture shows a wide expanse of beach with blue sea and sunny sky and lots of people. On the back of the postcard he writes:

12 This is one of the best beaches here. Not a patch on our beaches in Queensland. Too much litter and pollution. Love, Mike

The first clause is both Situation and Evaluation of Situation; the pronoun 'this' refers to the Situation represented by the photograph, and the superlative 'best' shows that the writer is further identifying this beach by matching it with other French beaches. The second, the verbless clause 'Not a patch on our beaches in Queensland' evaluates the first Situation by matching it unfavourably with beaches in Queensland (rival Situation).

Newcomers to clause relations might find the idea of an Evaluation of an Evaluation, as the second clause is of the first, difficult to accept – semantically slippery, as it were. The third clause offers a Basis for the unfavourable comparison in the second clause. We can account for the text structure here by considering its expected pattern of questions (as an Australian tourist visiting French beaches and writing home about them): 'How does this one (in the photograph) compare with other beaches here?' (= clause 1); 'How does this beach compare with our beaches in Queensland?' (= clause 2); and finally, 'What makes me say this?' (= clause 3).

There is, of course, nothing to stop the writer from ending his postcard at the second clause, but then his readers would have missed the expected Basis/Reason for the negative Evaluation of this French beach which would have justified the Evaluation. The important point to remember is that it is *not* the limited space on the postcard so much as it is that the space is sufficient for what he wishes to say to suit his purpose. It is sufficient for basic text structure. This is the principle upon which the practicalities of all writing (or speaking) operate, regardless of how complex and detailed it becomes. Space in this case is purely relative.

Cartoons as Situations to be evaluated

Another way of representing Situation is by picture. Take the art of cartooning, for instance. In just one drawing, the artist can do as much as words by presenting a frame of life. Although the drawing can go far to setting out a Situation, we have a long tradition of balloons in which the characters speak. The traditional balloons have been replaced by captions at the bottom of the drawing. Here are some cartoons from the *Punch* magazine, where the drawing itself may provide the humorous Situation, possibly with Problem/Solution, and the speech of the characters may provide the Evaluation of their Situation. Linguists have regularly paid lip-service to the notion of 'knowledge of the world' entering into sentences. Our appreciation of a cartoon certainly depends upon it.

In example 13a, we have a scene from a hospital mortuary where bodies presumably await their post-mortems. Two doctors are at a living man's bedside; one says: 'Mr Atkinson, we'd like to make a few more tests.' Mr Atkinson, with a fag in his mouth, is unconcernedly reading a newspaper as if at home with nothing to do. This cartoon is being presented in its original drawing, so that the reader can appreciate the true art of Haldane, one of the best cartoonists in *Punch*.

The Contrast by Evaluation of the same Situation is between the nonchalance of the live patient and the apparent concern of the two doctors. A definition of a fool is the kind of person who fails to Evaluate his Situation which is obvious to everybody else. This is the formula for the films of Charlie Chaplin, Buster Keaton, Laurel and Hardy, Norman Wisdom and others.

In example 13b below, we again have Situation and Evaluation, this time the Evaluation is by a single adjective 'Terrific!' from the young man with the

Example 13a 'Mr Atkinson, we'd like to make a few more tests.'

woman at the lakeside. He is exclaiming at the wonder of the super-claspknife rising out of the waters. 'Knowledge of the world' is what enables us to see the humour; we match our knowledge of the legendary King Arthur and Excalibur with this drawing and appreciate the incongruity of the two Situations. Much cartoon humour can be defined as matching incongruous Situations, with only one Situation present in the cartoon, another in the mind of the reader.

Next, consider the two sentences in example 14, where the would-be author is face to face with his prospective publisher. The Situation represented by the cartoon is the crucial moment for the author, whether or not the publisher will publish his book. This is the topic developed by the publisher. His first sentence evaluates the book favourably. The second sentence is a co-ordinated clause pair. Its first clause provides a favourable Basis for the

Example 13b

'Terrific!' (apologies to Punch)

Example 14

'We like your book, Mr Fryston. It nicely oversteps the bounds of decency, but to
get away with it could you work in a little sociology?'

Evaluation; the co-ordinator 'but' signals an unexpected snag to this Basis,
and its second clause suggests a little sociology as a Solution to overcome the
Problem of 'getting away with it'.

The text structure is congruent with the following pattern of questions:
'What's your feeling about my book?', 'What is it that you like about my
book?', (but) 'What is it you don't like about my book?' The implied negative
Basis for not liking the book can be seen when we make explicit the
underlying expectation which the co-ordinator 'but' is denying: 'Your book
nicely oversteps the bounds of decency *and* you *won't* get away with it.' In
this cartoon, I suggest it is the mixed Basis that provides the humour,
particularly the second clause of the co-ordination.

Summing up, the key linguistic features of this text structure can be
expressed from the encoding point of view: bearing in mind what our
audience knows, we tell them what we want them to know, framing it in an
acceptable linguistic or pictorial starting point called Situation. We tell them

what we think or feel about it, by picture or words, and then we give them a Reason or Basis for our thinking so.

We select lexical detail for our clauses which is relevant for our purpose in communicating within each member of the structure. As Jordan (1980, 1981, 1984) amply demonstrates, we can fulfil the linguistic requirements for the completion of our text structure with as little as one sentence per member of structure as the function of postcards and cartoons shows. In a conversation with me, Jordan noted in passing that the one-word road sign 'Danger' is an Evaluation of the real Situation for the motorist implying a Problem whose Solution is avoidance.

We now turn to the second basic text structure which contrasts with the first in respect of the kind of information it is offering. Instead of presenting the 'facts' of Situation, it now presents a 'hypothesis' about the likely facts or Situation.

BASIC TEXT STRUCTURE 2: HYPOTHETICAL AND REAL

In the Situation and Evaluation structure, we are concerned with a binary relation between what you (definitely) know, where 'definitely' is default (= Situation), and what you think about it (= Evaluation). The binary equivalent for hypothetical and real structure is hypothetical situation = hypothetical element, and Evaluation of Investigation into likely reality for hypothetical Situation = real element.

Unlike the Situation and Evaluation structure whose Situation presents something which 'exists' within the knowledge or experience of the encoder and perhaps shared with his decoders, we are speaking of the role of the encoder where the Situation is not known or controversial. In such a case, the Situation becomes the Hypothesis which the encoder has to signal explicitly as hypothetical, and do likewise when s/he is repeating somebody else's statement in order to communicate it.

The normal unmarked mode in present Situation is that for ordinary sentences; the absence of modals in the environment of finite tense, present and past tense, presents its clause on trust as true (Winter 1982: 46–8). But the moment the clause has modals or any other signal of suspension of fact we enter into hypotheticality of some kind. What this means is that hypothetical and real is the marked structure, with the hypothetical as the key sign that real is potentially next. It has to be signalled by items which 'say so'. In my work I try to name relations by their key lexical item, in this case, by the adjective 'hypothetical' and the adjective 'real', as in: 'Are you asking me a hypothetical question or do you want the facts (real)?' Note the adjective 'real' in the question: 'What is his *real* reason for resigning?'

The hypothetical element can be signalled by means of the lexical items such as *assertion, assumption, belief, claim, conclusion, expect, feel, guess, illusion, imagine, proposition, rumour, speculation, suggestion, suppose, theory, think*, etc. The real element can be signalled by evaluatory words such as:

(1) *Denial*: contradict, challenge, correct, deny, dismiss, disagree, dispute, false, lie, mistake, object to, refute, rebut, repudiate, not true, wrong, etc.
(2) *Affirmation*: affirm, agree, confirm, concur, evidence, fact, know, real, right, true etc.

(See Winter 1982: 196–200)

Basically, we can regard the hypothetical and real structure as the basic text structure which we use to report our response to the perceived truth of somebody else's or our own statements. In the two members of this structure, the hypothetical member presents the statement to be affirmed or denied as true. The real member presents the affirmation or Denial as true. (Or we have a directly explicit Evaluation of the hypothetical implying it is either true or not true.)

We can see the role of Real as answering such questions as: 'Is it true?' or 'How true is it?' A *yes/no* answer can predict the next clause relation of this structure as Basis: 'How do you know it is true?', 'What proof (evidence or facts) have you got?' Thus the ultimate linguistic function of the real member is to transmute the hypothetical Situation into real Situation as discovered by the encoder. This is what good science communication is about.

In what ways can the hypothetical and real structure be said to be explicitly controversial? We have already seen a list of words which signal either hypothetical or real, but we need to know a little more about how it works linguistically.

It is best understood by its function in argument or explicit controversy where we report and comment on somebody else's statements. What this person reports as his Situation (presented on trust as true, that is) we may contradict outright or reformulate as hypothetical and then contradict or deny it, stating what we see as the truth (real or rival Situation). In doing so, we have to mark out counter-text in some unmistakable way.

The signalling of the hypothetical element is simple enough. A newspaper journalist writes an article in a newspaper in which appears the following statement:

The Germans are planning a Third World War.

This is the *unmarked declarative clause* without modifying modals presenting its clause to be taken on trust as true. As a reader of this article, I can express my disbelief by writing a letter to the editor, attacking the statement by embedding it in a larger clause of my own which clearly signals hypotheticality:

Mr X has taken leave of his senses. He *imagines* that *the Germans are planning a Third World War.*

I have signalled the hypothetical member twice: first by an unspecific Evaluation of the coming statement: 'He has taken leave of his senses', and second, by its Evaluation being made further specific as: 'He imagines that the Germans are planning a Third World War.' The compatibility of unspecific and specific in both of my statements implies a denial as true, especially the notion of taking leave of his senses as equal to crazy, mad.

In its most fulfilled form, the real member can have two main patterns of basic clause relations according to whether the hypothetical clause is *affirmed* ('Yes, it is true'), or *denied* ('No, it is not true'). The Affirmation pattern can have two expected members, Affirmation and Basis/Reason as in example 15 below, where the lexical item, the verb 'expected', signals the *that*-clause as its hypothetical member:

15 The engineers expected *that the earthquake would have caused damage to their underground tunnel. It did*; it was at least the magnitude of 6 on the Richter Scale.

The substitute clause '*It did*' signals Affirmation as a 'Yes' – an answer to the stock question: 'Did it (cause damage to their underground tunnel)?' The second of the paired clauses provides a Basis supporting the Affirmation; that is, *definite information* about the *extent* of the earthquake.

The Denial pattern can have up to three members: Denial–Correction–Basis/Reason. In example 16, we have Denial–Basis for Denial which offers a Correction. Here the hypothetical is signalled by the verb 'thought'.

16 I always thought *that academic litigation was a peculiarity of modern America*, but *no*: one Paul Nicholas sued the University of Paris for withholding his degree. He lost, thereby achieving the distinction of becoming the first person in history who could be proved to have failed his degree. The year was 1426.

The co-ordinator 'but' indicates an unexpected change to the Hypothetical Clause. The negator '*no*' is a one-word Denial as true in the sense that America is not unique. The clause following 'no' is Basis for Denial. It and the rest of the paragraph offers **Evidence**, which is what Basis is. In example 17, the use of Denial and Correction rhetoric is shown in a historical electioneering pamphlet:

17   FARMERS!
                          BEWARE!
        The enemies of the King and the People, – of the
                       CONSTITUTION
                           AND
                    SIR FRANCIS HEAD
              ARE, DAY AND NIGHT, SPREADING
                           LIES.
    They say Sir Francis Head is recalled – Sir Francis Head is NOT recalled, but is supported by the King and his ministers.
    They say TITHES are to be claimed in Upper Canada... TITHES shall NOT be claimed in Upper Canada says a permanent Act of Parliament.

FARMERS

Believe not a word these Agitators say, but think for yourselves and SUPPORT SIR FRANCIS HEAD, friend of Constitutional Reform.

(1836; Election Notice, Toronto, Canada)

The unspecific verb of the imperative clause with vocative, 'Farmers! Beware!' signals some kind of trouble to come. Its specifics follow as the statements of the enemies of the king, of the people, of the constitution etc. The Evaluation of the source of statements as 'the enemies etc.' and of these statements as 'SPREADING LIES' predicts that its real will deny these 'lying' statements. The verb 'say' in this context signals hypothetical for its embedded clause: 'Sir Francis Head is recalled.' Notice how both of the Denials are emphasized by the use of capitalized 'NOT'.

The first 'say' relation is that of Denial and Correction: 'Sir Francis Head is NOT recalled, but is supported by the King and his ministers.' Here the Correction clause is 'but supported by the King and his ministers'.

The second 'say' relation is that of Denial combined with Basis for Denial: 'TITHES shall NOT be claimed in Upper Canada says a permanent Act of Parliament.' Here the Denial is followed by Basis for Denial; this last is signalled by the factual 'so says a permanent Act of Parliament'. Finally, notice the retrospective Evaluation of the first hypothetical clause, again signalling Denial as true: the imperative clause with vocative: 'Farmers. Believe not a word these Agitators say', where 'the enemies of the King and the People etc.' have now become *reformulated* as 'the Agitators'.

BASIC TEXT STRUCTURE 3: COMBINATIONS OF STRUCTURES 1 AND 2

Earlier, I mentioned that Evaluation of Situation implied a potential matching of this Situation with other Situations from the knowledge and experience of the encoder. When this happens, the basic structure may coalesce into one combined structure. In example 18 below, we see a common use of combined structure of Situation and Evaluation with hypothetical and real in letter-writing. The Situation here is represented in two matched hypothetical situations, in which sentence (1) is contrasted by sentence (2). This is comparative Denial: What is true of X is not true of Y. The Evaluation element is represented by sentences (3) and (4). The overall formula for this letter is (hypothetical) Situation 1 versus (hypothetical) Situation 2 followed by Evaluation. The role of Evaluation as interpretation is clearly demonstrated here.

18 Sir – (1) All the examples you quoted from Marjorie Schonfield's casebook in last week's article 'Out of Wedlock', are replete with infectious guilt and gloom. (2) It would be just as easy to make up a case-book to show that many illegitimate children are brought up in exceptional and favourable circumstances by rational, free-thinking and affectionate parents.

(3) It is only when illegitimacy is combined with personal guilt and financial inadequacy in the mother that guilt and gloom set in. (4) Nobody need mind being a bastard as long as he is not a *poor* bastard.

Love-child.

As part of the correspondence about Marjorie Schonfield's article on illegitimacy and its consequences for the illegitimate in later life, Sentence (1) refers to the topic of case-studies of illegitimacy and evaluates them as: 'replete with guilt and gloom'. The verb 'quoted' signals a hypotheticality for the writer. Thus, sentence (1) presents the Situation with an implied Problem of 'guilt and gloom'. The criterion for sentence (2) as a counterhypothesis is whether we can fit a Denial clause of some kind between sentences (1) and (2).

We find that something like 'That is not quite true' fits, which then makes sentence (2) into an Evaluated Basis (signalled by 'just as easy to make up') for this partial Denial. Thus we have Situation 2 being evaluated as being favourable without 'the problem of guilt and gloom' of Situation 1, and hence in matching Contrast with it. The hypotheticality is still there with the notion of making something up, but it is the more plausible hypothesis in the writer's view. Sentences (3) and (4) develop this Situation still further.

As the Evaluation element, sentences (3) and (4) progressively *reformulate* Situation 1 by narrowing down the scope of its influence. Sentence (3) initiates the narrowing down by restricting Situation 1 to 'personal and financial inadequacy in the mother'. In sentence (4), the writer concludes by reducing what is left of Situation 1 still further to a mere matter of avoiding poverty. Note this as the focus of the orthographic emphasis on the word '*poor*' used in two senses here, which includes the 'poor' meaning 'unfortunate'.

Summing up, the writer chooses not to deny outright the truth of Situation 1 for himself; instead he contrasts it with his own version of Situation 2 as its counterhypothesis, and then returns to progressively reformulate Situation 1, so that by sentence (4), he reduces it to a meaningless contrast with his Situation 2. This presumably was his intention. The aim of arguing against a case is either to reduce the truth of your opponent's Situation or to demolish the Basis from which Conclusion is drawn.

Like the newspaper poster in example 11, the postcard of example 12, the cartoons of examples 13 and 14, the election poster of example 17, we have in example 18 above a completion of basic text structure that we sense as corresponding with the completion of the writer's message to us. The writers have given us the minimal number of sentences as befits their different purposes for these particular kinds of message. As already mentioned, longer more detailed texts such as articles and books are no different in principle.

SUMMARY AND CONCLUSIONS LEADING TO A NOTION OF CO-RELEVANCE

The whole point of this chapter can be summed up as *the clause as a device of co-relevance*, once it communicates as a member of a clause relation in a text. To clarify this matter of relevance, we need to sum up what has been said about clauses and clause relations.

Earlier, we noted that we, expectedly as decoders, are sensitive to the lexis and grammar of the clause in any written texts, and that a study of written discourse structures should cover all lexis and grammar and other devices including the all-important repetition and replacement of the clause, on the assumption that all clauses in the text ultimately count in the total meaning.

We noted (a) that there are indeed powerful forces constraining the amounts of what we can say or write in a text in that we cannot say everything about anything by choosing to say *something* on a strict relevance principle, and (b) that the study of linguistics should at this stage be a study of how we actually use the discipline of the clause for saying less than everything.

We noted that using the clause to settle for saying less than everything was systematic in the sense that we, as communicators with one another, had a linguistic consensus about the form it should take. Example 11 demonstrated one of its common sequences, given our cultural expectations. We noted that the clause itself was our primary device of lexical and grammatical selection for what is considered relevant, and that somehow the relevance of lexical choice for the clause was narrowed down by what lexical choices had already been made for the immediately preceding clause relations of the text itself.

The theoretical point about clause relations is that relations between clauses are not random, but part of an expected finite consensus about their mutual interpretation. (See Winter 1977a: 5.) A description of basic text structure in English is therefore a description of its clause relations, and this includes its interactive basic clause relations.

We have noted that there are two main kinds of clause relation:

(1) The basic text (or message) structures with their relations of Situation and Evaluation, and hypothetical and real and combinations of these two;
(2) Basic clause relations of matching, logical sequence and their multiple and mixed relations. We noted briefly that basic clause relations interact with basic text structures. For instance, we noted that the demonstration of our consensus about the basic structure of Situation and Evaluation in example 11 depended upon our awareness of the 'weak' logical sequence of its three imperative clauses. Above all, we noted that what basic text structures had in common with basic clause relations is that its binary memberships could be realized by a mere two one-clause sentences. This last point about sentences is very important for our notion of linguistic relevance.

In systematically settling for saying less than everything, we can cut down our 'message structure' to what is relevant in as little as a one-clause sentence per member. This does not mean that our sentence is trivial or the simple sum of its words, but more importantly that one sentence will do because we can count on our decoder's very much vaster knowledge of the subject-matter which s/he brings to grasping the significance of the selections we have made for our clause. We can now revise the notion of relevance to include the more specific notion of co-relevance.

If we think of any text structure consisting of one or more clause relations, then we can say that the ideal coherence of this text would be where all the clauses are unbrokenly connected in the semantics of the topic development of its participants by the semantics of its clause relations. That is, all clauses that (i) present information (ii) must be seen as making sense of their (iii) clause relation, or as relevant to it.

However, once within the membership of a clause relation, a clause must be co-relevant; that is, it must make sense as a second member within the scope of the semantics of lexical and grammatical choice of the first member. Taking the matching Contrast of example 6, where we match the situations of men and women as co-operators in an experiment, we note that the lexical choice of the second sentence must be co-relevant with that of the first sentence; that is, it must make sense as a relevant contrast for the *same activity by expectedly different participants*. The repetition structure carries what is predetermined by the first sentence.

Finally, we could speculate from this that any text structure itself might be co-relevant with a larger known text structure (for instance, *New Scientist* may select information from science articles for popularization) which is either written or unwritten, spoken or as yet unspoken. It is the likelihood of such a linguistic context that makes it possible for us to select very small text structures of two sentences long, since our audience brings their knowledge of this larger context to 'fill in' what we might have otherwise selected from it. This is what ensures their understanding of the significance of our selections.

5 Predictive categories in expository text

Angele Tadros

The approach to text pragmatics presented here is based on research into the discourse structure of expository text. The initial corpus investigated was drawn from *A Textbook of Economics* (Hanson 1953 [1972]), and a model of discourse analysis was designed (Tadros 1981) using the notion of Prediction. The corpus was later expanded to include other areas such as law, stylistics and linguistics.

THEORETICAL ASSUMPTIONS

The model of discourse analysis presented here is based on two basic assumptions. The first is that written text is interactive since two participants are involved: writer and reader, although, of course, 'the exigencies of the medium oblige one of the participants to be only represented at the writing stage, thus complicating the process for both parties' (Sinclair 1980: 255). This means that the writer takes on the roles of both addressor and addressee and incorporates the interaction within the encoding process itself (see Widdowson 1978a: 21).

The second assumption is that the writer is in agreement with the propositions expressed in the text unless s/he specifically signals detachment. So, for instance, if the writer says, 'Every commodity is nothing more than a bundle of services', s/he will be taken to be in agreement with the proposition, but if s/he says 'It has been pointed out by some economists that every commodity is nothing more than a bundle of services', s/he is overtly detaching him/herself from the proposition and attributing it to some other entity. In this latter case, s/he will at a later point be expected to give an evaluation of the proposition expressed.

THE NOTION OF PREDICTION

The term **Prediction** has previously been used in a generalized sense to refer to the activity of guessing or anticipating what will come in the text, an activity based on the reader's common-sense knowledge of the world, of content and formal schemata (Carrell 1983; Swales 1986). As used here, however, the term is much more specific: it refers to an interactional phenomenon – a commitment made by the writer to the reader, the breaking of which will shake the credibility of the text.

Prediction is thus a prospective rhetorical device which commits the writer at one point in the text to a future discourse act. It is overtly signalled in the text and thus a piece of text which does not have a signal of Prediction cannot unambiguously commit the writer to a certain course of action.

To illustrate the notion of Prediction, let us look at the following example (the sentences have been numbered for convenience and the signals italicized).

> (1) *Two problems* arise in this case. (2) First, there is the universal alibi which exists as long as we have no independent indicator of a change in tastes . . .
> (3) Second, the possibility is admitted in theory that some demand curves might slope upwards.
>
> (Lipsey 1963: 154)

In sentence (1) above there a specific numeral, 'two', followed by a noun of the type I have called Enumerables (see table 5.1, p. 72), whose referents in the first instance are signalled as to follow in the text. The occurrence of such a signal commits the writer to enumeration, which, in this example, comes in sentences (2) and (3).

CATEGORIES OF PREDICTION

Six categories of Prediction were identified in the initial corpus (Hanson 1953 [1972]): Enumeration; Advance Labelling; Reporting; Recapitulation; Hypotheticality; Question. Each of these categories consists of a *pair*, the first, predictive, member (symbol V), signals the prediction which has to be fulfilled by the second, predicted, member (symbol D). A member may consist of one or more sentences in a member (see Tadros 1981, 1985).

But what do we mean by sentence? Here it is necessary to extend the notion of sentence to include not only what is traditionally conceived of as a sentence boundary, but also other stops not traditionally regarded as terminal signals – the dash and the colon – since these latter can be taken as sentential terminal signals when they separate a V from a D member. The reason for extending the traditional notion is that the dash and the colon are capable of marking major discourse patterns.

In what follows, the categories of Prediction will be discussed. Examples are drawn from the following texts:

(1) *The Sound Pattern of English*, Chomsky and Halle 1968 (C&H).
(2) *Salmond on Jurisprudence*, Fitzgerald 1966 (F).
(3) *A Textbook of Economics*, Hanson 1953 [1972] (H).
(4) *An Introduction to Positive Economics*, Lipsey 1963 (L).
(5) *Economics: an Introductory Analysis*, Samuelson 1948 [1964] (S).
(6) *Towards an Analysis of Discourse*, Sinclair and Coulthard 1975 (S&C).
(7) *Stylistics and the Teaching of Literature*, Widdowson 1975 (W).

Enumeration

Enumeration is a category of Prediction in which the V member carries a signal that commits the writer to enumerate. There is of necessity more than one D member.

Criteria for V membership of Enumeration

Each criterion is both a sufficient and a necessary condition.

(1) Where a structure has
  either
  (a) a plural subject followed by a verb which demands a complement followed by a colon,
  or
  (b) a free clause followed by a clause binder (a word which joins a bound clause to a free clause (Sinclair 1972: 25).
(2) Where a sentence includes a cataphoric textual place reference item such as *the following* or *as follows* in association with a plural noun.
(3) Where a sentence includes an Enumerable (see definition below, and table 5.1) in association with a numeral, provided the information is presented as new to the context.

Before proceeding further, let us explain some terms.

'Enumerable' comprises both what we might call 'sub-technical' nouns (e.g. *advantages*, *reasons*, *aspects*, etc. as distinct from *men*, *women* and *children*) as well as discourse reference nouns (e.g. *examples*, *definitions*, *classifications*). See table 5.1 below. The important point to bear in mind is that the referents of such nouns are, in the first instance, textual, that is, other stretches of language.

'Numeral' can be exact, such as *two*, *three*, *four*, or inexact, such as *a few*, *several*, *a number of*.

'New' is glossed as that which is assumed not to be recoverable from the context. For instance, 'There are three reasons for . . .' is presented as new to the context, whereas 'The three reasons mentioned above . . .' is presented as recoverable, and hence the structure does not predict Enumeration although this may still occur.

Three types of Enumeration have been established, using the criteria above:

Type (a) Enumeration: This is isolated on criterion 1.

The *major* points are:

(S&C, p. 61)

This is possible under *conditions when*:

(H, p. 157)

In the first example the Signal of Enumeration is the colon following a structure with a plural subject and a verb that demands a complement. In the second example the colon follows a bound clause binder, 'when'. In either case not only is Enumeration predicted, but also that fulfilment will follow straightaway. Thus a syntactically incomplete sentence terminating with a colon requires syntactic completion which is provided discoursally by the D member of Enumeration.

Type (b) Enumeration: This type is isolated on criterion 2. In type (b) the V member is a syntactically complete sentence, although it may have a colon. The signal is the occurrence of the textual place items *the following/as follows* when in association with a plural noun.

   The following, for example, are all short story openings:

(W, p. 64)

In the above example Enumeration is predicted and it will follow without delay since the colon allows no interruption.

Type (c) Enumeration: This type is isolated on criterion 3. The V member is a syntactically complete sentence, but unlike type (a), the colon is not crucial, although it may occur. What is crucial, however, is the occurrence of a numeral, exact or inexact, in association with the Enumerable. Enumerables found in the corpus are given in table 5.1.

Table 5.1 Enumerables

adjuncts	classes	effects	motives	sources
advantages	concepts	elements	objections	stages
angles	conditions	examples	periods	suggestions
aspects	consequences	factors	points	terms
attempts	courses	features	policies	things
branches	criticisms	forms	problems	trends
categories	difficulties	influences	propositions	types
causes	disadvantages	kinds	qualities	varieties
circumstances	drawbacks	meanings	reasons	views
			senses	ways

   The term 'question of law' is used in *three distinct* though related *senses*.

(F, p. 66)

It will be noted that in the example above there is an exact numeral *three*, whereas in the example below the numeral is inexact, *a number of*:

   In addition to insurance, there are *a number of ways* by which risks can be reduced.

(H, p. 17)

So far we have been concentrating on the V member. We will now briefly indicate how we recognize a D member of Enumeration.

Cognitively, of course, the D member will have to correspond to the V member – that is, a reason signalled must be a reason given. But to the unwary readers, of whom there are many, this might not be readily available, so, in order to help the reader recognize the enumerated text, the writer will use certain devices such as: special features of layout, numbering, punctuation, sequencing markers (*first*, *second*, etc.), lexical repetition and grammatical parallelism (identical sentence structures). In the example below the writer uses sequential markers (first, second) in the D members as well as grammatical parallelism and lexical repetition.

V It is useful to divide linguistic universals into *two categories*.
D (i) There are, first of all, certain 'formal universals' that determine the structure of grammars and the form and organization of rules;
D (ii) In addition, there are 'substantive universals' that define the sets of elements . . .

(C&H, p. 4)

Advance Labelling

Advance labelling is a term used here to refer to a category of Prediction in which the writer both labels and commits him/herself to perform a discourse act. Thus, if a writer says 'Let us distinguish between x and y', he is committed to showing us the distinction between the items concerned; if the writer says 'This can be illustrated by the following diagram', a prediction is set up that s/he will produce the promised diagram.

Criteria for V membership of Advance Labelling

Four criteria are given below, all of which must be satisfied to qualify for inclusion:

(1) The sentence must contain a labelling of an act of discourse.
(2) The labelling of the act must be prospective.
(3) The role of the actor is not assigned elsewhere, and, therefore, remains as the writer's.
(4) The sentence labelling the act must not include its performance. Advance Labelling is realized by (a) linear text, (b) by non-linear text, a 'table', 'diagram', 'graph' or the like, or (c) by non-linear text followed by linear text. We will now exemplify each type.

Type (a) *Advance Labelling*

V This analysis leads us *to make the important distinction* between real income and money income.
D Money income measures a person's income in terms of some monetary unit, . . .; real income measures a person's income in terms of the command over commodities which the money income confers.

(L, p. 140)

In the above example the act labelled in advance is 'to make the important distinction' and this sets up the prediction that the two terms 'real income' and 'money income' will be distinguished. The prediction is fulfilled in the D member.

Type (b) *Advance Labelling*

9   V We *can show* this in a simple *diagram* as follows:

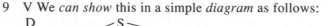
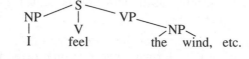

(W. p. 55)

Type (c) *Advance Labelling*

   V *Consider* now the following cost *schedule* of a firm:

TABLE XXVIII
The Cost Schedule of a Firm (2)

Da

Output	Total cost	Average cost	Marginal cost
Units	£	£	£
20	270	13.5	–
30	330	11.0	6
40	400	10.0	7
50	500	*10.0*	*10*
60	630	10.5	13
70	840	12.0	21

Db The table shows that if average cost is falling, marginal cost will be less than average cost; if, however, average cost is rising, the marginal cost will be greater than average cost. It also shows . . .

(H, p. 231)

Reporting

We mentioned earlier that a basic assumption is that the writer avers the opinions and ideas of the text so long as s/he does not specifically detach him/herself from the embedded propositions expressed. The writer detaches him/herself from propositions by attributing them to others. This detachment predicts involvement, which means that the writer will come again into the text in order to declare his/her state of knowledge as regards what s/he is reporting. I have termed this 'Evaluation' to be taken in the broad sense in which Labov and Fanshel (1977) use the term:

The term *evaluation* here appears as a superordinate term that includes agreement, disagreement and more extended types of evaluation; it comprises both cognitive and evaluative types of response.

(ibid.: 101)

Criteria for V membership of Reporting

All the criteria given below must be satisfied to qualify a sentence as a realization of Reporting:

(1) The sentence must contain at least one Report Structure. The typical Report Structure is a pair of reporting and reported clauses as in 'Those who support the bargaining Theory of Wages assert that . . .' (H, p. 315), but a quoting/quoted pair can also occur as in the example on p. 80 below, and a specialized adjunct as in 'In their view', or 'According to Alfred Marshall'.

(2) The sentence must contain propositional content which is attributed to others.

(3) The writer must detach himself from what he is reporting, i.e. if he says 'As x said' or 'x has rightly pointed out' there is no detachment here from the Report Structure. There is no Prediction of Evaluation because the evaluation has already occurred.

(4) The position of the reporting clause in its sentence and paragraph must be taken into account. Where the report is the only one in the paragraph and it comes at the end it is not predictive but is interpreted as a comment.

Reporting verbs and verb phrases that occurred in the corpus are given in table 5.2 in their base forms. A glance at the list in table 5.2 indicates its heterogeneous nature: while grammatically most of the items can take a *that* complement, quite a number take a nominal-group complement which may be followed by an appositional *that* clause, for example, 'He put forward the view that'; yet others are admitted to the group on condition that they combine with sub-technical or metadiscoursal nouns 'placing factors of production' and 'making points' or 'suggestions'.

Equally heterogeneous is their semantic behaviour. The list contains both factives (*show, realise, prove, know*) and non-factives (*claim, suggest, think, state*).

The distinction between factives and non-factives is significant for

Table 5.2 Reporting verbs and verb phrases

adopt	discuss	note	regard
agree	develop	notice	reiterate
argue	emphasize	observe	relate
assert	enunciate	oppose	say
assume	expound	place	show
base	formulate	point out	state
believe	imagine	propose	stress
boast	insist	prove	suggest
claim	know	put forward	support
consider	level	realize	think
contend	look (on, upon)	recognize	treat
declare	make	recommend	seek (to relate)
define	modify	refute	wish (to show)
disagree			

prediction. Factives, whether negative or affirmative, presuppose the truth of the proposition embedded in their complement clause, whereas with non-factives nothing is presupposed about the embedded propositions and hence the writer is not committed to their truth. (For more details see Tadros, 1981, 1985.)

The following example illustrates Reporting:

> V *Halliday's* (1970) *discussion* of language structure and function *is pitched* at a different level. *He is concerned . . . His approach . . .* Halliday *insists that . . . He finds . . .*
>
> (S&C, p. 12)

In the V member the writers are not presenting their own propositions, but rather they are attributing the proposition to Halliday by means of a series of detaching signals. The predicted member is the writers' evaluation, indicating their return to averral.

Recapitulation

The term 'Recapitulation' is used to refer to a member which predicts by recalling information from earlier in the text: 'It was mentioned/stated/ pointed out above/in the preceding section'; or by the inferential 'then'. Recapitulation predicts that there will be new information, but not what it will be – the predicted information may take the form of contrastive particulars, further elaboration or explanation. In the V member there is a verb or a nominalization that refers to a discourse act, and generally a textual time or place item such as *already, in chapter . . . , in the section above, so far*, etc.

Criteria for V membership of Recapitulation

(1) The sentence must contain either (a) a labelling of an act of discourse or (b) the inferential 'then'.
(2) If (a), the following further criteria apply:
　　(i)　the labelling must have a past-tense morpheme in the clause predicator;
　　(ii)　the role of the actor must not be assigned elsewhere, but remain the writer's.
(3) Whether (a) or (b) the sentence must not be paragraph-final, for in that case its function will be that of comment (i.e. reminder of relevance).

Table 5.3 lists verbs and verb phrases occurring in Recall signals.

In the example below, the Recall signal in the V member is 'We have said'. In the D member we find contrastive particulars, explicitly signalled by means of 'however'.

> V *We have said that* the underlying representations, lexical as well as phonological, are abstract as compared with phonetic features . . . .
> D There is, however, one very obvious sense in which the underlying representations are more abstract than the phonetic representations . . .
>
> (C&H, p. 11)

Table 5.3 Verbs and verb phrases in Recall signals

assume	examine	mention
consider	find out	note
deal with	give	notice
define	indicate	point out
discuss	make (+ a nominalization,	see
emphasize	e.g. reference)	

Hypotheticality

Like Reporting, Hypotheticality is based on the notion of authorial detachment, but here the writer detaches him/herself from the world of actuality through the creation of a hypothetical world. Hypotheticality presupposes that the writer is aware of the gap between his/her conceptual world and that of the reader, and by means of this device the writer is able to set up a world where there are only two countries, two linguistic theories, in order to confine him/herself to those aspects of a situation that will enable him/her to derive a generalization.

Criteria for V membership of Hypotheticality

Each of the characterizations given below is both a necessary and a sufficient condition for V membership of Hypotheticality:

(1) Where a sentence contains a verb like *assume*, *suppose*, *consider* and is subject to the following conditions:
    (i) the verb is either used in the imperative or is preceded by *let us*;
    (ii) in the case of *consider* the verb is followed by a nominalization which has no embedded propositional content (for a detailed treatment, see Tadros 1980).
(2) Where a sentence contains the structure common in mathematics of the setting up of variables: *let* + NP + *be* + NP.
(3) Where a sentence contains a fictitious proper name.
(4) Where a sentence contains 'if + NP + VP (past verb) + NP + VP (past modal)'.
(5) Where a sentence contains 'if + NP + VP (present verb) + NP + VP (present or past modal)', provided that:
    (i) the noun in the first NP does not make reference to an entity which is actual;
    (ii) 'if' is not paraphraseable by 'whenever' in that context.

V *Suppose* the legislator could draft rules that were absolutely clear in application: even so he could not foresee every possible situation that might arise, . . .
D As it is, legal uncertainty is counterbalanced by judicial flexibility.

(F, p. 40)

This example satisfies criterion 1. The signal of Hypotheticality is the imperative *suppose*.

V   In order to simplify discussion of the advantages . . .

> *Let the two countries be Atlantis and Erewhon*, and let the two commodities be cloth (typifying manufactured goods) and wheat (typifying agricultural products).

(H, p. 463)

This example illustrates criteria 2 and 3, since it has the structure *let* + NP + *be* + NP, together with the two fictitious names *Atlantis* and *Erewhon*.

> . . . but the patterns he creates express also the very elusiveness of what he perceives. *If it were not elusive, if it could be brought within the compass of what is conventionally communicable*, then . . .

(W, p.70)

This example illustrates 4 above. The use of the counterfactual conditional signals from the start an unreal world which is clearly at variance with the real world. This unreal world is demolished on the basis that it does not accurately mirror the real world.

In the example below, both the V and D members will be given. The V member meets criterion 5 above and the D member is a Generalization.

V   *If Spenlow* has an account with the *Eastern Bank*, Northampton, and draws a cheque for £25 in favour of *Drood*, who pays it into his account at the *Western Bank*, Exeter, this cheque will be cleared through the London Clearing House.
D   All cheques originating from banks in towns other than that where they have been paid in are sent each day to the Head Office of the payee's bank after which they go the London Clearing House.

(H, p. 405)

The signals of Hypotheticality in the V member are both the *if* clause and the fictitious entities: 'Spenlow', 'Drood', 'Eastern Bank' and 'Western Bank'. It is interesting to note that the fictitious banks are located in real cities. The moral of this tale comes in the D member.

In the D member, specific items in V are repeated in less specific terms. Now 'a cheque' or 'this cheque' becomes 'all cheques', 'the Eastern Bank' becomes 'banks' and so on. The function of the D member of Hypotheticality is, thus, to generalize from the Hypothetical statements.

Question

Question is a category of Prediction based on the underlying assumption of writer detachment. The writer detaches himself from the resolution of the disjunction of the proposition posed by the question he asks, and this detachment predicts that he will be involved at some later point to declare his state of knowledge as regards the question.

Criteria for V membership of Question

The following criteria are necessary for a V member of Question:

(1) The sentence must have interrogative syntax.
(2) It must occur at section level, not under the heading 'Questions'.
(3) There must not be more than two interrogative sentences in succession, otherwise there is the implication 'not now, but later'.

It will be observed that in some texts some questions are typographically detached by occupying the position of heading or sub-heading; others do not have the heading status. In the former case the predicted member does not come immediately after the question, there is always some intervening material to prepare the way for the writer's declaration of his state of knowledge. In the latter case, the question is similar to elicitation in that there is a tendency, though this is not always the case, for the D member to follow straightaway. These two types of question are illustrated by the two examples below.

V   *Is college worthwhile?*
D   Education is one of society's most profitable investments. Human capital yields a return as great or greater than capital in the form of tools and buildings . . .

(S, pp. 119–20)

V   *Can this statement* be reconciled with a theory of scarcity?
D   Indeed, it can since . . .

(H, p.7)

The question in the first example occupies heading status, which predicts a delayed D member. A question of this type foreshadows the existence of problems in communication. The writer eliminates the problems by trying to reduce the number of 'D-events' (Labov and Fanshel 1977), using the Socratic question technique. In other words, he tries to ensure that no terms or concepts required for the D member are unfamiliar to the reader. In the D member we find an answer to the question.

The question in the second example is different. It occurs at section level, and is not typographically detached from the rest of the text. The V member is followed by the D member straightaway, that is, there is no intervening material separating the V from the D.

Complex patterning

The six categories of Prediction discussed above should not leave the reader with the impression that texts are neatly structured into V and D members. The fact is that these members, through various combinations, are capable of yielding an interesting variety of complex patterning, when applied to long stretches of text. (For details see Tadros 1981, 1985.) Suffice it to give a few illustrations of the way Predictive categories are interrelated.

(i) Recapitulation preceding Advance Labelling:

V1 *We have examined* the economic forces operating to determine the level of national income – the balance of saving and investment.

V2 *We now turn* to the problems of how the level of national income has fluctuated, and how economists try to forecast the future.

(S, p. 250)

V1 *The previous section presented* a downward view showing how units at each rank had structures realised by units at the rank below.

V2 *This section begins* at the lowest rank and discusses the realisation and recognition of acts; . . .

(S&C, p. 62)

V1 *We have considered* aspects of literary use of language which depend on a combination of what is kept distinct in the code.

V2 *Let us now briefly review the converse*: aspects of literary discourse which depend on dividing what is normally compounded.

(W, p. 62)

(ii) Recapitulation preceding Question

V1 *So far we have been pointing out* certain linguistic peculiarities of this poem as a text.

V2 *What* relevance *do they have* for an understanding of the poem as discourse, as an act of communication?

(W, p. 57)

V1 *It has already been seen* that a change in demand can bring about a change in supply, and that a change in supply, may cause a change in demand.

V2 *Can it be* that the supply and demand curves are even more intimately related and, indeed are responsive to the same influences.

(H, p. 129)

(iii) Advance Labelling preceding Question

V1 *Now we must clarify* the term 'command'.

V2 *How do* commands differ from requests, wishes and so on?

(F, p. 26)

(iv) Reporting preceding Question

V1 *It is* frequently *asserted* today that we are living in an age of plenty, because larger quantities than ever before of all kinds of goods and services are being produced.

V2 *Can this statement* be reconciled with a theory of scarcity?

(H, p. 7)

(v) Advance Labelling preceding Hypotheticality

V1 *Let us be* somewhat more precise about Convention 2.

V2 *Suppose* that a formative belongs to the syntactic categories animate, nonhuman, exception to rule n.

(C&H, p. 174)

CONCLUSIONS

The approach to text pragmatics presented here has practical pedagogical applications, since it emphasizes the interactional relationship between writer and reader in discourse. The interaction is manifested through the use of the Predictive Categories examined. Since these Predictive Categories are common across a range of disciplines, they can be fruitfully exploited in the teaching of reading and writing to students of various disciplines.

In the area of reading, it is very important to make students aware of signals of Prediction in order to enhance their reading efficiency. They must be trained, for instance, to recognize signals of Advance Labelling so that they look for the fulfilment of the act labelled; or to exploit signals of Enumeration in order to get at the enumerated items. Through Recapitulation they are forewarned that they should link up bits of information or ideas so that they would not lose the thread of the argument; and by means of signals of Hypotheticality they are alerted to the Generalization at the end of the hypothetical excursion.

The idea of authorial detachment from propositions through Reporting is of particular significance in expository text. Students should thus be trained to distinguish between what a writer 'thinks', 'believes', 'claims', and what he says others 'think' 'believe' or 'claim'. Inability to recognize such signals leads the student to produce a statement like 'Television has made American life better' as a paraphrase of 'When television was first introduced into American society, *writers and social scientists thought* that this new invention would better American life'. From the above it is clear that the detaching signal was missed by the student.

Predictive Categories are also pertinent to the teaching of writing. Students must be trained to fulfil their commitments to the reader. For instance, if a student signals that s/he is going to compare X and Y, s/he should not simply produce separate descriptions of the items concerned, leaving it to the reader to arrive at the comparison him/herself; or if a student signals that there are three reasons for X, he should be committed to that number. And, when using visual material, students often throw in tables without warning or explanation. They rarely announce or interpret a table or graph: these things just occur in their writing without any reference.

The use of signals of writer detachment from propositions, or text reporting, is particularly important for students in the writing of theses or research papers. How often do students switch from text reporting to text averral without signalling! And, of course, it is an easy step from removing detaching signals, when reviewing your literature, to plagiarism. Thus it is crucial to train students to signal Reporting as well as to provide the predicted Evaluation.

There is no doubt that in the absence of signals of Prediction, the reader will have to work harder in order to find out the relationships intended by the writer. As Johns (this volume, p. 108) rightly observes, some texts are difficult to read not because of subject matter, but because they are 'badly written'. By 'badly written' he means that 'The writer fails to set up a basis for reader prediction, or fails without apparent reason to fulfil the predictions he appears to set up.'

6 Labelling discourse: an aspect of nominal-group lexical cohesion

Gill Francis

INTRODUCTION

The main aim of this chapter is to identify, describe and illustrate one of the principal ways in which nominal groups are used to connect and organize written discourse. This type of nominal-group lexical cohesion will be referred to as **labelling**. Two types of label will be identified: these will be termed **advance** and **retrospective labels**. The examples given to illustrate the use of these are all from the Bank of English collection of corpora held at Cobuild, Birmingham, and, in particular, the corpus containing a series of complete editions of *The Times*.

Within the category of labels, an important sub-set is further isolated and described: this set is referred to as **metalinguistic**. These are nominal groups which talk about a stretch of discourse as a linguistic act, labelling it as, say, an *argument*, a *point* or a *statement*. In other words, they are labels for stages of an argument, developed in and through the discourse itself as the writer presents and assesses his/her own propositions and those of other sources. Unlike, say, *problems* and *issues*, which exist in the world outside discourse, they are *ad hoc* characterizations of the language behaviour being carried out in the text.

LABELS

The main characteristic of what will be termed a label is that it requires lexical realization, or lexicalization, in its co-text: it is an inherently unspecific nominal element whose specific meaning in the discourse needs to be precisely spelled out (Winter 1982, 1992). Labels may function either cataphorically (forwards) or anaphorically (backwards). Where the label precedes its lexicalization, it will be termed an **advance label**;[1] where it follows its lexicalization, it will be called a **retrospective label**.

It should be noted that, while a label and its lexicalization often occur within a single clause, I will be considering only those which operate cohesively across clause boundaries.

Advance labels

In example 1 below, the italicized nominal group is an **advance label**:

1   I understand that approximately 12 per cent of the population is left-
handed. Why, then, should there be such a preponderance of right-handed
golfers which extends, I am informed, to club level? In reply to that
question a golfing colleague of mine offered *two reasons*.
    The first was that beginners usually start with handed-down clubs,
which are usually right-handed. The second was that, for technical
reasons, left-handed individuals make good right-handed golfers.

Two reasons, here, allows the reader to predict the precise information that
will follow, which is an explanation for 'the preponderance of right-handed
golfers'. In order to meet these expectations, the nominal group (including, of
course, *two*) has to be fully lexicalized in what follows, and these **replacement clauses** (Winter 1982) have to be fully compatible with the semantics of
reason. Thus the label clearly has an organizing role which extends over the
whole of the next paragraph.

If there are additional lexical modifiers or qualifiers within the nominal
group, they too have to be lexicalized in the replacement clause or clauses, as
in the next example:

2   The *New York Post*, which has been leading the tabloid pack, has added
two salacious details to this bare outline. It reported that the alleged attack
took place on a concrete staircase that runs from the Kennedy house to the
beach. More sensationally, the *Post* claimed on Friday that Ted Kennedy,
half naked, was romping round the estate with a second woman while the
alleged attack was taking place. This allegation was at best dubious and at
worst an outright fabrication.

The predictive and organizing functions of advance labels can be seen in
terms of the three Hallidayan metafunctions: ideational, interpersonal and
textual. In example 2, *two salacious details* has ideational meaning as a
participant in the material process of 'adding'. It is crucial to the accumulation
of meaning in the discourse, assigning to its replacement clauses a particular
status in the ongoing argument. The label also has interpersonal meaning: by
choosing *details* as the head noun, the writer suspends his/her evaluation: a
choice of, say, *allegations* would have pre-empted the ensuing negative
evaluation and thus would have had a different effect on the semantics of the
replacement clauses. *Salacious* as a modifier, too, is evaluative, and makes
predictions which are fulfilled by the compatible lexis of the sentence
beginning with 'More sensationally'.
    The label also has textual meaning: it is located in the Rheme of the clause
and is part of the focus of new information. As such it has the potential to be
taken up again in the development of the argument; only information
presented as new can be prospective.

Finally, it should be noted that the whole group *two salacious details* is itself part of a pattern of contrastive replacement in relation to *this bare outline*; the outline precedes the quoted paragraph of the text. A particular label, then, is not selected independently, but is one element in a configuration of compatible lexical and syntactic choices.

Retrospective labels

When an advance label is used, the motivation for its use has not yet been supplied and hence its unique lexicalization in the clauses which it replaces can be predicted: its function is to tell the reader what to expect. The use of a retrospective label, on the other hand, requires a different explanation, since it has already been lexicalized.

A retrospective label serves to **encapsulate** or package a stretch of discourse. My major criterion for identifying an anaphorically cohesive nominal group as a retrospective label is that there is no single nominal group to which it refers: it is not a repetition or a 'synonym' of any preceding element. Instead, it is *presented as equivalent to* the clause or clauses it replaces, while naming them for the first time. The label indicates to the reader exactly how that stretch of discourse is to be interpreted, and this provides the frame of reference within which the subsequent argument is developed. An example will make this clearer; again the label is italicized:

3   ... the patients' immune system recognised the mouse antibodies and rejected them. This meant they did not remain in the system long enough to be fully effective.
    The second generation antibody now under development is an attempt to get around *this problem* by 'humanising' the mouse antibodies, using a technique developed by ...

The retrospective label *this problem* is preceded by its lexicalization, and thus it tells the reader to interpret the rejection of the mouse antibodies as a *problem*. This characterization, which is anticipated by the description of the antibodies as not being 'fully effective', aligns the preceding clauses with what is to follow, and provides a framework for the solution to be described.

Retrospective labels as pro-forms

The head nouns of retrospective labels are almost always preceded by a specific deictic like *the*, *this*, *that* or *such*, and may have other modifiers and qualifiers too. The whole nominal group functions very much like a pro-form or reference item. In this respect labels are very similar to the **general nouns** identified by Halliday and Hasan (1976: 27); these include *man*, *creature*, *thing*, *stuff*, *matter*, *move*, *question*, *idea* and *fact*. These general nouns, they say, may have a cohesive function 'because a general noun is itself a borderline case between a lexical item (member of an open set) and a grammatical item (member of a closed system)'. From a grammatical point of view, 'the combination of general noun plus specific determiner, such as *the man*, *the thing*, is very similar to a reference item' (p. 275).

Like general nouns, too (and indeed like *this* and *that* without a following noun), retrospective labels have the ability to refer to 'text as fact': in Halliday and Hasan's terms 'the referent is not being taken up at face-value but is being transmuted into a fact or a report' (p. 52). A label refers to and names a stretch of discourse, aligning it with the ongoing argument, which now continues in terms of what has been presented as 'fact'.

In so far as it functions like a pro-form, the head noun of a retrospective label is always presented as the **given** information in its clause, in terms of which the new message, the information focus, is formulated. The term **presented** is important here, since the label does not have a 'synonym' in the preceding discourse, and its head is actually a new lexical item. It sums up and encapsulates what has gone before, re-entering it (Jordan 1985) in such a way that it has no prospective potential. If read aloud, *this problem* in example 3 would not be given tonic prominence; it falls into the post-tonic part of the tone group.

The head noun of a retrospective label may combine with a definite reference item in one of two ways: first, it may be modified by it as in example 3 above; second, it may be the complement of the reference item, as in the next example:

4   Anthony Burgess thinks hero worship is peculiar to the British. He explains it by our obsession with the past and our preference for believing in the supremacy of people over ideas. 'In contrast to Plutarch's Lives, which contain no real people, it is healthy on the part of the British to think that history is made by people going to the toilet or having indigestion.'

   While this is *an old-fashioned diagnosis*, in line with Carlyle's maxim that history is the essence of innumerable biographies, there is cogency in the notion that we, unlike Europeans, and especially the French, do not approve of seeing abstruse values exalted over individual achievement.

The organisational function of retrospective labels

Like advance labels, retrospective labels have an important organizational function: they signal that the writer is moving on to the next stage of his/her argument, having disposed of the preceding stage by encapsulating or packaging it in a single nominalization. This no longer has any prospective potential (though its modifiers may do, as will be argued on pp. 95–9 below).

Thus these labels have a clear topic-shifting and topic-linking function: they introduce changes of topic, or a shift within a topic, while preserving continuity by placing new information within a given framework. This signalling function is reinforced by an orthographic division: clauses containing retrospective labels are usually paragraph-initial.

A retrospective label may extend its topic-linking capacity over a very small stretch of discourse, in which case its organizational role is limited, as in the next example:

5 During the war Frisch was called up into the Swiss army and was on duty with the frontier forces. *This experience* tended to confirm him in his view that Switzerland's decision to remain neutral was a matter more of luck than judgement, and that it reflected a lack of commitment rather than a moral statement. Nevertheless Switzerland's neutral position did give him a unique vantage point from which to view the events of a war raging outside its borders.

In this example, the label *this experience* sums up the first quoted sentence only. In the second sentence, a rapid transition is made to a discussion of Frisch's view about Switzerland's neutrality, and the third sentence ends this discussion. Thus very little of the discourse is about *this experience*, and the label has a very local organizing role.

In other cases, the use of a retrospective label may help organize a much longer stretch of discourse, providing the main link that unifies two major structural elements, as in the next example:

6 Sir, As Lech Walesa visits London this week, I trust someone will raise with him the threat to women's rights in his so-called 'new democracy'.
  The Polish government is on the verge of outlawing abortion, which has been free on demand since 1956. *This move* in itself is deplorable, but is made far worse by the fact that contraception is virtually unobtainable. As in many eastern European countries, women have become accustomed, rightly or wrongly, to relying on abortion as a means of choosing their family size. Under the new Polish law doctors will face imprisonment if caught performing illegal terminations and women will only be permitted abortions if life is at risk . . .

The stretch of discourse which is labelled by *this move* is short, but the rest of the letter is of some length: it is devoted to an evaluation of the *move* as *deplorable*, and to giving the reasons why. The label, then, comes at the boundary between the Situation and Evaluation sections of a lengthy Situation–Evaluation–Basis for Evaluation discourse pattern (Winter 1982, 1992). It faces both backwards and forwards: backwards to encapsulate and re-enter as given the situation described in the preceding paragraph, and forwards to evaluate it. The whole letter, then, is about *this move* and nothing else.

Fuzzy reference

It is worth mentioning at this point that a retrospective label does not necessarily refer to a clearly delimited or identifiable stretch of discourse: it is not always possible to decide where the initial boundary of its referent lies. This may be explained in terms of the intrinsic cohesive function of retrospective labels: they are used, like the anaphoric *this*, to tell the reader to section off in his or her mind what has gone before. The precise extent of the stretch to be sectioned off may not matter: it is the shift in direction signalled by the label and its immediate environment which is of crucial importance for the development of the discourse. It could even be argued that referential indistinctness of this kind may be used strategically by the writer to creative or persuasive effect, perhaps providing scope for different interpretations, or blurring the lines of specious or spurious arguments.

Summary: the metafunctions

Like advance labels, retrospective labels can be seen as having ideational, interpersonal and textual meaning. For example, *this move* in example 6 has ideational meaning: its participant role is that of Carrier in an attributive intensive process where the Attribute is *deplorable*. The label also has interpersonal meaning: the choice of *move* is typical journalese for anything which has happened or will happen as a result of political decisions, and encodes the writer's acceptance that 'outlawing abortion' is definitely on the agenda. In terms of textual meaning, it is the Theme of its clause, and as is typical of thematic position, it is presented as given information.

THE LEXICAL RANGE OF ADVANCE AND RETROSPECTIVE LABELS

It is impossible to attempt any exhaustive listing of nominal-group heads which can function as labels in the ways described above. My recognition criteria are very simple: any noun can be the head noun of a label if it is unspecific and requires lexical realization in its immediate context, either beforehand or afterwards.

Labels also have much in common with what Widdowson (1983: 92) refers to as a general or 'procedural' vocabulary which structures and supports the more specific, field-related vocabulary of academic texts. This consists of 'words of a wide indexical range . . . useful for negotiating the conveyance of more specific concepts, for defining terms which relate to particular fields of reference'. Ivanic (1991) uses very similar criteria to identify her category of 'carrier nouns'. Peters (1985) also proposes a category of 'all-purpose' words like *aspect, fact, feature, procedure, sign* and *thing*. (The word 'all-purpose' is a misnomer, since even the most general and adaptable of these, *thing*, would be collocationally inappropriate as a label in any of the examples given above. It should be stressed again that the choice of a label is not an independent selection from a notional paradigm of words which have the same function: these items are highly context-dependent.)

Basically, however, what all head nouns of labels have in common is, in Winter's terms, the fact that they are all inherently unspecific: their specification is a unique choice from an infinity of possible lexicalizations, and is found in the clauses with which they enter into replacement relations. It is this concept which is the most helpful in specifying labels as a class, albeit an open-ended one.

Within the category of labels it is possible to isolate a set of nouns which have an important feature in common – they are **metalinguistic** in the sense that they label a stretch of discourse as being a particular type of **language**. They are used by the writer to forge relationships which are located entirely within the discourse itself; they instruct the reader to interpret the linguistic status of a proposition in a particular way. Farnes (1973) made a similar distinction between what he called 'structure' and 'content' signposts: he takes *point* to be a structure signpost, whereas *cause* is a content signpost. The next section attempts to classify these metalinguistic nouns further.

Before moving on, however, it is worth listing the head nouns which fall into the more general category. All of these were found as head nouns of labels at least twice in a small part of *The Times* corpus. The most common ones are listed first. It should be noted that retrospective labels are far commoner than advance labels, and not all the nouns listed occur as heads of advance labels. Some are typically plural, but only the labels that are always plural are listed as such.

> *Most common*: approach, area, aspect, case, matter, move, problem, stuff, thing, way.
>
> *Others*: accident, achievement, action, activity, advance, advantage, affair, agreement, anachronism, approach, arrangement, attempt, background, behaviour, blunder, calamity, cause, challenge, change, characteristic, circumstances, combination, complication, compromise, conditions, consequence, consideration, context, contingency, contradiction, deal, deed, development, device, difficulty, dilemma, disaster, effect, element, episode, event, evidence, exercise, experience, fact, factor, fate, feature, incident, information, issue, manner, measure, mess, method, mistake, mixture, news, objective, occasion, occurrence, operation, outcome, pattern, picture, plan, policy, possibility, practice, procedure, process, programme, project, prospect, purpose, question, reaction, reason, result, scenario, scheme, setback, sign, situation, solution, sphere, step, strategy, system, subject, tactic, task, technique, tendency, threat, topic, treatment, trend, truth.

Finally, it should be pointed out that many labels have a complex nominal-group structure, and can be seen as 'double-headed' (as in the terms set out by Sinclair 1989 for nominal groups containing *of*). Examples found in the data include *state of affairs*, *course of action* and *level of activity*.

Metalinguistic labels

Broadly speaking, the metalinguistic head nouns of labels fall into the following groups, though there is some blurring and overlap between them, as will become clear:

'illocutionary' nouns
'language activity' nouns
'mental process' nouns
'text' nouns

Again, the lists of exponents given below are those that were found at least twice in a small part of *The Times* corpus.

Illocutionary nouns

These are nominalizations of verbal processes, usually acts of communication; they typically have cognate illocutionary verbs. Head nouns of this type found in the data are:

accusation, admission, advice, affront, allegation, announcement, answer, appeal, argument, assertion, charge, claim, comment, complaint, compliment, conclusion, contention, criticism, decision, (level of) denial, disclosure, excuse, explanation, indication, objection, observation, pledge, point, prediction, projection, proposal, proposition, protestation, reassurance, recognition, recommendation, rejection, remark, reminder, reply, report, request, response, revelation, statement, suggestion, warning.

The next example illustrates the use of *explanation* and *level of denial* as the 'illocutionary' head nouns in labels:

7   As we left this meeting, my wife said: 'Potter has gone barmy, and they don't know what to do.' I could not bring myself to believe she was right. I only accepted *this explanation* when my wife confided her suspicions to a friend, a psychiatrist, who exclaimed: 'That's a terrible thing to say about your child's therapist.' *This level of denial* convinced me that it was true.

It must be emphasized that the selection of a particular noun as a label for someone else's proposition does not necessarily reflect the latter's original intention. Thus the choice of *explanation* here does not necessarily encode the original illocutionary force of writer's wife's utterance; rather, it is the way in which the writer chooses to interpret that force, just as he interprets the corresponding mental representations as *her suspicions*. (*Suspicion* is a 'mental process' head noun: see p. 92 below.) If he had chosen, say, *suggestion* or *pronouncement* instead, this would have involved a different interpretation. The same applies to *level of denial* in the next sentence of the example; the referent could have been labelled a *protest* or a *retort*, but the writer is free to choose any appropriate interpretation of the psychiatrist's illocutionary act. Of course, any choice of label cannot be seen independently from all the other lexical selections made: 'accept' is compatible with *explanation* and 'confide' with *suspicions*, while *denial* is typically juxtaposed contrastively with 'true'.

To summarize the point, the synonymity presented as given by the use of a label may be both partial and illusory, and reflects the writer's exploitation of the strategic resources of the device.

Language-activity nouns

These are nouns which refer to some kind of language activity or the results thereof. They are similar to illocutionary nouns, but they do not have cognate illocutionary verbs (though they may have cognate verbs). Head-nouns of this type found in the data are:

account, ambiguity, comparison, consensus, contrast, controversy, criterion, debate, defence, definition, description, detail, diagnosis, dispute, distinction, drivel, equation, example, formula, illustration, instance, language, message, myth, nonsense, proof, (line of) reasoning, reference, squabble, story, summary, tale, talk, theme, verdict, version, way (of putting it), (style of) writing

The next example illustrates the use of *description* as the 'language activity' head noun in a label:

8   Foster, the Fife-based organiser, said: 'So many great sporting cars are only seen as static exhibits in museums nowadays, so it is a great honour for Scotland that it has become one of the premier venues for using these wonderful machines.'
     This description is scarcely inflated. McLaren will be driving his Jaguar Lightweight E Type. John Coombes, now based in Monaco, will drive a Jaguar D Type . . .

Included in this group, too, are nouns referring to the results of discourse-patterning and stylistic operations carried out on language data, such as *conundrum, corollary, image, imagery, irony, metaphor* and *paradox*. Also included are nouns like *gossip* and *heresy* which are used primarily to evaluate verbal activity. The next example illustrates the use of *irony* as a retrospective label:

9   Rather as the great king of Babylon, Nebuchadnezzar, was obliged to listen to Daniel, the prophet of the oppressed people of Israel, so Saddam the tyrant of Baghdad has been forced to listen to the spokesmen of the Kurds, a people he despises. The Western powers should not spoil *this irony.*

Mental-process nouns

These are nouns which refer to cognitive states and processes and the results thereof. They include nominalizations of mental-process verbs of the type that are used to project ideas, like *think* and *believe*, but not all of them have cognate verbs. When they are used as head nouns in labels, their referents have of course been expressed verbally, but such expression is not a necessary part of their meaning. Many of them, like *belief* and *opinion*, refer to aspects of cognitive states arrived at as a result of the processing of thoughts and experiences. Others can refer either to the result or to the process: *interpretation*, for example, may refer both to the particular theory formulated as a result of interpreting, or to the process of interpreting.

Head nouns of this type found in the data are:

analysis, assessment, assumption, attitude, belief, concept, conviction, doctrine, doubt, finding, hypothesis, idea, insight, interpretation, knowl-edge, misconception, notion, opinion, philosophy, position, principle, rationale, reading, suspicion, theory, thesis, thinking, thought, (point of) view, vision

The next example illustrates the use of *view* as the 'mental process' head noun in a label:

10 At a press briefing in London during the inaugural meeting of the bank's board of governors, Henning Christophersen, vice-president of the Euro-pean Commission, said: 'The EBRD must not be a political institution, but plainly and simply a bank.'
    This view contrasted with that of Jacques Attali, the president of the European Bank, who regards the bank's role as political and economic.

It should be pointed out at this stage that there is some overlap between the illocutionary and language-activity types of label on the one hand, and the mental-process type on the other. The world of cognition is mirrored in the world of discourse, and the views and opinions we hold are often seen in terms of the way they are expressed. Thus all the nouns in these sets are in fact located on a cline, and their two aspects of meaning shade imperceptibly into each other. At one end of the cline are the purely verbal-process nouns (with illocutionary cognate verbs) like *claim* and *statement*, which must refer to illocutionary acts, and which encode the writer's chosen interpretation of these. At the other end are the purely cognitive nouns like *belief* and *idea*: it is no necessary part of their meaning that they be expressed in language, though of course as labels they do refer to their written or spoken expressions. In the middle of the cline can be located such nouns as *conclusion* and *observation*, which may refer either to an illocutionary act or a cognitive state or process, though naturally, again, when they have been used in labels they are interpreting expressed conclusions and observations. These have in fact been included in the illocutionary set, on the grounds that they have cognate illocutionary verbs.

In spite of the haziness of the boundaries, however, the basic distinction remains valid. At the core of it is the same distinction as that made by Halliday (1985) between verbal and mental processes, and between the projection of locutions and the projection of ideas, though of course, since we are dealing with nouns rather than verbs, the criteria for inclusion in each of the sets are rather different.

Text nouns

These are nouns which refer to the formal textual structure of discourse. There is no interpretation involved: they simply label stretches of preceding discourse whose precise boundaries they define.

Head nouns of this type found in the data are *phrase*, *question* (orthographically signalled), *sentence* and *words*, which, according to Leech (1983: 314), are in the 'syntactic mode of metalanguage' as opposed to the semantic mode. They also include nouns like *excerpt*, *page*, *paragraph*, *passage*, *quotation*, *section*, *term* and *terminology*, which similarly refer to formal structures, though these are not syntactic units.

The next example illustrates the use of *quotation* as the 'text' head noun in a label:

11 'Projects are also introducing changes in teaching styles. Increasingly these are geared towards providing students with the opportunity to develop initiative, motivation, problem-solving skills and other personal qualities. Central to this approach is the transfer to students themselves of the responsibility for managing their own learning and applying their own knowledge.'

    That quotation comes not from the Plowden report, but from the Technical and Vocational Education Initiative review of 1985. Is it very different from what we found in the best primary schools?

EVALUATIVE RETROSPECTIVE LABELS

It was suggested on pages 90–1 above that while retrospective labels are presented as given and therefore as synonymous with their preceding clause(s), such synonymity is a construct, a resource which the writer draws upon to serve the purposes of his/her argument. Although labels are presented as given pro-forms, they have interpersonal meaning, and may, in fact, add something new to the argument by signalling the writer's evaluation of the propositions which they encapsulate.

Some head nouns of labels, for example *statement*, *belief* and *view* can be termed 'attitudinally neutral', though they may well take on 'positive' or 'negative' meanings in discourse, according to the lexical environment in which they are used. Others necessarily indicate either a negative or a positive attitude towards the preceding propositions.

In the next example, the label *this claim* is clearly a distancing device, enabling the writer to convey scepticism as to its validity. This type of negative evaluation involves the interpretation of the illocutionary force of a statement in a way that its speaker would probably disagree with, especially in a political context like this:

12 . . . led me to wonder whether politicians are becoming more cavalier in their use of data. John Major, speaking of the government's new council tax in the Commons 10 days ago, said: 'Over 70 per cent of people will be gainers under the scheme.'

   As it happened, at the exact time he was making *this claim*, I and other correspondents were being briefed on the tax by senior Treasury officials.

In the next example, the label *nonsense* is a more explicitly negative evaluation of the preceding statement:

13 . . . I recall the late Shah telling me repeatedly during the 1978 revolution that the people believed that 'If you lifted up Khomeini's beard, you would find 'Made in England' written under his chin.' He half-believed *this nonsense* himself, in spite of my protestations that Anglo-Iranian relations had prospered as never before under his rule, and that the Ayatollah was demonstrably no admirer of Britain.

The next example shows the use of *squabble* as a signal of the writer's negative attitude towards the propositions it encapsulates. His choice of label is explicitly derisive: it would have been more 'objective' to use a word like *dispute*:

14 . . . Mr Fitzwater was in turn mocked by the American press and excoriated by British Tories anxious that their leader screw the maximum number of votes from his diplomatic rugby game. By yesterday morning the White House had a fax of the front page of London's Evening Standard, claiming that the relationship between President Bush and John Major is strained 'as never before'.

   Mr Bush was wise enough to see that *this squabble* was getting out of hand. Mr Fitzwater was asked to retract the statement which had caused the fuss . . .

There are few head nouns which, if unmodified, classify their referents in positive terms: those that can be termed positive usually indicate the writer's identification with the status and validity of the referent, such as *fact* and *finding*. In the next example, the results obtained by the Accident Research Unit are endorsed as *information*:

15 The Accident Research Unit at Birmingham University has been investigating the outcome of real-life car accidents for the past 25 years. Each year, the Cooperative Crash Injury Study (of which we are part) investigates 850 car accidents in which people are injured or killed.

We thoroughly examine the vehicle with particular reference to the occupant protection systems, of which the seatbelt forms a fundamental part. We combine *this information* with detailed medical and police records as well as information provided on questionnaires supplied voluntarily by the accident victims themselves.

MODIFICATION IN RETROSPECTIVE LABELS

It was pointed out on page 84 above that the cohesiveness of labels is a function of the whole nominal group, not just the head noun. It is now time to look at the various modifiers of the head nouns listed above, and to see what they contribute to the predictive and encapsulating roles of the labels in which they are used. I will confine this discussion to their role in retrospective labels, which are more common and more varied.

Like the head nouns of labels, their modifiers may have ideational, interpersonal and textual meaning. Those with primarily textual meaning are particularly interesting, and will be dealt with separately.

Ideational and interpersonal modification

First, there are modifiers whose functions are primarily ideational: they add to the meaning of the head noun by classifying it or defining it, making its participant role more explicit. Here is an example:

16 I was travelling today on the InterCity 125 from Plymouth to Paddington, seated within feet of a door which burst open as the train entered a tunnel at speed, just south of Taunton.

　　From my own observation and the opinions of the three deeply shocked people who were standing adjacent to the door, there is strong prima facie evidence that *this spontaneous incident* was due to a material failure.

Here, *spontaneous* has ideational meaning: it adds information about the *incident* by classifying it as *spontaneous*; this, of course, is compatible with, and recoverable from, the preceding paragraph, where the door is described as having 'burst open'.

The same applies to the modifiers of *concept* in the next example:

17 This week dentists up and down the country are being asked to hand out sweets as part of a 'tooth-friendly' promotion to boost sales of sweets being sold as 'kind to teeth'. Manufacturers of *this new confectionary concept* are providing dentists participating in this week's National Smile Week with free samples to give away on open days aimed at encouraging more people to visit their dentists.

Both *new* and *confectionary* are ideational modifiers in the sense that they are far more informative than *concept* would have been on its own in encapsulating the whole idea of the sweets being sold as 'kind to teeth'. The economy of the device, in allowing a lot of information to be presented as a single given package, is particularly apparent here.

In some cases the modifier seems to add little to the ideational meaning of the label, as in the next example:

18 The squeeze determines the swing, and while the squeeze may be predictable by good polling, it tells us nothing about any election other than today's in Monmouth.

   Nobody, however, has any interest in *this basic truth*. The political community is addicted to any horse race it can find . . .

Basic, here, does not add much to the concept of *truth*: it is not selected from a range of adjectives that could modify *truth*, and a *basic truth* cannot be contrasted with truths that are not basic. Here noun and modifier are relatively predictable collocates, where the function of the modifier is simply to add weight and dignity to *truth* by underlining or focusing on a facet of the way we would normally understand the noun (see Sinclair, this volume).

Some modifiers have both ideational and interpersonal meaning, as in the next example:

19 How free range is a free-range chicken? After months of deliberation, the European Commission has come up with an official answer, or rather three answers, to *this hotly-debated question*: there is free range, traditional free range and total free range. The Brussels mandarins have devised the three-part definition to satisfy a commendable desire for a common standard throughout the European Community while at the same time, and more questionably, enabling all the main types of free-range chicken on the market to qualify.

Perhaps the question is indeed *hotly debated*, and the modifier does have a certain classificatory role. But there is something hyperbolic about this particular choice of epithet which conveys the writer's attitude towards the issue.

The most common modifiers found in labels, however, are those which encode interpersonal meaning quite unequivocally: they evaluate the propositions they encapsulate. Where the nominal group acts as a single cohesive unit, this evaluation is slipped in as part of the given information, though it may in fact be a new indication of the writer's attitude. The next example makes this clear:

20 In 1970 he publicly compared the banks to a railway with too many uneconomic branch lines, arguing that many bank branches should become lightly-staffed satellites.

   But *this far-sighted recommendation* encountered strong resistance . . .

Recommendation is itself attitudinally neutral, and the writer's assessment of it as *far-sighted* is in fact new to the reader, while being presented as part of a given package.

Sometimes the attitude has already been indicated, and the function of the modifiers is to spell it out more fully, as in the case of the negatively evaluative modifiers in the next example:

21 London's cab drivers take an aristocratic thrashing in the current edition of their magazine *Taxi*. The Earl of Winchilsea and Nottingham, the Liberal Democrat peer and staunch defender of cabbies, writes in warm terms about the trade in general but blasts those drivers who refuse to pick up fares in Parliament Square because they do not like the destinations.

'Because of *this thoughtless and stupid attitude*, it is becoming more difficult to continue the fight against minicabs', thunders the earl.

Here, *thoughtless and stupid* is predictable from the compatible lexis of the previous sentences, in particular 'an aristocratic thrashing' and 'blasts'. Again, however, the head noun *attitude* is itself neutral, and this brings us to an important observation. Writers seem to choose the labelling device because of the modification options it offers: by choosing a nominalization like *attitude* they can get in their evaluation without having to make a special point of it. *Attitude*, then, unlike *truth* in example 18 above, is primarily a carrier for its modifiers. In other words, it is easy to see here what the motivation is for choosing a lexically cohesive device rather than a grammatical one like 'Because of *this*, it is becoming more difficult . . .'

So far in this section, we have seen only examples in which head and modifiers function as a single cohesive unit. In some cases the modifiers seem to be simply an extension of the meaning of the head, and in others they seem to be more important in encoding the writer's message than the heads which carry them. In all the cases, however, the heads cannot be omitted, however minimal their independent participant role, as the result would be ungrammatical ('because of this thoughtless and stupid' in example 21).

This applies to all those retrospective labels which are modified by *this* or another specific deictic. However, this is not always the case: very often the label is the Complement of the deictic. In such cases, the label does not function as a single cohesive pro-form: only the head is presented as given, while the modifiers are presented as new, and have prospective meaning. Here is an example:

22 'I feel mentally like a pink worm fed on pink nougat', he observed.

Readers of his later books might suppose *this* to be *an accurate description* of his mental state from cradle to grave, but in fact, as an Oxford undergraduate just after the first world war (in which, extraordinarily, he had been a military instructor), Nichols was a brilliant success.

Here the modifier *accurate* is prospective in a way that it would not be in a label like *this accurate description*: it is precisely the word *accurate* which carries the discourse forward. If read aloud it would be intonationally prominent. *Description*, here, just seems to be a convenient carrier for this modifier. The test of this is that the head and modifier could be separated without altering the information structure: 'Readers . . . might suppose this description to be an accurate one.'

It is worth noting that part of the lexicogrammar of *thing* is that when it is used as the head noun of a retrospective label, it is always used in the structure 'This is a (modifier) thing', where the modifier has prospective potential, rather than in the alternative structure 'This (modifier) thing is . . .' This is the extreme case of a head noun of a label being used as a neutral carrier for highly evaluative and prospectively oriented modifiers. Here is an example:

23 He has the charisma of a wet fish. This is probably *the most memorable thing* anyone has said about Graham Gooch, the England cricket captain, and it was, of course, said by Ted Dexter, now chairman of the selectors . . .

Textual modification

Textual modifiers are those which contribute directly to the organizational role of labels: they help to order messages with respect to each other and signal the relationships between them. These modifiers include post-deictics like *same*, *similar*, *different*, *next*, *further*, *other* and *another*, and numeratives like *second* and *third*. Of these, *another* is by far the most common.

Textual modifiers differ from ideational and interpersonal modifiers in important respects. First, they are always presented as new information, even when the rest of the nominal group is presented as given, and even when they occur clause-initially in unmarked Themes. Second, and obviously related, the labels in which they occur are not co-referential with the preceding text. In Hasan's (1984) terms, they participate in similarity chains, but not identity chains. Consider this example:

24 In his inauguration speech, for example, Mr Walesa stressed the need for good relations with neighbours, but forgot to mention Czechoslovakia. This reminded Prague of the sourness that has crept into relations between their president, Vaclav Havel, and Mr Walesa since the revolution of 1989. *Another blunder*: the outgoing president, General Jaruzelski, was not invited to the inauguration ceremony.

Here, *blunder* encapsulates Mr Walesa's failure to mention Czechoslovakia. While *blunder* is presented as given, however, *another* is new and refers forwards to another omission of the same sort. In other words, the head noun is retrospective, but the nominal group as a whole is predictive. In this example, the nominal group is structurally cataphoric, that is, cohesive within the clause (Halliday and Hasan 1976: 78). Where the prospective reference extends beyond the clause, however, such nominal groups may be both retrospective labels (excluding the textual modifier) and advance labels, as in this example:

25 Mr Budd has had no direct connection with politics or the Tory party but, like Sir Terry, he was closely identified with the monetarism of the early Thatcher years.

   A similar argument may work against Gavyn Davies, chief UK economist at Goldman Sachs, the US investment bank. Mr Davies has been widely identified with Labour although his only links were a stint 15 years ago in Jim Callaghan's office, and marriage to Neil Kinnock's private secretary.

It is easy to find any number of texts in which the transitions between sections are signalled by textual modifiers, usually in thematic position. They are extremely useful as discourse-organizers. First, they establish a wide range of degrees of contrast, from 'sameness' to 'difference' between the co-classified items. At the same time they can be used to sequence the stages of an argument: the numeratives like *first* and *second*, in particular, sequence quite explicitly. Hence these modifiers have a metalinguistic function: they may sequence the points in an argument or events in the world, but even in the latter case, the progression is determined by textual considerations. What the writer is asking and answering is not 'How many things happened, and in what order?', but rather 'How many events do I need to cite, and in what order shall I present them?'

Comparative epithets as modifiers

Comparative epithets, and to a lesser extent equatives and superlatives as well, are similar to textual modifiers in that they may have both retrospective and prospective functions. Consider this example:

26 He always pronounced the word 'heard', as if spelt with a double e, 'heerd', instead of sounding it 'herd', as Boswell recorded was most usually done. Perhaps this was partly a hangover from Sam's early Staffordshire pronunciation, but, characteristically, he had *a more bombastic explanation* when challenged: 'He said his reason was that if it were pronounced "herd", there would be a single exception from the English pronunciation of the syllable "ear", and he thought it better not to have that exception.'

Here, *explanation* encapsulates the sentence beginning 'perhaps', which counts as a partial explanation of Johnson's pronunciation, to be contrasted with the *more bombastic* one then attributed to Johnson himself. Therefore the nominal group, while its head is a retrospective label, has a prospective function as an advance label.

It is worth noting, however, that the head plus modifiers in *a more bombastic explanation* does not convey the message that the previously suggested explanation is *less* bombastic on a scale of relative bombast, but that it is not bombastic at all: what organizes this bit of discourse is a direct contrast between types of explanation, or a relation of comparative denial

(Hoey 1983). Only the use of *even* before *more*, as in the next example, signals a relation of comparative affirmation:

27 According to a report submitted to an east–west migration conference in Vienna earlier this year, some 1.4 million people left the post-communist countries last year. Figures submitted to the European Commission in Brussels suggest that 800,000 a year could be entering western Europe from the east. There are *even more drastic projections* emerging from the Soviet Union: between 1.5 million and eight million Soviet citizens are said to be ready to move westwards.

Here both *projections* are presented as being on a scale, from *drastic* to *more drastic*.

CONCLUSION

The type of cohesion discussed in this chapter is extremely common in the press and in all discourse of an argumentative nature: Francis (1986) investigated the use of metalinguistic retrospective labels in journals like *Encounter*, but without the benefit of a corpus. Now, with the availability in Birmingham of large corpora of naturally occurring text (the Bank of English will expand from 100 million to 200 million words by the end of 1993), it has become possible to study text in detail with sophisticated concordancing tools, and to list the wide range of non-specific nominal-group heads, and their modifiers, that realize the labelling function. Further studies in this area could concentrate on its incidence in various genres, and in particular, could compare the range of lexis used as labels in spoken as opposed to written genres. It would also be useful to know which heads and modifiers are used as advance labels: it was pointed out above that these are less common and more restricted in range than retrospective labels, but I have not carried out any detailed investigation of this.

These studies are important not least because labelling is a way of classifying cultural experience in stereotypical ways: the range of realizations of an *idea* or a *proposal*, for example, is vast, but it is not unlimited. The relationship between a label and the clause(s) it replaces is not a random process of naming, but an encoding of shared, or sharable, perceptions of the world. With access to large corpora, we are in a position to understand how experience is processed through discourse into nameable entities which, although often very similar, are by no means interchangeable.

It was also pointed out above that there is a tendency for the selection of a label to be associated with common collocations. Many labels are built into a fixed phrase or 'idiom' (in the widest sense of the word), representing a single choice. Frequent collocations include, for example, 'the move follows . . .', '. . . rejected/denied the allegations', '. . . to solve this problem', and '. . . to reverse this trend', where the retrospective label is found in predictable company. These clusters are readily available, to be drawn on as the common currency of written and spoken communication. Even where the collocations are less fixed, the label occurs in a compatible lexical environment. It would be useful, I believe, to study all labels in their lexical and syntactic contexts; arguably this is the only way they can be studied if we are to increase our knowledge of significant patterning in language. In this chapter I have attempted to do only the basic groundwork.

NOTE

1 The term **advance labelling** is used rather differently by Tadros (1985) to refer to the category of prediction in which 'the writer labels, and thereby commits himself to perform, an act of discourse', and includes verbal groups like 'let us define'. I am using the term **advance label** in a more restricted way, to refer to predictive nominal groups only.

7   The text and its message

Tim Johns

In recent years one of the most important developments in the teaching of
English as a Foreign Language has been the attention given to the development of a reading knowledge of the language for students who need
access to information published in English. The need has been created by the
worldwide increase in the number of students in secondary and tertiary
education and by the unique position of English at the higher levels of
education as the medium of written instruction in text-books and as the
dominant language of international communication. In many countries
English-language teaching at school may have been poor preparation for
reading in the student's subject-area. In a more traditional syllabus reading
will have been of literary texts, and will probably have involved reading
aloud, translation and close examination of difficult points of vocabulary,
idiom and syntax. More 'modern' methods will probably have concentrated
on the development of oral skills by means of 'habit-formation' drills within
a restricted vocabulary and a limited range of syntactic patterns. The frequent
failure of both such methods to produce competent readers of English may be
contrasted with the success of self-taught learners who, determined or obliged
to read English texts on their subject, develop their own methods for
'puzzling them out'. It would seen that among the characteristics of self-
taught learners that give them advantages over the school-taught learners are
their motivation: familiarity with the subject-matter, which allows them to
exploit redundancy and guess successfully; and concentration on the message
conveyed by a text rather than on details of the code. In this they would have
a good deal in common with the successful language-learners whose reading
strategies Hosenfeld has compared with those of unsuccessful language-
learners (Hosenfeld 1977). Hosenfeld found that her successful language-
learners tended to have a 'positive self-image' in approaching a reading task,
to be able to keep the developing overall message within their span of
attention and memory, and to be able to use the context of that message to
guess unknown words and phrases, or to realize that it is unnecessary to know
a particular word or phrase. Her unsuccessful language-learners, on the other
hand, tended to have a negative self-image, and to be easily discouraged, to
refer to the glossary or dictionary immediately when they came up against a

difficulty, and to have poorly developed guessing strategies, and, processing the text in very small chunks, not to have its overall message within their span of attention or memory.

One inference to be drawn from Hosenfeld's research, as from the work of psycholinguists such as Goodman (1967) and Smith (1971), who see the reading process as a type of 'guessing-game' in which readers are constantly matching their predictions against the unfolding text, is that it may be possible to train learners in successful reading strategies. In the field of EAP (English for Academic Purposes), what may be called the 'traditional' method – for example, in published materials such as the Oxford University Press *English Studies Series* – is to select a number of reading texts, usually simplified, within a particular subject-area, and to append word-lists, 'comprehension questions' and 'language practice exercises' to them. There are two main criticisms that can be levelled at this approach. First, in looking for passages which are short and self-contained and which will not cause too much alarm or embarrassment to the language-teacher without specialist training in the subject-area, the tendency is to select 'semi-popular' texts (the writer communicating with a wider audience, for example in scientific journalism) rather than 'academic' texts (the writer communicating with students of the subject, for example in a text-book; or with his/her peers, for example in a research paper) although it is the latter the student will have to read and not the former. Second, there is the danger that the materials may, by emphasizing small points of linguistic and factual detail, and by encouraging reference to the glossary, be training students in exactly those strategies which Hosenfeld has shown to be associated with unsuccessful language learning. A newer generation of materials – for example, those prepared by the University of Malaya English for Special Purposes Project (UMESPP) team at the University of Malaya – have attempted to overcome these drawbacks by selecting a proportion of texts from the text-books which students will have to read in their courses, and by training students explicitly in the strategies of successful reading: for example, in perceiving the overall structure of the message, in developing the ability to predict and guess from context and in 'skimming' and 'scanning' for information. While this work undoubtedly represents a considerable advance on what went before, there remain many unresolved practical and theoretical problems.

The first group of problems relates to the question of *authenticity*. It is by now generally accepted by practitioners of EAP that texts used to teach reading should be tampered with as little as possible, and that any simplified text should be used only as a stepping-stone to the 'real thing'. However, there are two senses in which a text exploited for teaching purposes remains inauthentic. In the first place, it has been *selected* by the teacher or materials writer as being 'interesting' or as exemplifying a particular point or points which s/he wishes to get across. There is the danger that if the factors which lead to the rejection of a certain text as 'unusable' or 'unteachable' are in any way related to the factors which make that text difficult for a student, a powerful – and probably unnoticed – source of distortion has already been introduced. Second, the text, by being incorporated in a language-teaching rather than a subject-teaching programme, is deprived of its authenticity of *purpose*. Within a subject-teaching programme a text takes its place in a *sequence* of other teaching/learning activities (e.g. lectures, tutorials and other texts), and has a certain *significance* in that sequence in terms of what is given and new, what the student is expected to do or to know as a result of reading the text, and so forth. A language-teaching programme deprives a text of these factors and these linkages which are always present when 'real' comprehension takes place. In the course of a full-time presessional programme it may be possible to stimulate the pedagogical 'placing' of a text (Candlin, Kirkwood and Moore 1978); a part-time 'withdrawal' programme hardly allows such a simulation.

The second group of problems is related to the first, and revolves around the question of *design*. In general, the practice of 'communicative language teaching' and attempts to systematize that practice (e.g. Munby 1978) have outrun our understanding of how language is used to communicate, and how people acquire an ability to communicate in their mother tongue or in a foreign language. In this connection, one of the major questions raised by the Hosenfeld research remains unanswered. If understanding and predicting the 'overall message' conveyed by a text is crucial, how should that message best be described? In recent work, two main approaches may be discerned: following the distinction made by Kempson (1975) mainly at sentence level; and by van Dijk (1977) at text level. We may describe one approach as being based on *text pragmatics* and the other as being based on *text semantics*.[1]

The text-pragmatics approach has, in its outlines, a good deal in common with the Classical and Renaissance theory of rhetoric (Kelly 1969), its 'rediscovery' owing much to speech-act theory (Austin 1962; Searle 1969) and the analysis of spoken discourse (Sinclair and Coulthard 1975). It views text as a type of conventionalized interaction between writer and reader, and attempts to analyse it in terms of strings of 'discourse functions', for example 'statement + justification' or 'generalization + exemplification'. One of the many problems facing this approach is the tendency for functional labels to proliferate in the absence of a clear theoretical basis for establishing a 'hierarchy of functions' and for distinguishing their realizations in text: for example, in the labels above drawn from different teaching materials, should 'exemplification' be classified separately from, or as a sub-variety of, 'justification'? An approach to text pragmatics which finds a theoretical basis for avoiding the heedless scattering of labels is the work of Angela Tadros (1978 and this volume), who, working with texts drawn from a particular subject-area – economics – has examined the discoursal expectancies set up by the writer. Apart from explicit predictive markers (e.g. 'There are three reasons why this should be so . . .'), she identifies implicit markers which derive from reader–writer interaction and the nature of argument in the subject. One example is the system of 'writer involvement and withdrawal', which allows the reader to predict from the statement 'It has been claimed by many authors that . . .' (writer's withdrawal) that 'writer's rebuttal' will follow. Another general system identified by Tadros derives from the use by economists of a 'real' and an 'imaginary' world, the latter being set up to simplify the features of reality for the sake of argument, so that marking a section of text as 'hypothetical' (e.g. 'Let us assume . . .') predicts that the writer will move towards a generalization which can be applied to the real world. In this connection it may be suggested that there is a related system of 'real' vs 'imaginary' common in the applied social sciences in which the writer negotiates the argument between what *does* happen in the world (descriptive) and what *ought to* happen (evaluative). Tadros' work, which is still in progress, is, in the present writer's opinion, an example of the hard analysis which remains to be done if text pragmatics is to provide an adequate basis for the teaching of reading.

The second approach – that of text semantics – is concerned centrally with the truth and falsity of statements which can be derived, not from individual propositions in the text, but from the text as a whole and, crucially, from the cross-referential relationships (equivalence, inclusion, exclusion) set up within the text (Palek 1968). While the text-pragmatic approach, being concerned with the moment-by-moment interaction between writer and reader, has to date been described basically in *linear* terms, the structure of semantic relationships (from now on referred to as the *information structure* of the text) can be described adequately only in *non-linear* terms, and may be modelled by means of an n-dimensional diagram. This is, in fact, a concept already implicit and familiar in the 'information-transfer' type of exercise incorporated in many recent EAP teaching materials (e.g. the *Focus* series edited by Widdowson and Allen and *Nucleus* edited by Bates and Dudley-Evans, as well as in the UMESPP materials). In these materials three main types of information structure are identified, the corresponding diagrams being the *tree-diagram*, the *matrix* and the *flow-chart*:

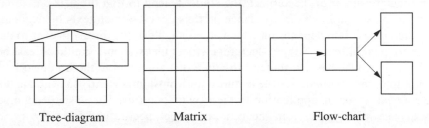

Tree-diagram   Matrix   Flow-chart

One of the unresolved problems raised by this approach is that it tends to take for granted the relationship between the non-linear structure of information and its realization in linear text: that is to say, the way in which the writer *negotiates* his/her way through that structure, and the effect this has on the pragmatic organization of the text, and on its predictability.

The remainder of this chapter outlines an attempt to solve some of the problems indicated above within the framework of one class provided by the English for Overseas Students Unit of Birmingham University (Johns 1975). The students are drawn from those following a one-year course for the Diploma in Development Administration in the Development Administration Group of the Institute of Local Government Studies. The course is 'post-experience', most of the participants being administrators in their late twenties to their early forties from Africa, Latin America, the Indian subcontinent and the Far East. A majority have English as a second language rather than as a foreign language, and many have used English as a medium of written communication; nevertheless even these may have difficulties with the linguistic demands of the course. One participant showed considerable insight into his problem with reading as follows:

> When I came to Britain I thought it would at least be easy to do the reading required, since every day in my Ministry at home I have to read and act on numbers of memoranda written in English. However, I have found it difficult to get through everything on our reading-lists. The problem is that I know how memos are written, and what I am supposed to do as a result of reading them; but I don't understand the sort of English used in the books recommended by our lecturers, and I don't know what I'm supposed to do with them.

From discussion with students and members of staff (including the departmental librarians), and from some previous research in observing and recording seminars in the Development Administration Group, it has been possible to reach some general conclusions about the sequence and significance of reading in the course. While there is a good deal of variation between different subjects and different lecturers, it appears that the most usual pattern is for reading to be regarded as follow-up to lectures and as input to seminars and writing. Most lecturers supply fairly lengthy reading-lists, and also some indication of which are the most important texts, and which deal with particular aspects of the subject: the students tend to find the lists daunting, and many would like more guidance on these lines. Which texts the student, in fact, reads often depends on which are available at the time s/he goes to the departmental library. Subject-lecturers expect that students should at least be able to grasp the basic argument; to relate that argument to the framework of the subject as expounded in the lectures; and, most importantly to evaluate the argument or see its application to their own countries. The basic pedagogic sequence tends to be from the general to the specific and from theory to practice although some teachers in the field of development studies advocate reversing these priorities to some extent through a 'case-study' approach (Henderson and Rado 1980).

In the light of the above background information it was decided, in setting up a subject-specific English class for the Development Administration Group, to concentrate on reading skills in the first term, and on the training of writing skills in the second term. The second term's work involves team-teaching between the subject-teachers and the language-teacher and has been described elsewhere (Johns and Dudley-Evans 1980). The time available for subject-specific English teaching is limited (45 minutes a week in the first term, making a total of seven-and-a-half contact hours) and in view of the intensive nature of the work and the need for feedback from individual students it is necessary to restrict the numbers attending to a maximum of ten from the fifty to sixty students on the course. When the number of students who wish to attend the class is greater than ten, we select those with the lowest scores on the Assessment and Diagnostic Test taken by all overseas students on arrival at the university. If, as may be charged, we are giving an unfair advantage to certain students, at least they will, we believe, include those most at risk of failing the course without some additional assistance.

In the first four or five sessions of the first term training is given in basic reading strategies: in 1978 these included guessing of vocabulary from context, prediction of writer's intention (the work here heavily influenced by the Tadros' research into text pragmatics), and perception of information structure underlying text. These strategies are then applied to texts selected by the students themselves on a week-to-week basis as ones which they have found particularly difficult to understand, the principle of student selection solving at a stroke many of the problems of teacher selection and full authenticity previously mentioned. Since the difficulties revealed in the second half of the term are the basis for modifying, on a year-by-year basis, the basic training in the first half, and all the texts used for that training have previously been student-selected (examples are shown in texts A–D at the end of this chapter), it may be useful to start from the features of those texts and the difficulties revealed by discussion with the students.

The first general feature of the texts worth noting is that they cover a wide range of subjects in the fields of administration, economics, finance, politics and sociology, written by authors with a wide range of academic back-grounds. In 1977, for example, one of the texts selected was written by a geologist on the appraisal of land resources. The difficulty was not simply that he used a large number of unfamiliar technical terms for types of rocks, land-forms and so forth, but that the students found it difficult to perceive the conceptual framework – or, more particularly, the taxonomic system – underlying those terms. This wide spread of subject-matter reflects our experience from other postgraduate courses for which the Unit provides subject-specific English classes. Students in the Department of Transportation and Environmental Planning, for example, find their engineering texts relatively easy: their difficulties lie with the novel areas of economics, sociology and 'applied aesthetics'. The pedagogic implication is clear, though often overlooked: such students need a good deal of *flexibility* in their approach to reading and learning, and any presessional language training or testing programme which identifies them as 'administration students' and 'engineering students' respectively and concentrates on texts within the narrow definition of those subjects will fail to provide that flexibility. This conclusion supports the approach of programmes (such as the UMESPP materials) which include a considerable 'common-core' component for students of all subjects, and which also train 'learning to learn from reading' as inseparable from 'learning to read'.

Investigating *why* the texts are difficult for the students is the central and most delicate task of the teacher. Initially, students will identify their difficulty in terms of the words they do not know or are unsure of, and hope that if the language-teacher teaches them enough words all their problems will disappear. This is a point of view which should not be dismissed lightly. As has been said, the approach to the teaching of vocabulary in the basic training period is through the development of guessing strategies, the main technique used being to force students to guess, and then to get them to compare the evidence for their guesses, the teacher not at first saying which guesses are 'right' and which 'wrong'. However, there seems to be a 'threshold effect' by which, when more than approximately 50 per 1,000 words are unknown, perception of overall structure may be effectively blocked, which in turn means that there is not enough in the way of context to allow successful guessing. Another vocabulary difficulty worth noting arises from the density of metaphorical usage in many of the texts. If, as Vico first proposed, metaphor is an essential step in the development of man's understanding of the world about him, it is natural that the social sciences – most of which have developed their conceptual framework relatively recently – should be rich in metaphorical use of language: see, for example, 'give too free a rein to' (text B, line 25), one of the interesting set of metaphors concerned with the concept of 'control' which derive from horse-riding.

One of the most striking features of a number of the student-selected texts is that they are difficult to read both for the overseas student and for the native speaker; their difficulty lying not so much in the subject-matter, but – to put the matter baldly – in their being badly written. There has in this century been a distaste among linguists and applied linguists for labelling language as 'good' or 'bad'; however, the notion of pragmatic prediction may allow us to put such value judgements on a securer basis, the 'bad' text from this point of view being one in which the writer fails to set up a basis for reader prediction, or fails without apparent reason to fulfil the predictions s/he appears to set up. From this point of view consider the short and relatively painless chapter opening of text A. The reader might like to try the experiment of covering up the second sentence and trying to guess what it will be from the evidence of the first. Most native and non-native speakers on whom this writer has tried the experiment have predicted that the author will continue with some sort of 'expansion' or 'justification' beginning, for example 'Only from such a viewpoint is it possible to see that . . .'; none have come anywhere near the author's actual continuation with its apparent contrast (but why is it being made?) and its tautologous proposition, which the present writer is unable to relate semantically to what goes before or what comes after. The challenge of such a text to the teacher of reading strategies is that the only effective strategy is to abandon rapidly any attempt to process the first two sentences, and to pick out a string of lexical items to represent what appears to be the message of the remainder: (all) large cities – ferment and change: (e.g.) old cities – obsolescence and shifting populations; new cities – staggering growth and demands for new facilities.

Turning to the main body of student-selected texts which are at least readable in the sense that the opening of text A is not, experience to date suggests that providing the density of unknown vocabulary falls – or can be reduced – below the 'threshold level', the main problem lies in the area of text semantics, and in particular the non-linear structuring of information. In the texts studied, the types of information structure represented by the tree-diagram, the matrix and the flow-chart appear to be very common.[2] The problem of training students to handle the comprehension of text above the level of the sentence involves developing a 'set' towards information structure, and the negotiation of that structure in text. Some typical problems are illustrated by texts A–D.

Texts B and C are similar in that for both the information structure is a 3 x 3 matrix, the major difference being that text B shows 'vertical negotiation' of the matrix, and text C 'horizontal negotiation'. Text B may be diagrammed as in Figure 7.1, the dotted line indicating the negotiation. In general, vertically negotiated matrix structure may be more difficult to grasp than horizontally negotiated structure. Notice, in particular, the greater dependence on cross-reference to obtain correct matching of what is being talked about. In the second column, as students have pointed out, the matching of the examples would have been easier if 'respectively' had been inserted in line 19, while the third column shows an interesting but potentially confusing type of 'elegant variation' in which the author departs from the expected 'downward' nego-tiation. In so doing, he issues a challenge to the reader's processing of the information structure up to that point by using different means of cross-reference for each cell: 'the third system' (line 21: cross-reference to enumeration); 'At the other extreme, the principle of universality' (line 24:

	Powers of local authorities	Examples	Disadvantages for developing country
1	'universal'	Germany	Gives too much freedom
2	'statutory'	Britain	Requires special legislation for local needs
3	'integrated'	France	Inhibits independent action

Figure 7.1 Negotiating the information structure in text B

double cross-reference to the structure of the matrix and to the description of the systems in the first column); and 'The British system' (lines 25–6: cross-reference to the example in the second column). These difficulties of cross-reference are such that even native speakers, when untrained in looking for information structure, find it hard to answer a question which requires reference to the reader's conceptualization of the matrix rather than to the linear organization of information in the text (e.g. 'What are the disadvantages for a developing country of the German system of local government?').

Text C, with its horizontal negotiation (readers may care to try drawing the diagram for themselves) appears to be easier than text B. The problem here (as with any matrix horizontally negotiated) lies not in the matching of what is being talked about but in matching what is ascribed to each system (in this text, as in many others, the advantages and disadvantages of each). Unless the reader grasps the matrix structure of the argument, s/he is unlikely to notice that both the advantages and disadvantages given for the second and third methods of representation have a number of points in common, or that in discussing the third method the author 'shifts' the nature of his argument, the advantages now being implicitly evaluated against the disadvantages since the former are hypothetical (lines 26–7: 'Such an arrangement depends on the hypothesis that . . .') and the latter, from the experience of Pakistan, are real.

Text D is an example of information structure which may be represented by a flow-chart: here, a 'backward-chained' argument of some complexity. Also, the text is typical of many in which the student finds it difficult to see the relationship between the main line of the argument and supporting evidence and examples. As a general method for handling texts of this sort, a diagramming method is presented by which the main line is identified first as represented on the vertical dimension, and supporting evidence shown on the horizontal dimension. On the basis of the resulting diagram (see Figure 7.2) it is possible to discuss general questions such as:

(1) Which of the 'information boxes' are least important, and which could be omitted without disturbing the writer's argument?
(2) Where could the student insert information of his own from his country (cf. the general importance in the course of relating 'writer's argument' to 'student's experience')?
(3) How does the author negotiate the argument in paragraph structure and in interparagraph relationships (note, for example, the parallelism between the first three paragraphs, and the shift in the fourth paragraph)?

More particular questions which can be raised include:

(4) The predictive significance of the 'empty box'.
(5) The ambiguity of 'basic economic improvements' (lines 50–1) which can be inserted into the diagram in more than one way.

It should be emphasized that, as with most research done 'on the ground'

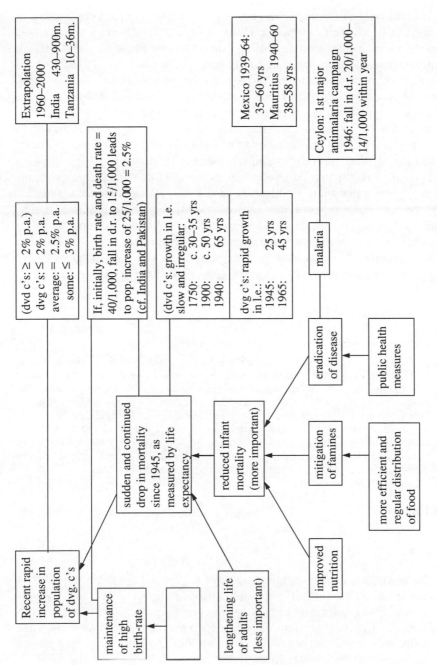

Figure 7.2 A flow chart of the information structure in text D

for immediate application to a teaching situation, the work reported in this chapter and the conclusions reached are tentative. Among the questions which may be worth pursuing are, first, the use of the approach for improving writing skills as well as reading skills. In the second term's work in the Development Administration Group, there has been some 'spin-off' in improvement of the students' ability to plan writing through the use of non-linear diagramming techniques, and to organize paragraph structure. Second, it would be interesting to know how far the crucial feature of student selection of texts is applicable at other levels (for example secondary level or with undergraduates) and how far the training of 'set' towards information structure of argument is applicable to other subject areas. As far as the latter is concerned, work on lecture comprehension with students of Plant Biology and Transportation and Highway engineering (Johns and Dudley-Evans 1980) suggests that their problems lie in very much the same area, and also that the three basic types of information structure have a similar importance. Finally, and more speculatively, it would be valuable to know how far students' reading problems, when seen in this perspective, may be related to cross-cultural differences in underlying patterns of argument (Kaplan 1966). The author would be grateful for comments on these or any other points raised.

NOTES

1 In the author's view, text is describable in *formal* terms, both text pragmatics and text semantics being regarded as *functions* of text, to be related to the formal description through interpretation and realization rules. Compare this with Widdowson's distinction between 'text' and 'discourse' (Widdowson 1973).
2 It may be suggested, not too seriously, that the particular prevalence of matrix-structure in texts in the field of administration (see, for example, texts A and B) may derive from the tendency of writers on administration themselves to be administrators or former administrators, and for the matrix to be particularly attractive to the methodical and pigeon-holing bureaucratic mind.

APPENDIX

Text A

To be comprehended in its entirety, the metropolis must be viewed from the air. Back on earth, its pulsing heart lies in the central city. Large and vital cities have ferment and change in common, regardless of their shape, wealth, or political system. Obsolescence and shifting populations chal-
5 lenge the capabilities of old cities. New cities confront staggering growth and demands for new facilities.

(Annemarie Hauck Walsh, *The Urban Challenge to Government* (New York: Praeger, for the Institute of Public Administration, 1969))

Text B

In constructing or re-constructing the local government system the first
question to be settled is the definition of the powers of local authorities. For
the brief general description, which alone is possible here, three broad
varieties will be mentioned. The first is where the constitution grants
5 'universal' powers – that is, local authorities may perform any function not
specifically forbidden them by law or not exclusively the power of another
authority. There is also a further general limitation to these powers,
namely that the powers exercised by a local council must be within the
conception of being for the good government of the locality. This is a
10 system which, short of complete independence which is impossible if
government is to be *local*, gives the greatest scope for the growth of local
government functions and is the easiest way in which each authority can
extend its obligatory functions to include activities which seem particularly appropriate for the local area. The second broad category is where
15 the local authorities can only perform those functions specifically granted
them by general statute – any extensions for particular localities must have
a specific statute for that district. The third division is where the local
authority is an integrated part of the hierarchy of administration, subject to
ministerial orders as well as statutes. These divisions are broadly typified
20 by the systems of Germany, Britain and France, and given the objectives
already outlined, none is entirely satisfactory for whole-sale transfer to
developing countries. The third system inhibits the independent action of
local authorities, subordinating them too strictly to the ministries of central
government, not only in the early – the embryonic – stages of the system,
25 but as a long term plan. At the other extreme, the principle of universality
would give too free a rein to most growing local government systems. The
British system on the other hand is not satisfactory as it requires the
passing of special legislation by individual authorities for variations to suit
local needs and abilities.

(H. Maddick, *Democracy, Decentralisation and Development*
(Bombay: Asia Publishing House, 1963))

Text C

The composition and forms of representation of representative bodies
frequently adopted in developing countries have a number of special
features, the most striking being the following:
1 Members of the central government field administration (health officer,
5 education officer, community development officer, representatives of the
Ministry of Public Works, etc.) are *ex-officio* members of local councils.
This system is widespread. It provides the necessary expertise for council
decisions, promotes deliberations between local representatives and technical staff, and facilitates proper coordination between local and central
10 policy-making. Its disadvantage, of course, is the considerable risk that
officials will dominate the local representatives.

2   The central government or its regional representatives choose some or all council members from the local community. This is by no means a new method, having been used in many European countries (especially France)
15   until as late as the middle of the 19th century. Its advantages are that it reduces the chances of political strife between the commune and the central authorities, and that, as is often claimed, the councillors thus appointed are more likely to be of good calibre. On the other hand it tends to decrease responsibility, and possibly responsiveness; council members
20   may also be only marginally representative of the local community, if at all, and may therefore pursue policies contrary to the general interest. Moreover, governments often tend to appoint people of a conservative cast of mind, thus introducing a devitalising element into local government.

3   Finally, developing nations show a notable leaning towards indirect
25   representation, i.e. a council composed of representatives of councils on the next lower level situated in its territory. Such an arrangement depends on the hypothesis that: a) indirect representation ensures better quality of the higher councils; b) it promotes coordination between the two levels of local government.
30   There are several examples of indirect representation being introduced as part of new local government systems in developing nations. Perhaps its most systematic application was found in Pakistan before 1969 when the chairmen of the lower councils (union councils and town councils) were *ex-officio* members of the higher *Tehsil* or *Thana* councils, the
35   chairmen of which were in turn *ex-officio* members of the district councils.
   However, the disturbances in Pakistan in early 1969 seem to have brought to light some basic weaknesses in this highly systematised indirect representation. Firstly, it reduces the total number of elected
40   representatives. Second, it may create an elected elite which is insufficiently responsive to the needs and wishes of the local population. And, finally, a general disadvantage is that elected officials in a number of councils are overburdened.
                   (A.F. Leemans, *Changing Patterns of Local Government*
             (The Hague: International Union of Local Authorities, 1970))

Text D

It is well known that the population of the world is increasing faster than ever before and that the present, rapid rate of growth is a very recent phenomenon, going back no more than twenty years or so. Although some of the industrial countries have also seen an increase in the rate of
5   population growth, this has only exceptionally been as much as 2 per cent per year, whilst in the underdeveloped countries the rate of increase has been almost uniformly at rates of 2 per cent or more. By the mid-60s it was

rising typically by 2.5 per cent whilst in some countries the increase was
proceeding at a rate of 3 per cent and even higher. If present rates were to
10 continue then the population of India, for instance, which was some 430
million in 1960 would rise to over 900 million by the end of the century
and that of Tanzania would increase ten million to thirty-six million over
the same period.

What has unleashed the great demographic acceleration in the under-
15 developed countries has been a rather sudden and continued drop in
mortality after the Second World War. Since the crude death rate is
influenced by the age structure, the fall in mortality is better measured by
the life expectancy at birth which expresses the average length of life of a
new born infant under prevailing conditions of mortality. In the Western
20 world the increase in life expectancy was slow and irregular. It was
probably 30–35 years in the middle of the eighteenth century; in 1900 it
was about fifty years and not until 1940 did it reach sixty-five. In the
underdeveloped countries that increase in life expectancy has come about
much more quickly. For example in Mexico it rose from thirty-six years to
25 sixty years between 1939 and 1964, and in Mauritius it is thought to have
gone from thirty-eight years in 1940 to fifty-eight years in 1960. Taking
underdeveloped countries as a whole it has been estimated that the average
expectation of life at birth rose from twenty-five years to forty-five years
during the twenty years following the end of the Second World War.
30   The remarkable increase in population in the underdeveloped countries
has come about, broadly, as a result of a marked fall in the death rate
without any corresponding fall in the birth rate. If, as was not untypical,
both birth and death rates were around forty per thousand of the
population to start with, and the death rate then falls to fifteen per thousand,
35 this would lead to an increase in the population by twenty-five per
thousand, or 2.5 per cent. Although these figures are merely illustrative
they do in fact correspond to what has happened since the Second World
War in many underdeveloped countries, including some of the largest and
most densely populated such as India and Pakistan.
40   Both the rapid fall in the death rate and the maintenance of the previous
high birth rate require explanation. The fall in the death rate has really to
be seen as comprising two elements: a lengthening of the life of adults and
a fall in infant mortality. The life span of adults is not so very different
from what it was before and the fall in the death rate has been particularly
45 concentrated in the first year of life. The rapid rise in population must
therefore be seen primarily as a consequence of the fall in infant mortality
and to a lesser extent as resulting from a greater expectation of life once
the critical first year of life has been survived.

The marked increase in life expectancy at birth cannot be attributed to
50 one 'explanatory variable' alone. Part of it is due to basic economic
improvements. More efficient and regular distribution of food has averted
food shortages and mitigated famines, and improved nutrition may

account for much of the spectacular reduction of infant mortality. But post-
war public health measures have also been extremely effective in under-
55 developed areas. The eradication of malaria by spraying with insecticides
has had spectacular effects in many countries in which malaria was
previously endemic and lethal, especially for children. In Ceylon, where
the death rate had already fallen to twenty per thousand, the first major
antimalaria campaign with DDT in 1946 coincided with a fall in the death
60 rate from twenty to fourteen per thousand within a year.

(Walter Elkan, *An Introduction to Development Economics*
(Harmondsworth: Penguin, 1973))

8 The analysis of fixed expressions in text

Rosamund Moon

In general, studies of fixed expressions – idioms, formulae such as proverbs and catchphrases, and anomalous or ill-formed collocations – concentrate on their typological and syntagmatic properties. Attention is given to such things as the degree of their lexical and syntactic frozenness, or their transformation potential; and even the primary characteristic of idioms, their non-compositionality as lexical units, may be seen as a matter of the interpretation of a syntagm. However, it is their paradigmatic properties which are of importance in relation to interaction. Fixed expressions represent meaningful choices on the part of the speaker/writer. They are single choices (see Sinclair 1987b: 321 and *passim*), and, as with other kinds of lexical item, their precise values and force should be considered in terms of the paradigm operating at each slot or choice. By taking into account paradigmatic as well as syntagmatic aspects, it is possible to assess the way in which fixed expressions contribute to the content, structure and development of a text.

Fixed expressions, especially highly colourful and metaphorical idioms and proverbs, are comparatively infrequent. They appear to be more frequent in spoken text than written, although to date there are few extensive studies of their actual distribution. Strässler assesses the frequency of idioms, excluding phrasal verbs, in spoken discourse as around one per 4.5 minutes of conversation (1982: 81). A survey of 240 English proverbs (Arnaud and Moon, forthcoming) finds that there are around 33 instances of proverbs per million words of OHPC,[1] and that the average frequency of each of the proverbs is much less than one occurrence per million words: this list of proverbs consists of those best known to informants in a small survey, and it should be pointed out that the more frequent of these proverbs nearly always occur in exploited or truncated forms, not the canonical citation forms. So in setting out to evaluate the textual contribution of fixed expressions, it is in fact difficult to find a text where their density is sufficiently high to make valid observations. A densely populated text would be atypical; while a densely populated section of a text would be unrepresentative by being decontextualized. With these caveats, I want to consider an editorial from *The Guardian* as a basis for discussion. The choice of this text is governed by the fact that it is fairly short, and contains a sufficient number of fixed expressions for commentary. It is a complete text in its own right, although as an excerpt from a newspaper it is also part of a 'colony' (see Hoey 1986), requiring intertextual knowledge for full decoding and understanding. Sentences in the text have been numbered for ease of reference in the following discussion.

THE TEXT

A warmish goodbye to all that

(1.1) It is, of course, very nice to be told how wonderful you are; to bathe in a scented foam of admiration; to feel good and to be made to feel good. (1.2) It doesn't happen nearly enough in this harsh, frenetic world: and – who knows? – it may also from time to time be true.

(2.1) Mr Ronald Reagan wasn't the Dr Strangelove clone of earlier legend as he passed through London yesterday. (2.2) He was Dr Feelgood, delivering, with all the sincerity he could muster, a farewell bouquet to Britain and to the world's newly designated senior statesperson. (2.3) There are – by golly, there are – all manner of hardened cynics who have found the Guildhall TV experience rather like rolling in a puddle of warm fudge. (2.4) But it was more interesting than that, on several levels.

(3.1) Level One, purely practically, was the exposure of a British audience to a full-dress Reagan occasion; which may finally have helped to explain, late in the day, why he has been such a popular President. (3.2) The blend of wry humour, folksy anecdote and simple belief was toasted to a turn and delivered with real eloquence. (3.3) He makes a formidable pitch.

(4.1) Level Two revealed some fascinating things about the Britain that Mr Reagan sees from afar. (4.2) The Britain of Tennyson and El Alamein and Churchill and GIs from Iowa turning up with Christmas presents for a 'songfest' in a Second-World-War pub; the Britain of Arnhem ('A Bridge Too Far') and Eric Liddell ('Chariots of Fire'). (4.3) Not a word about privatisation or top tax rates; or, indeed, any of the policies of Britain in the 1980s. (4.4) We are a gallant bulldog breed, washed forever in the words and battles of the past.

(5.1) And then there was Level Three, the post-Moscow view of the world. (5.2) Benign and hopeful, replete with achievement; but watchful, too, because the crusade for peace and freedom is constant. (5.3) It cannot be carried forward by mere co-existence, by live-and-let-live with the forces of alien ideology. (5.4) It must be fervently pursued so that, in time, the contradictions of Communism precipitate its collapse and the spread of democracy itself brings a peaceful world. (5.5) QED.

(6.1) Mr Reagan, in short, has changed and been changed by his summit experiences. (6.2) He has seen the Soviet people close to, and knows now that they are not demons. (6.3) He has seen the glum queues of Moscow, and believes that this economic system will not inherit the earth. (6.4) He has felt the pall of Russian bureaucracy. (6.5) He understands more and is more confused. (6.6) But the struggle, for him, is still there, to be continued by other means; the memory of the second world war, the clash of good and evil, defines the natural cast of his mind.

(7.1) He talked, too, of the need for 'public candour'. (7.2) That is a two-way street. (7.3) Candidly, the progress of the past four summits has not, in essence, flowed from the White House. (7.4) Mr Gorbachev has been the indispensable catalyst of change. (7.5) Candidly, Moscow would have achieved much more if the dissonant wings of the American administration had been led to the summit negotiating tables rather than paraded there. (7.6) Candidly, the strength of the Western Alliance hymned in hushed tones yesterday is fraught with doubts and rivalries. (7.7) Candidly, when the president dreams of a world free from nuclear weapons, Mrs Thatcher pulls the hat down over her eyes. (7.8) Candidly, it is all very well to be told what a great chum you are; but great chummyness butters no parsnips in a world of trade frictions and budget deficits and soaring defence burdens. (7.9) Ronald Reagan already has a place in history. (7.10) It will probably conclude that he deserves to be remembered not because of what he did but because of what he was: the arch conservative who changed minds back home because his own mind changed a little. (7.11) He bade Britain a benevolent farewell yesterday. (7.12) It would be foolish to cast it off churlishly; but foolish, too, to remember it as more than a segment of eloquence set in a finite time and space.

(© *The Guardian*, 4 June 1988)

A brief note on the historical background: the editorial discusses and evaluates a meeting between Reagan and Thatcher during a London stopover by Reagan while returning home from a meeting in Moscow with Gorbachev. The London meeting was televised and therefore high profile: it was a meeting for showmanship rather than statesmanship. It was also known to be one of Reagan's last meetings as US president.

From a stylistic or literary point of view, this editorial is a florid and highly marked piece of writing, and rhetorical strategies overwhelm the message to the extent of clouding it. Curiously enough, this in fact appears to reflect or counterpoint the message, which is, crudely, that the ostentatious, ritualistic meeting and the exchange of compliments were in danger of disguising the fact that there were still problems in the course of world peace and east–west *détente*.

TEXTURE, STRUCTURE AND LEXIS

Before considering the lexical choices made in this text, and in particular its fixed expressions, it is worth looking at some of its textural aspects, following the sort of model described by Halliday (1985: *passim*). These include choices made in the text concerning the organization of theme and rheme and placement of topic, and cohesive ties.

Different paragraphs are foregrounded by different devices, but throughout the text there are many clauses in which the subject and topic is realized either by a pro-form or by a dummy, thus forcing the reader's attention towards the rheme. For example, in paragraph 6, sentences (6.2)–(6.5) all begin with *he*, relating to *Mr Reagan*, the subject, topic and theme of (6.1), and forming a sequence of five successive sentences which state and evaluate Reagan's thinking. This parallelism then contrasts all the more markedly with sentence (6.6) that thematizes contrastive or adversative *but*, and has *the struggle* as topic. Paragraph 1 begins with *it* as dummy theme, the displaced theme/topic *very nice*, and then four, fairly lengthy, parallel infinitive groups as rhemes. In paragraph 4, sentences (4.2) and (4.3) are characterized by ellipsis of subjects and main verbs, thus forcing the natural rhemes of the sentence into prominence.

Paragraph 7 is characterized by the striking thematization of *candidly* in sentences (3), (5), (6), (7) and (8). As well as the obvious parallelism of the structure, *candidly* is tied cohesively to *candour* in (7.1), while effectively foregrounding the status of the editorial as opinion. Sentences (7.2) and (7.4), intervening in this highly marked sequence, are adversative or contrastive, and they could easily have been linked hypotactically or paratactically to their preceding sentences. The fact that they were not leads to a fore-grounding of the contrast they contain.

Crystal and Davy point out (1984: 184) that 'connectedness' of newspaper discourse, clarity of organization, is a feature of key importance: 'the story once begun should carry the reader through to the end'. The connectedness of this text shows tight control of the discourse. In it, cohesion is provided in many ways. There is striking lexical repetition: (1.1) *to feel good and to be made to feel good*; (6.1) *has changed and been changed*; (6.2, 6.3) *He has seen . . . . He has seen*; (7.12) *It would be foolish to cast it off churlishly; but foolish, too, to remember it . . .*, as well as the recurrent conjunct-like disjunct *candidly* in the final paragraph. *Level One, Level Two* and *Level Three*, the opening topics of paragraphs 3, 4 and 5, make structure explicit by a foregrounding of the levels of analysis, and they are cohesive with *on several levels* at the end of paragraph 2. Patterns of statement and contrast also contribute to cohesion with such formulations as (5.2) *Benign and hopeful . . . but watchful too*; (5.3, 5.4) *it cannot be carried forward . . . . It must be fervently pursued*; and the pair of sentences (1.1) *it is of course very nice to be told how wonderful you are* and (7.8) *it is all very well to be told what a great chum you are, but . . . .* In addition to these, there are simple cases of relexicalization and parallelism: (title) *A warmish goodbye to all that*; (2.2) *a farewell bouquet*; (7.11) *a benevolent farewell*; and also perhaps (1.1) *to bathe in a scented foam of admiration*; (2.3) *rolling in a puddle of warm fudge*.

Turning to the lexis of the text, two initial points are worth making. First, a consideration of the verbal processes in the text (after Halliday 1985: 102ff.) shows that material and relational processes feature most strongly. The dominance of relational processes, together with mental and existential once, is entirely consistent with the *modus operandi* of the text – the promotion of an evaluation by means of stating the way things are, or seem to be, to both the writer and, by projection, to Reagan, the chief participant in the text. This is reinforced by the tenses selected: many simple presents and an almost total absence of continuous forms. The material processes are more interesting. In fact, many of them are grammatical metaphors (in Halliday's terms: see 1985: 319ff. for relational or mental processes), and occur in lexicosemantic metaphors, both instantial ones and the institutionalized stereotypes: I shall return to this point below.

Second, there are many evaluative epithets in the passage, and more are positive than negative in orientation: that is, more lexical items have 'positive' than 'negative' as a componential feature. Yet the overall effect of the editorial's evaluation is negative – it functions cumulatively as a concealed performative of which the illocutionary force is 'warning'. This mismatch between overt feature and covert effect, surface and sub-text, once again reflects the overall message.

THE FIXED EXPRESSIONS

The uses of the fixed expressions in this text cannot be entirely divorced from other marked lexical selections. In particular, there is the use of allusion: *Dr Strangelove, Mr Feelgood, Tennyson, El Alamein, Arnhem ('A Bridge Too Far'), Eric Liddell ('Chariots of Fire')* and so on. If these references are not understood, parts of the evaluation of Reagan's behaviour and attitudes will not be understood. There is the use of (exploited) quotation: *A warmish goodbye to all that*, drawn from the title of Robert Graves' autobiography, and *in this harsh . . . world*, drawn from *Hamlet* V.2; and the use of strong collocations and binomials such as *good and evil, in hushed tones, time and space*. Compare the investigations by Cowie into the collocations and stereotyped formulae used in newspaper reporting (1992: 1–12); he attributes these at least in part to time constraints and sees them as reflecting 'the central role of ready-made complex units in spoken and written communication' (*ibid.*: 11). There is a plethora of non-institutionalized metaphors such as *bathe in a scented foam of admiration, like rolling in a puddle of warm fudge, washed forever in the words and battles of the past, a two-way street*. These contribute to an important aim or strategy of the text: the encouragement or even presumption of shared values by the careful setting up of cultural icons that extend the connotations of the evaluation expressed. This extensive use of assumed cultural knowledge, without which a substantial proportion of the message will be missed, is insiderism, elitism. But it is not necessarily intended to *exclude*: it may simply be intended to encourage agreement or pre-empt disagreement by flattering and stroking the reader in its assumption of a certain cultural milieu.[2] This is rather like a use of elaborated versus restricted codes, in a Bernsteinian sense.

The twenty-three fixed expressions in the text that I shall be considering vary typologically from proverbs and idioms to simple institutionalized collocations; from the highly marked (because of exploitation) to the unmarked (because of frequency). In the following discussion, I shall comment briefly on each fixed expression, in the order in which they appear in the text. I shall describe some characteristics and properties of the canonical forms of each expression and any special peculiarities of the particular instance of the expression in this text. I shall limit classification of their forms to simple categories such as 'metaphors' (largely idioms, institutionalized metaphors); 'formulae' (fixed strings that are decodable compositionally but are institutionalized as strings and may well have pragmatic meaning); 'anomalous collocations' (collocations that are grammatically ill-formed, or restricted, or contain a word or use of a word that is unique to the combination); and the familiar categories 'proverb' and 'phrasal verb'. References to functions such as 'modalize' or 'convey information' are explained further in a later section.

> *of course* (1.1): an anomalous collocation, grammatically ill-formed. It functions as a modalizer, emphasizing by reinforcing the message. It also has organizing properties, as it may be used as a preface to an opinion or line of argument, and pre-empts disagreement by appealing to shared values. In ordinary discourse, it is typically a response to something previously said, or has at least some cohesion with the preceding text, rather than as here, an opening with cataphoric range. Its function here is therefore more emphatic and pre-emptive.
>
> *who knows?* (1.2): a formula, interpolated as a parenthetical comment. It functions as a modalizer, indicating that the writer is distancing him/ herself from the utterance – expressing possibility, but indicating uncertainty or a refraining from commitment to categorical opinion. It reinforces the following epistemic modal *may* in this text.
>
> *from time to time* (1.2): a collocation that is grammatically ill-formed if considered in relation to the relevant, countable, sense of *time*, although it fits into the phraseological frame *from (countable noun) to (countable noun)*: cf. *from day to day, from house to house*, etc. *From time to time* is semantically different from these, and indicates frequency rather than recurrence or repetition. It can be considered an epistemic modalizer.
>
> *by golly* (2.3): an anomalous collocation since the item *golly* is highly restricted, occurring only in interjections if its homonym meaning 'golliwog' is ignored. It functions as a modalizer by emphasizing. In this particular case the emphasis is intensified by its position in parentheses and the repetition of *there are*. The expression is very dated.
>
> *all manner of* (2.3): an anomalous collocation, grammatically ill-formed. It functions as a quantifier, with a following plural or mass noun. *All manner of* is more marked than the synonymous and commoner expressions *all kinds of* and *all sorts of*, and it is slightly more disparaging. It may therefore have a subsidiary evaluative function.
>
> *late in the day* (3.1): an institutionalized collocation and transparent

metaphor. Its primary function is to convey information, although there is also a negatively evaluative component implied by *late*: compare pure evaluative uses such as 'It is a bit late in the day to . . .' or 'The problems don't go away just by being ignored. It is only now, rather late in the day, that the Government is waking up to the enormity of the problems it has indolently built for itself' (OHPC).

toasted to a turn (3.2): ultimately a metaphor, though *to a turn* is anomalous in relation to the noun *turn*. This particular instance can be considered an exploitation of the canonical form *done to a turn*, rather than a variation. The exploitation reinforces a positive evaluation.

make a – pitch (3.3): a transparent metaphor, though tied to an established sense of *pitch* meaning '(exaggerated) sales talk, appeal'. It evaluates, and in this context summarizes and relexicalizes the previous statements. *Make a pitch* more often appears in the frame 'make a pitch for (something or someone)': that is, a direct appeal where the desideratum is mentioned explicitly. Here, however, it is only implied, and the action is evaluated by means of an epithet.

from afar (4.2): an anomalous collocation in so far as in current English *afar* occurs almost entirely after the preposition *from*. It conveys information.

turn up (4.2): a highly frequent phrasal verb, idiomatic in meaning. It conveys information, and can be distinguished from its more formal quasi-synonyms *arrive* and *appear* by its implication of casualness.

live-and-let-live (5.3): a compound noun, based on and alluding to the proverb *Live and let live*. This proverb is amongst the ten commonest proverbs found in OHPC, with twelve occurrences in various forms: seven of these occurrences are adjectival and two more are nominal, as in the text under discussion. It therefore appears to be the case that the locution *live and let live* is changing formally, shifting from proverb to allusive expression. Conventionally, proverbs are didactic and hortatory, but this use in the text above seems primarily to convey information. However, it also relexicalizes the previous nominal group *mere co-existence*, and its apparent redundancy can be explained by taking into account the ideological didacticism of the proverb on which it is based.

in time (5.4): a collocation that can be considered anomalous simply because the reference is so vague. When associated with future time reference, it can be seen as an epistemic modalizer. Cf. the commoner circumstantial adjunct *in time* = 'not late, before the deadline'.

QED (5.5): a formulaicized foreign borrowing. It functions as an organizer in that it shows the status and result of a preceding argument.

in short (6.1): a grammatically ill-formed collocation. It organizes by signalling a summary; it could also be said to modalize by indicating the generality of the associated proposition.

close to (6.2): an anomalous collocation, scarcely a fixed expression at all except on the grounds that it contains a rare adverbial (or absolute) use of *to*; this, however, may be seen as a transformation with shifting or ellipsis of the prepositional object ('He has seen the Soviet people by being close to them'). It conveys information.

inherit the earth (6.3): a metaphor, with biblical allusion. The subject of the metaphor is, curiously, *economic system* – a metonym for people (or countries) within that system. Canonically, the subject is lexicalized by a nominal referring to people who have or will have taken control or been given power. It is primarily informative, although there is an evaluative component as hangover from the original biblical context.

by other means (6.6): a fixed formula, or discontinuous collocation if considered in terms of the frame *by – means*, which is filled from only a small range of possibilities. It conveys information, but does so with vagueness, through the slot-filler *other*.

in essence (7.3): a grammatically ill-formed collocation. It organizes by signalling a summary and the centrality of a piece of information, but, like *in short* it can be said to modalize by indicating generality.

pull the hat down over one's eyes (7.7): this is barely an institutionalized metaphor, and there is only very slight evidence for it: it could perhaps have been grouped with the freely coined metaphors listed above. It conveys information, although the body-language described in the metaphor carries an implication of secrecy or refusal to pay attention, and this suggests criticism of the action. The expression is interesting since it appears to pick up on the idiom *pull the wool over someone's eyes*, which evaluates negatively an action or situation.

all very well (7.8): a fixed formula, though it is hard to decode compositionally. It evaluates and acts as a signal of a following adversative statement.

great chummyness butters no parsnips (7.8): an exploitation of the proverb *fine words butter no parsnips*. It conveys an evaluation. It is tied cohesively with *chum* in the preceding clause, and both *chum* and *chummyness* demonstrate a deliberate selection of a dated word, suggestive of outdated camaraderie, or the camaraderie of a restricted social group. Cf. *by golly* and *all manner of*.

change (some)one's mind, one's mind changes (7.10): a restricted collocation. Its primary function is to convey information.

cast off (7.12): a phrasal verb. Its function is to convey information. In many occurrences, the object of the phrasal verb has negative connotations, and the action of ridding is evaluated as a positive action.

This is summarized and represented in table 8.1. The items are arranged in descending order of frequency, according to their occurrences per million tokens in OHPC. Polysemous items have been disambiguated, and the frequencies given are those for the sense appearing in the text. Frequencies above 1 are rounded to the nearest whole number; < 1 means less than 1 occurrence per 1 million tokens, and < 0.5 means less than 1 occurrence per

Table 8.1

Fixed expression and reference	Frequency per million	Function	Syntax	Type
of course 1.1	242	modalize, (organize)	sentence adverb	anomalous collocation
turn up 4.2	23	inform	P+A	phrasal verb
change (some)one's mind, etc. 7.10	12	inform	P+C	anomalous collocation
from time to time 1.2	11	modalize	adjunct	formula
in short 6.1	9	organize, (modalize)	sentence adverb	anomalous collocation
in time 5.4	6	modalize	adjunct	anomalous collocation
who knows? 1.2	5	modalize	sentence adverb	formula
in essence 7.3	4	organize, (modalize)	sentence adverb	anomalous collocation
all manner of 2.3	3	inform, (evaluate)	quantifier	anomalous collocation
all very well 7.8	3	organize, (evaluate)	complement	formula
by other means 6.6	<1	inform	adjunct	formula
cast off 7.12	<1	inform, (evaluate)	P+A	phrasal verb
from afar 4.1	<1	inform	adjunct	anomalous collocat on
late in the day 3.1	<1	inform, (evaluate)	adjunct	metaphor
live-and-let-live 5.3	<1	inform, (evaluate)	noun group	formula/proverb
make a – pitch 3.3	<1	evaluate	P+O	metaphor
by golly 2.3	<0.5	modalize	sentence adverb	anomalous collocation
close to 6.2	<0.5	inform	adjunct	anomalous collocation
(fine words) butter no parsnips 7.8	<0.5	evaluate	S+P–O	metaphor/proverb
inherit the earth 6.3	<0.5	inform, (evaluate)	P+O	metaphor
pull the hat down over one's eyes 7.7	<0.5	inform, (evaluate)	P+O+A	metaphor
[pull the wool over someone's eyes 7.7	<0.5	inform, (evaluate)	P+O+A	metaphor]
QED 5.5	<0.5	organize	convention	formula
(toasted) to a turn 3.2	<0.5	evaluate	complement	metaphor

2 million tokens. 'Syntax' represents the clause function of the whole expression, or, in the cases of predicators and arguments, in terms of a SPOCA analysis (SPOCA = subject/predicator/object/complement/adjunct).

FUNCTIONS AND TEXTUAL BEHAVIOUR OF FIXED EXPRESSIONS

The text functions of fixed expressions may be classified according to the way in which they contribute to the content and structure of a text. In the text under consideration, four functions are seen, according to whether the expression primarily informs (conveys new information), evaluates (conveys speaker/writer's opinion or attitude), modalizes (conveys speaker/writer's attitude towards the truth value of his/her utterance) or organizes and functions as a discourse signal. To these four functions may be added a fifth, situationally bound, typically found in spoken interaction, and typically lexicalized as a convention or closed-set turn: this covers fixed expressions that show a speaker's reaction to something in the extralinguistic situation, for example a greeting, valediction, apology, request or warning such as *So long!*, *Excuse me*, *A penny for them* and *Talk of the devil . . .*

The handful of fixed expressions in the above text and table 8.1 suggest a number of correlations between discourse function, type, syntactic form and frequency. Apart from the phrasal verb *turn up* and the restricted collocation *change someone's mind*, the commonest expressions are textual operators: 'functional' or 'grammatical' as opposed to 'lexical' or 'content' items. This is true of the lexicon as a whole, where the very commonest items are virtually all functional rather than lexical. It is perhaps inevitable that the metaphorical items, the most marked, are the least frequent, since lack of general frequency is a key property of markedness. With respect to function and syntactic realization, it is predictable that modalizers and organizers will be lexicalized formally as sentence adverbs or adjuncts; informational as predicators and their arguments, or adjuncts; and evaluative as complements or as predicator/argument combinations. Such a relationship is reflected in the general information structure of text, and may be set out in the following way:

informational	rheme (or component of rheme)
evaluative	rheme (or component of rheme)
organizational	conjunctive adjunct
modalizing	modal adjunct

Functions of fixed expressions can be related to Halliday's model of the semantic components of language (for example, in Halliday 1978: 116ff.), but they are not identical to it. Halliday's model views text in terms of its semantic stratification into ideational, interpersonal and textu(r)al components: it is a model for the interpretation of ongoing dynamic discourse. At each selection point, a choice has repercussions at all levels, and the levels are simultaneous. At the same time, Halliday shows how specific items are primarily linked to specific macro-functions, listing, for example, many such as conjunctive or modal adjuncts (1985: 50), including multi-word items.

Fixed expressions certainly contribute to all the components. In particular the selection of a fixed expression is nearly always significant with respect to the interpersonal component, either directly, because it is communicating an attitudinal point or a reaction, or, less directly, because it lexicalizes a mitigation of the message or pre-emption of disagreement: by choosing to use a stereotyped formula, the speaker/writer can be deliberately vague, less directly assertive, but less open to question or refutation by appealing to shared cultural values: see further below.

Ideational, interpersonal and textual components operate at the highest level – at the level of the whole discourse. The text functions of fixed expressions as described above are lower-level functions and intended to provide a tool for the assessment of the effect of an expression on its immediate co-text. The following chart attempts to show how fixed expression functions cluster with respect to the ideational and interpersonal components:

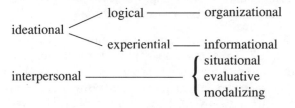

The textual component, the 'enabling function', is best considered instantially in terms of the ways in which fixed expressions are placed topically and thematically. For example, the position of *of course* and *by golly*:

(1.1) It is, *of course*, very nice to be told how wonderful you are; to bathe in a scented foam of admiration; to feel good and to be made to feel good.

(2.3) There are – *by golly*, there are – all manner of hardened cynics who have found the Guildhall TV experience rather like rolling in a puddle of warm fudge.

where they intervene between dummy subject/themes and displaced topics, so that the emphasis they convey is itself thematized and foregrounded. In contrast, classical tournure idioms, fixed expressions such as *kick the bucket*, *spill the beans* and *rock the boat*, consist entirely of rheme, ostensibly new information. This is their natural text position, and thematization is improbable. Hence:

She spilt the beans.
She spilt the peas.
*The beans were what she spilt.
The peas were what she spilt.
*It was the beans she spilt.

It was the peas she spilt.
?What she did was spill the beans.
What she did was spill the peas.
?Spilling the beans was what she did.
Spilling the peas was what she did.
*Spilling was what she did to the beans.
Spilling was what she did to the peas.

In fact thematization of either *spill* or *the beans* on its own breaks the gestalt of the idiom and the decontextualized utterance is likely to be interpreted as literal.

As far as cohesion and fixed expressions are concerned, the situation is more complex. Looking just at rhematic idioms, they are noted for their superficial lack of cohesion with their co-texts. Frequently, they contain a grammatical object that is prefaced with *the* signalling shared or given knowledge, but an antecedent or referent must be inferred through knowledge of the meaning of the idiom as a holistic unit. For example (examples with Roman numerals are taken from sources other than the text under examination, and if not otherwise stated, they are drawn from OHPC):

I.   They build on the introduction of general management into the NHS five years ago, which has seen all managers from region down to hospital move on to rolling contracts and performance-related pay. That has undoubtedly improved the management of the service. But it has also reduced the managers' willingness to *rock the boat* in public – over resources, for example – however hard they may argue in private.

where there is no apparent reference for *boat* or explanation of the reference, though its meaning fits perfectly into the context and is relexicalized as *argue* in the following clause.

The exception to the rule of lack of lexical cohesion is, of course, in punning, but then it is the chain of cohesive-but-incongruent lexis that provides the fun:

II. And God knows the press will cooperate. They are making so much money now that they will *drown* the first man who tries to *rock the boat*.
III. The impression created by Topol is that anything is fair game, in or out of government, Civic Forum or not. It is better, he believes, to *rock the boat* than keep it *on an even keel*.
IV. Ron Todd, Transport and General Workers Union general secretary, was applauded as he reaffirmed his union's commitment to unilateralism. 'I am convinced that we need to push the British disarmament *boat* out from the *shore*. Once it's properly *launched*, where everyone can see it, you won't have to worry too much about *rocking the boat*', he said.

An examination of the fixed expressions in a text and their functions – what they are intended to do – can throw light on such matters as the textual rhetoric. If two comparable texts have identical densities of fixed expression, but one has mainly organizers and modalizers, and the other mainly informational and evaluative idioms, the first will appear more controlled and the second more marked. There are five fixed expressions in the first two paragraphs of the text under analysis (here labelled as T, and there are also five in V, an excerpt from a longer report in *The Manchester Guardian Weekly*:

(T.1) It is, *of course*, very nice to be told how wonderful you are; to bathe in a scented foam of admiration; to feel good and to be made to feel good. It doesn't happen nearly enough in this harsh, frenetic world: and – *who knows?* – it may also *from time to time* be true.

(T.2) Mr Ronald Reagan wasn't the Dr Strangelove clone of earlier legend as he passed through London yesterday. He was Dr Feelgood, delivering, with all the sincerity he could muster, a farewell bouquet to Britain and to the world's newly designated senior statesperson. There are – *by golly*, there are – *all manner of* hardened cynics who have found the Guildhall TV experience rather like rolling in a puddle of warm fudge. But it was more interesting than that, on several levels.

(V.1) Vietnam's special relationship with its Soviet 'comrades' of old is now *as dead as a dodo*. The failure of last August's bid to oust Gorbachev and the banning of the Soviet Communist Party made even the more conservative Vietnamese apparatchiks realise *the writing was on the wall*.

(V.2) Some of them would have liked to see reconciliation with China *go hand in hand* with an ideological alliance between their two parties. But Beijing was not interested in heading a cartel of last-ditch Communists, partly because it did not want *to put the wind up* other South East Asian regimes, with which China is keen to keep *on the best of terms*.

(*The Manchester Guardian Weekly*, 9 February 1992)

In T, the fixed expressions reinforce the message and convey modal attitudes; in V, they convey new information and evaluation.

One consequence of the examination of the functions of fixed expressions is the emergence of an interesting phenomenon. Fixed expressions cross-function: that is, they take on another function instantly and thereby develop a different importance or prominence in relation to the structure of the text. For example:

VI. Kempson . . . opts for a conventional mapping of one on to the other set of categories whereas I prefer . . . to *go the whole* pragmatic *hog*, and attempt an explanation entirely in terms of Interpersonal Rhetoric.

(Leech 1983: 117–18)

Go the whole hog functions as a discourse signal and prelexicalizes the contrasting part of an argument. Note that there is insufficient ideational content in the expression itself to convey the message successfully, and so the expansion is necessary. Similarly with the following three examples of idioms used as prefaces: the first two are openings of articles:

VII.   I must *nail my colours to the mast*. I'm a very keen advocate of all sorts of sport for all sorts of people at all ages, but intensive sport or intensive training for sport could surprisingly, [*sic*] have side-effects.

(*Daily News* (Birmingham), 4 June 1987)

VIII. To the question, what are universities for? I would shake *the bees from my bonnet* and answer from under it that they exist in order to advance knowledge and understanding of three great provinces of thought and learning: the human world (including the past and present states of civilization), the natural world, and the technologies, which enable us to put our science at the disposal of our civilization.

(*University of Birmingham Bulletin*, 16 November 1987)

IX.   A rather common fault among shamans [i.e. language prescriptivists] is to *let the* grammatical *tail wag the* usage *dog*. A rule – learned too well from a sixth- or seventh-grade grammar lesson – gets stuck in the head and influences judgments of right and wrong. Take the following . . .

(Bolinger 1980: 169)

In the next example, an idiom is used to clarify, summarize and evaluate:

X.   Then only last week, the Director of Public Prosecutions for Northern Ireland and Sir Patrick Mayhew, the Attorney General (both, incidentally, with spotless criminal records) agreed that no one should be prosecuted for attempting to pervert the course of justice – not because these things hadn't happened, but because putting them in the spotlight of British Justice would 'not be in the public interest'. That is to say: it might open up *a can of worms*.

(*The Guardian*, 3 February 1988)

Compare the way in which proverbs are used not only didactically (their original purpose), but also to evaluate and summarize or preface, as pointed out, for example, by Schegloff and Sacks (1973: 306–7) and Stubbs (1983: 24).

XI.   But tinkering with basic rates is unlikely to *butter any parsnips* in a dispute which this week could become distinctly less civilised, with suspensions and pay cuts following tonight's intensification of industrial action.

XII.   *Fine words butter no parsnips!* High flying philosophies and esoteric ethics may give you plenty of thought but will they put bread on the table this Thursday? Intersperse intuitive, introspective imaginings with spells of diligent and determined effort.

(a horoscope)

XIII. Disciplines, unlike cows, yield least when most contented. *Necessity is the mother of invention* and a stimulus to thought – or it can be. The ideas in this book evolved under pressure from outside.

(G. Kress and R. Hodge 1979: preface)

XIV. But sometimes, uneasily, I recall what this director once told me. He was putting on *Macbeth* with an actor notorious for his often drunken belligerence playing the name part. He said every night he had to crouch in the wings and, when it came to the fight between Macbeth and Macduff, cup his hands over his mouth and hiss at Macbeth 'You've got to lose, you've *got* to *lose*.'

Well, some of us have got to, eventually. *The show must go on.*

(The Guardian, 10 September 1990)

THE METAPHORS OF FIXED EXPRESSIONS

There are several aspects of the metaphoricity of fixed expressions, especially idioms, sayings and proverbs, which might be considered: the degrees of transparency or opacity, historical development, the nature of the images. I want to consider the relationship between the surface lexis and deep meaning of the metaphor, and to do so by examining the verbal processes involved, following Halliday's classificatory scheme (1985: 101ff.). For example:

Fixed expression	Surface process	Meaning	Deep process
spill the beans	material (action)	'reveal a secret'	verbal
kick the bucket	material (action)	'die'	material (event)
have a bee in one's bonnet	relational (attribution)	'be occupied with something trivial'	mental
give someone the eye	material (action)	leer at	behavioural

This provides a framework within which it is possible to look formally at how institutionalized metaphors work. As indicated above, there is a tendency for the surface process to be more material, more action-like, and the meaning process to be more abstract. This is not surprising since a chief trait of metaphor is that it aims to make concrete, vivid or clear a more abstract or less familiar idea. Looking at the fixed expressions in the text which contain predicators:

Fixed expression	Surface process	Meaning	Deep process
be toasted to a turn	material (action)	'be good'	relational (attribution)
make a . . . pitch	material (action) (process + range)	'speak forcefully'	verbal, behavioural
turn up	material (event)	'arrive'	material (event)
inherit the earth	material (action)	'become rich'	relational (attribution)
pull the hat over one's eyes	material (action)	'ignore'	mental
(fine words) butter no parsnips	material (action)	'...are meaningless without action'	relational (attribution)
change (some)one's mind	material (action)	'cause to think differently'	material, mental
cast off	material (action)	'dismiss (idea)'	mental

the distribution of meaning processes is often different from that of lexis processes.

This sort of analysis is useful because it provides a means of identifying the ways in which the real message of a text is expressed: cf. the kind of analysis of verb processes undertaken by Benson and Greaves with respect to Poe and Melville, and how this affects such things as the development of the plot and character (1987: 133–43). There is a great difference between a text where the processes are material, contributing to a narrative and presenting clear statements about cause, circumstance and so on, and a text where the processes are superficially material but actually grammatical metaphors for, say, mental and relational processes. Material processes are inevitably associated with fact and objective report, whereas mental and relational processes are associated more with evaluation and subjective comment. By disguising – or rather lexicalizing – the second as the first, subjective opinions may appear more objective, more purely descriptive of some actual, physical situation, although in reality they communicate an interpretation and evaluation of that situation. Vivid idioms such as *lose one's bottle*, *breathe down someone's neck* and *make heavy weather of something* use material processes as metaphors for relational ones, and others such as *get hold of the wrong end of the stick*, *sweep something under the carpet* and *change one's tune* use material processes as metaphors for mental ones.

XV.   England achieved their prime objective, scoring 225 runs, after 70 minutes' batting in the morning, but *made heavy weather of* it.

XVI. Even the opponents of an 'imperialist' war *changed their tune* at the prospect of alliance with 'the Socialist sixth of the world'.

By doing so, the narrative or description is more colourful, but colour in any narrative or description is the result of interpretation and selection, not straight observation. Even in cases of a fairly simple mismatch of processes, such as that between a material action process and a material event process (for example, *kick the bucket* and 'die'), the mismatch can be seen as representing a concretization or transitization, implying action and causation where there is in fact none.

This is consistent with one of the effects, already mentioned, that fixed expressions have on a text. Idioms, proverbs and other sayings present familiar ideas in stereotyped form. The stereotyping, prepackaging, of the item encourages acceptance on the part of the hearer/reader, pre-empts disagreement and aims to avoid misunderstanding. Such expressions invoke shared cultural schemata, values and interpretations; because they are general and non-specific yet concrete, there is less room for the negotiation of meaning between speaker/writer and hearer/reader. They are, in a Barthian sense, closed metaphors. All such items express an ideological perspective, institutionalized in the culture. This is clear with respect to proverbs and other didactic sayings – *Fine words butter no parsnips*, *live and let live*, *you can't have your cake and eat it, it's an ill wind that blows nobody any good, the best things in life are free*:

XVII. Sir, *It is an ill wind that blows nobody any good.* After the Prime Minister's espousal of the policy of forcible repatriation of the boat people, even she may be constrained from lecturing the French on the superiority of the British record in promoting and defending human rights in this bicentennial year of the Declaration of the Rights of Man.

(letter in newspaper)

XVIII. *The best things in life are free* and the joys of a happy home and peace-giving partnership are amongst your most treasured possessions.

Similarly, with expressions such as *inherit the earth, the strai(gh)t and narrow, stand up and be counted,* with their philosophical and theological overtones. It is the case with evaluative, metaphorical idioms:

XIX. Rich though it was, the Comstock Lode *could not hold a candle to* the Cerro Rico, the 'Hill of Silver' at Potosi in Bolivia, which was discovered in 1544, almost immediately after the Spanish conquest of Peru.

XX. Gerry Healy could indeed claim to have made a unique addition to an identifiable left tradition, though not the global revolutionary one to which he aspired, but rather that of sectarian *big fish in little* British *ponds.*

So too with expressions such as *pull the hat over one's eyes, spill the beans, jump on the bandwagon,* which all represent sociocultural schemata, shared evaluations of what it means to ignore or be indiscreet or take advantage of a fad. Overt evaluation is avoided, and concealed behind the stereotyped, culturally institutionalized, image. The editorial by its very nature promotes an ideologically grounded perspective: its purpose is to evaluate events, to establish the corporate view and to elicit the support and agreement of a readership – at the very lowest level, for financial or political reasons – and it uses lexis as well as structure to achieve this end.

SELECTION AND SUBSTITUTION

A crude way of assessing the effect of a fixed expression on its text is to substitute another, broadly synonymous, item. For example, the first paragraph of the editorial might have read:

(T.1) It is, (naturally), very nice to be told how wonderful you are; to bathe in a scented foam of admiration; to feel good and to be made to feel good. It doesn't happen nearly enough in this harsh, frenetic world: and – (perhaps) – it may also (occasionally) be true.

The substitution of *perhaps* for *who knows?* reads strangely, if only because of the positioning and prominence: it breaks the rhythm. Otherwise, there is very little change in either the effect of the text or its message. The fixed expressions and their substitutes are high-frequency items and more-or-less unmarked. In contrast, consider substitutions for more marked items:

(T.5.3) It cannot be carried forward by mere co-existence, by (tolerance of) the forces of alien ideology.

(T.6.3) He has seen the glum queues of Moscow, and believes that this economic system will not (succeed).

(T.7.8) Candidly, it is all very well to be told what a great chum you are; but (that will have little effect) in a world of trade frictions and budget deficits and soaring defence burdens.

(V.1) Vietnam's special relationship with its Soviet 'comrades' of old is now (over). The failure of last August's bid to oust Gorbachev and the banning of the Soviet Communist Party made even the more conservative Vietnamese apparatchiks realise (it could not last).

The difference is striking. The connotations of the fixed expressions and the sociocultural schemata that they represent have gone entirely. This is at least partly due to their status as fixed expressions and stereotypes. Substitution of non-institutionalized items in a text are more likely simply to reduce a text's 'literary' qualities such as expressiveness:

(T.1.1) It is, of course, very nice to be told how wonderful you are; to (be the object of admiration); to feel good and to be made to feel good.

(T.2.3) There are – by golly, there are – all manner of hardened cynics who have found the Guildhall TV experience rather (cloying).

The sentences have become blander, and in the first the parallelism seems just tautological. But what is lost is as much individualistic connotation as shared, predetermined cultural views. There is also a phonological point to be made. The rhythms and tonic patterns are affected when fixed expressions are replaced, since in spite of their superficially appearing to give new information, they are not stressed in that way. Non-institutionalized metaphors receive normal phonological prominences and so on.

In conclusion, the analysis of fixed expressions in a text is useful for several reasons. Most basically, it provides a simple count of population and typology: compare Ure's work on measuring lexical density and the relationship between this and discourse type (1969: 443–52). It reveals something about the discourse itself and the strategies adopted by the speaker/writer to communicate his/her message. An examination of the nature of the fixed expressions in the text provides data concerning the overtness or otherwise of the message – the speaker/writer's presentation of information and the way in which this relates to objective statement or subjective interpretation. The evaluations expressed and the connotations carried may be related to overall patterns in the text and its other lexical and grammatical choices. Fixed expressions, especially organizers and highly marked metaphors, are rhetorical tropes as well as lexical realizations of specific meanings. The above editorial uses clever, witty devices to communicate the message and even to make a joke of the message. Without these devices, it would be less readable and its message more open to question. Though the internal ideational content of its fixed expressions may be nothing more than trivial, they are none the less significant, not trivial, enablers of the discoursal message.

NOTES

1 OHPC is the Oxford–Hector Pilot Corpus: a subset of the Oxford Pilot Corpus in use at Oxford University Press. It consists of approximately 18 million words of English, with a high proportion of journalism and comparatively little spoken text. Data concerning frequencies and distribution will not necessarily be replicated in other corpus investigations: for example, the 1 million-word LOB corpus has significantly higher relative frequencies for *of course*, *in short* and *from afar*, whereas the AP newswire corpora have lower ones. OHPC frequencies should therefore be regarded as benchmarks rather than universal truths. I am very grateful to Kenneth W. Church at AT & T Bell Labs for making available information concerning the frequencies of these items in the AP newswire corpora.
2 I am grateful to Valerie for this observation made during a conference discussion.

9 The construction of knowledge and value in the grammar of scientific discourse, with reference to Charles Darwin's *The Origin of Species*

M. A. K. Halliday

THEME AND INFORMATION IN SCIENTIFIC DISCOURSE

Our text for this symposium is 'verbal and iconic representations: aesthetic and functional values'. I shall start from verbal representations and functional values; but I shall suggest that functional values may also be aesthetic, and verbal representations may also be iconic. The first part of this chapter will be a general discussion of certain features of the grammar of scientific English. In the second part, I shall focus on one particular text, the final two paragraphs of Darwin's *Origin of Species*. I shall assume the concept of **register**, or functional (diatypic) variation in language. It is convenient to talk of 'a register', in the same way that one talks of 'a dialect': in reality, of course, dialectal variation is typically continuous, along many dimensions (that is, with many features varying simultaneously), and what we call 'a dialect' is a syndrome of variants that tend to co-occur. Those feature combinations that actually do occur – what we recognize as 'the dialects of English', for example, or 'the dialects of Italian' – are only a tiny fraction of the combinations that would be theoretically possible within the given language. Similarly, 'a register' is a syndrome, or a cluster of associated variants; and again only a small fraction of the theoretically possible combinations will actually be found to occur.[1]

What is the essential difference between dialectal variation and diatypic or register variation?[2] Prototypically, dialects differ in expression; our notion of them is that they are 'different ways of saying the same thing'. Of course, this is not without exception; dialectal variation arises from either geographical conditions (distance and physical barriers) or social–historical conditions (political, e.g. national boundaries; or hierarchical, e.g. class, caste, age, generation and sex), and, as Hasan has shown (see Hasan, forthcoming) dialects that are primarily social in origin can and do also differ semantically. This is in fact what makes it possible for dialect variation to play such an important part in creating and maintaining (and also in transforming) these hierarchical structures. Nevertheless dialectal variation is primarily variation in expression: in phonology, and in the morphological formations of the grammar.

Registers, on the other hand, are not different ways of saying the same thing; they are ways of saying different things. Prototypically, therefore, they differ in content. The features that go together in a register go together for semantic reasons; they are meanings that typically co-occur. For this reason, we can translate different registers into a foreign language. We cannot translate different dialects; we can only mimic dialect variation.

Like dialects, registers are treated as realities by the members of the culture. We recognize 'British English', 'American English', 'Australian English', 'Yorkshire dialect', 'Cockney' etc.; and likewise 'journalese', 'fairy tales', 'business English', 'scientific English' and so on. These are best thought of as spaces within which the speakers and writers are moving; spaces that may be defined with varying depth of focus (the dialect of a particular village versus the dialect of an entire region or nation; the register of high school physics textbooks versus the register of natural science), and whose boundaries are in any case permeable, hence constantly changing and evolving. A register persists through time because it achieves a contingent equilibrium, being held together by tension among different forces whose conflicting demands have to be met.[3] To give a brief example, grossly oversimplified but also highly typical: what we call 'scientific English' has to reconcile the need to create new knowledge with the need to restrict access to that knowledge (that is, make access to it conditional on participating in the power structures and value systems within which it is located and defined).

In a short paper on the language of physical science I set out to identify, describe and explain a typical syndrome of grammatical features in the register of scientific English (Halliday 1988a). I cited a short paragraph from the *Scientific American* and focused particularly on the pattern represented in the following two clauses:

The rate of crack growth depends . . . on the chemical environment.
The development of a . . . model . . . requires an understanding of how stress accelerates the bond rupture reaction.

In their most general form, these clauses represent the two related motifs of '*a* causes/is caused by *x*', '*b* proves/is proved by *y*'. Let me cite another pair of examples taken from a different text:

These results cannot be handled by purely structural models of laterality effects . . . [*b* + prove + *y*]
(if . . .) both word recognition and concurrent verbal memory produce more left than right hemisphere activation. [*a* + cause + *x*]

Taken together: '*b* cannot be explained by *y* if *a* causes *x*'. At the level of the syntagm (sequence of classes), each of these consists of two nominal groups linked by a verbal group whose lexical verb is of the 'relational' class, in this case *handle*, *produce*. Their analysis in systemic–functional grammar, taking account of just those features that are relevant to the present discussion, is as set out in Figure 9.1:[4]

	these results	cannot	be handled	by	purely structural models of laterality effects

transitivity	Value/ Identified	Process: relational/circumstantial: cause (internal)			Token/Identifier

mood

Mood		Residue	
Subject	Finite	Predicator	Adjunct

theme

Theme	Rheme

information

Given	◄ – – – – – – – – – – – – – – New

	both word recognition and concurrent verbal memory	produce		more left than right hemisphere activation

transitivity	Token/Identified	Process: relational/ circumstantial: cause (external)	Value/Identifier

mood

Mood		Residue	
Subject	Finite	Predicator	Complement

theme

Theme	Rheme

information

Given	◄ – – – – – – – – – – – – – New

Figure 9.1 Transitivity (ideational), mood (interpersonal), and theme and information (textual) structures in the 'favourite' clause type

In that paper I tried to show how and why this pattern evolved to become the dominant grammatical motif in modern scientific English. Historically the process is one of dialectic engagement between the nominal group and the clause. It is a continuous process, moving across the boundary between different languages: it began in ancient Greek, was continued in classical and then in medieval Latin, and then transmitted to Italian, English and the other languages of modern Europe. Table 9.1 is a summary of the relevant grammatical features that led up to this dominant motif, as they appear in two influential early scientific texts: Chaucer's *Treatise on the Astrolabe* (*c*. 1390) and Newton's *Opticks* from 300 years later. What is not found in Chaucer's text, but is found in Newton, is this particular syndrome of clausal and nominal features: a clause of the type analysed in Figure 9.1 above, in which the nominal elements functioning as Token and Value are nominalizations of processes or properties; for example,

The unusual Refraction is therefore perform'd by an original property of the Rays.

(*Opticks*, p. 358)

This is still very much a minority type in Newton's writing; but it is available when the context demands. In order to see when the context does

Table 9.1 Some grammatical features in the scientific writings of Chaucer and Newton

	Grammatical features	Typical contexts
Chaucer: *Treatise on the Astrolabe*		
1: nominal	nouns:	technical terms:
	noun roots	technological (parts of instrument)
	nouns derived from verbs and adjectives	astronomical and mathematical
	nominal groups (with prepositional phrase and clause Qualifiers)	mathematical expressions
2: clausal	material and mental; imperative	instructions ('do this', 'observe'/'reckon that')
	relational ('be', 'be called'); indicative	observations; names and their explanations
Newton: *Opticks*		
1: nominal	nouns:	technical terms:
	noun roots	general concepts; experimental apparatus
	nouns derived from verbs and adjectives	physical and mathematical
	nominal groups (with prepositional phrase and clause Qualifiers)	mathematical expressions
	*nominalizations of processes and properties	logical argumentation; explanations and conclusions
2: clausal	material and mental; indicative	description of experiments ('I did this', 'I saw/reasoned that')
	*relational ('cause', 'prove'); indicative	logical argumentation; explanations and conclusions

Note: * = not found in Chaucer's text

demand it, let me cite the immediately preceding text:

> . . . there is an original Difference in the Rays of Light, by means of which some Rays are . . . constantly refracted after the usual manner, and others constantly after the unusual manner. For the difference be not original, but arises from new Modifications impress'd on the Rays at their first Refraction, it would be er'd by new Modifications in the three following Refractions; where it suffers no alteration, but is constant, . . . The unusual Refraction is therefore perform'd by an original property of the Rays.

Note in particular the sequence [*are*] *constantly* [*refracted*] *after the unusual manner . . . . The unusual Refraction is therefore perform'd by* . . . Formulaically: '*a* happens . . . . The happening of *a* is caused by . . . The nominalization *the unusual Refraction* refers back to the earlier formulation *are refracted after the unusual manner*, in such a way as to make it the starting point for a new piece of information explaining how it is brought about.

This grammatical pattern exploits the universal **metafunctional** principle of clause structure: that the clause, in every language, is a mapping of three distinct kinds of meaning – interpersonal, ideational and textual (clause as action, clause as reflection, clause as information). The structural mechanism for this mapping, as it is worked out in English, was shown in Figure 9.1. What concerns us here first and foremost is the textual component. In English the clause is organized textually into two simultaneous message lines, one of Theme + Rheme, and one of Given + New. The former presents the information from the speaker's angle: the Theme is 'what I am starting out from'. The latter presents the information from the listener's angle – still, of course, as constructed for the listener by the speaker: the New is 'what you are to attend to'. The two prominent functions, Theme and New, are realized in quite distinct ways: the Theme segmentally, by first position in the clause; the New prosodically, by greatest pitch movement in the tone group. Because of the different ways in which the two are constituted, it is possible for both to be mapped on to the same element. But the typical pattern is for the two to contrast, with tension set up between them, so that the clause enacts a dynamic progression from one to the other: from a speaker–Theme, which is also 'given' (intelligence already shared by the listener), to a listener–New, which is also 'rhematic' (a move away from the speaker's starting point). This pattern obviously provides a powerful resource for constructing and developing an argument.[5]

We could refer to this in gestalt terminology as a move from 'ground' to 'figure', but that sets up too great a discontinuity between them, and I shall prefer the 'backgrounding–foregrounding' form of the metaphor since it suggests something more relative and continuous. The type of clause that is beginning to emerge in the Newtonian discourse, then, constructs a movement from a **backgrounded** element which summarizes what has gone before to a **foregrounded** element which moves on to a new plane. But there has to be a third component of the pattern, namely the relationship that is set up between the two; and it is this that provides the key to the potentiality of the whole, enabling the clause to function effectively in constructing knowledge and value. We have said that the relationship is typically one of cause or proof, as in the examples so far considered (*depends on, accelerates, produce, arises from, is performed by*; *requires an understanding of, cannot be handled by*). That was an oversimplification, and we now need to consider this relationship a little more closely.

The grammar of natural languages constructs a set of logical-semantic relations: relations such as 'i.e.', 'e.g.', 'and', 'or', 'but', 'then', 'thus', 'so'. These are grammaticalized in various ways, typically (in English) by conjunctions and prepositions. There are many possible ways of categorizing these relations, depending on the criteria adopted; one schema that I find useful in applying the model of the grammar to discourse analysis is that shown in table 9.2.[6] In the type of clause that we are considering here, however, these relationships come to be lexicalized as verbs; for example, the verbs *produce, arise from, depend on, lead to* as expressions of the causal relationship. Furthermore, this logical-semantic space is then crosscut along another dimension, according to whether the relationship is being set up *in rebus* or *in verbis*;[7] thus the causal relationship may be either (*in rebus*) '*a* causes *x*' or (*in verbis*) '*b* proves (= causes one to say) *y*'. Not all the logical-semantic relationships are lexicalized to the same extent; nor is this last distinction between relations in the events and relations in the discourse equally applicable to all. But the general pattern is as shown, with the experiential content entirely located within the two nominal groups and the verbal group setting up the relation between them. Table 9.3 lists some of the common verbs by which these logical-semantic relations are construed in lexical form.

Only a handful of these verbs occur in Newton's writings. The number has noticeably increased half a century later, in Joseph Priestley's *History and*

Table 9.2 Common types of logical-semantic relation, with typical realizations as conjunction and preposition

Expansion type	Category	Typical Conjunction	Typical preposition
1 elaborating	expository	in other words; i.e.	namely
	exemplificatory	for example; e.g.	such as
2 extending	additive	and	besides
	alternative	or	instead of
	adversative	but	despite (in contrast)
3 enhancing	temporal	then (at that time)	after
	causal	so (for that reason)	because of
	conditional	then (in that case)	in the event of
	concessive	yet	despite (contrary to expectation)
	comparative	so (in that way)	like

Table 9.3 Examples of lexicalization of logical-semantic relations (as verbs)

Category	Examples of lexicalization (verbs)
expository	be, represent, constitute, comprise, signal, reflect
exemplificatory	be, exemplify, illustrate
additive	accompany, complement, combine with
alternative	replace, alternate with, supplant
adversative	contrast with, distinguish
temporal	follow, precede, anticipate, co-occur with
causal	cause, produce, arise from, lead to, result in, prove
conditional	correlate with, be associated with, apply to
concessive	contradict, conflict with, preclude
comparative	resemble, compare with, approximate to, simulate

Note: Verbs in the same category are not, of course, synonymous, since they embody other features such as negative, causative. No distinction is shown here between 'external' (in rebus) and 'internal' (in verbis).

Present State of Electricity; and by the time of James Clerk Maxwell's *An Elementary Treatise on Electricity*, after another hundred years, there are some hundreds of them in current use. My guess is that in modern scientific writing there are somewhere around 2,000, although in the early twentieth century a countertendency arose whereby the logical-semantic relationship is relexicalized, this time as a noun, and the verb is simply *be* or another lexical lightweight such as *have, bring, need*. The pattern is then '*a* is the cause of *x*', '*b* is the proof of *y*'; thus *is the cause of, is the result of, is a concomitant of, has as a consequence, is a representation of, is an alternative to, is the proof of, needs explanation as, is an illustration of, serves as evidence for*, and so on. Figure 9.2 displays some examples from a text in the *Scientific American*.

We can appreciate, I think, how such verbal representations are themselves also iconic. (1) There is a movement from a given Theme (background) to a

1	Theme	nominal group	the theoretical program of devising models of atomic nuclei
	Relation (extending: additive)	verbal group	has of course been ⬚complemented⬚ by
	New	nominal group (noun: process)	experimental investigations
2	Theme	nominal group	the resulting energy level diagram
	Relation (elaborating: expositive)	<u>be</u> + nominal group (noun: relation)	is in essence a ⬚representation⬚ of '<u>b</u> represents <u>y</u>'
	New	nominalization (rankshifted clause)	what nature allows the nucleus to do
3	Theme	nominal group (noun: process)	the <u>resolution</u> of the experimental difficulties
	Relation (enhancing: causal)	<u>come</u> + nominal group (noun: relation)	came in the ⬚form⬚ of '<u>a</u> was resolved by <u>x</u>'
	New	nominal group	an on-line isotope separation system

Figure 9.2 Examples showing logical-semantic relations lexicalized (1) as verb, (2) and (3) as noun (from J. H. Hamilton and J. A. Maruhn, 'Exotic atomic nuclei', *Scientific American*, July 1986)

rhematic New (foreground); this movement in time construes iconically the flow of information. (2) New semiotic entities are created by these nominal packages, like *rate of crack growth*, *left/right hemisphere activation*, *unusual refraction*, *resolution of the experimental difficulties*; the nominal expression in the grammar construes iconically an objectified entity in the real world. (3) The combination of (1) and (2) construes iconically the total reality in which we now live, a reality consisting of semiotic entities in a periodic flow of information – a flow that one might well say has now become a flood. The grammar constructs this world, as it has constructed (and continues to construct) other worlds; and it does so, in this case, by this complex of semogenic strategies; 'packaging' into extended nominal groups, nominalizing processes and properties, lexicalizing logical-semantic relations first as verbs and then as nouns, and constructing the whole into the sort of clause we meet with everywhere not just in academic writing but in the newspapers, in the bureaucracy and in our school textbooks – typified by the following from a primary-school science text: *Lung cancer death rates are clearly associated with increased smoking*. The grammar of a natural language is a theory of experience, a metalanguage of daily life; and the forms of verbal representation that evolved as part of modern science have penetrated into almost every domain of our semiotic practice.

THE FINAL PARAGRAPHS OF *THE ORIGIN OF SPECIES*

Let me now move to the second part of the chapter, which I realize will appear somewhat detached from the first, although I hope the overall direction will soon become clear. I am still taking as my 'text' the language of science, but now contextualizing it within a more literary frame of reference. I said earlier that the concept of register, as functional variation in language, implies that our domain of enquiry is a text type rather than an individual text; we are interested in what is typical of this or that variety. In stylistics, on the other hand, we have traditionally been interested in the highly valued text as something that is unique, with the aim of showing precisely that it is not like any other texts. There are of course more or less codified genres of literature, text types showing similar text structures such as narrative fiction or lyric poetry; but there is no such thing as a literary register, or 'literary English' as a functional variety of English.

Does this mean that we cannot have a highly valued text in some definable register such as the language of science? Clearly it does not. For one thing, we can treat any text as a unique semiotic object/event. If we take a piece of scientific writing and 'read' it as a work of literature, we locate it in two value systems which intersect a series of complementarities: (1) between the text as representing a register or type and the text as something unique; (2) between the traditional 'two cultures', scientific and humanistic, the one privileging ideational meaning, the other privileging interpersonal; (3) within the scientific, an analogous opposition between (in terms of eighteenth-century thought) the uniformity of the system and the diversity of natural processes, or (re-interpreted in modern terms) between order and chaos.[8]

But there are some texts which by their own birthright lie at the intersection of science and verbal art: which are not merely reconstituted in this dual mode by us as readers, but are themselves constituted out of the impact between scientific and poetic forces of meaning. I have written elsewhere (Halliday 1988a) about the crucial stanzas of Tennyson's *In Memoriam*, those which seem to me to lie at the epicentre of one such semiotic impact. That is a text that would be categorized, in traditional terms, as elegiac poetry but containing certain passages with a scientific flavour or motif; and by studying its grammar we can get a sense of what that implies. In the text I am concerned with here, this relationship of 'science' to 'literature' is reversed: *The Origin of Species* will be classified in the library under 'science', whereas in certain lights it appears as a highly poetic text. Interestingly, while in the Tennyson poem this impact is most strongly felt at a point more or less halfway through the text, here it is most striking at the very end – in the final two paragraphs, according to my own reading of the book. Text 1 reproduces the two paragraphs in question.

Text 1
Authors of the highest eminence seem to be fully satisfied with the view that each species has been independently created. To my mind it accords better with what we know of the laws impressed on matter by the Creator, that the production and extinction of the past and present inhabitants of the world should have been due to secondary causes, like those determining the birth and death of the individual. When I view all beings not as special creations, but as the lineal descendants of some few beings which lived long before the first bed of the Silurian system was deposited, they seem to me to become ennobled. Judging from the past, we may safely infer that not one living species will transmit its unaltered likeness to a distant futurity. And of the species now living very few will transmit progeny of any kind to a far distant futurity; for the manner in which all organic beings are grouped, shows that the greater number of species of each genus, and all the species of many genera, have left no descendants, but have become utterly extinct. We can so far take a prophetic glance into futurity as to fortell that it will be the common and widely-spread species, belonging to the larger and dominant groups, which will ultimately prevail and procreate new and dominant species. As all the living forms of life are the lineal descendants of those which lived long before the Silurian epoch, we may feel certain that the ordinary succession by generation has never once been broken, and that no cataclysm has desolated the whole world. Hence we may look with some confidence to a secure future of equally inappreciable length. And as natural selection works solely by and for the good of each being, all corporeal and mental endowments will tend to progress towards perfection.

It is interesting to contemplate an entangled bank, clothed with many plants of many kinds, with birds singing on the bushes, with various insects flitting about, and with worms crawling through the damp earth, and to reflect that these elaborately constructed forms, so different from each other, and dependent on each other in so complex a manner, have all been produced by laws acting around us. These laws, taken in the largest sense, being Growth with Reproduction; Inheritance which is almost implied by reproduction; Variability from the indirect and direct action of the external conditions of life, and from use and disuse; a Ratio of Increase so high as to lead to a Struggle for Life, and as a consequence to Natural Selection, entailing Divergence of Character and the Extinction of less-improved forms. Thus, from the war of nature, from famine and death, the most exalted object which we are capable of conceiving, namely, the production of higher animals, directly follows. There is grandeur in this view of life, with its several powers, having been originally breathed into a few forms or into one; and that, whilst this planet has gone cycling on according to the fixed law of gravity, from so simple a beginning endless forms most beautiful and most wonderful have been, and are being, evolved.

(Darwin, 1859)

Here Darwin not only sums up the position for which he has been arguing (over some 450 pages, in my edition (Darwin 1979)) but also defends it against the opposition and ridicule which he knew it was bound to evoke. The initial clause in the last sentence of all, *There is grandeur in this view of life*, presents a defiant, if perhaps rather forlorn, challenge to those whose only after-image of the text would be (as he foresaw) the humiliation of finding that they were descended from the apes.

I shall offer a very partial grammatical analysis of these paragraphs, taking account just of the two features discussed above: the 'textual' organization of the clause in terms (1) of Theme–Rheme and (2) of Given–New. In embarking on this analysis, I was interested in finding out what rhetorical or discursive strategies Darwin was using, as he summed up his case and worked up to the resounding climax of that final clause: *from so simple a beginning endless forms most beautiful and most wonderful have been, and are being, evolved.* The patterning is not at all obvious; to me, at least, it did not stand out on the surface of the text. On the contrary, perhaps; one thing that makes this passage so effective may be that the reader is not presented with any explicit signal that 'this is the nature of my argument'.

Why then did I think that the clause-by-clause analysis of Theme and of New would be likely to reveal anything of interest? In general, these features of the clause grammar play a significant part in constructing the flow of the discourse. We have seen above, first, how they give texture to a single clause and, second, how they construe a pair of clauses into a coherent logical sequence, interacting with referential and lexical cohesion. In addition to this, the ongoing selection of elements functioning as Theme, and elements functioning as New, throughout a portion of a text is a major source of continuity and discursive power. In a seminal article written some ten years ago, on the status of Theme in discourse, Peter Fries (1981) showed that it was possible to relate Theme in the clause to the concepts of 'method of development' and 'main point' in composition theory.[9] Any motif that figured regularly as clause Theme could be seen to function as 'method of development' in the text, while any motif that figured regularly as Rheme was likely to be functioning as 'main point'. Fries was concerned specifically with the category of Theme and so based his interpretation on the straightforward division of each clause into two parts, the Theme and the Rheme, treating the Rheme as equal in prominence with the Theme. This has the advantage with a written text that one does not need to give it the 'implication of utterance', as is necessary if one wants to identify the element that is New. But the category of New is more appropriate, since it identifies prominence that is of a different kind and would therefore be expected to have a distinct function in the discourse; it is also more constraining, since not everything that is outside the Theme will fall within the New.[10] Here therefore I shall take it that what constitutes the 'main point' of the discourse is any motif that figures regularly as New. The third reason for analysing this aspect of the grammar of the text, then, is that the analysis reveals a great deal about the organization of the discourse. All these considerations would of course apply to any text. But in many texts these patterns are near the surface, and emerge very quickly once one begins to read them carefully; whereas here they come to light only when one consciously attends to the grammatical structure.

Text 2 shows the Theme in each ranking clause throughout the text.[11]

Text 2
the text showing Theme–Rheme structure (Theme italicized)
Authors of the highest eminence seem to be fully satisfied with the view *that each species* has been independently created. *To my mind it accords better with what we know of the laws impressed on matter by the Creator, that the production and extinction of the past and present inhabitants of the world* should have been due to secondary causes, like those determining the birth and death of the individual. *When I* view all beings not as special creations, but as the lineal descendants of some few beings which lived long before the first bed of the Silurian system was deposited, *they* seem to me to become ennobled. *Judging from the past, we* may safely infer *that not one living species* will transmit its unaltered likeness to a distant futurity. *And of the species now living* very few will transmit progeny of any kind to a far distant futurity; *for the manner in which all organic beings are grouped*, shows *that the greater number of species of each genus, and all the species of many genera*, have left no descendants, but have become utterly extinct. *We* can so far take a prophetic glance into futurity as to fortell that it will be the *common and widely-spread species, belonging to the larger and dominant groups*, which will ultimately prevail and procreate new and dominant species. *As all the living forms of life* are

the lineal descendants of those which lived long before the Silurian epoch, *we* may feel certain *that the ordinary succession by generation* has never once been broken, and *that no cataclysm* has desolated the whole world. *Hence we* may look with some confidence to a secure future of equally inappreciable length. *And as natural selection works* solely by and for the good of each being, *all corporeal and mental endowments* will tend to progress towards perfection.

It is interesting to contemplate an entangled bank, clothed with many plants of many kinds, with *birds* singing on the bushes, with *various insects* flitting about, and with *worms* crawling through the damp earth, and to reflect *that these elaborately constructed forms*, so different from each other, and dependent on each other in so complex a manner, have all been produced by laws acting around us. *These laws*, taken in the largest sense, being Growth with Reproduction; Inheritance which is almost implied by reproduction; Variability from the indirect and direct action of the external conditions of life, and from use and disuse; a Ratio of Increase so high as to lead to a Struggle for Life, and as a consequence to Natural Selection, entailing Divergence of Character and the Extinction of less-improved forms. *Thus, from the war of nature, from famine and death*, the most exalted object which we are capable of conceiving, namely, the production of higher animals, directly follows. *There is grandeur* in this view *of life*, with its several powers, having been originally breathed into a few forms or into one; *and that, whilst this planet* has gone cycling on according to the fixed law of gravity, *from so simple a beginning* endless forms most beautiful and most wonderful have been, and are being, evolved.

The grouping of these into motifs is set out in diagrammatic form in Figure 9.3. The first motif that emerges (number I in Figure 9.3) is very clearly that of authority, beginning with the Theme of the first clause *authors of the highest eminence*. This, when followed by *seem to be fully satisfied*, becomes solidary with a passage in the final paragraph of an earlier chapter where, mentioning a number of authorities who have (*contra* Darwin) *maintained the immutability of species*, he then goes on: *But I have reason to believe that one great authority, Sir Charles Lyell, from further reflexion entertains grave doubts on this subject*. The motif of authority is thus already given, constructed out of the morphological relationship of *authors = authorities*. Darwin now extends it in a sequence of clause Themes as follows:

authors of the highest eminence – the Creator [to my mind] – I – we

By this thematic progression Darwin establishes his own claim to authority, wherewith to dispute and override these authors of the highest eminence. He first appeals to the Creator – but being careful to precede this with the interpersonal Theme *to my mind*, which both protects him against the arrogance of claiming to know the Creator's purposes and, by a neat

THEME/METHOD OF DEVELOPMENT

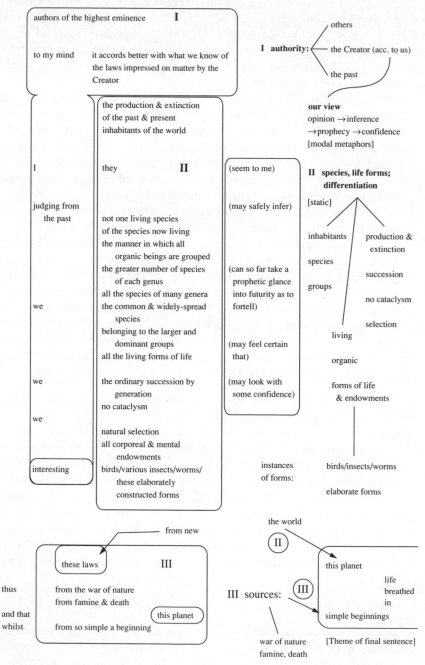

Figure 9.3 Charles Darwin, *The Origin of Species*: Thematic and informational motifs of last two paragraphs

'NEW' (= FOCUS OF ATTENTION)/ MAIN POINT

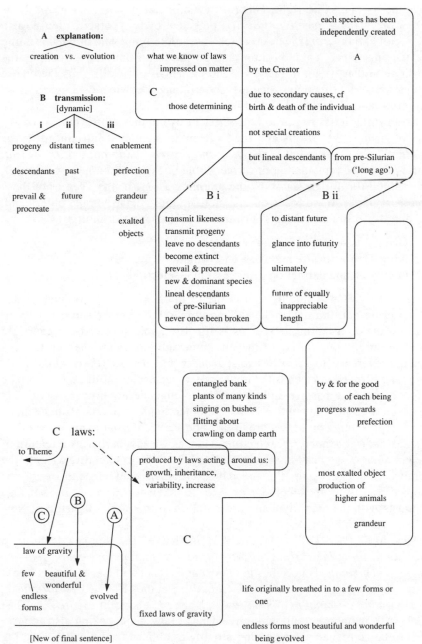

A   **explanation:**

creation vs. evolution

what we know of laws
impressed on matter

C

those determining

each species has been
independently created

A

by the Creator

due to secondary causes, cf
birth & death of the individual

not special creations

B   **transmission:**
[dynamic]

i   ii   iii

progeny   distant times   enablement

descendants   past   perfection

prevail &   future   grandeur
procreate

exalted
objects

but lineal descendants | from pre-Silurian
('long ago')

B i

transmit likeness
transmit progeny
leave no descendants
become extinct
prevail & procreate
new & dominant species
lineal descendants
   of pre-Silurian
never once been broken

B ii

to distant future

glance into futurity

ultimately

future of equally
inappreciable
length

entangled bank
plants of many kinds
singing on bushes
flitting about
crawling on damp earth

by & for the good
   of each being
progress towards
   prefection

C   **laws:**

to Theme

produced by laws acting | around us:
growth, inheritance,
variability, increase

most exalted object
production of
   higher animals

grandeur

C

B

A

C

law of gravity

few   beautiful &
   wonderful
endless   evolved
forms

fixed laws of gravity

[New of final sentence]

life originally breathed in to a few forms or
one

endless forms most beautiful and wonderful
being evolved

Figure 9.4

metafunctional slip (from interpersonal 'me' to ideational 'me'),[12] leads naturally from his role as interpreter of the Creator's design to his position as an authority in his own right. This *I* is then modulated to *we*, in *we can so far take a prophetic glance into futurity*; preceded by a hypotactic clause (also thematic) *judging from the past*, which – without saying who or what is doing the judging (since it is non-finite and so needs no Subject) – justifies the assumption that 'I' am in fact speaking on behalf of us all. Thus the clause Themes have by this point securely underpinned Darwin's own status as an authority; and this thematic motif is now abandoned.

Meanwhile, it has begun to be overtaken by another motif (numbered II), that of species, life forms and their differentiation; first introduced as *the production and extinction of the past and present inhabitants of the world*. Since this is the principal motif of the whole book (as embodied in the title), it is natural for it to be set up by the grammar as one of the Themes of these final paragraphs. If we focus on this motif in more detail, on the other hand, we find that it is constructed out of three interlocking sub-motifs:

(a) inhabitants – species – groups
(b) living – forms of life and their endowments
(c) production and extinction – succession – selection

These are developed side by side in the form of fairly long nominal groups which bring out, through their lexicogrammar, the number and diversity of species, the collocation of 'species' with 'life', and the steady, irreversible forward progression through time; the three sub-motifs are then united in a specific reference to *birds*, *various insects* and *worms* (*these elaborately constructed forms*), which is the final appearance of this motif as Theme. The effect is one of a massive and powerful life-engendering process – which is however presented synoptically as an objectified 'state of affairs', since words representing processes are in fact nominalized: *production*, *extinction*, *succession*, (*no*) *cataclysm*, *selection*. This, as we saw earlier, is a feature of the grammar of the most highly favoured clause type in scientific writing: the nominalization picks up the preceding argument and presents it in this 'objectified' form as something now to be taken for granted. Here it also contrasts with the more dynamic presentation of the motifs figuring as New (see B below in Figure 9.4).

The third motif (III in Figure 9.3) is that of the sources leading to speciation: *these laws*; *from the war of nature, famine and death*; *from so simple a beginning*. This comes in almost at the end; and Darwin leads into it by taking over *laws* into the Theme from the previous Rheme (. . . *produced by laws acting around us. These laws* . . .; see C above in Figure 9.4). The effect is to juxtapose, both within the Theme (and hence, being also 'given', both to be construed as something already established), the two conflicting principles in nature – its lawfulness, and its lawlessness – which together by their dialectic interaction account for the origin of species.

I shall return below to the extraordinary final sentence of the text.

Meanwhile let us consider the motifs that constitute the 'main point' of the argument, as these appear clause by clause with the grammatical function of the New.[13] These are shown in text 3 and set out diagrammatically in Figure 9.4.

Text 3

Authors of the highest eminence seem to be fully satisfied with the view that each species *has been independently created*. To my mind it accords better with *what we know of the laws impressed on matter by the Creator*, that the production and extinction of the past and present inhabitants of the world should have been *due to secondary causes*, like *those determining the birth and death of the individual*. When I view all beings *not as special creations*, but as *the lineal descendants* of some few beings which lived *long before the first bed of the Silurian system was deposited*, they seem to me to become *ennobled*. Judging from *the past*, we may safely infer that not one living species will transmit *its unaltered likeness to a distant futurity*. And of the species now living very few will transmit *progeny of any kind* to a far distant futurity; for the manner in which all organic beings are grouped, shows that the greater number of species of each genus, and all the species of many genera, have left *no descendants*, but have become *utterly extinct*. We can so far take a *prophetic glance into futurity* as to fortell that it will be the common and widely-spread species, belonging to the larger and dominant groups, which will ultimately *prevail* and procreate *new and dominant species*. As all the living forms of life are *the lineal descendants of those which lived long before the Silurian epoch*, we may feel certain that the ordinary succession by generation *has never once been broken*, and that no cataclysm has desolated *the whole world*. Hence we may look with some confidence *to a secure future of equally inappreciable length*. And as natural selection works solely *by and for the good of each being*, all corporeal and mental endowments will tend to progress *towards perfection*.

It is interesting to contemplate *an entangled bank*, clothed with *many plants of many kinds*, with birds singing *on the bushes*, with various insects *flitting about*, and with worms crawling *through the damp earth*, and to reflect that these elaborately constructed forms, so different from each other, and dependent on each other in so complex a manner, have all been produced *by laws acting around us*. These laws, taken in the largest sense, being

> Growth with Reproduction; Inheritance which is almost implied by reproduction; Variability from the indirect and direct action of the external conditions of life, and from use and disuse; a Ratio of Increase so high as to lead to a Struggle for Life, and as a consequence to Natural Selection, entailing Divergence of Character and the Extinction of less-improved forms.

Thus, from the war of nature, from famine and death, *the most exalted object which we are capable of conceiving*, namely, *the production of higher animals*, directly *follows*. There is *grandeur* in this view of life, with its several powers, having been originally breathed *into a few forms or into one*; and that, whilst this planet has gone cycling on *according to the fixed law of gravity,* from so simple a beginning *endless forms most beautiful and most wonderful have been, and are being, evolved.*

The first such motif (lettered A in Figure 9.4) is that of alternative explanations: specifically, creation versus evolution. It may be helpful to set the wordings out in a list:

has been independently created
due to secondary causes
those [causes] determining the birth and death of the individual
not as special creation (but as . . .)
the lineal descendants
long before the first bed of the Silurian system was deposited

The final one of these is the last appearance of this motif until the very last words of the text (. . . *have been, and are being, evolved*); meanwhile, via the two semantic features of generation (*lineal descendants*) and antiquity (*long before the first bed* . . .), it leads us into the second of the 'New' motifs, that of transmission – or better, transmitting, since the way the grammar constructs it is at least as much clausal as nominal.[14]

Like the second of the thematic motifs, this second motif within the New (B in Figure 9.4) is also constructed out of three sub-motifs:

(a) progeny: (leave) descendants – (become) extinct – (procreate) new and dominant species
(b) time: remote past – distant futurity (*a secure future of inappreciable length*)
(c) ennoblement: (become) ennobled – (progress) towards perfection – most exalted object – the production of higher animals

The first two of these co-occur; the third is introduced at the beginning of this motif (*become ennobled*), then left aside and taken up again after the sub-motifs of progeny and time have been established. The message line is that descendancy across the ages equals ennoblement, and that this process will continue in the future as it has done in the past. The effect of associating the 'evolutionary' motifs of progeny and time with this one of ennoblement is to collocate evolution with positively loaded interpersonal expressions like *by and for the good of each being, towards perfection* and so on; this might serve to make such an unpalatable concept slightly less threatening and more acceptable.

There is then a short, transitional motif comprised of the environment in which the diversity of species (the birds, insects etc. of II above) can be appreciated: *an entangled bank, plants of many kinds, (singing) on bushes, flitting about, (crawling) through the damp earth.* This could perhaps be seen as an appendage to B above (see Figure 9.4), illustrating the progress towards perfection; but it is also transitional, via the search for explanation (*have all been produced by*), to the final motif (lettered C in Figure 9.4) which is broached as *laws acting around us*. These laws are then enumerated, as a long list of nominal groups (shown in the box in text 3), all with embedded phrases and/or clauses in them and all functioning as the final element in the one ranking clause – a clause which is (anomalously) non-finite, despite being the main and only clause in the sentence.[15]

Up to this point, then (that is, up to the final sentence of the final paragraph), the clauses are rather clearly organized, through their textual functions of Theme (in Theme–Rheme) and New (in Given–New), around a small number of distinct but interlocking motifs. We could summarize this pattern as in table 9.4. Then, in the final sentence, the motifs of II, III, B and C are all brought together: and in an extremely complex pattern. The sentence begins with *There is grandeur in this view of life* . . . . Here *grandeur*, which relates to B(iii), is unusual in being at the same time both Theme and New; hence it is doubly prominent.[16] On a first reading, *in this view of life* seems to complete the clause; and since it is anaphorically cohesive (by reference of *this*, and by lexical repetition of *life*) it is read as not only Rheme but also Given. It then turns out that Darwin has misled us with a grammatical pun, and that *life* actually begins a new clause, *life . . . having been originally breathed into a few forms or into one*, all of which is a projected Qualifier to *view* ('the view that life was originally breathed . . .'). This makes *life* thematic, and (since no longer anaphoric) a continuation of the motif of life forms in II(ii); this motif is then carried on into the New, in *(breathed) into a few forms or into one*. The next clause turns out to be another projected Qualifier to *view*, paratactically related to the last, yet finite where the other was non-finite; furthermore it is a hypotactic clause complex in which the dependent clause comes first. The dependent clause has as Theme *this planet*, relating cohesively to *the world* at the very beginning of II(i): and as New *(has gone cycling on) according to the fixed law of gravity*, where *law of gravity* derives from motif C (natural laws) but shifts the attention from the temporally organized world of biology to the timeless universe of physics. The final clause, the culmination of the projected 'view' in which there is grandeur, has the theme from III (*from so simple a beginning*, with anaphoric *so*); the Rheme takes up the motifs of II, *endless forms*, and B(iii), *most beautiful and most wonderful*, leading to the final New element, the verbal group *have been, and are being, evolved*.

Table 9.4 Summary of motifs constructing Theme and New of ranking clauses in final two paragraphs of *The Origin of Species*

Theme ('method of development')		New ('main point')		
I	authorities	A		explanation
II	the phenomenon of species:	B		the process of evolution:
(i)	inhabitants and groups		(i)	transmission and procreation
(ii)	life forms and endowments		(ii)	time: past–future
(iii)	variation		(iii)	ennoblement
III	sources (laws/war of nature)	C		law (natural selection)

This resounding lexicogrammatical cadence brings the clause, the sentence, the paragraph, the chapter and the book to a crashing conclusion with a momentum to which I can think of no parallel elsewhere in literature – perhaps only Beethoven has produced comparable effects, and that in another medium altogether. Phonologically, the co-ordination of *have been, and are being,* forces a break in the rhythm (further reinforced by the surrounding commas) that directs maximum bodyweight on to the final word *evolved.* Grammatically, the word *evolved* has to resolve the expectation set up by the ellipsis in the uncompleted verbal group *have been.* Semantically, *evolved* has to resolve the conflict between *so simple a beginning* and *endless forms most beautiful and most wonderful.* All that is only what the word is expected to achieve within its own clause. In addition, within the projected clause complex, it has to complete the complex proportion between physical and biological processes:

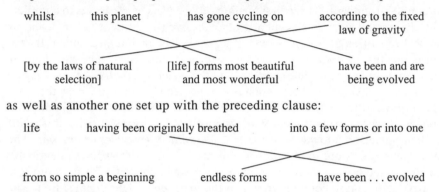

as well as another one set up with the preceding clause:

Within the sentence, the word *evolved* has to carry a culminative prominence to match the initiating prominence carried by *grandeur* (as Theme/New) at the beginning. Within these two paragraphs, it has to pick up the thematic motif of explanation, and to secure total commitment to one explanation and rejection of the other. It is here that the selection of voice becomes important: since the verbal group is passive, the responsibility for evolution is clearly lodged with the Creator (there is an external agency at hand; it is not . . . *have been, and are, evolving*). Yet all this load of work is hardly worth mentioning beside the major responsibility the word *evolved* has to bear, along with the verbal group of which it is a part: that of sustaining the climax of 450 pages of intense scientific argument. This is the culmination towards which the entire text has been building up. It would be hard to find anywhere in English a sentence, or a clause, or a group, or a word that has been made to carry such an awesome semiotic load.

I do not know how long it took Darwin to compose these two paragraphs, or whether he reflected consciously on their construction as he was doing it – I imagine not. I certainly had no idea, when starting the analysis, of what I was going to find. I had the sense of a remarkable and powerful piece of writing, as the climax to a remarkable and powerful book; and it struck me that something of the effect of these two paragraphs might lie in the patterning of the Theme and of the New – that is, in the textual component within the grammar of the clause. It is important to stress that that is in fact all that I have been looking at in this chapter; I have said almost nothing about cohesion or transitivity or mood or the clause complex or any of the other lexicogrammatical systems/processes that go into the make-up of a text. Some, at least, of these other features would undoubtedly show interesting and significant patterns if we were to analyse them with this or some comparable kind of functional grammatics.

It is pointless to try and classify a text such as this – to ask whether it 'is' a scientific treatise or a declaration of faith or an entertaining work of literature. It is a product of the impact between an intellectual giant and a moment in the space-time continuum of our culture, with all the complexity of meaning that that implies. With this very partial analysis – a fragment of the grammar of a fragment of the text – I have tried to suggest something of how this text takes its place in semo-history. Some of the thematic patterning here is like that which I described in the first part of the chapter, which evolved primarily (I think) in the context of scientific endeavour; we can recognize instances where Darwin is backgrounding some point already covered, so getting it taken for granted, and moving on from it, by a logical-semantic 'process', to a foregrounded next stage; for example *from the war of nature . . . the production of the higher animals directly follows*. (There are more of this type in the more strictly 'scientific' passages; for example the account of the honeycomb in Chapter 7, pp. 255–6.) But the pattern has rather a different value here from that which it typically has in the context in which it evolved; Darwin's strategy is that of accumulating masses of evidence rather than moving forward logically one step at a time. And particularly at critical moments he moves into a more monumental mode, that of a writer producing a text which he knows is unique and will have a unique place in the history of ideas. What is important is that we should be able to use the same theory and method of linguistic analysis – the same 'grammatics' – whatever kind of text (or sub-text) we are trying to interpret, whether Tennyson or Darwin, Mother Goose or the *Scientific American*. Otherwise, if we simply approach each text with an *ad hoc* do-it-yourself kit of private commentary, we have no way of explaining their similarities and their differences – the aesthetic and functional values that differentiate one text from another, or one voice from another within the frontiers of the same text.

NOTES

1 That is, there are many 'disjunctions'; see Lemke (1984: esp. 132ff.). Dialectal disjunctions are mainly phonetic; cf. the Prague school's concept of functional equilibrium in phonology.
2 The term 'diatypic' is taken from Gregory (1967). The term 'register' was first used in this sense by Reid (1956); cf. Halliday, McIntosh and Strevens (1964).
3 The concept of register should therefore be defined so as to make explicit the dimension of power, as pointed out by Kress (1988), Fairclough (1988).

4 For this and other aspects of the systemic–functional grammar referred to throughout this paper see Halliday (1985).

5 The Given + New structure is not, in fact, a structure of the clause; it constructs a separate unit (the 'information unit') realized by intonation as a tone group. In spoken English the typical (unmarked) discourse pattern is that where one information unit is mapped on to one clause; further semantic contrasts are then created by departure from this unmarked mapping. In written English there are of course no direct signals of the information unit; while the unmarked mapping may be taken as the typical pattern, a great deal of systematic variation will show up if the text is read aloud.

6 This is, obviously, a very sketchy and selective account. See Halliday (1985: Chapters 7, 9; and Table 9(3), pp. 306–7).

7 For this distinction see Halliday and Hasan (1976: Chapter 5, esp. pp. 240–4). Here we refer to 'external' (*in rebus*) and 'internal' (*in verbis*) conjunctive relations.

8 We do not of course transcend these oppositions; the nearest we get to a position of neutrality, in the sense of being able to accommodate the complementarities on a higher stratum, is in the discourse of mathematics and of linguistics – as thematic rather than disciplinary discourses (perhaps now computer science and semiotics).

9 For a more recent discussion see the same author's 'Toward a discussion of the flow of information in a written English text' (1992).

10 The boundary between Given and New is in any case fairly indeterminate. What is clearly marked by the intonation contour is the information focus: that is, the culmination of the New (signalled by tonic prominence). There is some prosodic indication where the New element begins, but it is much less clear (hence the move from Given to New is often regarded as continuous). See also note 14 below.

11 Ranking clauses are those which are not embedded (rank-shifted); they enter as clauses (either alone, or in paratactic or hypotactic relation with others) into clause complexes (sentences). Embedded clauses are not considered, because they do not enter into clause complexes but function inside the structure of a nominal group, and present little choice of textual (thematic or informational) organization; thus their Theme–Rheme and Given–New structure has no significance for the overall patterning of the discourse.

12 In *to my mind* the 'me' has no role in the transitivity structure (no ideational function). In *when I view* . . . , the same 'me' has been transformed into a thinker, with a highly significant role in transitivity – as Senser in a mental process; note here also the lexical slip from *view* = 'observe', suggested by *when I view all beings*, to *view* = 'opine', a re-interpretation forced on the reader by the subsequent *as*.

13 Based on my own reading of the text: on the construction into information units and location of information focus.

14 This option is not available to a motif functioning as Theme, since (almost) all thematic elements are nominals (any clause functioning as Theme has first to be nominalized). Instances such as *transmit likeness*, *transmit progeny*, *have left no descendants* and so on illustrate the point made in note 10 above; in my reading the New could be heard as beginning with the verb in each case. I have used the more cautious interpretation, restricting it in most instances to the final (culminative) element.

15 I have treated all these as falling within the New, rather than attempting to analyse them further; a list tends to have special rhythmic and tonal properties of its own.

16 That is, it clearly represents a 'marked' mapping of information structure on to thematic structure, characteristic of such existential clauses.

10 Frames of reference: contextual monitoring and the interpretation of narrative discourse

Catherine Emmott

INTRODUCTION: TEXT-SPECIFIC MENTAL STRUCTURES

This chapter argues that there are features of narrative discourse that cannot be accounted for without cognitive modelling. Cognitive modelling requires us to postulate mental stores of information. These mental structures enable a reader of narrative to interpret pronouns and other pro-forms which lack recent antecedents. Mental structures also help the reader to construct a fictional world and to process narrative flashback.

Mental structures are of various kinds. A distinction can be drawn between **general knowledge mental structures** and **text-specific mental structures**. A general knowledge structure (or 'schema' (Bartlett 1932)) consists of information which we bring to a text. A text-specific mental structure, by contrast, is built up of information that comes from the particular text we are reading and for this reason should be of particular interest to discourse analysts.

Much work has already been done on general knowledge structures (e.g. Minsky 1977; Schank and Abelson 1977). One often quoted example is the 'restaurant script' (Schank and Abelson 1977). This accounts, amongst other things, for our expectation that when we enter a restaurant a waiter or waitress will come to give us the menu and take our order and that we will have to pay for our meal before we leave. Such schemata are necessary in theories of both reality processing and text processing. Another type of general knowledge structure is the story schema (e.g. Rumelhart 1975; Mandler and Johnson 1977; Thorndyke 1977). Story schemata account for our expectations about narrative text in general, such as our awareness of the typical structure of a fairy story.

Interest in text-specific mental structures is more recent. One such mental structure is the **character construct**.[1] This is an information store which we build for any one character in a story from explicit statements in the text about that character or from inferences drawn from these statements (Brown and Yule 1983; Emmott 1989). Likewise, all the information that we have accumulated about any one fictional place can be stored in what may be termed a **location construct** (Emmott 1989). Another and very different type of text-specific mental structure is described in this chapter. This is the **frame**.[2] The frame monitors fictional context. It consists not of stores of information about particular entities, such as characters or locations, but of a tracking system which monitors which particular characters are 'present'[3] in a location at any one point. The frame can be likened to both a school timetable and a school register[4] for it shows the grouping of people in a place without giving us any detailed information, this detailed information being held in the character constructs and the appropriate location construct.

The notion of the frame was introduced in Emmott (1989) and derived from my examination of forty full-length texts, both novels and short stories (see also Emmott 1992, forthcoming). The idea draws partly on Ballmer's (1981) discussion of contextual 'book-keeping' in sign language for the deaf and its implications for natural-language processing, whilst the term comes from Goffman's (1975) work in sociology which bears some parallels. Some similar independent research on narrative has been carried out in artificial intelligence (e.g. Nakhimovsky and Rapaport 1989) using such terms as 'Event–Situation Structure'.

THE FRAME AS A CONTEXTUAL MONITOR IN NARRATIVE

Interpreting pro-forms

One reason why the reader of narrative needs to store contextual information mentally in a frame is that many pro-forms can only be interpreted if this information is readily to hand. The characters in a story, for example, in direct speech or in first-person narration, use words such as *here*, *we* and *everyone* which look, on the surface, as if they are exophoric. Exophoric pro-forms are, however, interpreted by looking around the real-world context for a suitable referent. For the reader of narrative text, the characters' pro-forms cannot be classed as exophoric since they refer not to the real but to a fictional world. The reader is not part of the fictional world and so cannot physically look around him/herself for the referent.

Halliday and Hasan (1976) suggest that in narrative fiction pro-forms such as *we* are endophoric (and hence usually anaphoric):

> In narration the context of situation includes a 'context of reference', a fiction that is to be constructed from the text itself, so that all reference within it must ultimately be endophoric. Somewhere or other in the narrative will be names or designations to which we can relate the [pro-forms] of the dialogue.

> (p. 50)

The phrase 'somewhere or other' is significant, for the antecedents of such pro-forms will often be distant and/or complex. The characters who are present at any one point in a story may form a grouping which has been built up gradually, with characters having entered separately and account having to be taken of characters who have since left. If we were to use Halliday and Hasan's 1976 model of backwards anaphoric reference,[5] then we would have to see 'group' pro-forms such as *we* or *everyone* as being interpreted by the reader searching for mentions of each individual character in the previous text. These mentions might be scattered and it would be difficult to know when to stop searching, for the pro-form could denote any number of characters. The alternative to a distant and complex backward search in these cases is, on the first occasion that characters are mentioned as being in a particular location, to build a frame. The frame monitors which characters are involved in the current action, bringing this information forward to each new sentence so that it can be used in the interpretation of such pro-forms. Because of the frame, the mind already knows 'who?' and 'where?' and has all the information about the relevant people and the relevant place ready to hand. Indeed many readers seem to carry forward their mental constructs as a quasi-visual image, monitoring characters, location and contextual connections in 'the mind's eye' as they read through the text. It is because this information is already known that pro-forms function so effectively as shorthand forms. This type of reference can still be classed as endophoric because the clues to interpreting 'group' pro-forms exist in the text.[6] However, as these clues are held in the mental frame, we do not need to access the prior text at the point of processing the pro-form.

Reading between the lines

We have, in the previous section, been concentrating on how the reader interprets words such as *here* and *everyone*. These words represent slots which must be filled (with a location construct or with character constructs) and the problem for the linguist is accounting for how the reader does this. The reader must, however, go beyond slot-filling of this kind. The following example demonstrates this:

1 (1) 'Ruminating', replied Meesh, and a merry smile threatened to break at the corner of his mouth.

(2) 'Whatinating?' asked Annie, blankly.

(3) 'Ruminating', repeated Meesh. Then he obligingly spelt it.

(4) 'R U M spelt rum when I was at school', said Annie. 'Take it from me, your days for ruminating are over. If you're staying at home you'll keep sober, and you'll do some work about the place.'

(Grant, 1989: 4; my numbering)

The sentences in the first and third paragraphs of this extract do not make any mention of Annie by lexical item or by pronoun. We would normally say that she is not being referred to in these sentences. Standard reference theory is, however, a rather blunt instrument. It offers just two possibilities: a sentence either refers to a character (pronominally or lexically) or it does not.

Yet our common-sense experience of reading suggests that something rather more complex is happening. Although Annie is not mentioned in the first and third paragraphs we know that she is 'there' with Meesh. If we were to dispute this and say that Annie is only present when she is pronominally or lexically referred to, we would be unable to explain how she comes to make such apt replies in the second and fourth paragraphs of the extract.

Reference theory does not tell us how a character who is not referred to in a sentence can be perceived as being 'there'. Yet we need to be able to distinguish between a character who, although not referred to, is present in the current location and a character who is not present at all at that point. Knowing who is listening to a character when they speak and act and who is not is of importance in our reading of a text.

Let us consider an extension of reference theory which would enable us to take account of the above common-sense intuitions about the reading process. I propose that we consider narrative reference to be a two-stage process comprising **priming** (Emmott 1989) and **focusing** (Sidner 1983a, b). Priming involves a mention of the character which establishes that character as being present in the current fictional context. A priming reference acts as a trigger. The reader must work on the principle that once a character has been mentioned as being in the current location, that character is assumed to remain 'there' until the text tells us otherwise. Such assumptions are monitored by the frame. So although subsequent sentences may not refer to the character, the initial priming reference has a sustained effect, made possible by the frame. Frames make a referent available whether mention is made of that referent or not.

From the point of view of letting us know who is present in a context, any mention of a participant whilst primed is superfluous. Such mentions simply re-affirm the presence of someone whom we know to be already there. In other respects, of course, these mentions are not superfluous. Subsequent mentions focus the reader's attention on one or more of the primed participants, telling us whose actions in particular are being described. A character for whom there is a structural slot in the sentence (whether lexical, pronominal or elided) is an **overt participant** (Emmott 1989) in that sentence. A character for whom there is no structural slot in a sentence is a **covert participant** (Emmott 1989) in that sentence.

CONTEXTUAL MONITORING BY THE BLIND

We have seen that (as in example 1) a text will not normally mention in every sentence every character who is present in a fictional context. The reader must therefore build a mental model of the context which can be used to fill the gaps. The reader can be likened in this respect to a blind person.[7] Blind people do not have information about their surroundings available constantly through the eyes. They receive only intermittent signalling of the context through the non-visual senses. This means that those around the blind person are only 'in focus' when speaking, moving audibly, touching, etc. The rest of the time the participants are covert rather than overt. The blind must compensate for this shortfall by mentally monitoring the context. This is achieved by priming contextual information into a frame.

Blind people will often be in the position where they address what, from the evidence of their senses at any one point in time, might as well be an empty room. Although a blind person can enquire who is around them, it would be socially unacceptable for them to keep asking. The blind person can, nevertheless, work on the assumption that whoever has been in the room is still present unless there has been any evidence to the contrary.

There will of course be occasions when the blind person is unaware of others coming and going either because they make no noise or because, in a crowded room, there is too much other noise. As a result a blind person may, for example, address someone who was in the room but has left. This indicates that the blind person is working with a mental model of the context which may or may not match the real context. It provides evidence that the human mind works by monitoring and making assumptions rather than by continually checking the context.

FRAMES AND FLASHBACKS

In narrative the frame can be used not only to interpret certain types of pro-form and to monitor the full participant set, but also to explain how we read flashback.

Verbs at the opening of a flashback are usually in the past perfect, but not all sentences of a flashback are marked in this way, as shown below. The example starts part way through a flashback.

2   'But what sort of study is it supposed to be?' Richard had pursued. 'Is it history? Physics? Philosophy? What?'
    'Well', said Reg, slowly, 'since you're interested, the chair was originally instituted by King George III, who, as you know, entertained a number of amusing notions, including the belief that one of the trees in Windsor Great Park was in fact Frederick the Great.'
    'It was his own appointment, hence "Regius". His own idea as well, which is somewhat more unusual.'
    Sunlight played along the River Cam. People in punts happily shouted at each other . . .

(Adams 1987: 12–13)

All these events take place in flashback. The verb form, however, switches from past perfect ('had pursued') to simple past ('said', 'played', 'shouted'). The sentences in the simple past are linguistically indistinguishable from sentences of the main narrative. At this point, the fact that we are in flashback is covert. The reader knows, however, that these sentences denote flashback events because on entry to the flashback s/he has set up a flashback frame. As well as monitoring people and location, a flashback frame monitors time, either the precise time or the fact that the action is set at a time prior to the main narrative. Until there is an indication that the flashback has come to an end the reader assumes, by means of the frame, that s/he is still in flashback.

DISTINCTION BETWEEN FRAME MODIFICATION AND FRAME SWITCH

In the main narrative, too, the assumptions of the reader about the current context remain in force until there is some signal that the context has changed. For the reader there are two quite different types of change: **frame modification** and **frame switch**.

Frame modification is the less extreme of the two. This happens when we are told that one or more characters enter or leave the current location. Our assumptions change about these characters. Our assumptions about the other characters, however, remain as before. So the frame remains in force despite having been modified.

Let us look at an example of frame modification. The example opens with a discussion in progress between the 'I' narrator and Bobbie and Bobbie's husband, Pete. During the course of this conversation Pete leaves the current location.

3   *Frame modification*
    'Oh, for Christ's sake, Pete, lay off, at least while I'm here', I said.
        'Why? You like to think of yourself as an old friend of the family . . . .'
    He got up and left the house.
        'Well, it's just like a year ago', said Bobbie. 'When you came to call on us last Christmas?'

                                                    (O'Hara 1986: 117; my omission marks)

In this example our assumptions about Pete change because we are told that he leaves the frame. Our assumptions about the presence of Bobbie and the 'I' narrator, however, continue, whether or not they are mentioned pronominally or lexically in the immediately succeeding text.

Frame switch differs from frame modification in that in frame switch our attention turns to a new frame, with no assumptions from the previous frame remaining actively in force. Example 4 illustrates this, the frame switch occurring at the beginning of the second paragraph with the words 'Five hundred yards away'.

4   *Frame switch*
    Anton looked along the upturned faces for Martha. She was not there and must have gone home. Andrew was thinking of Maisie: he had reasons to be with her tonight. But both men knew that because of their rivalry they would stay out the meeting to its end, and afterwards take Jack Dobie off for coffee . . . . Unless it rained and although the thunder rolled above the tin roof, often drumming out the sound of Jack's voice, there was no sign of rain, there would be no excuse to go home.

Five hundred yards away in a small bright hot room, Maisie Gale, briefly Maisie York, briefly Maisie Denham, now Maisie McGrew, a girl of twenty-four in the full of her pregnancy, sat with her belly resting on her sweaty thighs on the bed . . . . Opposite her on a stiff chair sat Athen the Greek.

(Lessing 1966: 231–2; my omission marks)

With the switch of location Anton, Andrew and Jack cease to be primed. Our assumptions about these characters have changed and, significantly, this has been achieved without any reference being made to them at the point of change. The result is that we no longer assume them to be present in the current context.

STORED FRAMES AND THEIR RECALL

We saw in example 4 that after a frame switch the characters from the old frame are no longer present in the context that the reader is actively monitoring. They are not there in the 'small bright hot room' where the reader's attention is now centred.

At another level of consciousness, however, the reader is aware that Anton, Andrew and Jack are together at a meeting. This information remains stored away in the reader's mind as s/he reads about Maisie and Athen. The reader is aware of a stored frame as s/he actively monitors the action in the current frame. The characters in the stored frame are *bound* (Emmott 1989) to their context but are not primed as the reader's attention is not on this context.

There is always a possibility that a stored frame may be recalled. We might return to a location that we had temporarily left. In particular, we might re-enter the present after temporarily leaving it to witness some past action. *Frame recall* is of particular interest because, as the characters are bound to their location, we need only mention a small amount of information about the stored context in order to re-instate the full frame (see example 5 below).

Frame recall can account for certain pronouns which are otherwise difficult to explain. The following example shows a plural pronoun, 'they', which has an incomplete antecedent, just the singular form 'Jim'. The reader of the novel,[8] who, unlike the reader of this example, has read all of the preceding text, can identify 'they' as being Jim and Peter, in spite of the fact that the only character other than Jim who has been recently mentioned is Clark Mulligan.

5   *Frame recall hair*[9]
    and Clark Mulligan, who had been showing two weeks of science-fiction and horror pictures and had a full head of lurid images – *you can show it, man, but nobody makes you watch it* – walked out of the Rialto for the fresh air in the middle of a reel and thought he saw in the sudden black-out a man who was a wolf lope across the street, on a fierce errand, in an evil hurry to get somewhere (*nobody makes you watch the stuff, man*).

8

Housebreaking, Part Two
Jim stopped the car half a block away from the house. 'If only the god-
damned lights didn't go off.' They were both looking at the building's
blank facade, the curtainless windows behind which no figure moved, no
candle shone.

(Straub 1979: 279; Straub's italics)

In an earlier section of this novel, entitled 'Housebreaking, Part One', a frame
which had Jim and Peter as sole participants had been built up. This frame is
then stored away as we switch to a sequence of new frames in which Jim and
Peter are not present. The heading 'Housebreaking, Part Two' can be seen as
triggering the recall of the stored frame. We can also see the mention of items
of contextual information from the stored frame as being instrumental in the
recall. When we last encountered Jim and Peter in 'Housebreaking, Part One'
they were travelling in Jim's car. Reference to Jim and to the car is sufficient
to re-instate Peter in the context and to make intelligible the pronominal
reference. The frame recall is also made possible because it is anticipated. At
the end of 'Housebreaking, Part One' we leave Jim and Peter about to embark
on an escapade which will put them in danger of their lives and the reader is,
therefore, eagerly awaiting a continuation of this strand of the story.

The implications of example 5 for reference theory are that frame recall can
reprime characters into the current context so that 'group' pronominals can be
interpreted in the absence of a full antecedent (or, indeed, any recent
antecedent (Emmott 1989: 128)). A 'group' pronoun denotes everyone in a
specific frame. In interpreting the 'group' pronoun, recent mentions of
characters are ignored if these characters were part of a different frame, as is
the case with Clark Mulligan in example 5. This means that our 'group'
pronoun can be interpreted even though there is a 'wrong antecedent' in the
immediate vicinity.[10]

PRIMING AND FOCUSING

The frame, although a powerful monitor, has its limitations. It primes all of
those characters who are present in a fictional location, but it does not tell us
which of these characters the narrative is treating as the linguistic focus
(Sidner 1983a, b) of attention in a particular sentence. So the frame tells us
everyone who is in the group and can help us interpret 'group pronouns' but
does not tell us who is overt and who is covert at any one point. This is
significant because many pronouns refer not to the entire group of characters
who are present in a frame but to a 'sub-set' consisting of one or more of these
individuals. These are usually characters who have been mentioned recently
– in other words, characters who have recently been overt participants.

The **focuser** is a separate mental structure which monitors these recent
mentions. When a character is referred to lexically s/he moves into focus

(Sidner 1983a, b). We expect that a subsequent 'sub-set' pronoun will refer to the character(s) in focus. This expectation is based on the assumption that if another character had been intended then the reference would have been by a lexical item rather than by a pronoun. This means that instead of regarding the interpretation of 'sub-set' pronouns as involving a backward search for an antecedent, the antecedent prompts us to carry forward (Harris 1980; Ballmer 1981; Sidner 1983a, b; Emmott 1985, 1989, forthcoming) a default character construct. So in focusing, as in priming, endophoric reference is mediated by a mental monitor, although this monitor, the focuser, is only a short-term monitor compared with the frame. In both cases, the clue to interpreting the pronoun exists in the text, but the text does not have to be accessed at the point of processing because the clue has already been extracted from the text and stored in the mind.

CONCLUSION

The frame compensates for the lack of contextual detail in any one sentence of a text. This is achieved by bringing forward information about the fictional context from the earlier text. This allows us to interpret 'group' pronouns, distinguish flashback sentences from main narrative sentences, and be aware of the covert participants in any situation. We cannot read individual sentences or groups of sentences in isolation from the whole text. The mind acts as a bridge between different parts of the text. This bridging[11] is the essence of reading.

APPENDIX: TEXTS DISCUSSED OR REFERRED TO

Adams, D. (1987), *Dirk Gently's Holistic Detective Agency*, London: Pan.
Grant, J.S. (1989), *Enchanted Island*, Stornoway: Stornoway Gazette.
Halliday, M.A.K. and R. Hasan (1976), *Cohesion in English*, London: Longman.
Lessing, D. (1966), *A Ripple from the Storm*, London: Grafton.
O'Hara, J. (1986), 'Imagine kissing Pete', in *The Collected Stories of John O'Hara*, London: Pan, 109–57.
Straub, P. (1979), *Ghost Story*, London: Jonathan Cape.

NOTES

1   *Character construct* is my own term for Brown and Yule's (1983) 'mental representation'. In my view there are types of mental representation other than the character construct (e.g. the frame) so the term *mental representation* is too broad in this usage. The term *character construct* can be replaced by *entity construct* on occasions when objects rather than people are being discussed.
2   *Frame* is used widely in work on cognition. Minsky (1977) uses the term for general knowledge structures (i.e. schemata), whereas I have used the term for one particular kind of text-specific structure. Frederiksen (1986) uses the term 'narrative frame' for a text-specific monitor which charts place and time but not participant relations.
3   Fictional characters cannot actually be present in a particular place at a particular

time. They can only be represented as being so by means of the words on the page, the conventions of narrative and the reader's capacity to synthesize mentally information given by the text.

4 The aim of this analogy is to stress the difference between a location construct and a contextual construct (frame). The analogy should not, however, be taken too literally. Whilst a school register and, sometimes, a school timetable are written texts, a frame is a mental store existing beyond the text. Also, whereas a timetable specifies where a group of people ought to be, the frame monitors where they actually are.

5 Halliday and Hasan have of course reworked their theory of reference since 1976 (for example, in Halliday and Hasan 1989). Their 1976 work has, however, been so influential amongst discourse analysts that it still represents the dominant paradigm for many non-specialists in reference theory.

6 In Emmott (1989: 300) I suggested the term 'psychophoric reference' for this type of reference. Here I have decided still to use the name *endophora* since this keeps the terminology in line with work on reference theory in artificial intelligence.

7 These remarks are based on my own informal observations at Queen Alexandra College for the Blind, Birmingham; the Royal National Institute for the Blind Commercial Training College, London (now Loughborough); and the City and Hackney Talking Newspaper for the Blind, London.
   Whilst the reader is blind to the fictional world (for it is non-existent), s/he builds a mental model of that world which can be quasi-visual. Similarly a non-congenitally blind person may, whilst having no sight, build a quasi-visual image in their 'mind's eye'. Congenitally blind people seem also to use mental models but these models are unlikely to be quasi-visual.

8 We must as analysts approach the text as a reader would. Harris (1980) makes the same point.

9 The first paragraph begins mid-sentence in the original text. The subsequent heading 'Housebreaking, Part Two' is in large typeface in the original. The number 8, above this heading, also appears in the original, marking the new section.

10 Fox (1987a, b) notes similar data but does not offer a cognitive explanation.

11 Clark (1977) uses this term for inferences made across adjacent sentences. In my own work I am particularly interested in inferences made over longer stretches of text, for this shows that long-term mental storage is taking place.

11 Inferences in discourse comprehension

Martha Shiro

Although many scholars in different disciplines – logic, psychology, linguistics – have shown an interest in inferencing, very few studies concern themselves with the inferential process in connected discourse. Even then, the inferences studied are generally those made by the analyst him/herself or those generated by isolated sentences. Very few studies analyse the inferences actually drawn by different individuals.

One of the assumptions behind the analysis of isolated sentences is that the inferences drawn from a text will be the sum of the inferences drawn on its corresponding sentences. Another assumption is that skilful readers make basically the same inferences. Thus, variation in inferencing is attributed to differences in readers' abilities in text processing. However, as will be shown below, neither of these assumptions can be supported when actual readers are observed. The majority of the inferences drawn from a text are the result of combining textual elements with themselves and/or with contextual elements. Hence the interpretation of the whole differs from the interpretation of each element in isolation (i.e. taken out of context). Similarly, in addition to readers' abilities, there are other variables which account for different interpretations, for example the reader's previous knowledge, reading purpose, motivation or concentration.

A text takes shape (or different shapes) in the reader's mind during the reading process. A textual world is being built by combining textual information with inferences to form a coherent whole. In this view, inferences are understood as information that is necessarily added to textual information in order to create new meaning.

The analyst faces certain difficulties in the study of inferences. For example, inferences are elusive because once they have been drawn they do not appear to be inferences any more. It is difficult for the reader (and it is not required in the reading process) to discriminate between what is stated explicitly and what is inferred. The reader becomes aware of the need to draw an inference only when his/her interpretation requires unusual effort. A further problem for the analyst is that inferences are the outcome of textual interpretation but, by definition, they are not present *in* the text. The analyst must, therefore, investigate how the text is used as input by the reader to produce inferences and what role these inferences play in the processing of texts.

I am suggesting here that the most useful way, though paved with difficulties, is to study the inferential process as it occurs in real-life text processing instead of speculating about possible inferences drawn from made-up sentences or artificially contrived texts. This field of enquiry is full of unanswered questions and complex problems. In this chapter, I am going to raise some of these questions, mainly the problem of coherence and the distinction between the explicit and the implicit, discussing their place in the field of the comprehension of written text.

The discussion will be illustrated with examples taken from an experiment (see Shiro 1988), where a text was analysed in terms of readers' inferences. The readers were divided into six different groups on the basis of three variables: reading ability, native language and the task used to elicit the inferences. Regarding their reading ability, a group of eighteen expert readers and a group of nine less skilled readers gave their interpretations of the text. The native language of the expert readers was English, and the native language of the non-experts was Spanish. Half of the first group and all the second group answered comprehension questions based on the text. The other half of the first group went through a 'think aloud' process. In individual interviews, readers paraphrased sentence by sentence and answered questions asked by the interviewer as necessary for the analysis of the protocols. These verbal reports (see Cohen 1987; Shiro 1988) were compared with the other two groups' answers to the comprehension questions.

The text below was chosen because it was published in a widely read British journal (*The Listener*) and it did not seem to require any specialized knowledge on the reader's part. For the purposes of this research, the readers were given the whole text (which is only an extract of the article that appeared in *The Listener*), but the analysis was based only on the passage under the title Text 1, where each sentence was marked with a letter (A–F).

Echoes of a desert song
JUNE KNOX-MAWER

Crocodiles in the bath, visits to the royal harem and sheep's eyes for supper are just a few of the sights to be seen along the way in June Knox-Mawer's search for survivors of the British heyday in Arabia.

'The look-out reported a bunch of Arabs approaching by camel from the East . . .'

Yorkshire-born veteran of the Imperial Camel Corps Rory Moore launched into his first story reliving his first days as a very young Signals Corporal at the height of the First World War, helping to blow up the Turkish railway at Hedjaz.

'I saw their leader was an obvious European, dressed in Arab clothes, but with no attempt otherwise at disguise – a fair haired chap, blue eyes, rather slightly built, dressed in a brown "aba" over an immaculate white robe, the head-dress held down with the traditional band of black and gold . . .'

The mysterious European was, of course, to become known throughout the world as Lawrence of Arabia. Then he was simply a brilliant, if unconventional, intelligence officer, engaged in mustering the Arabs in a revolt against the Turks.

To Rory Moore, one of the minor mysteries about Lawrence was the whiteness of his linen. 'I don't know who did his laundry, but it was always impeccable.'

Text 1

(A) 'Schoolboys with red knees' was how Lawrence saw the young British soldiers. (B) Fortunately, Rory Moore was a highly observant schoolboy, remembering how his hero would settle down with one of the books he carried in his saddle-bags, whenever the camel-lines halted on the long treks between engagements. (C) Malory was Lawrence's favourite reading, as the group took shelter from the midday sun under their makeshift tents of blankets and signal-flags. (D) At one point Moore sprang up in horror as he saw one of the Arabs stealthily raising his rifle in Lawrence's direction. (E) But even as the bullet whizzed past his ear, Lawrence remained immersed in his book. (F) The Arab retrieved his sand-grouse for the supper and Corporal Moore learned another lesson of desert life.

THE EXPLICIT AND THE IMPLICIT

To distinguish inferences from what is stated, it is necessary to identify what is explicit and what implicit information in a text. Although most studies take this distinction for granted, no sufficiently accurate criteria can be found to differentiate the explicit content from the implicit import in a text.

Sperber and Wilson (1986) studied communication as an inferential process. They define inference as 'the process by which an assumption is accepted as true or probably true on the strength of the truth or probable truth of other assumptions. It is thus a form of fixation of belief' (Sperber and Wilson 1986: 68).

The quotation above clearly implies that communication is basically inferential, in other words, language used to communicate cannot be totally explicit. From this perspective, 'human intentional communication is never a mere matter of coding and decoding . . . . Linguistically encoded semantic representations are abstract mental structures which must be inferentially enriched before they can be taken to represent anything of interest' (Sperber and Wilson 1986: 174).

Thus, communication is achieved by producing and interpreting evidence and comprehension is brought about by making assumptions that result from the interaction between linguistic structure and non-linguistic information. Sperber and Wilson follow Grice's inferential theory of communication. They suggest that the interpretation of both explicit and implicit information requires inferencing. The addressee forms several assumptions based on a sentence (or, more precisely, a proposition). These assumptions can be combined to form other assumptions. Being assumptions, they carry a certain strength. In the following sentence:

(A)'Schoolboys with red knees' was how Lawrence saw the young British soldiers.

most readers thought that 'schoolboys with red knees' referred to the fact that the British soldiers were very young. However, as they are explicitly described as 'young British soldiers' in the same sentence, the expression 'schoolboys with red knees' stresses one particular aspect of their youth, probably their inexperience, the fact that they were immature. Moreover, some readers interpreted 'red knees' as referring to the fact that the British soldiers wore shorts and their knees were sunburnt. Others understood 'schoolboys with red knees' as one semantic unit and, therefore, 'red knees' made reference to the schoolboys whose knees were always red because they wore shorts.

The first point to be noted is that 'schoolboys with red knees' is open to at least two interpretations. In one, the expression is taken as one unit and, as a result, the 'red knees' belong to the schoolboys. In the other, the comparison between 'schoolboys with red knees' and the British soldiers has two parts: one in which the British soldiers are described as young and inexperienced like schoolboys and another part where 'red knees' is taken as an allusion to the soldiers' uniforms in the desert and the effect of the desert sun on their white skin. Both interpretations are possible within the text and it would be unnecessary to ask which reflects the writer's intention as they both fit the textual world.

The second point to be noted is that the assumption derived from the comparison between 'schoolboys' and the British soldiers is much stronger than the one derived from 'red knees'. This is due to the fact that the former is confirmed twice in the text: first, in the expression 'the *young* British soldiers'; and second, in sentence (B), where a British soldier, Rory Moore, is described as 'a highly observant schoolboy'.

It is worth pointing out that most readers agreed on the stronger assumption (i.e. that the British soldiers were young and inexperienced), whereas the weaker assumption derived from 'red knees' tended to vary from one reader to another.

Although Sperber and Wilson (1986) believe that all communication requires inferencing, they still distinguish between implicit and explicit information. They draw a line between the 'explicatures' and 'implicatures' based on an utterance. An assumption is an 'explicature' when it is derived from the explicit information in the text. They define an 'explicature' as follows:

An assumption communicated by an utterance 'U' is explicit if and only if it is a development of a logical form encoded by 'U'.

(Sperber and Wilson 1986: 182)

A logical form is a well formed formula, a structured set of constituents, which undergoes formal logical operations determined by its structure. Logical operations are truth preserving.

(Sperber and Wilson 1986: 72)

If my interpretation of this definition is correct, explicit information consists of the assumptions which can be logically deduced from the utterance. According to this definition, any assumption based on an utterance is either an explicature or an implicature. However, there can be degrees of explicitness. In the example above, the comparison between 'schoolboys' and the British soldiers is an explicature only if the verb 'saw' is thought to contain among its literal senses one that expresses some mental perception (e.g. become aware of something) or opinion forming, in addition to its meaning of visual perception.

Implicatures, as described by Sperber and Wilson, 'are recovered by reference to the speaker's manifest expectations about how her utterance should achieve optimal relevance' (Sperber and Wilson 1986: 195). This definition implies that the implicit information is interpreted on the basis of the addresser's intentions. However, it is problematic to describe the comprehender's behaviour in terms of the addresser's intentions as the entire comprehension process consists of the presumed understanding of these intentions.

As can be seen in the example analysed above and in Sperber and Wilson's definition of 'implicatures', there is no clear-cut division between the implicit and the explicit. However, it becomes clear that there are degrees of 'explicitness' or 'implicitness'. Therefore, instead of a distinction between the explicit and the implicit, it would be more appropriate to consider the difference as only a matter of degree, closer to the textual information when 'more explicit' and relying more on the reader's contextual knowledge when 'less explicit'.

Let us take an example from the text to illustrate this point:

(D) . . . one of the Arabs stealthily raising his rifle in Lawrence's direction . . .

All readers, without exception, interpreted 'raising his rifle' as 'shooting'. It is not explicitly stated that the Arab shot his rifle, and, in theory, a rifle can be raised for many different purposes. However, the reader is forced to draw this inference in this particular context and the assumption becomes so strong that it merges into the text and considerable effort is required to notice that it is not explicitly stated. As a matter of fact, the assumption is confirmed in the following sentence when 'the bullet' is mentioned, which will naturally lead to the inference that the bullet was shot from the Arab's rifle.

These assumptions are so strong that there is no need for confirmation in the text to accept them as valid. In the following example,

(B) . . . his hero would settle down with one of the books he carried in his saddle-bags, whenever the camel-lines halted on the long treks between engagements.

the expression 'settle down with one of the books' was interpreted as 'to read' and again, the inference is so tightly related to the textual information that it is difficult to detect that it is not explicitly stated.

What do these two examples have in common? In both, an event is stated and the reader is expected to infer the purpose of that event:

(a) 'raise his rifle' – what for? – to shoot.
(b) 'settle down with a book' – what for? – to read.

Let us compare these with another example taken from the text:

(E) But even as the bullet whizzed past his ear, Lawrence remained immersed in his book.

The readers offered different interpretations of this sentence. Some inferred that Lawrence trusted the Arabs and, as a result, he knew that the bullet was not meant for him. Others understood that he was concentrating so hard on his reading that he simply did not notice the shot. Others suggested both these alternatives as their interpretation.

Several conclusions can be drawn from these inferences. In the first place, although the readers' interpretations varied, basically in three different directions, they all had something in common. All the inferences tried to explain *why* Lawrence 'remained immersed in his book' and did not move when the bullet flew near him. This information falls into the category of 'non-event' because it states what did not happen or what continued the way it was. To express that something has not changed tends to be evaluative in discourse (see Labov and Waletzky 1967, Grimes 1975, for the difference between 'event' and 'non-event' and their relation to evaluation). Evaluation in discourse tends to be accompanied by the 'basis for the evaluation' (see Hoey 1983). If the 'basis for the evaluation' is not explicit, it needs to be inferred. Similarly, it was found in other cases in the sample (see Shiro 1988) that the readers tended to look for a purpose for events and for a reason for evaluations, when these are not explicitly stated in the text. Therefore, it seems to be the case that the type of inference drawn on certain textual information depends on the 'function' of that information in the text, that is, how the information is related to the rest of the text.

In the second place, it is important to point out that, even though some readers chose *one* alternative for their interpretation, other readers kept *two* alternatives for their inferences. These alternatives – that Lawrence did not fear an Arab attack and that he was concentrating too hard to notice what was going on – are contradictory because one implies that Lawrence was aware of what was going on around him and the other implies that he was not. However, this contradiction does not seem to disturb the readers and it appears that they keep both assumptions unless, as the reading proceeds, one (or both) is rejected on the basis of some counter-evidence found in the text. It can be concluded, then, that readers can maintain parallel interpretations of the same textual element.

It can be assumed, then, that the explicit information is closer to the propositional content of an utterance. The implicit information is not confined to utterances. It can be recovered from several, as is often the case, or from only parts of an utterance combined with some contextual element (i.e. the reader's world knowledge). The implicit import is freer from the linguistic conventions that govern the structure of the utterance than is the explicit content. Thus, the propositional content of an utterance would be its main explicature. This would not mean that the processing of the propositional content does not require a considerable amount of interpretation (disambiguation, reference assignment and enrichment, as Sperber and Wilson suggest). In addition, there is an extraordinarily vast area of information that a reader can process while reading a text, which would constitute the implicit information.

To summarize, my suggestion has been that, even though there is a distinction between explicit and implicit information, the difference is a matter of degree. Comprehension of any text requires inferencing to some extent but some texts require more processing than others and are, therefore, more implicit. Thus, 'explicit' and 'implicit' are textual features. A text cannot be more explicit for one reader and more implicit for another. Readers only differ in the ease with which they derive meaning from these texts. Likewise, the meaning that the reader gleans from the text constitutes the textual world, which will show certain variations that can be explained either as a result of ambiguity caused by the combination of the textual elements or as a consequence of variation in the readers' interpretations caused by differences in the readers' characteristics.

COHESION AND COHERENCE

We have already seen that most existing studies of inferencing tend to deal with assumptions generated from single sentences. This poses a theoretical problem due to the fact that an indefinite number of inferences can be drawn from an isolated sentence. However, this is not the way it actually happens when a text is being processed. Therefore, it can be assumed that inferences drawn on the basis of a series of sentences which jointly form a text are limited by the context (in both its senses: co-text – see Brown and Yule, 1983 – and context of situation). On the other hand, the text formed by sentences generates inferences which would not have been made had each sentence been taken individually.

In the text above, the inference 'Lawrence did not trust the British soldiers' could easily be drawn from sentence (A). Nevertheless, it was not mentioned as a possible inference because it did not fit into the textual world. On the other hand, the question of whether Lawrence trusted the Arabs was mentioned, in spite of the fact that this inference cannot be derived from any particular sentence. It is probably activated by some readers' previous knowledge when it is needed to explain information contained in sentences (D) and (E) and solved in an unexpected way in sentence (F). Thus, this inference, together with many others, is derived from the combination of several sentences in the text.

A more striking example of inferences beyond sentence boundaries is derived from the combination of sentences (D), (E) and (F). In sentence (F), the interpretation of 'his sand-grouse for the supper' forces the reader to reconsider the assumption that Lawrence's life was in danger and to conclude that the peaceful Arab was only hunting.

The fact that the text is coherent results to a large extent from the reader's ability to infer the relations beyond sentence level that keep the text together. Halliday and Hasan (1976) suggest that texts possess 'texture', namely, they hang together: 'A text has texture, and this is what distinguishes it from something that is not a text. It derives this texture from the fact that it functions as a unity with respect to its environment' (Halliday and Hasan 1976: 2). Texture is the result of the cohesion of a text in addition to its register. Halliday and Hasan claim that cohesion is formed by the formal ties which bind one sentence to another: reference, substitution, ellipsis, conjunction and lexical cohesion. These ties are semantic or lexicogrammatical. On closer examination, however, the coherence of the text is not guaranteed by the presence of these cohesive ties:

> I bought a Ford. A car in which President Wilson rode down the Champs Elysées was black. Black English has been widely discussed. The discussions between the presidents ended last week. A week has seven days. Every day I feed my cat. Cats have four legs. The cat is on the mat. Mat has three letters.
>
> (Brown and Yule 1983: 197)

Although there is apparent cohesion (mainly lexical reiteration) in the text above, it is difficult to accept it as coherent.

On the other hand, the following is a very well known example of a text where there are no explicit cohesive ties but which is coherent:

A: The phone is ringing.
B: I'm in the bath.

> (Widdowson 1978b)

In opposition to Halliday and Hasan's view, Morgan and Sellner (1980) argue that formal cohesion is a natural effect of textual coherence rather than the cause. On the same lines, Urquhart (1975) takes Grice's Co-operative Principle as the basis for text processing:

> Grice's Relevance maxim is essential when we attempt a process analysis. The reader must assume that what he has facing him is a 'real' text, i.e. a

real piece of communication. He must then assume that any utterance in the text is relevant in the context of surrounding utterances. He will often have to *make* the utterance relevant by supplying information of his own, etc.

(Urquhart 1975: 60)

The following illustrates this point:

John and Bill were sailing on Mystic Pond, and they saw a coffee can floating in the distance. Bill said, 'Let's go over and pick it up.' When they reached it, John picked it up and looking inside said, 'Wow, there are rocks in the can.' Bill said, 'Oh, I guess somebody wanted the can to float there.'

(Collins *et al.* 1980: 387)

This text was given to several subjects, who, apparently, did not question the coherence of the text, even though it contains information that could easily contradict our expectations of how cans usually float. Instead, they tried to find a suitable explanation for the passage because, despite the fact that they were participating in an experiment, they assumed that the text represented a 'real' piece of communication.

It follows, then, that the coherence of a text cannot be described independently of the reader.

Apparently, the dichotomy cohesion/coherence is fraught with the same problems as those described in relation to the explicit/implicit. It seems that the main difficulty is to decide how much is found in the text and how much in the readers' minds. If it is supposed that the coherence of a text comes about when the reader provides the missing links to build the textual world, is cohesion independent of the reader's processing ability? Can the cohesive ties of a text be interpreted merely on the basis of formal considerations?

We shall take reference assignment as an example of the relation between cohesive ties and understanding. The following examples illustrate some problematic aspects:

1 John and Mary went for a walk because he needed it.
2 ?John and Paul went for a walk because he needed it.
3 John lent Paul some money because he needed it.
4 ?John wrote Paul a letter because he needed it.

In example 1 there is no doubt who needed the walk, but example 2 is so ambiguous that it is unlikely to appear in any real context. The interpretation of 'he' in example 3 seems obvious (it should refer to Paul), but there can be cases where the context will yield a different interpretation (e.g. that John needs the money in the future and the only way he can save it is if he lends it to someone). Example 4 is again ambiguous and it is too obscure unless it is disambiguated by the context where it appears. Thus, reference assignment is more complex and more demanding on the reader than it would seem from Halliday and Hasan's analysis.

Is, then, coherence a textual feature or is it in the mind of the reader? What distinguishes a coherent text from an incoherent sequence of sentences? Can an authentic text be incoherent or do incoherent texts only exist when a linguist invents them to illustrate a point? When we call a text coherent, is it from the addressee's point of view, or can it be from the addresser's point of view? Is a text incoherent when it is not understood and must be made more explicit? Would the same text become coherent for an addressee who shares more knowledge with the addresser? If a text is always coherent from the producer's point of view and can vary in coherence from one reader to another, we can assume that coherence is not a textual characteristic. It is rather the result of the interpretative process and as such it depends on the relation between reader and text. An immediate implication of this assumption is that no authentic text is incoherent. It should always means something for the speaker/writer. It is the degree of successful interpretation which makes a text more or less coherent from the addressee's point of view.

This issue takes us to the question of whether the reader recovers meaning from the text or whether s/he looks for the writer's intention. When connected discourse is interpreted, a combination of different factors comes into play and these factors are difficult to separate. As written discourse is verbally expressed, the linguistic factors are obviously important but not sufficient. As we have seen, language does not offer the possibility of being totally explicit. Therefore, the reader must also use other abilities to understand what is meant. When using these processing skills, the reader should start out with the assumption that the text which s/he is confronting makes sense, is meaningful, is connected in a certain purposeful way, and is coherent, as suggested by Urquhart (1975) above. It follows, then, that the reader will assume an intention behind the text which s/he will try to recover using all the available clues, linguistic or other. Therefore, the reader's interpretation results from decoding the linguistic signs that appear in the text combined with other processing strategies based on his/her world knowledge and other cognitive abilities. Thus, given the differences that exist between individuals and the variety of processes involved in understanding a text, the outcome of the reader's comprehension will not coincide totally with the writer's original intention.

In the extract taken from 'Echoes of a desert song' the importance of sentence (F) is twofold. In the first place, the information in the first clause changes the interpretation of the previous sentences. Second, the conclusion that 'Corporal Moore learned another lesson of desert life' seems to justify the whole anecdote. But what is meant by this statement? The readers' interpretations of this statement varied significantly:

(a) One should not jump to conclusions.
(b) You need to catch your food to eat in the desert.
(c) You should not think that somebody is going to be killed.
(d) Things are not what they seem to be.
(e) Life in the desert is different.

Most readers expressed their inference as a general statement that included some recommendation (probably because of the presence of the lexical item 'lesson'). However, the content of their inferences differs. Are all these inferences 'acceptable'? Which is nearer what the writer intended the readers to understand?

Furthermore, different reading purposes yield different interpretations of the same text. Therefore, there can even be variation among the interpretations resulting from several readings of the same text carried out by one individual at different times with different purposes. If the text analysed above is read for a second time, the reading process will differ from the first. Even with the same purpose, a second reading cannot repeat the first because the reader's expectations change the balance between anticipation and retrospection (see Iser 1978: 149).

CONCLUSIONS AND IMPLICATIONS

The discussion above can be summed up in the following points:

1 Inferences result from connecting meaning beyond the sentence level. Apparently they result from relating a sentence or parts of a sentence with other sentences in the text and/or previous knowledge.

2 Inferring implies supplying *missing links*. As Thorndike states (quoted in Urquhart 1981: 1): 'understanding a paragraph is like solving a problem in mathematics. It consists in selecting the right elements of the situation and putting them together in the right relations.'

3 A large amount of textual meaning is constructed in this way.

4 Inferences are the primary result of the interaction between the reader and the text. Therefore, they are not constant (they vary, within limits, from reader to reader), they are elusive – difficult to analyse – because they are mental constructs, but, because they are based on a text, they can be taken as more or less acceptable, coherent or fitting into the textual world. The reader's understanding of a text depends on how appropriate his/her inferences are. However, we all know that there is no such thing as complete understanding, only levels of understanding. So a reader can interact with a text and fulfil a certain purpose without drawing *all* the inferences that would, to the analyst, seem necessary for the interpretation of the text. Moreover, some readers infer information that other readers do not find in the same text. It can be concluded that there are two important extratextual aspects that affect inferencing:

(a) *reader variability*:
   experience in reading;
   sufficient knowledge of the world to understand the text.

(b) *reading purpose*: which will determine the depth of the processing reached in a text. It is not the same to read for pleasure, for information, for an examination, for criticism, for survival, etc.

It is possible for a reader to make an inference at a certain point in the text and discard it as the reading proceeds. One can easily imagine that the inferences made *during* the reading process will not always coincide with the end product. The point being made here is that the study of inferences should focus on what actually happens when 'real' readers are faced with 'real' texts. Elsewhere (Shiro 1988) I have followed this approach and obtained interesting results related to issues in comprehension like:

the ways in which readers combine linguistic and contextual information in text processing;
the degree to which the interpretation of a text varies from one reader to another;
problems with the acceptability of different interpretations;
comparison between inferences in first and second language.

The main argument of this chapter has been that inferencing should be studied from the 'comprehender's' perspective, as it is the 'comprehender' who is faced with the problem of drawing the appropriate inferences from a certain text. Furthermore, when studying comprehension, there is little interest in speculating on the possible inferences that might be drawn from an artificially contrived decontextualized sentence because, as has been argued, inferences are generated and constrained by the text as a whole.

12 Narratives of science and nature in popularizing molecular genetics

Greg Myers

Today the BBC radio news reported that a study showed that a high-fat diet actually prolonged life. On hearing this, some listeners may have breathed a sigh of relief (it was broadcast just before Christmas and the attendant overeating). Others may have been sceptical. Others may have wondered just what form the study took. But there was no time for that in a one-minute report. Every day the newspaper or radio news asks us to believe new pieces of scientific knowledge like this. People may believe and act on some of them: parents turn their babies over to reduce the risk of cot death; cooks use more olive oil to increase their intake of mono-saturated fats; or green consumers boycott deodorant sprays that contain CFCs that might harm the ozone layer. Or they may doubt what they hear, despite the scientific label on the facts: sheep farmers may remain sceptical about the uptake of Chernobyl radiation by their lambs, and diabetics may refuse to accept assurances about genetically engineered insulin being identical in its effects to the animal insulin they had been taking.

Our attitudes towards the authority of scientific facts are shaped in part by the discourses in which we encounter them. I will argue here that facts in popular science are endowed with an authority they did not always have within the specialist discourse from which they emerged. In the BBC report, for instance, the finding of the study was separated from any methods or sample that could limit the claim. This happens, not because of any desire to misrepresent, but because the narrative style of much of popular science – television documentaries, newspaper features, popular science magazine articles – emphasizes the immediate encounter of the scientist with nature,[1] whereas the narrative style of most scientific research reports emphasizes the concepts and techniques through which the scientist conceives of and delimits nature. Thus, despite the sense of impersonality and abstraction they may convey to non-scientists, scientific texts do, in fact, foreground the human and social elements of science.[2] One effect is that popular science texts do not suggest how scientific facts could be questioned or modified. That is one reason why non-scientists can have such difficulty in understanding scientific controversy or changes in scientific thinking.

In an earlier study (Myers 1990a: ch. 5) I compared scientific articles in

Nature and *Proceedings of the National Academy of Sciences* with popular-izations of the same findings by the same authors published in *New Scientist* and *Scientific American*. I also looked at the revisions made by editors in the scientists' submitted drafts. I argued that many of the linguistic differences between research articles and popularizations, and many of the revisions made by editors, could be described in terms of contrasting underlying narratives.

> Textual differences in narrative structure, in syntax, and in vocabulary help define two contrasting views of science. The professional articles create what I call a *narrative of science*; they follow the argument of the scientist, arrange time into a parallel series of simultaneous events all supporting their claim, and emphasize in their syntax and vocabulary the conceptual structure of the discipline. The popularizing articles, on the other hand, present a sequential *narrative of nature* in which the plant or animal, not the scientific activity, is the subject, the narrative is chrono-logical, and the syntax and vocabulary emphasize the externality of nature to scientific practices.
>
> (Myers 1990a: 142)[3]

For instance, the title of an article by Geoffrey Parker in *Evolution*, a specialized scientific journal, was 'The reproductive behavior and the nature of sexual selection in *Scatophaga stercoraria* L. (Diptera. Scatophagidae), IX. Spatial distribution of fertilization rates and evolution of male search strategy within the reproductive area'. The editor gave Parker's *New Scientist* article the title 'Sex around the cow-pats'.

I was looking at scientists who could say they were studying hormonal controls and environment, game-theoretical approaches to sexual selection and co-evolution; that is, they could present their work entirely in terms of scientific concepts. But for the purposes of popularization, they could be presented as studying garter snakes, or dungflies, or butterflies and vines. For their work, the neat dichotomy between a narrative of science and a narrative of nature worked pretty well.

But this neatness concealed some limitations in my narrative analysis. For one thing, I had chosen texts with two main kinds of actors – scientists and organisms. We could find much more complex narratives with other kinds of actors involved – for instance, in reports that link scientific innovations to social concerns.

Similarly, I was looking at a limited set of events. Every popularization needs a story, but I was looking only at discovery stories involving observa-tion in the field or laboratory.[4] There are other devices for making science news – personalities, oddities, extremes of scale and, most important, links to defence or medicine.

In my earlier study, I deliberately limited my selection of popularizations to those written by the scientific researchers themselves. That way I could avoid accusations that some ignorant journalist was simply misinterpreting the scientist's work. But that meant I was looking only at *Scientific American* and *New Scientist* publications that are primarily aimed at and read by people with some scientific education. So, in my comparisons, the popularizations may not have seemed very popular. Most of us get our information about science from newspapers, general-interest magazines, or television documentaries, publications where science stories have to compete with other sorts of news for editorial space and readers' attention.

More fundamentally, I limited my definition of narrative to sequences of events that could be identified in the structure of the text, that is, in surface features. This definition would not apply to most expository writing, nor to the complex stories within stories of some news articles. We need to recognize at least two levels, as do most approaches to narrative.[5] The textual organization I was tracing is called by some approaches to narrative the **plot**; this plot may carry another series of events called the **story**. For instance, the plot of a detective novel follows the detective in his/her search for clues, but the point is to reconstruct the story of the crime investigated. To take a scientific example, Stephen Jay Gould's *Wonderful Life* explicitly marks its plot about scientists with sections treated as the acts of a drama, while his story deals with Cambrian life forms.

Many of the devices I described are common to all sorts of popularization. But the focus on the narrative of organisms may well be a feature of those scientific fields that can be made into natural history. Other fields may require other narratives. In this chapter I would like to look at popularizations of another area of biology, one where the popularizer cannot focus on the organisms themselves. I have been analysing various textual features of a collection of about 100 texts published between 1977 and 1987, all related in some way to one important discovery in molecular genetics.[6] Here I will look at two major scientific events, choosing for each of them a research article, an article in a magazine devoted to popular science and a news report in a general-interest publication.

The first of these stories was the discovery in 1987 that the genes in higher organisms could be split, with sections of nonsense message intervening in the code, sections that have to be cut out of the RNA before it is translated into a protein. Several different groups reported aspects of this discovery more or less simultaneously; I will look at one of these first reports, an article by Pierre Chambon and his collaborators in *Nature* (BMC). I will compare it to an article in *Scientific American* (*SA*), also written by Pierre Chambon, and to one of the first newspaper reports, by Harold Schmeck in *The New York Times* (*NYT*). The discovery required a major change in thinking about genetics and evolution. But this change in scientific concepts was hard to present as news to a public that never thought genes were continuous, so they would not be surprised to be told they were in fact split. Some popularizations showed pictures of the chickens, yeast cells and other organisms from which the nucleic acids had been taken. But the discovery was at the molecular level, not at the level of whole organisms, so it could not be presented in the natural history narrative I had studied before.

One of the researchers involved in the discovery of split genes, Alec Jeffreys, later continued work on one kind of intervening sequence, looking for sequences that were highly variable between members of a species. In 1985 he and his group announced that they had found a probe that would locate many highly variable regions, and that these regions, once located, could serve as the basis for DNA 'fingerprints'. I will consider the original article in *Nature* by Jeffreys and his group (JWT), a popularization in *New Scientist* (*NS*) by Jeremy Cherfas, and a news report in *The Economist* (*EC*). There have of course been a number of other popularizations as DNA fingerprinting has become a widely used technique in forensic science, immigration cases, pedigree research, diagnosis of hereditary diseases and research on evolution. Here the journalistic problem was different. This was not just a shift of scientific concepts – though it was that too – it was a new technique touching on many aspects of society.

As in the earlier study of biologists' texts, I will compare the scientific and popular articles on three levels, looking at organization, syntax and vocabulary.

ORGANIZATION

Like most scientific research articles, the *Nature* articles considered here open by situating the claim within the existing literature on a topic.[7] Unlike most articles, though, they give an answer that goes beyond the question posed in their introductions: Chambon introduces the topic of cell differentiation, but makes a claim about split genes, while Jeffreys introduces the topic of DNA polymorphisms, but goes on to make a claim for DNA fingerprinting.

We can see the re-orientation of the BMC article in its introduction. The first paragraph is about the usefulness of ovalbumin in pursuing the issue of cell differentiation. The first three sentences of the second paragraph describe the recombinant DNA technology used for the study. Only in the last sentence of this section does it come to the main claim, that the sequences are split.

> Unexpectedly, we have found that the DNA sequences complementary to ovalbumin mRNA are split into several fragments in oviduct DNA, and that the same peculiar ovalbumin gene organization is present in laying hen oviduct and erythrocyte DNA.

> (BMC, *Nature*)

This marks a sudden turn from the rest of the introduction. Since the organization is the same in both kinds of cells studied, the research does not lead the authors to a claim about cell differentiation issue. But it does enable them to make a claim that is relevant to research on RNA processing mechanisms.

Perhaps because of this shift of focus, the BMC article does not follow the conventional format of introduction–methods–results–discussion. But within each section its organization is more conventional, with the arrangement of a number of actions into a structure emphasizing their simultaneity. This is best seen in the section of the article where they were presenting their novel claim that the gene is split. The paragraph is highly technical, but this passage gives some idea of how a number of experiments involving different kinds of fragments are juxtaposed, on the autoradiograph gel and in the text:

> Irrespective of the combination of restriction endonucleases, there was always one fragment which hybridised strongly to *Pst*B, but not to *Pst*A or *Hinf*A: band 'b' for the *Eco*RI/*Hin*dIII digest (compare lanes 1, 4, 6 and 8) and for the *Hin*dIII/*Pst*I digest (lane 3, hybridisation with *Pst*A, *Pst*B, and *Hinf*A probes are not shown) band 'c' for the *Eco*RI/*Pst*I digest (compare lanes 2, 5, 7, and 9). From the hybridisation pattern with P*st*A and *Hinf*A, it is clear that . . . But . . . Since . . . therefore . . . But . . . therefore.
>
> (BMC, *Nature*)

This dense prose (readable only with the figure of the autoradiograph) results from the assembling of a number of different results to close off possible objections that could arise (and that probably had arisen in conference presentations of the results before publication).[8]

In his *Scientific American* article, in contrast, Chambon represents these experiments in a sequence. The *Scientific American* passage corresponding to the research article sentence I have just quoted stresses chronological links

> Breathnach, Jean-Louis Mandel and I began to map the ovalbumin sequence in the chicken genome. By probing the genome with restriction enzymes that had target sites both in the complementary DNA and in the chromosomal DNA we could relate corresponding sites in the two DNA's to each other. In this way we found, for example, that the chromosomal *Eco*RI fragment we had designated *b* includes the sequence coding for the first 500 nucleotides of the messenger RNA, whereas the sequence coding for the last part of the messenger molecule is in fragment *a*. We went on to develop a detailed restriction-enzyme map of the gene.
>
> (*Scientific American*)

Professor Chambon is well aware of the difference in structure between his research articles and his popularizations. He noted in an interview that new research assistants usually had to be taught that in writing a research article, they were constructing an argument, not telling the whole story in chronological order. Perhaps they must then learn when they write popularizations how to tell it as a story again.

One change that often occurs in the narrative between the research article and the popularization is that the researchers become actors and the claim becomes a discovery event. For instance, in his *Scientific American* article, Chambon gives his group's response to the results as they developed: 'To our great surprise we saw several bands on the film' (*Scientific American*). In the *New York Times* article, in contrast, the discovery is stressed at the outset. The discoverers are mentioned only a third of the way through. And the techniques that make up most of the *Scientific American* article are mentioned only in passing, and in a last short anticlimactic paragraph. Mentioning or not mentioning the techniques used could have been significant in the political climate of the time, when recombinant techniques were the subject of public controversy about possible hazards. Journalists might play down such technical matters, but the researchers themselves lost no chance to stress that these techniques made their findings possible.

These same sorts of changes in organization occur between research articles and popularizations on DNA fingerprinting. Again, the introduction to the research article in *Nature* stresses a claim different from that for which it became famous – it does not mention DNA fingerprinting at all. The abstract of the JWT article gives a sense of its movement from problem to application:

> The human genome contains many dispersed tandem-repetitive 'mini-satellite' regions detected via a shared 10–15 base pair 'core' sequence similar to the generalized recombination symbol (chi) of *Escherichia coli*. Many minisatellites are highly polymorphic due to allelic variation in repeat copy number in the minisatellite. A probe based on a tandem-repeat of the core sequence can detect many highly variable loci simultaneously and can provide an individual-specific DNA 'fingerprint' of general use in human genetic analysis.

The scientific issue is foregrounded. But with a commercially applicable discovery like this, it is important to establish the researchers' awareness of the implications of their finding – otherwise someone else could patent it. JWT actually present a whole series of related findings, leading from the sequence itself, to the discovery of the probe, its application to a library and to a pedigree study. So this article does not just present simultaneous results supporting one claim. Within each section, though, it is structured like the BMC article, with the juxtaposition of tightly linked statements, not in idealized chronological order but in a structure of argument.

There were two *New Scientist* articles on the work of Jeffreys' group soon after its publication. One, by Mark Ridley, mentions the possibility of a test for pedigrees only in passing. It is reporting the findings in the same way that popularizers had reported split genes, within the domain of evolutionary concepts. Another article, by Jeremy Cherfas, makes more of the fingerprinting. It follows the structure of the *Nature* article closely, almost paragraph by paragraph, but begins and ends with the possible applications. The title, 'Geneticists develop DNA fingerprinting', emphasizes the activity of the scientists (and also highlights the striking use of 'fingerprinting', to which I will return).

One early report on the technique in a general magazine was in *The Economist* (where contributions are not attributed). It starts with the evident need for a test to distinguish individuals: 'Every human being is unique, but intangibly so.' Three paragraphs are devoted to this as a problem. Then Jeffreys is introduced to solve the problem. The relation of basic and applied research suggested by the original report has been reversed – for Jeffreys the discovery of a probe, while he was doing purely scientific work, led to the application in an identity test, while in *The Economist* account the need for the test leads to the probe. In fact, Jeffreys stressed in all his interviews that he had been doing 'pure' research when he hit this commercial jackpot. So just as Chambon's emphasis on recombinant DNA techniques might be related to public fears at the time, so Jeffreys' defence of pure science might be seen as reflecting a time of cutbacks in funding and emphasis on commercial applications.

SYNTAX

There have been many studies of the syntax of scientific articles, but most take the social function of these texts as a given, rather than as a topic for investigation.[9] I am particularly interested in those features that seem to vary with different audiences, between the specialized scientific articles and the popularizations. We might begin with active and passive voice, since it is a heavily studied feature and we would expect to find more passive sentences in the scientific articles.[10] Indeed, in the earlier study I showed how the editors of the popular magazines would rewrite the researchers' drafts to make the passive sentences active where possible.

The contrast in grammatical voice between research articles and popularizations is not as striking as we might expect. There are active sentences with personal subjects in the research articles:

> Unexpectedly, we have found that the DNA sequences complementary to ovalbumin mRNA are split into several fragments . . .
>
> (BMC, *Nature*)

> We show here that the myoglobin 33-bp repeat is indeed capable of detecting other human minisatellites . . .
>
> (JWT, *Nature*)

If we look at a wider range of research articles in this field, we will see that such sentences occur rarely, but occur at crucial points in the introduction and discussion, where the authors state their main claims. Similarly, there are many passives in the popularizations, even after the editors have gone over them. But the typical pattern is that a paragraph describing technical work begins in the active and then switches to the passive, so the personal work of the scientists is still foregrounded. 'We *did so* [found the ovalbumin gene] by applying a "blotting" technique devised by E. M. Southern of the University of Edinburgh. The DNA fragments on the gel *were denatured* and then *were transferred* . . .' This suggests that the location of shifts in grammatical voice may tell us more than a simple comparison of the numbers of passive and active sentences. The overall narrative of the research articles emphasizes the entities studied, so the explicit mention of the researchers marks an important act. Similarly, the focus on the researchers in the popularizations is maintained even when they are describing general techniques.

I have suggested that the organization of each section of the research articles involves juxtaposition of several related statements into a simultaneous order of argument, while the popularizations tend to organize the statements into a sequence. The related observation on the syntactic level is that the research articles tend to use complex sentences, and complex phrases that bring a number of clauses into the same sentence, asserting them at once. Similar (though not exactly the same) content may be conveyed in the popularizations with a series of simpler sentences. We can see this by looking for a complex sentence in a research article and comparing it to a corresponding part of the popularization, a comparison that is easier where the popularizer follows the form of the research article, as Cherfas does.

> This core region in each cloned minisatellite suggests strongly that this sequence might help to generate minisatellites by promoting the initial tandem duplication of unique sequence DNA and/or by stimulating the subsequent unequal exchanges required to amplify the duplication in a minisatellite. As polymorphic minisatellites may also be recombination hotspots (see above), it might be significant that the core sequence is similar in length and in G content to the *chi* sequence, a signal for generalized recombination in *E. coli*.
>
> (JWT, *Nature*)

> This core identity of the different minisatellites would certainly help to promote reduplication of the region by unequal exchange. It might also actively promote recombination. Certainly the sequence resembles a region called *chi* found in the DNA of the bacterium *Escherichia coli*. The *chi* region is believed to be the signal that causes recombination . . .
>
> (*New Scientist*)

There are many differences here – for instance, Cherfas fills in background information, and omits some evidence and some qualifications. But for our purposes, in looking for a narrative, what is interesting is that Cherfas separates out some statements in JWT's complex sentences, so that they appear one after another in shorter sentences.

This last example involved unpacking clauses. Popularizers also unpack the nominalized verbs that are characteristic of scientific writing.

> Briefly, this involves *cleavage* of the DNA with various restriction endonucleases, *fractionation* of the fragments by electrophoresis, their *transfer* to nitrocellulose sheets, *hybridization* to a specific probe labelled in vitro by nick-translation to high specific activity and *location* of the gene fragments by autoradiography.
>
> (BMC, *Nature*)

We *cleaved* samples of DNA . . .
We *subjected* the fragmented chromosomal DNA to electrophoresis on an
agarose gel . . .
The DNA fragments on the gel were denatured and then *were transferred* . . .
Next *the probe was applied*: ovalbumin complementary DNA, strongly
labelled with a radioactive isotope, was poured over the filter paper.
Probe molecules . . . became annealed . . .
Autoradiography *revealed the location* of the labelled probe.

(*Scientific American*)

The heavily nominalized scientific style clearly has the advantage of economy.
The BMC article is not asking other researchers to imagine a series of actions,
but is checking off the techniques used, for comparison with other lines of
research on the topic. But when Chambon rewrites it for a general audience,
he turns the nouns into verbs, so the effect is of a series of actions. The *Nature*
article presents the selection of techniques, while the *Scientific American*
article presents a series of steps necessary to pursue the gene.

There are other syntactic patterns that might be related to the narrative of
nature. For instance, in my earlier study I noted the tendency for the
popularizations to use question and answer patterns (a traditional technique in
pedagogical literature). But there were few of them here. I have also noted the
much wider range of cohesive devices in the popularizations. These strengthen
the sense of following the chain of a continuous story, while the research
articles could be thought of as a construction of blocks, with the connections
filled in by the informed readers.

VOCABULARY

We have already seen examples in which the popularization substitutes for
some scientific term an explanation or a rough equivalent in the general
vocabulary. Researchers who write popularizations often have to battle with
editors to try to preserve some of their specialized terminology. As with any
translation, associated meanings can be lost as equivalents are found for
specialized terms. The coining and acceptance of a term is a crucial step in
forming a disciplinary concept. For instance, when JWT uses the terms
'heterozygousity' and 'hypervariable region', the popularizers' explanations
or substitutes may subtly alter the sequence of information.

. . . the mean heterozygousity of human DNA is low ($\approx$0.001 per base
pair). . . . Genetic analysis in man could be simplified considerably by the
availability of probes for hypervariable regions of human DNA showing
multiallelic variation and correspondingly high heterozygousities.

(JWT, *Nature*)

Human DNA does not vary much between different members of the species:
roughly 999 out of every 1000 base pairs (the letters of the genetic code) are

the same in two unrelated individuals. There are, however, some regions that seem to be more variable, with a different structure in different individuals. . . . All of these so-called hypervariable regions have a similar structure.

(New Scientist)

Of every 1,000 'letters' of DNA, 999 are the same in two different people. Dr Alec Jeffreys and his colleagues at the University of Leicester have now found a way to seek out the few parts of the genetic code that vary greatly among individuals. They found that many such 'hypervariable' regions are similar . . .

(Economist)

There may be a slight difference between saying that DNA varies, and saying it has a low heterozygousity. Making it into a ratio, given in a certain form, treats it as an inherent part of the description of DNA, the way litres are part of the description of an engine.

The terminology plays a role in narrative because many of the terms are unpacked in the form of narratives of laboratory techniques. For instance, near the end of the BMC article, the authors mention some possible implications for the use of bacterial systems in biotechnology, and say that they may require the use of bacterial regulatory elements with 'ds cDNA'. The equivalent of this abbreviation is given by a whole sentence in Chambon's *Scientific American* article:

The ovalbumin messenger RNA was copied (by means of a viral enzyme, reverse transcriptase) to form a complementary strand of DNA, which in turn was copied (by means of a DNA polymerase) to form a double-strand DNA – in effect an artificial ovalbumin gene made by working backward from messenger RNA to DNA.

(Scientific American)

The same sort of encapsulation of a narrative in a term happens with such terms as *hybridization* or for that matter, *popularization*.

One term that makes a process into an entity, *DNA fingerprint*, is clearly a key in the JWT article. It seems like the sort of catchy journalistic name that might be added in the popularizations. But in fact Alec Jeffreys introduced it at the outset. There have been other processes in molecular biology with similar names, but this is the first to have entered the general vocabulary. Just as Jeffreys recognized early on that he had a marketable application, he realized it would need a non-technical name with the right associations. 'Probe for hypervariable regions' would not do.

CONCLUSION

My argument here is that the different styles of research articles and popularizations construct different views of science. Scientists see their work as much more tentative and mediated than does the public. It might be argued that the sort of authority accorded to a concept like *split genes* does not matter very much – it remains in the realm of specialized concepts, and does not affect those people who do not care about evolutionary theory or genetics. The same cannot be said about *DNA fingerprinting*. Interestingly, public attitudes towards the technique have gone from one extreme to the other. When it was introduced in widely publicized criminal and immigration cases, it was treated as infallible proof of identity backed by scientific authority. Later, when geneticists and molecular biologists testified for the defence in one test case, it was treated as dependent on the skills and interpretations of laboratory technicians.[11] Part of the problem in assessing the technique, and its more recent and more precise replacements, is that the laboratory processes behind it remain for most members of the public a black box, with samples put in and answers coming out. With that view, any errors must be due to incompetence or fraud. There is no room for results that lie between total certainty and error. The same issue arises with many scientific findings relevant to social issues – like the report on eating fat that I heard on the radio today.

Who needs to do this sort of analysis? Students and teachers do, if they are to follow the entry of students into a research community. But I think such analyses could also be a part of the public's critical interpretation of science. Of course I do not expect the radio audience to go out and read the articles that form the basis for the findings they hear reported. But it would be useful if they had some notion of the processes that go on in science and in popularization. Discourse analysis can help by focusing our attention on textual features that can help us to see in concrete forms how knowledge changes as it moves from one discourse to another.

APPENDIX

Texts discussed

Breathnach, R, J. L. Mandel and P. Chambon (1977), 'Ovalbumin gene is split in chicken DNA', *Nature* 270: 314–19. [BMC, *Nature*]
Chambon, P. (1981), 'Split genes', *Scientific American* (May): 48–59. [*SA*]
Cherfas, Jeremy (1985), 'Geneticists develop DNA fingerprinting', *New Scientist* (28 March): 21. [*NS*]
Economist (1986), 'Genetic fingerprints: cherchez la gene', *Economist* (4 January): 68–9. [*Economist*]
Jeffreys, Alec J., Victoria Wilson and Swee Lay Thein (1985), 'Hypervariable "minisatellite" regions in human DNA', *Nature* 314: 67–73. [JWT]
Schmeck, Harold (1978), 'Intervening pieces discovered in genes', *New York Times* (12 February). [*NYT*]

Papers on the split genes collection of texts

'The pragmatics of politeness in scientific texts', *Applied Linguistics*, 10, 1 (March 1989): 1–35.

'Making a discovery: narratives of split genes', in Christopher Nash (ed.), *Narrative in Culture*, London: Routledge, 1990, pp. 102–26.

[With Tony Hartley] 'Modelling lexical cohesion and focus in naturally-occurring written texts: popular science articles and the naive reader', in Ulrich Schmitz, Rüdiger Schütz and Andreas Kunz (eds), *Linguistic Approaches to Artificial Intelligence*, Frankfurt: Peter Lang, 1990, pp. 201–42.

'Story and style in two review articles', in Charles Bazerman and James Paradis (eds), *Textual Dynamics of the Professions*, Madison: University of Wisconsin Press, 1990, pp. 45–75.

'Lexical cohesion and specialized knowledge in science and popular science texts', *Discourse Processes* 14 (1991): 1–26.

'Scientific speculation and literary style in a molecular genetics article', *Science in Context* 4 (1991): 321–46.

'Textbooks and the sociology of scientific knowledge', *English for Specific Purposes*, 11 (1992): 3–17.

'Speech acts and scientific claims', *Journal of Pragmatics*, 17 (1992): 321–46.

NOTES

1 For sociological background on popularization, see Nelkin (1988); Silverstone (1985); La Follette (1990). For other textual studies of popularization, see Fahnestock (1986, 1989). Bastide (forthcoming); Myers (1988, 1990b), and other articles on molecular genetics texts that I have listed above.

2 Ludwik Fleck, in his classic study of thought communities in science (Fleck 1935 [1979]) pointed out this paradox – that scientific texts, which seem so impersonal, still convey more of the personal and provisional than popular texts or textbooks.

3 This article is a brief review of the argument of that chapter, applying it to new data.

4 On the structure of news texts, see van Dijk (1988), Fowler (1991), Bell (1991).

5 For reviews of approaches to narrative, see Jameson (1971), Chatman (1978), Brooks (1984) (all by literary critics); or in linguistic studies, Toolan (1988).

6 Rather than fill this chapter with self-citations, I have listed other studies of this collection in a separate appendix.

7 For reviews of the genre of research articles, see Swales (1990) (for linguistic studies) and Bazerman (1988) (for sociological and historical context).

8 For an analysis of the rhetoric of such passages, see Latour (1987).

9 See, for instance, Gopnik (1972), Huddleston (1971), Halliday (1988b).

10 An influential study on the use of passive voice in context is Tarone *et al.* (1981).

13 Evaluation and organization in a sample of written academic discourse

Susan Hunston

INTRODUCTION

To evaluate something is to have an opinion about it, particularly in terms of how good or bad it is. The terms of reference for the judgement may be essentially personal, such as when readers decide they find a particular novelist 'boring', or they may occur within an institutionalized framework, such as when teachers decide whether a particular text-book is suitable for a particular group of students. (Of course, the 'personal' evaluation is itself influenced by cultural considerations, socialization, philosophical background and so on.)

While this evaluation is a mental process, its linguistic expression forms an essential component of discourse. That is, for a text – an exemplum of discourse – to work as communication, there must be frequent indications of attitudes held towards information given in the text and towards the communicative value of the discourse itself. This is a major finding of various approaches to discourse, such as Winter (1982), Hoey (1979), Sinclair and Coulthard (1975), Sinclair (1981), Labov (1972). Expressing evaluation in a text involves both a statement of personal judgement and an appeal to shared norms and values. In that it creates a shared point of view of speaker/writer and hearer/reader, its meaning is essentially interpersonal.

Here I wish to present a way of looking at evaluation which allows texts to be analysed in terms of their evaluative language alone. The method of analysis will be demonstrated with one article, reprinted as an appendix at the end of this chapter. The resulting analysis will be used to illustrate the kind of information that can be obtained in this way, with especial reference to the issue of text organization.

The text that has been chosen for analysis is 'The spontaneous use of *thank you* by preschoolers as a function of sex, socioeconomic status, and listener status', hereafter referred to as SUTY, written by Becker and Smenner and published in the journal *Language in Society* in 1986. It is essentially the report of experimental work undertaken by the writers, and is thus a useful vehicle for demonstrating this approach to evaluation, which was developed originally with scientific experimental research articles (Hunston 1989).

The SUTY text can be summarized as follows. Some work has been done on the acquisition of sociolinguistic competence in the use of politeness formulae by young children, but the results are inconclusive. Becker and Smenner carried out an experiment in day care centres, with children aged about four. The children took part in a game organized by their teachers, in the course of which each child in turn won a prize. The children then went next door where they were given their prize by either an adult or a child. The adult recorded whether or not the recipient of the prize said *thank you*. The variables which were then considered were the sex of the child, the socio-economic status of the child and the status (adult or child) of the prize-giver. The study found that the girls said *thank you* more often than the boys, that the children of low-income families said *thank you* more often than those of middle-income families and that the children said *thank you* more often to the adult than to the child.

AN APPROACH TO EVALUATION

It may seem surprising to claim that evaluation is an essential component of the academic research article, because such articles are typically considered to be factual and impersonal, their only purpose being to report and draw inferences from a series of events. Bazerman (1984: 163–5), for example, lists (ironically) the advice given to writers of scientific articles:

(1) the scientist must remove himself from reports of his own work and thus avoid all use of the first person;
(2) scientific writing should be objective and precise, with mathematics as its model;
(3) scientific writing should shun metaphor and other flights of rhetorical fancy to seek a univocal relationship between word and object; and
(4) the scientific article should support its claims with empirical evidence from nature, preferably experimental.

Although, of course, the nature of the 'object' of investigation in the social sciences is somewhat different from that investigated by scientists, two central concerns remain the same: that models must be tested against observation, and that the language of the article must be objective and impersonal.

If it were true that the sole function of the research article was to give an account of a procedure without any kind of value judgement, then it might indeed be counterproductive to assign a central role to evaluation. The main goal of experimental reports, however, is persuasion. Their aim is to persuade the academic community to accept the new knowledge claims (Latour and Woolgar 1979) and to adjust its network of consensual knowledge in order to accommodate those claims – potentially a radical and face-threatening operation (Collins 1985; Myers 1989). Where an experiment is involved, the persuasion takes place by evaluating the experiment and its knowledge-claim outcome as superior to rival claims. Each part of the traditional experimental research article uses evaluation in order to carry out part of this persuasion. In the SUTY text, the persuasive goal of each section of the text can be summarized thus:

Section	Persuades the reader that ...
Introduction	the research undertaken is necessary and worthwhile, on the grounds that there exist some gaps in knowledge on a topic which is important.
Method	the research was well done, specifically that the subjects represented the groups they were intended to represent and the experimental method avoided distortion.
Results	the statistical packages used were useful and informative.
Discussion	the results make sense and fit with other examples of research, leading to a consistent body of knowledge.

How, then, can this persuasive goal, with its concomitant evaluation, be reconciled with the apparently objective nature of the research article? Latour and Woolgar point out that 'The result of the *construction* of a fact is that it appears unconstructed by anyone; the result of rhetorical *persuasion* in the agnostic field is that participants are convinced that they have not been convinced' (Latour and Woolgar 1979: 240). In other words, to be convincing, what is persuasion must appear to be only reportage. It follows that the evaluation through which the persuasion is carried out must be highly implicit and will, in fact, avoid the attitudinal language normally associated with interpersonal meaning (Halliday 1985). To illustrate this, I shall consider Paragraph 27, from the end of the Discussion section of SUTY.

Paragraph 27
(1) The present results can also be used to address Piaget's (1959) claims. (2) Piaget argued that children under the age of seven years, especially between the ages of three and five years, find it difficult to accommodate the perspectives of their listeners. (3) The results of the present study, however, indicate that children between the ages of 3½ and 4½ years do adapt to differences in listener status and say 'thank you' more frequently to adults than to peers. (4) This finding supports the results of previous studies in which preschoolers recognized differences in listener status and adjusted their use of politeness routines accordingly [references].

This paragraph contains no single sentence that can uniquely be assigned the function *evaluation*, nor does it contain any attitudinal language. On the other hand, we are left in no doubt by the end of the paragraph what the writers' views of Piaget and of their own experiment are. Furthermore, by sharing in this view of the world, we, as readers, are persuaded to alter our perceptions of what is known about children's communicative competence to take these findings into account.

I propose that evaluation be viewed as being of three kinds, or alternatively, since the same language is used for each kind, as performing three distinct functions: that of status, value and relevance. These will now be addressed in turn.

Status

Returning to paragraph 27 (quoted above), it is clear that each of the four sentences represents a different activity on the part of the writers, each of which represents a different attitude towards the reality of what is being said: S1 (Sentence 1) is an assessment of the present results; S2 reports the conclusions that someone else has made about his own research; S3 interprets the writers' findings; S4 takes that interpretation a stage further. These different activities represent differing degrees of certainty and commitment towards the propositions in the sentences. Although there are no modal verbs here, a form of modality is being expressed. (Compare Halliday's notion of interpersonal metaphor; Halliday 1985 and Hunston 1993b.) We know, from the use of the words *claims* and *argued* that although Piaget thought that *children find it difficult to accommodate the perspectives of their listeners* was probably true, these writers think it is probably not true. On the other hand, we know from the selection of *indicate* rather than *show* or *suggest* in S3 that the writers think that their interpretation of their own findings is probably, although not certainly, true (see Thompson and Ye 1991). S3 and S4 represent a progression towards what Pinch (1985) calls greater **externality** in the interpretation of experimental results.[1] That is, from the 'raw data' of the figures, the writers can draw a series of conclusions, each of which moves progressively away from the figures themselves and involves a greater degree of interpretation, in Pinch's terms, becoming more external. An imaginary example of such a sequence of increasing externality might be as follows:

(1) Twenty-seven children said *thank you* to the child, forty-one children said *thank you* to the adult.
(2) Therefore, more children said *thank you* to the adult than to the child.
(3) Therefore, these children showed an awareness of listener status.
(4) Therefore, (all) children show awareness of listener status when they are four.
(5) Therefore, models of child language development which allow for this are correct.

As the interpretation moves along the externality scale, progressively greater risk is attached to making the knowledge claim and correspondingly lower degrees of certainty are likely to be expressed by the writer.

The distinguishing features of the status function of evaluation are:

the scale of evaluation is *certain–uncertain*
status is identified by writer **activity**, modified by the ascribed **source** of
    the proposition (Piaget in S2, experimental data in S3, the writers

themselves in S4) and by **modifications** such as modal verbs, report verbs and meta-linguistic labelling.[2]

status is attached to each clause – each clause must have one status or another, so that the whole text is evaluative in this sense.

The status of a proposition shows the writer's perception of the relation between that proposition and the world. A 'fact' represents the world, an interpretation or a hypothesis represents a possible world. Furthermore, the ascribed status of items in academic discourse has important intertextual consequences. Items which are presented as 'facts', such as experimental results, cannot be subsequently denied, as to do so would be to accuse the researcher of lying. (Note that in paragraph 27, quoted above, the things that Piaget has said are labelled as 'claims' rather than 'results'.) Interpretations, on the other hand, can be argued against, as to do so is simply to present an alternative reworking of the consensual network.

When approaching an analysis of the status evaluation in a text, two main options must be considered, depending on what is taken as the unit of analysis: the clause or the proposition. In S4 of paragraph 27, for example, there are at least four propositions, each of which carries an assessment of status:

(1) What has gone before is a finding. (Status: *assignment of status to another proposition.*)
(2) This finding supports the results of previous studies. (Status: *interpretation.*)
(3) Preschoolers recognized differences in listener status. (Status: *result.*)
(4) Preschoolers adjusted their use of politeness routines. (Status: *result.*)

It would be possible to show iconically the role of proposition (2) in providing an interpretative link between the finding described in proposition (1) and the results of propositions (3) and (4). A true representation of S4 would thereby be achieved. Such a representation would, however, provide more information than is manageable or desirable if one's aim is to analyse a complete text and to talk about the organization of that text. In terms of the text as a whole, what is important in S4 is that the interpretation of proposition (2) is made grammatically more salient than the results of propositions (3) and (4). This represents a sentence-level contribution to the organization of the text.

The second alternative is therefore adopted here, which is to treat each (non-rank-shifted) clause as a single entity, ignoring the individual propositions it contains. For each clause, the following information is given:

the activity of the writer, e.g. *interpret result*;
the source of the information, e.g. *citation*;
any modification, e.g. use of a report verb;
the resulting place on the certainty scale, e.g. *possible*.[3]

Each example of the activity *interpretation of results* is given a number (1–6) to indicate the degree of externality involved. For example, *result 3* means a generalization involving the findings from the current experiment only, in the past tense, whereas *result 4* means a more generalized interpretation, using present tense. Projecting clauses are identified as such, but are not analysed further, as their function is to state the source and the level of certainty of the subsequent proposition.

The contribution of status to organization will be discussed in detail below. For the present, it may be noted that a change in status can indicate a transition from one part of an argument to the next. This can be exemplified by looking at the status analysis of paragraph 9. (See table 13.1.) The analysis suggests that the paragraph is organized in three parts: S9.1 is an **assessment** by the writers, S9.2–9.6 present **results** from citations and S9.7 is a **recommendation** from the writers. Furthermore, S9.2–9.5 present a progression in status concerning one set of results, with S9.6 introducing another set of results. If we look at the actual paragraph, this three-part division works nicely, corresponding to a Problem (S1), two exceptions to the Problem (S2–6) and an outcome of (or response to) the Problem (S7).

Table 13.1 Status analysis of paragraph 9

Sentence	Activity	Source	Modification	Certainty
9.1a	assess research	writers	–	certain
9.1b	assess research	writers	–	certain
9.2a	project			
9.2b	result 4 – interpret	citation	*show*	certain
9.3	result 3 – generalize	citation	*report*	known
9.4	result 2 – compare	citation	–	known
9.5a	project			
9.5b	result 4 – interpret	citation	*suggest*	possible
9.6a	project			
9.6b	result 4 – interpret	citation	*found*	certain
9.7	recommend	writers	–	certain

Value

The more common meaning of the term *evaluation* is a judgement of good or bad, an assessment of worth or value. In paragraph 27, several items are given value. The 'present results' are assessed as being useful because they can be used to test Piaget's hypotheses. These results and those quoted in S4 are judged as likely to be accurate because they fit with each other, whereas Piaget's claims are given negative value because they do not fit the results. The change in evaluative footing is indicated by *however* (S3), but there is no attitudinal language to signal the evaluation itself. How, then, is the evaluation achieved? I suggest that the phenomenon needs to be investigated with the aid of a concept of goals (see Hunston 1985 for further details). Each status category carries implicitly a set of goals, which are criteria by which the item is judged. A *hypothesis*, for instance, carries with it the goal that it should fit with experimental findings, with other, more accepted, hypotheses and with more general beliefs, common sense and so on. It will be further valued if it explains a number of phenomena and if it is unique in its explicative power. Whenever a hypothesis is mentioned, then, subsequent sentences which give such information about it will count as grounds for evaluation of value. (Hunston (1993a) gives further examples of the value criteria for items of various statuses.)

In paragraph 27, the hypotheses in S2 are evaluated in S3, and the findings in S3 are evaluated in S4. As a further point, however, note that Piaget's hypotheses have already been evaluated, prior to S3, by the very words which give them their status (*claims* and *argued*). In other words, the negative evaluation in S3 is prefigured by the status category of the item evaluated, which pre-empts certain evaluative options. Status and value are therefore inextricably linked.

The distinguishing features of the value function of evaluation are:

the scale of evaluation is *good–bad*.

evaluation of value depends on the goals of the community within which the text has been produced. Anything which refers to these goals is evaluative, even if it does not contain what is commonly thought of as evaluative language.

what constitutes evaluation of value depends on what is being evaluated, and in particular its status.

Value categories may be divided into those assessing the **fit** between aspects of theory and practice and the **usefulness** of a piece of information.

the expression of evaluation of value may not be confined to a single sentence but may occur as an accumulation of items over several sentences.

when an item is evaluated in terms of its value, that item is effectively highlighted, that is, made more important than items which are not so evaluated.

Turning to the analysis of value, there are, as with status, several possibilities. One could, for example, select a key item, and show it gradually collecting positive value. In this text, for instance, the hypothesis that preschool children have a considerable amount of sociolinguistic awareness gathers positive value as the text progresses. Such a selection would mean, however, that the whole text was not being analysed. The analysis exemplified below (figures 13.1 and 13.2) attempts to include all evaluation of value in the text. The item given value is shown in bold, the category of value, from the list determined by each status category, in italics. Sentences which together form a single item to be evaluated or which together carry out evaluation of a single item are boxed together.

In organizational terms, evaluation of value has a text-chunking function.

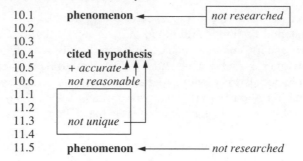

Figure 13.1 Value analysis of paragraphs 10 and 11

                    results (in preceding text)
                                ↑
    27.1   + *useful*

    27.2   **cited hypothesis**
                                ↑
    27.3   *not accurate*   **results**
                                                    ↑
    27.4   + *consistent*

Figure 13.2 Value analysis of paragraph 27

The value analysis for paragraphs 10 and 11 of SUTY, for instance, shows S10.4 to S11.4 chunked by evaluation of value, in that the whole section evaluates the hypothesis presented in S10.4. Text-chunking is also illustrated by S1 of paragraph 27, which gives value to much of the preceding article (*The present results*). In addition, the analysis of paragraph 27 illustrates a commonly used chaining pattern of organization, where S27.2 is evaluated in S27.3, which in turn is evaluated in S27.4.

Relevance

An important function of evaluation in academic research articles is the evaluation of *relevance*. While all the information given in such articles must be shown by writers to be important, the exact nature of the significance may be stated in a *Relevance Marker*. Relevance Markers have an important organizational role and occur at the beginnings or ends of units, typically, although by no means always, coinciding with the beginnings or ends of paragraphs. Paragraph 6 of SUTY, for instance, has Relevance Markers as its first and last sentences. S6.1 is a prospective Relevance Marker, which states the significance of the section of text which follows. S6.7 is a retrospective Relevance Marker, assessing the significance of the preceding section of text.

    To illustrate what constitutes a Relevance Marker, I shall consider S13.6:

These studies demonstrate that preschoolers are affected by status variables, and adjust their use of politeness when addressing their listeners.

This sentence summarizes the preceding stretch of text, in this case using a noun phrase, *these studies*, which is similar in function to Francis' category of anaphoric noun (see Francis, this volume). The verb *demonstrate* is a near-synonym of *mean* and places the summarized preceding text within a category of significance. This is the 'Mean' type of Relevance Marker. Other types of Relevance Marker perform the same function but use different linguistic resources, as the following table (13.2) shows. Prospective Relevance Markers have slightly different identification criteria, but as these are less important to my argument, they need not be discussed here.

Table 13.2 Retrospective relevance markers

Type	Preceding text	Means	Significant category
Token value	This	provided	an appropriate context in which to say *thank you*
Mean	These studies	demonstrate	that preschoolers are affected by status variables
Conclude	The data of Figure 3D	make it apparent	that our dichroism signal arises from overall orientation of a rigid particle
Thus	Therefore		these studies may not be representative of behavior in settings which are familiar . . .

Note: Because there is no example of the 'Conclude' type in this text, an example from another text has been used here.

The distinguishing features of the relevance function of evaluation are:

the scale of evaluation is *important–unimportant*.

Relevance Markers may be prospective or retrospective. Retrospective Relevance Markers have an anaphoric element and place the preceding text within a category of significance; prospective Relevance Markers have a cataphoric element and state the significance of the subsequent text.

Relevance Markers overtly mark the relevance of preceding, or subsequent, stretches of text. Their absence does not mean that the text is not significant, but rather that its significance is being indicated in an implicit manner, or left to the deductive powers of the reader. A sentence that is not a Relevance Marker is not, of course, irrelevant.

Relevance Markers are metadiscoursal in that they give information about the progression of the discourse, and take the discourse itself as the item to be evaluated.

Relevance Markers have an important organizational role in that, by referring to stretches of text of anything from a sentence to a paragraph or a whole article, they divide the text into *ad hoc* sections.

Analysing a text for evaluation of relevance is a fairly simple matter of identifying Relevance Markers and the extent of the stretch of text that they

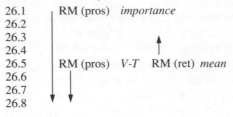

Figure 13.3 Relevance analysis of paragraph 26

evaluate. Relevance Markers, of course, chunk the text, and a hierarchy can thereby be created. Figure 13.3 shows an example.

One interesting question which arises from the comparative paucity of Relevance Markers is why they often do not occur in places where they could appropriately be used. It is possible to postulate a variety of motives for the absence of Relevance Markers. A strong motive would be that the potential Relevance Marker would be embarrassing, as may happen if a rival researcher is being criticized. A weak motive would be to leave the inference of relevance to the reader. For example, paragraph 8 of the text gives the relevance of the preceding section (paragraphs 3–7), but it is not stated in terms of a Relevance Marker. This is particularly likely to happen when the organizational function of the potential retrospective Relevance Marker has already been fulfilled by a prospective Relevance Marker, as occurs in S3.1. Where the progression of the argument becomes more important, in the Discussion section, there are more retrospective Relevance Markers.

Particles and waves

The above discussion, with its identification of discrete items which evaluate status, value and relevance, assumes that a text may be analysed as a series of *particles*, joined together linearly or hierarchically. Halliday, however, using Pike's adaptation of physics terminology, notes that the metaphors of *wave* and of *field* may be equally applicable to the analysis of both clause and text (Pike, 1959; Halliday 1982). The metaphor of the wave is particularly illuminating in discussing evaluation, which may have a cumulative effect.

Examples of the usefulness of the wave metaphor may be given for each of the categories of evaluation. With respect to status, for example, there is a pattern particularly common in scientific experimental research articles, where results are given further and further degrees of interpretation, thereby representing a gradual movement away from what is certain, (and, incidentally, towards what is significant, coinciding with evaluation of relevance). A version of this pattern occurs in paragraphs 20 and 21 of SUTY, where a method is described, followed by its interpretation. There is a movement through the paragraphs from a certainty – the application of the statistical package – to what is less certain, more interpretative.

Value is the evaluation type for which the wave metaphor is most illuminating. Throughout paragraphs 3–7, for example, the evidence against existing studies of children's sociolinguistic competence grows in a cumulative fashion. Similarly, in paragraph 25, the evidence against Greif and Gleason's findings increases as the paragraph progresses. The same phenomenon is found in paragraph 27, where Piaget's hypotheses are given negative value at the beginning by being assessed as *claims* and are then further evaluated negatively by the assertion that the current research does not confirm them. The positive evaluation of the current research further adds to the strength of the evidence against Piaget. Again, the effect is cumulative, wave-like.

Relevance may also be said to be cumulative in a way that coincides with status or value, as illustrated above. However, prospective Relevance Markers may mean that the crest of the relevance wave occurs at the beginning of the unit rather than, or as well as, at the end. The final paragraph of SUTY, paragraph 28, is an interesting case. There are retrospective Relevance Markers in S28.1 and S28.4b, and the final two sentences of the paragraph, in recommending future research, may be said to have a particular relevance. Intuitively, then, I would say that there is strong relevance in sentence 1, which decreases in S2, 3 and 4a and increases again in S4b, 5 and 6, giving a double-crested wave pattern.

Although this metaphor is in principle revealing, and at the very least reminds us that the particle metaphor is also precisely that, an analysis which attempts to represent waves is impressionistic and somewhat uninformative. Such an analysis will not be attempted here, therefore, and in what follows I shall return to the particle metaphor.

WHAT AN ANALYSIS SHOWS

The study of evaluation can give a considerable amount of information about a text. Following an analysis of status evaluation, a count may be made of various categories in each section of the text. The status figures for the SUTY text (table 13.3), for example, confirm what is known about the nature of the Introduction, Method, Results and Discussion sections of experimental research articles. For example, the Method section in this text consists entirely of the activity *narrate event*. The Results section contains many of the lower-level interpretation of results, whereas the Discussion section contains the higher-level interpretations. The first eight paragraphs of the text in the status analysis show a predominance first of facts, then results, then hypotheses. This corresponds to the traditional notion of the Introduction consisting of background information, followed by a discussion of other research, followed by the hypotheses of the current research (e.g. Swales 1981).

In addition, texts can be compared in terms of what is evaluated and how. It is possible, for example, to distinguish between texts produced when a field of research is in its infancy, and observation predominates over the discussion of a theoretical model, and those produced when the field is more advanced

Table 13.3 Status figures for SUTY

Total non-projecting clauses in each section

Introduction	84
Method	16
Results	22
Discussion	35
Total	157

Sources

	Writers	Received knowledge	Citation	Data	Text
Introduction	38	7	37	0	1
Method	16	0	0	0	0
Results	19	0	0	3	0
Discussion	17	0	6	7	3

Activities

	Fact	Event	Results 1–3	Results 4+	Hypothesis
Introduction	18 (21%)	5 (10%)	17 (20%)	16 (19%)	6 (7%)
Method	0	16 (100%)	0	0	0
Results	0	8 (36%)	13 (59%)	0	0
Discussion	1 (3%)	1 (3%)	4 (11%)	17 (49%)	5 (14%)

and there is a clearer development of a model, or of conflicting models (see Bazerman 1984). The useful relevant questions to ask seem to concern (a) the degree of interpretation of results involved, shown by an analysis of status; (b) the degree of intertextuality, shown by status, and the importance of the cited statements, shown by an analysis of value; (c) the degree of complexity of the argument constructed in the text, shown by analyses of value and of relevance. Characterizing this text in this way, we can see that it belongs near the infancy stage of a field of study, although there is a fair amount of intertextuality. The interpretation of results, however, stops short of confirmation of a theoretical model, and the analyses of value and of relevance show little of the complex cross-referencing and creation of hierarchies found in more 'advanced' fields.

Finally, the nature of the evaluation tells us about the value-system of the discipline (see Hunston 1993a). Using this text, for example, we can compare this discipline with science disciplines, such as biochemistry (Hunston 1989). One aspect of note is the way that controversy or conflict is dealt with. In the SUTY text, for example, there are reports of results (paragraphs 3–6) which conflict with the writers' own results. A comparable situation in a bio-chemistry context is when researchers extract and test a particular substance. It can happen that researchers in different laboratories obtain results that are diametrically opposite (see Hunston 1989 for examples). The conflict between results is a more problematic issue for the biochemists than for the linguists, in ways which pinpoint the different approaches to replicability, general-izability and accuracy in experimentation. When the scientist takes a sample of naturally occurring substance x and tests it in the laboratory, the sample is assumed to represent the whole of substance, x, and the laboratory conditions must replicate the *in vivo* conditions in all important respects, otherwise the results are worthless. If two laboratories perform the same tests but do not obtain the same results, one set of results must be in error, and that which has been stated as a fact must be discredited, a very serious matter indeed. These conflicts are typically dealt with in terms of both value and status. It is implied that the other researchers had distortion in their figures due to interference from instruments, contamination of material, mistaken assumptions in calculations and so on, so that what was stated as a fact was actually a mistaken interpretation.

Where the subject of the research is children's language, however, there is no necessary assumption that a sample stands for all (unless statistical claims are made). If results conflict, it can be shown that a feature of the other researchers' experiment made their results ungeneralizable, as is done in SUTY, without suggesting that the results themselves are at fault. In Myers' (1989) terms, the inconsistency is much less face-threatening, and can be dealt with more casually.

This illustrates two different attitudes towards results and towards models – ultimately towards what counts as knowledge. In the scientific articles on which the above observations are based, the models which the results were used to support were mutually exclusive, and the scientific community had to agree on one of them. For this reason, the papers were model-(dis)proving. In the SUTY text, conflicting results provide a context for further research but do not represent a serious problem. The theories under discussion are not polar opposites, but are centred around ages of children, with margins for disagreement and individual difference. With the exception of paragraph 27, there is no 'model of child development' visibly at issue.

Whether these differences truly represent ideological differences between sciences and social sciences, or whether they reflect disciplines at different stages of development, must be a question for further research.

THE ROLE OF EVALUATION IN ORGANIZATION

Approaches to discourse organization

If discourse is seen as sharing features of paradigm and syntagm with other levels of language organization, then the analysis of discourse necessarily involves the identification, characterization and accountability of the units that make up a text. As evaluation has an organizing role in discourse, the analysis of evaluation is crucial to the analysis of discourse units. It is worth remembering, for example, that the influential Problem–Response pattern (Hoey 1979) is essentially an evaluative one.

The identification of such units is an issue of distinguishing borders, that is, of identifying those linguistic criteria which mark a change from one unit to the next. Halliday, for example, argues that a consistent grammatical choice, such as declarative clauses, forms a text 'phase' which changes when the choice changes, for example to imperative (Gregory 1985; Halliday 1988a). Sinclair suggests that such changes may be supplemented by other, lexical indicators and that the markers of unit boundaries may be register-specific (Sinclair 1987a).

The establishment of paradigmatic and syntagmatic constraints and choices within and between units is an issue of structure. It involves also the development of a taxonomy of unit types, which is an issue of classification. Both structure and classification may be accounted for in terms of the social construction of the text. Salient features of the social context may be described in terms of Field, Tenor and Mode (Halliday and Hasan 1985) or, alternatively, in terms of the participants' roles as interactants and joint text-constructors (Sinclair 1981).

The contribution of evaluation of status, value and relevance to the organization of discourse has been pointed out in general terms above. It has also been noted that, for evaluation, the 'wave' metaphor of organization is at least as appropriate as the more commonly applied 'particle' metaphor (Halliday 1982). Below I shall consider in more specific terms the uses of the analysis of evaluation to considerations of discourse organization.

Boundaries

In this discussion of the role played by evaluation in discourse organization, I shall begin by considering how units may be identified externally, that is, in terms of the boundaries between them.

By way of illustration, I shall consider paragraphs 3–8 of the sample text, proposing first a 'common-sense' account of the organization of this section, in order to identify probable unit boundaries (figure 13.4). The account presupposes a hierarchical pattern of organization and further presumes that paragraph 8 is connected to the preceding paragraphs by constituting the consequence or outcome of the Problem outlined in them (level 1). As an example of how the figure is to be interpreted: sentences 3.2–4.3 form part of one of the units which specify the problem generalized in S3.1 (level 2); they constitute results which are then interpreted (level 3); they are subdivided into two sets of results (level 4). From this account, it might be expected that, in general, unit boundaries will coincide with paragraph boundaries, as a change in label at some level co-occurs with every paragraph boundary. In addition, S3.1 may be expected to be different from S3.2–3 and paragraph 7 may be expected to have several boundaries within it.

Figure 13.5 then presents partial analyses of the status, value and relevance of the same text section. (Each analysis will of necessity be incomplete, given that all three are to be included in the same figure.) The first column of figure 13.5 shows that change of status activity coincides with boundaries between paragraphs 4 and 5, 6 and 7, and 7 and 8. Between paragraphs 3 and 4 there is a change in source. Within each paragraph there is approximate unity of status activity and/or source, except that boundaries are suggested between

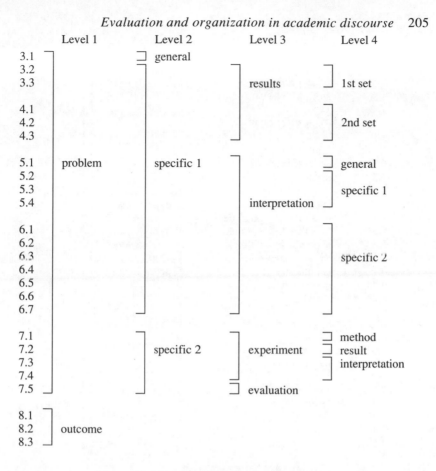

Figure 13.4 Paragraphs 3–8, general account

S3.1 and S3.2 and within paragraph 6. The first of these coincides with a proposed boundary in figure 13.4. Paragraph 6 is united, and separated from paragraph 5, by evaluation of value and by the presence of Relevance Markers. These two also serve to unite paragraphs 3–7, while value also unites paragraph 7.

In paragraph 7 there is a progression of status, that is, a progressive movement towards externality and away from certainty. From S7.1 to S7.3, each sentence re-interprets the preceding one in a way that is more external, or less certain. S7.1 gives a known fact about an experiment; S7.2 interprets a result of that experiment in terms of a generalization about the children's performance; S7.3 takes the interpretation a step further, making a deduction about the internal system developed by the children, with S7.4 providing evidence. Had the writers of the article agreed with Eisenberg's experiment, S7.5 would no doubt have been a further interpretation; as it is, it gives a judgement on the study as a whole, which maintains the increasing uncertainty but without becoming more external.

	Status	Value	Relevance
3.1	assess research	**results**	RM pros
3.2	result 3 – G&W	– *consistent*	
3.3a	result 1 – G&W		
3.3b	result 3 – G&W		
4.1a	result 3 – G&G		
4.1b	result 1 – G&G		
4.2a	result 1 – G&G		
4.2b	result 1 – G&G		
4.3	result 2 – G&G		
5.1	hypothesize – possible	**hypothesis**	
5.2	hypothesize – possible	+ *reasonable*	
5.3	hypothesize – possible	**hypothesis**	
5.4	hypothesize – unlikely	+ *reasonable*	
6.1	hypothesize	**procedure**	RM pros
6.2a	narrate event	–*verity*	
6.2b	state fact		
6.3	state fact		
6.4	assess research		
6.5	hypothesize		
6.6	hypothesize		
6.7	hypothesize	–*verity*	RM ret
7.1	narrate event	**procedure**	
7.2a	result 3		
7.3b	result 3	**interpretation**	
7.4	result 3	+ *accurate*	
7.5	assess research	– *useful*	
8.1	recommend		
8.2	hypothesize		
8.3	hypothesize		

Figure 13.5 Paragraphs 3–8, evaluation in units

Thus, figures 13.4 and 13.5 together suggest that status, value and relevance identify unit boundaries in different ways. Changes in status coincide with transitions from one unit to the next, while value and relevance serve to bind together sections that may cover several status categories.

Point

Units are not identified solely by boundaries, however. The internal development of a unit may be seen in terms of its evaluative 'point', which in turn is determined by the social role of the article. This points to one way in which the social context of the article influences its organization.

One of the key functions of evaluation in any genre is to indicate the 'point' of the text, or part of the text, to the hearer or reader (Labov 1972; Polanyi 1979). What that point may be is determined by the culture within which the text is produced (Polanyi 1979), and how the text is related to its co-text (Schiffrin 1984). In other words, evaluation has the function of relating what is being said to the concerns of the hearer/reader, concerns which are both socially determined, and determined by the nature of the text itself. Although these observations have traditionally been made with respect to narrative occurring in conversation, they apply equally well to the research article. Each unit in the article makes an evaluative point, which is relatable to the social context of an academic paper (the ideological concerns of academic research) and to the specific argument which the article propounds.

The most obvious indicator of 'point' is of course the Relevance Marker, in that Relevance Markers potentially tell the reader *why* a fact has been given. In S24.6, for example, the retrospective Relevance Marker

Thus, these results replicate those of Gleason and Weintraub (1976) for middle income children,

indicates that the reason the preceding information has been given is to account for an apparent discrepancy between the writers' results and those of earlier researchers. What appear to be incompatible results turn out to be mutually supportive. Similarly, S26.1, as a prospective Relevance Marker, tells us in advance that what follows is one of a list of important factors:

A second factor shown to be of importance is socioeconomic status.

The point of a unit may be implied by other types of evaluation, however. This may be illustrated by paragraphs 3–8 of the sample text. In this section there is a point in terms of value, a point which is stated at the outset in S3.1. In addition, however, there is a point with respect to status. How far preschool children have sociolinguistic competence with respect to politeness routines with 'thank you' is, by the end of paragraph 7, established as unknown or at least as unproven, leaving the field open for the research described in paragraph 8. The movement in status and value in 3–7 therefore determines the relevance or point of those paragraphs. This point is socially determined, in the sense that the notions that any gap in knowledge should be filled, and that research is not valuable unless it fills gaps, lie within the ideological perspective of academic research. It is also crucial to the writers' argument construction: in Swales' terms, paragraphs 3–7 form a niche which paragraph 8 can fill.

Of course, it would have been possible for this relevance to have been marked, at the end of paragraph 7, with a Relevance Marker. Compare, for example, S13.6, which states explicitly, in the form of a Relevance Marker, what the point of the preceding sentences has been, even though the content of S13.6, as opposed to its summarizing function, repeats almost word for word that given in S13.2.

For examples of units built around value as their point, consider paragraphs 14 and 15, each of which constitutes one unit. In this part of the article, the writers are describing the method of their experiment, evaluating it consistently as successfully achieving its goals.

Paragraph 14. The item to be given value is presented in S14.2. It has the status of *experimental design*. In S14.3, the basis or criterion by which the design may be evaluated is given: 'It is necessary to study the spontaneous use of *thank you* by preschoolers in a setting that is familiar to the children and in the absence of the parents.' (For the identification of goals or criteria for evaluation, see Hunston 1985.) The fact that this criterion has been met is then stated in S14.4: 'Thus, the present study took place in day care centers, a setting that meets these criteria.' S14.5 provides further evidence of positively valued design, as the procedure of using both an adult and a child to give the gift is judged with the positive-value terms *provide* and *appropriate*.

Paragraph 15. Here the value is less explicitly expressed. The paragraph describes part of the experimental procedure, with the status of *event*. Specifically, it describes the selection of subjects for the experiment. One of the goals of such a procedure is to ensure that the subjects are actually representative of the socioeconomic classes that comprise the experimental variables. From the information in S15.3–5 it may be inferred that the sample of subjects is indeed representative, and the validity of this is asserted in S15.6: 'This information was obtained by a telephone survey and an interview with the director at each center.' In other words, the reader is given information from which the value of the experiment may be inferred, using shared knowledge about the goals of experimental procedure in this context. The 'point' of this unit is then that the experiment was carried out in such a way as to guarantee the validity of the results obtained.

Crystalline and choreographic

Halliday suggests that the structure of clause complexes may be discussed in terms of a choreographic mode and a crystalline mode (Halliday 1987). In choreographic mode, typical of spoken language, clauses are joined by parataxis and hypotaxis in an *ad hoc* way, such that it is not possible to predict accurately the end of the complex from the beginning. In crystalline mode all the information is packed into a single, lexically dense clause, or a set of clauses joined by hypotaxis, so that it is possible to predict the end of the clause (complex) from the beginning. The metaphor here is one of shape rather than of sequence.

Although the parallel is not exact, the twin metaphors of choreographic and crystalline may be applied to discourse units as well as to clauses, in a way that brings together the notions of 'point' and of organization. In a crystalline unit, the direction of the unit is prefigured by the initial statement: the 'topic sentence' or prospective Relevance Marker. An example from the SUTY text is paragraphs 3–7. Everything in these paragraphs is subsumed under the judgement of inconsistency made in S3.1 and, as indicated above, this sentence contains (partly) the point of the unit. In a choreographic unit, the point, or the direction of the unit, is not apparent until its end, as in paragraph 26. Although this paragraph also begins with a 'topic sentence', the paragraph, in exploring possible explanations for a particular result, goes beyond the information contained in S26.1. The paragraph, in fact, ends with an evaluation (value, although a Relevance Marker could also have occurred) of the possibility that the children's degree of affluence affects their response to the offered gift. Note that, in this case, the organizational property of the evaluation of value that closes the paragraph overrides that of the prospective Relevance Marker at the beginning.

Evaluation as termination

To conclude this discussion of the modes of association between evaluation and discourse organization, I shall consider models of discourse which argue that structural units or organizational patterns are terminated by evaluation. One example is Hoey's (1979) discussion of the Situation–Problem–Response–Evaluation pattern, where the final section evaluates the Response in terms of how effective it is (which appears to be classifiable as *value* in my terms). Another is Sinclair's proposal that discourse is tripartite and hierarchical in structure, and that units are terminated by evaluation (Sinclair 1987a). For example, teaching exchanges normally end with the teacher evaluating the student's response as right or wrong (this is also *value*, in my terms). Sinclair's generalized discourse model finds expression in the IRF structure proposed for spoken dialogue (Sinclair and Coulthard 1975) and the PRD structure proposed for written monologue (Sinclair 1987a).

Parts of the text which has been analysed here would seem to lend support to such models. For example, a unit comprising paragraphs 3–6 could be said to consist of a focusing statement (S3.1) and a statement of findings (S3.2–4.3), concluded by an assessment of negative value (S5.1–6.7).

I have argued, however, for a view of evaluation that identifies it as much more pervasive than the above models suggest, occurring, as status, in all clauses and, as value, cumulatively across large sections of text. I have also argued for a crucial organizing role belonging to evaluation of relevance, not of value. This alternative viewpoint corresponds more closely with Sinclair's argument that discourse structure operates on the interactional place (Sinclair 1981), because it is in Relevance Markers that the topic discussed becomes the text itself and the writer talks directly to the reader, standing outside the text: *This is why I am telling you this.*

Paragraphs 3–6 of the sample text may be reconsidered in the light of this. I would argue that it is the function of S6.7 as a Relevance Marker that is crucial to the closure of the unit. Yet S6.7 also participates in the evaluation of value. Only the overlap of value and relevance in this particular case gives the false impression of the role of value in unit termination.

Given that by no means every unit is terminated by a Relevance Marker, it is obvious that in some cases, value does indeed 'stand in for' relevance as a unit-terminator. I would argue, however, that value terminates a unit only coincidentally, in those cases where it alone indicates relevance. To give a more complete picture, it is evaluation of relevance, and the specific occurrence of the Relevance Marker, which must be seen as unit-terminating.

CONCLUSION

Three main claims have been made in this chapter. The first is that evaluation is a unified concept but may be seen as having three aspects – status, value and relevance – which necessitates three types of analysis.

Second, evaluation, while being personal, is also dependent upon the value-system of the community in which the text is produced. In academic writing, that value-system is largely concerned with what constitutes knowledge. Observations which arise out of an analysis of evaluation, such as that lack of certainty is seen as problematic, or that experimental results may be cited as legitimate sources for knowledge claims, tell us a great deal about how the academic community sees the world.

Finally, evaluation is an essential contributor to discourse structure. Evaluation of status and of value are important to the establishment of boundaries between units, but it is evaluation of relevance which has the most crucial role as a unit organiser. This is partly because it seems that each unit must have an evaluative point or relevance, and partly because of the unit-determining role of the Relevance Marker. The matter of prediction in units is complicated by the fact that while the point of some units, which may be described as crystalline, is determined in advance, for others, which may be termed choreographic, the point is not apparent until the end of the unit.

*

APPENDIX

The spontaneous use of *thank you* by preschoolers as a function of sex, socioeconomic status, and listener status*

JUDITH A. BECKER AND PATRICIA C. SMENNER
Department of Psychology
University of South Florida

ABSTRACT

This study investigated whether preschoolers would spontaneously say *thank you* in a familiar context without their parents' presence. Two hundred and fifty 3½- to 4½-year-olds played a game with their teachers and received a reward from either an unfamiliar peer or adult. Across conditions, 37 percent of the children said *thank you* spontaneously, more than in previous studies. The frequency of the spontaneous use of *thank you* was assessed as a function of sex, socioeconomic status, and listener status. Preschool-aged girls said *thank you* spontaneously more than boys, χ^2 (1) = 7.95, $p < .01$. Also, children from families of low economic status said *thank you* spontaneously more than children from middle income families, χ^2 (1) = 7.17, $p < .01$. This finding does not appear to be due to racial differences. Finally, the preschoolers said *thank you* spontaneously more to the adult than to the peer, χ^2 (1) = 4.27, $p < .05$. These results are discussed in terms of their implications for pragmatic socialization and the acquisition of politeness formulas such as *thank you*. (Routines, politeness formulas, pragmatic socialization, sex differences, socioeconomic differences, language and status)

INTRODUCTION

1 (1) The study of pragmatics in language acquisition has emerged from the recognition that much of language cannot be understood without knowledge of the context in which a verbal exchange occurs. (2) Context involves the listener's relationship to the speaker, the speaker's goal, and the physical setting in which the exchange occurs. (3) Some of the pragmatic language skills children must develop to become effective communicators include knowing when it is appropriate to request rather than demand of a listener, taking turns speaking, and knowing when to use particular social phrases. (4) As Eisenberg (1982) pointed out, learning to say the 'right' thing at the 'right' time means knowing when the 'right' time is. (5) Knowing when to use a social phrase such as *thank you* involves the ability to perceive differences in the context of situations and the knowledge of rules governing social interaction. (6) This is because the 'meaning' of *thank you* lies in the context in which it is used rather than in its representation of an object or person.

2 (1) Ritualized communications such as those involving *thank you* are universal in human languages and are important in the regulation of interactions within a society (Ferguson 1976; Goffman 1971; Goody 1978). (2) *Thank you* is the accepted way of showing appreciation in the United States and may convey respect for a listener who has contributed to, assisted in, or alleviated a condition for the speaker. (3) Failure to use phrases such as *thank you* correctly can have socially disruptive consequences for the individual (Apte 1974; Ervin-Tripp 1969; Hymes 1973). (4) While politeness routines have been discussed in terms of adult use (Apte 1974; Ferguson 1976; Goody 1978), research on how and when children learn to use them is sparse.

3 (1) The results of research on the use of *thank you* by preschoolers are inconsistent. (2) Gleason and Weintraub (1976) showed that middle-class children under six years of age tended not to say *thank you* spontaneously when given candy on Halloween. (3) Twenty-one percent of the children said *thank you*, typically while being prompted by parents.

4 (1) Greif and Gleason (1980) found spontaneous production of *thank you* by preschoolers to be even more rare, with middle-class children responding spontaneously in only 7 percent of the appropriate opportunities observed in the laboratory. (2) Following prompting by their parents (which occurred 51 percent of the time), 86 percent of the children said *thank you*. (3) Greif and

Gleason noted that *thank you*, as compared to *hi* and *goodbye*, was the least likely to be produced spontaneously and appropriately, and most likely to be prompted by parents.

5 (1) It may be that the children's infrequent use of *thank you* resulted from factors other than their ignorance of the context involved in its appropriate use. (2) One explanation for the infrequent spontaneous use is that children become accustomed to prompts by their parents. (3) Children may view the prompt as an integral part of the ritual. (4) It is unlikely, with parents prompting them over 50 percent of the time and persisting in prompting until the child says *thank you*, that prompts are having no effect on the children.

6 (1) Another factor which may have influenced the low frequency of the spontaneous use of *thank you* by the children in these studies is the fact that both were conducted in unusual situations. (2) The study by Gleason and Weintraub (1976) was conducted on Halloween, which occurs only once a year. (3) A three- to four-year-old has had minimal experience with this ritual. (4) The laboratory (used in Greif & Gleason 1980) is also a unique setting for the majority of children of this age. (5) It may be that, in novel social situations, children attend to the unfamiliar aspects of the situation. (6) Familiar and understood aspects of the situation may be neglected in an attempt to actively learn new information. (7) Therefore, these studies may not be representative of behavior in settings which are familiar and social situations which are more common to the children's experiences.

7 (1) In fact, Eisenberg (1982) observed preschoolers in their homes. (2) By age three, the children had a number of politeness formulas in their repertoires and used them spontaneously and appropriately quite frequently. (3) Eisenberg concluded that children had formed a 'category' of polite expressions and that errors indicated that the children were attempting to analyze the situational components governing the appropriate context in which to use the routines. (4) Children never confused politeness routines involving *please*, *thank you*, *excuse me*, and *sorry* with greetings such as *hello* and *goodbye*. (5) Unfortunately, this study has limitations in that it involved children from only three Mexican-American families who may not be representative of the population in general.

8 (1) Additional research is necessary to determine whether preschoolers are aware of the contexts in which *thank you* is appropriate and whether this knowledge was masked by the presence of the parents or the unfamiliarity of the situation in previous studies. (2) Furthermore, there may be other factors which affect the use of *thank you*. (3) These include the sex of the child, the socioeconomic status of the child's family, and the relative status of speaker and listener.

Sex differences in the spontaneous use of thank you

9 (1) There has been an abundance of research on sex differences in children's use of language, but relatively little deals with pragmatics. (2) Most of the

literature (e.g., Clarke-Stewart 1973; Maccoby & Jacklin 1974; Nelson 1973) shows that girls are more advanced than boys in many language skills. (3) Greif and Gleason (1980) reported the only sex difference found in the use of social phrases by children of preschool age: (4) A higher percentage of boys (41%) than girls (18%) spontaneously said *hi* to the experimenter. (5) Gleason (1980) suggested that this difference may be because girls are more shy than boys and Western culture puts more emphasis on males providing greetings. (6) However, Greif and Gleason (1980) also found that boys and girls are equally likely to say *thank you* and *goodbye*. (7) Further research is in order on the spontaneous use of *thank you* by boys and girls of preschool age.

The spontaneous use of thank you *and socioeconomic status*

10 (1) The relation between preschoolers' use of *thank you* and their socioeconomic status has not been directly addressed. (2) Of the few studies conducted on the use of *thank you*, one involved families of low income (Eisenberg 1982) and two involved middle-income families exclusively (Gleason & Weintraub 1976; Greif & Gleason 1980). (3) While both middle- and low-income parents were found to prompt their children to say *thank you* (Eisenberg 1982; Greif & Gleason 1980; Gleason & Weintraub 1976), there is evidence of socioeconomic differences in the ways parents teach their children pragmatic skills. (4) Greif and Gleason (1980) suggested that middle-income families may be more permissive and concern themselves less with pragmatic routines. (5) Researchers have noted that lower-class, black families tend to emphasize different pragmatic skills (Heath 1983), such as making 'ritual insults' (Labov 1972; Sullivan 1972), and even encouraging pragmatic behaviors, such as profanity, that are often punished by middle-class, white parents (Ward 1971). (6) Unfortunately, however, such comparisons are complicated by the confounding of class with race.

11 (1) It may be that both middle- and low-income parents stress the acquisition of politeness routines, but not for the same reasons (Chilman 1980; Kohn 1963). (2) Middle-income parents may stress politeness routines to allow their children to become socially effective communicators and develop beneficial affiliations; (3) they emphasize social achievement. (4) Low-income parents may stress politeness routines in order to insure conformity and to gratify needs as conveniently as possible by avoiding social conflicts (Hess 1970). (5) The extent to which teaching styles and the amount of prompting of politeness routines by middle- and low-income parents differ, and the effect these differences may have on children's spontaneous use of *thank you*, have not yet been studied.

Listener status and the spontaneous use of thank you

12 (1) Authority (or status) is a natural concomitant of age. (2) Status also includes relative power by virtue of control of resources, size, or sex. (3)

These and other factors that affect children's use of language include social distance or intimacy, what the speaker desires from the listener, and the formality of the setting in which an encounter takes place (Becker 1982; Brown & Levinson 1978; Ervin-Tripp 1969; Goody 1978; Wood & Gardner 1980). (4) It is not clear at what age children begin to recognize and respond appropriately to listener status. (5) Shatz and Gelman (1973), for example, found that four-year-olds were sensitive to their listeners' status and verbal abilities. (6) The children used more polite and indirect speech with adults than with peers or two-year-olds.

13   (1) The relationship of preschoolers' use of *thank you* to listener status has not been directly studied. (2) There is evidence, though, that children of this age recognize differences in listener status and adjust their use of other politeness routines accordingly. (3) For example, Bates (1976) found preschoolers to be more polite and indirect when requesting of an adult than a peer. (4) Preschoolers also address dominant, higher-status peers with indirect requests, as they do adults (Ervin-Tripp 1969). (5) Similarly, dominant children tend to use more direct requests with less dominant, lower-status peers (Wood & Gardner 1980). (6) These studies demonstrate that preschoolers are affected by status variables, and adjust their use of politeness when addressing their listeners.

14   (1) Previous research has provided much information about children's understanding and use of pragmatic skills. (2) The present study focused on the spontaneous use of *thank you* by preschoolers and its relationship to sex, socioeconomic status, and listener status. (3) It is necessary to study the spontaneous use of *thank you* by preschoolers in a setting that is familiar to the children and in the absence of the parents. (4) Thus, the present study took place in day care centers, a setting that meets these criteria. (5) The children received a gift from either an adult or child model and this provided an appropriate context in which to say *thank you*.

METHODS

Subjects

15   (1) Two hundred and fifty children (121 boys, 129 girls) between the ages of 3½ and 4½ years participated in this study. (2) Subjects were drawn from day care centers in a southeastern metropolitan area. (3) Children came from middle and low income families, as measured by the cost per week to the family of the day care center which the child attended. (4) The 146 children from low-income families attended day care centers which charge nothing to the family. (5) The 104 children from middle-income families attended day care centers which charge the highest rates in the area (approximately $40.00 per week), and had parents employed in professional occupations. (6) This information was obtained by a telephone survey and an interview with the director at each center.

Procedure

16 (1) Teachers were given colored cards and asked to play a color-naming game with the children. (2) The teachers explained that if the children correctly guessed the color on the card, they would receive a reward from a guest helper in the adjoining room. (3) The teachers alternately called on boys and girls.

17 (1) After guessing, children went individually into the next room where they each received a sticker from either a child model or an adult model. (2) As each child approached, the model said only 'Hi, here's your sticker.' (3) Both the child (a 4½-year-old girl) and the adult (the second author) were unfamiliar to the children. (4) Half of the children of each sex and socioeconomic group received the sticker from the child model and half from the adult model. (5) Both models were seen first an equal number of times in each socioeconomic level. (6) All responses were audio-tape recorded and the adult model also kept a record of them.

RESULTS

18 (1) Inter-rater agreement was assessed conservatively. (2) Three additional raters, blind to the purposes and conditions of the study, listened to the audiotapes and noted whether each subject said *thank you* or some derivative (e.g. *thanks*). (3) Because of the high level of agreement among the four raters (96.4%), the experimenter's original coding was used for statistical analysis.

19 (1) The overall frequency with which children said *thank you* was relatively low. (2) Only 37 percent of the children across conditions responded this way. (3) A number of analyses were conducted to see whether children's responses varied as a function of sex, socioeconomic status, or listener status.

TABLE 1. *Number of children responding* thank you
in each condition

	Children responding *thank you*			
	Boys		Girls	
	Peer	Adult	Peer	Adult
Low SES	7 (19%)	13 (41%)	12 (34%)	17 (40%)
Mid SES	2 (8%)	1 (4%)	6 (21%)	10 (42%)
	Children not responding			
	Boys		Girls	
	Peer	Adult	Peer	Adult
Low SES	30 (81%)	19 (59%)	23 (66%)	25 (60%)
Mid SED	24 (92%)	25 (96%)	22 (79%)	14 (58%)

20 (1) In order to determine whether there were any main effects or interactions among the three independent variables, an analysis of variancelike version of the Chi square test was utilized. (2) A 2 (sex: male, female) x 2 (socioeconomic status: low, middle) x 2 (model: peer, adult) distribution-free test of analysis of variance (Wilson 1956) was performed on children's responses. (3) Table 1 shows the number of children in each condition who did and did not respond *thank you*.

21 (1) The analysis revealed that girls were more likely to respond *thank you* than were boys, χ^2 (1) = 7.95, $p < .01$. (2) This effect was not qualified by any statistically significant higher order interactions. (3) None the less, the sex difference tended to be more pronounced for children of middle income families.

22 (1) Socioeconomic status also had a significant impact on the use of *thank you*. (2) Children from low-income families said *thank you* more frequently than the other children, χ^2 (1) = 7.17, $p < .01$. (3) Because children from middle-income families were predominantly white and children from low-income families were predominantly nonwhite, a Chi square test of independence was also performed using socioeconomic status and race as variables. (4) No significant effects were found for race. (5) In addition, the effect of socioeconomic status was not qualified by any other higher order interactions.

23 (1) Finally, there was a significant effect of listener status. (2) Children said *thank you* more frequently to the adult than to the peer model, χ^2 (1) = 4.27, $p < .05$. (3) This effect was not qualified by any higher order interactions, although it tended to be stronger for children of low socioeconomic status.

DISCUSSION

24 (1) Gleason and Weintraub (1976) found that children under six years of age tended to say *thank you* spontaneously only 21 percent of the time. (2) In a similar study, Greif and Gleason (1980) also found the spontaneous production of *thank you* by preschoolers in the laboratory to be rare (7%) in the presence of the parents. (3) In contrast, the results of the present study indicate that, in the absence of prompting adults, a greater number of 3½- to 4½-year-old children are able to recognize the appropriate context in which to say *thank you*. (4) However, this difference can be accounted for by the effect of socioeconomic status: (5) only 18 percent of the middle income children said *thank you* in contrast with 34 percent of the low income children. (6) Thus, these results replicate those of Gleason and Weintraub (1976) for middle income children. (7) The absence of parents and the familiar context do not appear to promote their use of *thank you*; (8) parental prompts may thus be seen as a necessary part of the routine.

25 (1) Greif and Gleason (1980) also found that preschool-aged boys and girls were equally likely to say *thank you* spontaneously. (2) The present results indicate that preschool-aged girls say *thank you* spontaneously more frequently than boys. (3) This finding is in accord with other research which

supports sex differences in language development (Clarke-Stewart 1973; Maccoby & Jacklin 1974; Nelson 1973). (4) Moss (1974) has suggested that girls receive more social training from adults than do boys and this may result in faster acquisition of the more social aspects of language. (5) Sex differences in the spontaneous use of *thank you* by preschoolers may also have a cultural basis, with Western culture placing more emphasis on the use of politeness routines such as *thank you* by females.

26 (1) A second factor shown to be of importance is socioeconomic status. (2) Both parents of middle and low income status have been observed to prompt their children to say *thank you* (Eisenberg 1982; Gleason & Weintraub 1976; Greif & Gleason 1980), but there are differences in their styles of teaching. (3) The finding that children of low-income families said *thank you* more frequently than children of middle-income families supports the idea that low income families stress certain pragmatic routines more. (4) This effect was not a function of race, which was confounded with socioeconomic status. (5) An alternative explanation for these results is that they reflected children's degree of appreciation, which may have varied according to the perceived magnitude of the reward. (6) That is, because families of low income are unable to provide their children with as many luxury items as families of middle income, the value of the reward (the stickers) may have been greater for the low-income preschoolers. (7) Therefore, they exhibited greater appreciation by saying *thank you* more frequently than children of middle-income status. (8) In support of this idea, the adult model observed that the low-income children showed greater excitement about the stickers than did the other children.

27 (1) The present results can also be used to address Piaget's (1959) claims. (2) Piaget argued that children under the age of seven years, especially between the ages of three and five years, find it difficult to accommodate the perspectives of their listeners. (3) The results of the present study, however, indicate that children between the ages of 3½ and 4½ years do adapt to differences in listener status and say *thank you* more frequently to adults than to peers. (4) This finding supports the results of previous studies in which preschoolers recognized differences in listener status and adjusted their use of politeness routines accordingly (Bates 1976; Becker 1982; Ervin-Tripp 1969; Schatz & Gelman 1973; Wood & Gardner 1980).

28 (1) The present study indicates that under certain circumstances, preschoolers exhibit greater competence in the use of *thank you* than prior research has revealed. (2) Nonetheless, fewer than half of the children in this study said *thank you*. (3) It is not clear how these children differed from those who failed to say *thank you* in the appropriate context. (4) The results show that sex, socioeconomic status, and status of listener affect children's use of *thank you*, and this suggests that individual differences in socialization play an important role. (5) Further research is needed to investigate the role of socialization and how it influences the development of the use of *thank you* and other pragmatic skills. (6) Additional research also needs to be done to explore how conversational contexts allow children to exhibit their abilities.

218   *Advances in written text analysis*

NOTES

* The article presented here is reprinted from *Language in Society*, by the kind permission of the author and the publishers, CUP.

1 Pinch (1985: 8–9) refers to 'the fundamental ambiguity over just what has been observed', resulting from the degree of interpretation involved in the reporting of results. The reliance upon assumptions and interpretation in observation is termed 'externalization of observation' by Pinch. He gives an example of an experiment, as a result of which there are marks on a graph. These are interpreted as indicating the presence of Argon atoms, which in turn are interpreted as indicating the presence of solar neutrinos. The researcher can report that 'splodges on a graph', or 'Ar^{37} atoms' or 'solar neutrinos' have been observed. Pinch comments: 'The difference between the possible observational reports of the experiment can be characterized by their *degree of externality*'.
2 *Activity*. The activities identified in the SUTY text are: state fact; interpret result; assess; narrate event; hypothesize; recommend; assert status; describe figure.
   Source. The possible sources are: received knowledge, data, writers, text.
   Modification. Modification may be effected by: modal verbs (*must*, *may*, etc.); modal constructions (*It is possible/clear/plausible that*; *We believe that*; *probably*; *possibly*, etc.); modal copulas (*appear*, *seem*); projecting verbs (*demonstrate*, *suggest*, *claim*, etc).
   For further details, see Hunston (1989).
3 The categories of certainty are: Known; Certain; Probable; Possible; Unlikely; Untrue; Unknown. For further details, see Hunston (1989).

14 Genre analysis: an approach to text analysis for ESP

Tony Dudley-Evans

INTRODUCTION

Genre analysis has become an important approach to text analysis, especially in the field of English for Specific Purposes (ESP). The work of Swales (1981, 1990), in particular, has generated a more focused approach to the teaching of academic writing to non-native postgraduate students or young academics learning to write in their subject. This approach has been much influenced by the work of writing scholars (e.g. Bazerman 1988; Myers 1990a) who have taken on board the findings of the sociology of science, but remains within the ESP and discourse analysis tradition.

The term **genre** was first used in an ESP context by Tarone *et al.* (1981) in an article that investigated the use of the active and passive forms in astrophysics journal articles. That article established the principle that within the conventions of the genre studied it was the writer's **communicative purpose** that governs choice at the grammatical and lexical levels. Communicative purpose is, in fact, the defining feature by which a genre such as the academic article is distinguished from other genres and by which the consideration of genre is distinguished from the consideration of register. The use of genre in ESP or applied linguistics is thus distinct from its use in literary criticism, where a particular genre, for example a tragedy, a comedy or a novel, is distinguished by its form.[1]

The view of genre adopted in ESP is much influenced by the definitions given by Miller (1984) and Martin (1989). The assumption is that a genre is a means of achieving a communicative goal that has evolved in response to particular rhetorical needs and that a genre will change and evolve in response to changes in those needs. The emphasis is thus on the means by which a text realizes its communicative purpose rather than on establishing a system for the classification of genres.

In ESP we are interested, often for pedagogical reasons, in exploring established but not necessarily codified conventions in certain key genres about style of presentation of content, the order of presentation of that content and all the myriad rhetorical factors that affect the plausibility for readers of the argument presented. We are also interested in the role of the genre within the discourse community that regularly uses it. The discourse community is that group of people within a discipline or area of special interest that communicates with each other in part through the genres which they 'possess' (Swales, 1990: 26), and which has expectations of what is permissible within the genre or genres that it uses.

Here, as in much genre analysis, we will be concerned with written text. The fact that most genre studies have been concerned with written text should not, however, be taken to imply that genre analysis is exclusively concerned with written text. Spoken genres, such as the board meeting, the business negotiation, the slide presentation and the inaugural lecture, are just as much of interest. It is the availability and the 'portability' of written text (Myers, 1990: 6) that have made it the main focus of genre analysis.

Following Swales' pioneering work on the introductions to academic articles (Swales 1981, 1990) much genre analysis has been concerned with the analysis of the various **moves** that writers use to write a given section of a text or to develop their argument. In this chapter we will be presenting an approach to the analysis of the Discussion section that draws its inspiration from Swales' original work. However, genre analysis is not always concerned with the analysis of 'moves'; it also embraces, for example, studies of tense usage (e.g. Oster 1981; Malcolm 1987), lexical frequency (Henderson and Hewings 1990) and classification of reporting verbs used in academic text (Thomas 1991; Thompson and Ye Yiyun 1991). These analyses, when placed within the context of the study of writers' communicative purpose and rhetorical strategies, play an important role in the higher-level analysis of the conventions of genres.

THE DISCUSSION SECTION

I present below an example of a move analysis of part of the Discussion section of an MSc dissertation written by a native speaker as part of the MSc course in Conservation and Utilization of Plant Genetic Resources run by the School of Biological Sciences at the University of Birmingham. I have decided to concentrate on the Discussion as this section of the article or thesis has had less attention than the Introduction, and also because it is the section that students claim to have the greatest difficulty with. For a full description of the analysis of article introductions and an outline of various textual studies of the article see Swales (1990: esp. 131–2 and 137–66).

Moves	*Discussion*
1 Statement of aims	[The aim of this research was to study the viability behaviour of cocoa seeds, and to apply any knowledge gained to devising possible methods for long-term storage of the material for the purposes
2 Work carried out	of genetic conservation.] [Various aspects were

examıned, with particular emphasis on the factors known to prolong viability in orthodox seeds, namely reductions in moisture content and temperature (Roberts 1960 and 1961; Roberts and Abdalla 1968; Harrington 1973) and oxygen levels (Roberts 1961; Roberts and Abdalla 1968; Villiers 1973) and on the possibilities of storage of seeds fully imbibed (Villiers 1973 and 1975; Villiers and Edgcumbe 1975).]

3 Finding

[Firstly, an examination of the reaction of the seeds to drying revealed that they may be reduced to a lower moisture content than previously reported, and still survive.]

4 Reference to previous research (comparison)

[Hunter (1959) and Ashiru (1970) both reported that seeds with or without testas could not be reduced below 50% + 2% moisture, without serious loss of viability. Since Hunter (1959) also reported that his seeds without testas had an initial, unreduced moisture content of 50.02%, then this implied that seeds without testas could not be dried at all without adverse effects.]

5 Statement of result

[In this study, seeds after removal of testas were found to have initial moisture contents of between 37.94 and 44.57%, for different seed batches.]

6 Explanation

[This range may have been due to the fact that various amounts of desiccation occurred during transport of the seeds to Britain, since some pods were only in transit for two days, while others took up to seven days to arrive.]

7 Reference to previous research (comparison)

[This initial moisture level is also lower than that of Hunter (1959)]

8 Explanation
9 Information move

[and this may be because of differences in the cocoa genotype or clone used.] [Hunter does not state the details of his material in this respect, but he may have used pods of a different clone from that used in this study, and it is possible that the initial moisture content varies with different types.]

10 Statement of result

[It was found that seeds may lose moisture down to a threshold value of between 17 and 20%, before suffering damage due to desiccation. Desiccation damage occurred in both the cotyledons and the embryonic axis. Cell contents pulled away from the cell walls, and condensed in the centre of the cells, and the pith region of the axis broke down completely at very low moisture.]

11 Reference to previous research

[Little attempt has been made in the past to explain why some seeds are recalcitrant, and non-tolerant of drying, while others are orthodox, and may be reduced in moisture content to very low levels, without adverse effect.]

12 Claim

[It is possible that the cell reaction seen here, in which the contents condense and leave the cell walls, may be a characteristic of recalcitrant seeds generally, while the cells of orthodox seeds may show a more generalized decrease in size, without such damage to the contents.]

13 Recommendation

[This hypothesis requires further investigation.]

14 Reference to previous research (comparison)

[The fact that in this study the moisture level of cocoa seeds could be substantially reduced without adverse effect, is contrary to the findings of previous workers, and could be a reflection of the drying method used. Hunter (1959) dried his seed samples by suspending them over various concentrations of sulphuric acid in glass jars, while Ashiru (1970) passed a current of dried air over the seeds.]

15 Explanation

[This study used silica gel as the desiccant and it is possible that this was less harsh as a drying agent, and therefore that the previous workers may also have obtained a reduction in moisture level while still maintaining viability, had other drying methods been attempted.]

16 Statement of result

[An important point noticed when the seeds were dried was that the embryonic axes of seeds always appeared to have dried more than the cotyledons. Therefore while the overall moisture of the seed at the threshold desiccation level was found to be 17–20%, it is possible that the axes were actually at a lower moisture level.]

17 Claim

[If the moisture content was in the region of 10–17%, there are possibilities here for the storage of the embryonic axis at very low temperatures, possibly as low as −196 C, in liquid nitrogen, since if the axis contains little moisture then little damage would be caused as a result of the formation of ice crystals.]

18 Reference to previous research (support)

[Roberts (1975) states that 15% moisture is the critical value in this respect. Grout (unpublished) working on tomato, and Grout and Mumford (unpublished) working on *Citrus* species, have recently shown that seeds can survive even with a moisture content of up to 20%,]

19 Limitation (of claim)

[provided that freezing is performed carefully, and with the use of suitable cryo-protectants. The success of such storage with cocoa would be dependent not only on a low moisture level

in the axis, but also on the ability of the cell contents
to withstand low temperatures.]

(Brett, 1979)

Here we notice that in paragraph 1 the writer begins by introducing the reader to the discussion by summarizing the aim of the work and stating what research has been carried out. As Huckin (1987) has noted, the discussion frequently reverses the order of moves that Swales posits for the introduction section by beginning with a restatement of the aim, whereas in the introduction the statement of aim is normally the final move. I see this paragraph as an example of an introduction to the discussion. In Dudley-Evans (1986: 141) I suggested that there are in general terms three parts to a discussion: (1) Introduction, (2) Evaluation of Results, (3) Conclusions and Future Work.

The writer then moves on to the results of the research. In paragraph 2 she reports one of the main **findings**, the fact that cocoa seeds could be reduced to a lower moisture level than previously reported and still survive. She then **compares** the finding with **previous research**. This is followed by the presentation of a **result**, this time a statement of the initial moisture level of the seeds. This result is then **explained** in some detail, which involves accounting for differences with previous research. In the final sentence of the paragraph the writer presents a short **information move** that is linked to the comparison with previous research in the preceding sentence. The final clause of the paragraph has some of the signals of a claim, notably the phrase 'it is possible that . . .'. My initial reaction was to classify the clause as a **claim**, but further consideration of the meaning of the text suggested that this is a low-level claim that is embedded in the **information move**.

In paragraph 3 she reports more detailed results. This is followed by a very interesting move: she refers to a lack of previous research in this particular area, thereby attempting to raise the status of the reported results by claiming originality for them. The fact that she feels a need to mention this lack of previous research would seem to indicate an awareness of the importance of following up a **statement of result** with a **reference to previous research** in order to validate the result. This then leads into the first of the writer's **claims** recognizable by the use of a hedged expression: 'it is possible that . . .'. This cycle is rounded off by a short **recommendation** that the claim needs further investigation.

Paragraph 4 presents a **reference to previous research** and an **explanation** of the differences. In paragraph 5 she states another **result**, which leads into the second of her **claims**, recognizable again from the hedged clause: 'there are possibilities here for the storage of the embryonic axis'. This **claim** is then **supported** by **reference** to various examples of **previous research**. Here the references to previous research are acting as both a support for and a limitation of the claim just made. The cycle is rounded off with a statement **limiting the claim** that specifies the conditions under which the claim is likely to be valid. This cycle of **claim** followed by **support from previous research** is very common in this and other data (e.g. McKinlay 1982).

The discussion proceeds in similar fashion for the next eight pages until it reaches the concluding section immediately below.

1 Summary of main findings	[Despite the fact that cocoa seeds are recalcitrant, and no successful method has yet been found for storage of the material long-term, certain of the conditions examined here suggest that there is some hope for storage in the future. It has been shown that the embryonic axes of the seeds will survive low temperatures for several weeks, with no damage, and therefore there may be potential in the method suggested of drying the seeds to a particular level, and subsequent storage of the axes in liquid
2 Recommendation	nitrogen.] [An examination is needed of the effects of cold on the axes after much longer time periods, and a study is also required on how far the moisture content of the axes alone (rather than the whole seeds) may be reduced before they lose viability. After storage in this way, the axes would have to be grown in culture, and again more work is needed on culture techniques.]
3 Recommendation	[The other major line which seems worthy of further consideration is the possibility of storage of fully imbibed seeds, with the application of germination inhibitors. The most important approach to follow here at present is the identification of the inhibitory substance in the cocoa pod itself.]
4 Recommendation	[Bearing these possibilities in mind, the problem of long-term storage of cocoa seeds for genetic conservation may not be insoluble.]

Here the writer summarizes the main **results** and **claims** before presenting a list of **recommendations** for future work, which are rounded off by a short conclusion.

MOVE CYCLES

Two aspects of this analysis are particularly worthy of comment. The first is that there seems to be an overarching three-part framework to the Discussion: **Introduction–Evaluation–Conclusion**. The introduction here sets the scene for the whole discussion by **restating the aim** and briefly describing **the work carried out**. In other examples we have noted **summary of the method used**, **restatement of the relevant theory** or **previous research** or, in some cases, **a statement of the main results/findings of the research**. The main body of the discussion provides detailed **comment** on the key results and the writer's main **claims**. The conclusion summarizes the main **results** and **claims** before making **recommendations** about future work.

The second point is that the main part of the discussion, the evaluation of results, can be analysed into a series of move cycles that combine two or more of the following moves:

(1) **Information Move**: the writers present background information about theory, the aim of the research, the methodology used, previous research that is felt to be necessary for the understanding of what follows in the move cycle.

(2) **Statement of Result**: this is frequently the first move in a cycle and is followed by one or more moves that comment on the result. A statement of result either presents a numerical value or refers to a graph or table of results.

(3) **Finding**: the function of a finding is essentially the same as a **statement of result** in that it is followed by a series of moves that comment on it. The basic difference is that a finding does not present actual figures but rather an observation arising from the research.

(4) **(Un)expected outcome**: the writers make a comment on the fact that a result is expected or, much more frequently, unexpected or surprising. The fact that the result is unexpected or surprising creates a need for a comment.

(5) **Reference to Previous Research**: the writers either **compare** their results with those found in previous research or use the previous research as a **support** for their own **claims** or **explanations**.

(6) **Explanation**: the writers give reasons for an unexpected result or one that differs significantly from previous research.

(7) **Claim**: the writers make a generalization arising from their results which is their contribution to the ongoing research on the topic. This is often referred to as a **knowledge claim**. In previous articles on this topic I and others (e.g. Hopkins and Dudley-Evans 1988; Peng 1987), have referred to a **hypothesis**, which is a hedged claim, and a **deduction**, which is a more confidently presented (i.e. unhedged) claim. I now prefer to combine these into one move. Claims tend to be presented cautiously, that is, using modal or other hedged phrases.[2]

(8) **Limitation**: the writers introduce one or more caveats about the findings, the methodology followed or the claims made.

(9) **Recommendation**: the writers make suggestions for future lines of research in the topic, or for improvements in the methodology followed in the research reported in the article.

The key move cycles are those involving **Statement of results** or **Findings** followed by a **Reference to previous research**, or a **Claim** also followed by a **Reference to previous research**. Sometimes the focus is on the Result, Finding or Claim with the Reference to previous research acting as an evaluation of those moves.[3] This was the case in the extract from the MSc thesis quoted above. The similarity to the clause relation Claim + Basis (Thomas 1991) will be clear.

At other times the order is reversed and the result or finding is presented as confirming a particular claim made by previous researchers. An example of this is provided in a text found by Hozayen (work in progress):

> Metastases to the central airways from extrathoracic tumours are rare, being present in 2 percent of patients who die with solid tumours. Renal and colorectal carcinomas are reportedly the most common tumours giving rise to such metastases . . . . This study provides further evidence that such metastases do occur and that combination therapy including Nd – Yag laser debulking offers not only symptomatic relief in most cases, but also some instances of improved survival.
>
> (Carlin *et al.* 1989: 1110–14)

The basis for an author's claim is sometimes provided by the presentation of results or findings from the author's own research, as in the following example found by Hozayen (work in progress):

> An improvement in the distribution of VA/Q may also improve the Pa O_2. In normal subjects, an increase in the VA/Q inequality contributes to a worsening in the alveolar–arterial oxygen gradient during severe exercise. In our patients mean P $(A - a)O_2$ increased from rest (19.7 ± 2.6 mm Hg) to peak exercise (25.2 ± 3.1 mm Hg) significantly ($p < 0.04$).
>
> (Forkert *et al.* 1989: 1100)

We see the role of referring to previous research or the presentation of results or findings in support of a Claim as increasing the plausibility of that claim. The use of referencing in academic articles as a means of persuading the reader of the accuracy or plausibility of one's claims, results or findings is well attested in the literature of the sociology of science.[4] Thomas (1991) has shown in detail how authors use reports of previous research in a variety of ways to increase the plausibility of the claims they wish to make. We believe that the move analysis outlined in this chapter shows the same processes at work; it is part of what Myers (1990a) refers to as the creation of a 'narrative' about the experimental data presented in the article or dissertation.

DISCUSSION

Two questions about this approach to analysis are pertinent: first, how do we make decisions about the classification of moves; and, second, how can we be confident of the validity of the moves and move cycles that are posited? Decisions about the classification of the moves are made on the basis of linguistic evidence, comprehension of the text and understanding of the expectations that both the general academic community and the particular discourse community have of the text. In most cases it is possible to classify the moves on the basis of linguistic evidence. In the analysis shown on page 221, it was very easy in the second paragraph to make decisions on the basis of such evidence. In the first sentence the lexical items *an examination . . . . revealed* clearly indicate a finding; in the second and third the citation of *Hunter (1959) and Ashiru (1970)* show that this is a reference to previous research; in the fourth the lexical items *in this study* and *were found* plus the quoting of actual data for moisture contents tells us that this is a statement of result; in the fifth sentence the phrase *may have been due to* is a strong signal of an explanation. In the sixth the comparison with previous research is signalled by the phrase *is also lower than that of Hunter (1959)*, and the actual citation of Hunter; in the second half of the sentence the explanation is signalled by the phrase *may be because*. The final sentence is more difficult to classify; the phrase *it is possible that* is a signal of a claim, but, as noted above, it was decided on the basis of our understanding of the text that the role of this clause is subsidiary to the information move presented in the first half of the sentence. It was therefore decided that the whole sentence should be classified as an information move.

At other times the lexical clues are less obvious and one needs to make use of one's understanding of the text itself and of the way that the genre is generally expressed. For example, the second sentence in the second paragraph is, as stated above, clearly a reference to previous research. It is less immediately clear whether it is acting as a comparison with or as a support for the finding that precedes it; at least there are no linguistic signals indicating which of the two it is. However, two factors indicate that it is a comparison: the first is the fact that it follows the presentation of a finding; second, it has been found in these analyses that a reference to previous research acting as a comparison frequently follows a statement of result or finding without any overt linguistic signal of comparison. Knowledge of the genre conventions helps both the reader of the text and the analyst to understand this. Similarly, as discussed above on page 223, a knowledge of the conventions helps the analyst to realize why the writer sees the need to mention the lack of previous work in paragraph 3.

The second question is about the validity of the analysis. How can we be confident that the moves and move cycles that we have posited have any concrete reality and are not 'little more than a reflection of my own perceptual predispositions' (Swales 1981: 14)? There are a number of approaches to validation of the analysis. Crookes (1986) has argued that the accuracy of this type of analysis can be tested by showing that the moves can be defined in such a way that a group of raters can agree on their classification with a sufficiently high level of agreement. He states that if a system represents an accurate reflection of the text, it should be possible to reach such agreement. Following this procedure with the Swales 4-Move model for article introductions, Crookes was able to obtain agreement at above 0.6 (Crookes 1986: 65). With the analysis reported in this chapter, the approach was rather different. The categories and the actual analysis of selected discussions were checked with a specialist informant from the Plant Biology department. Other parts of the analysis were validated by comparing the results with the analysis produced by other approaches, notably clause relations. In Dudley-Evans (1986) I reported that there is considerable overlap between the boundaries for categories generated by separate analyses based on clause relations and genre analysis. It is assumed that if the two systems of analysis agree on the boundaries between the various chunks of text, this indicates that both analyses are capturing something real in the text. Mauranen (1993) has also shown that there is a relation between the moves found in the introduction and discussion sections of a journal article and a theme/rheme analysis of those texts.

This brief introduction to the methods of genre analysis has, I hope, shown some of the advantages of the approach. Perhaps still the strongest argument in its favour is that it provides input to the increasingly important and popular courses in academic writing run for those aspiring to be full members of the academic community, that is, thesis writers and newly appointed members of academic departments. The sophistication of a recent text-book *Writing up Research* (Weissberg and Buker 1990), which draws directly on the findings of genre analysis, provides evidence of its pedagogical value. But this is not the only claim I am making. I have tried to show that the detailed and perhaps rather laborious findings that come from the analysis of particular sections of the academic article or thesis provide concrete evidence that supports the claims of those working in the areas of rhetoric and sociology of science. I have argued elsewhere (Johns and Dudley-Evans 1991) that this type of analysis may have a role in the demystification of the epistemological conventions of certain disciplines. This work shows applied linguistics bringing particular insights and a certain rigour to the investigation of both the general academic culture and particular disciplinary variations of that culture.

APPENDIX: ARTICLES/THESIS REFERRED TO

Brett, A. C. (1979), 'A study of the viability of cocoa seeds (*Theobroma Cacao* L.)', unpublished MSc thesis, University of Birmingham, UK.
Carlin, B. W., J. H. Harrell, L. K. Olsen and K. M. Moser (1989), 'Endobronchial metastases due to colectoral carcinoma', *Chest* 96: 1110–14.
Forkert, L.F., R.D. Wigle, P.W. Munt and J.M. Todesco (1989), 'Oxygenation in patients with chronic airflow obstruction after cessation of exercise', *Chest* 96: 1099–103.

NOTES

1 For a full discussion of the use of the term genre in various disciplines, see Swales (1990, pp. 33–49).
2 For a full discussion of hedging in academic articles see Myers (1989).
3 See Hunston (1989) for a full discussion of the role of evaluation in scientific articles.
4 See especially Gilbert (1977) and Latour and Woolgar (1979).

15 On Theme, Rheme and discourse goals

Peter H. Fries

THEMATIC STRUCTURE AND RELATED ISSUES

In recent years, a number of linguists have been interested in the flow of information in texts.[1] I have been using a systemic–functional approach to discourse analysis to demonstrate the usefulness of the concept of Theme. As a part of that endeavour, it is necessary to develop a better description of Theme. Halliday has defined Theme in the following terms.

> The English clause consists of a 'theme' and a 'rheme' . . . [the theme] is, as it were, the peg on which the message is hung, . . . The theme of the clause is the element which, in English, is put in first position; . . .
>
> (Halliday 1970: 161)

> The Theme is a function of the CLAUSE AS MESSAGE. It is what the message is concerned with: the point of departure for what the speaker is going to say.
>
> (Halliday 1985: 36)

It is useful to notice that 'pegs' and 'points of departure' are semantic notions. The statement that Theme occurs in first position in English is a realizational statement for English, not a definition of the notion of Theme. Further, the definitions quoted here describe Theme as an element of structure of the clause, although elsewhere Halliday makes it clear that he believes other structures, such as clause complexes (1985: 56–9) and nominal and verbal groups (1977: 183; 1985: 158, 166, 176), also have Thematic structures. Following Halliday's suggestion, I have found it useful to treat Thematic structures in independent conjoinable clause complexes. This structure consists of an independent clause together with all hypotactically related clauses which are dependent on it. The independent conjoinable clause complex is very similar to the T-unit of American educational literature (see Hunt 1965), and so I will use the term 'T-Unit', since it is so much shorter.

In Fries (forthcoming a), I have also rephrased Halliday's definition of the meaning of Theme somewhat less metaphorically in the following terms:

The Theme of a T-unit provides a framework within which the Rheme of that T-unit can be interpreted.[2]

Text 1 illustrates the use of Thematic information.

Text 1
1   What does the term *culture* mean throughout this book?
2   *As used by anthropologists*, the term *culture* means any human behavior that is learned rather than biologically transmitted.

(Gregg 1985: 2)

In text 1, the author is obviously aware that the word *culture* is often used with radically different interpretations from the one she intends to use. By placing the restriction *as used by anthropologists* first in sentence 2, she 'prevents' the response 'That's not what *culture* means to me'.

Before continuing with a discussion of Theme, it is useful to point out two related concepts – information structure and participant reference – which should not be confused with Thematic meanings. Information structure includes the division of what is said into units of information and the signalling of which portions of those information units are most important. In the spoken language, units of information are signalled by the location of tone-group boundaries, while the location of tonic prominence indicates the culmination of the information that is being presented as New. Halliday defines New information as 'information which is being presented by the speaker as . . . not recoverable by the listener' (1985: 277). New information is contrasted with Given information, which is defined as 'information which is being presented by the speaker as recoverable . . . to the listener' (1985: 277). I prefer to rephrase Halliday's definition of New positively, as 'information which is being presented as "newsworthy"'. (Indeed, this re-phrasing is in keeping with Halliday's intent, since he elaborates on the meaning of New by saying, 'the meaning [of New] is: attend to this; this is news' (1985: 277).) The revised description of New has the added advantage of being quite different from the description of a related factor, the notion of participant identification.

Participant identification refers to the ways the various participants are introduced and referred to in the development of a text. In text 2, for example, Alice has the task of introducing two new participants (*a book* and *a newspaper*) into the discourse, while Betty needs to refer to one of those participants (*the book*) as already on stage and in attention.

Text 2
Alice: I have a book and a newspaper. Which do you want?
Betty: Could you give me the book?

Alice achieves her task by introducing the participants with indefinite articles, while Betty achieves her task by referring to the participant with a definite article. Many linguists describe the use of the indefinite article as

Introducing a referent which is not recoverable from the context, while definite articles are said to introduce referents which are recoverable from the context. Of course, these descriptions introduce an ambiguity, since 'recoverability' has already been used to describe the difference between Given and New information. Since the two concepts are similar, this is a serious ambiguity. In the case of participant identification, we are concerned with referential identity. In the case of information structure, referential identity is not a primary focus. We are, rather, concerned with what is considered 'news'. One way to avoid the confusions inherent in the different interpretations of 'recoverability' is to avoid that term altogether. I have already chosen to use the term 'newsworthiness' to describe the meaning of New in information structure. In the issue of participant reference, I will follow Martin (1992) in distinguishing presenting and presuming reference. Presenting reference introduces new referents into the discourse, and, in English, is associated with indefiniteness. Presuming reference, on the other hand, introduces participants which are familiar to the audience, and, in English, is associated with definiteness.

It has long been noticed that a correlation exists between the concepts discussed so far. Many linguists (including Halliday 1967, 1985; Chafe 1980, 1984) have noted that each new intonation contour signals a new chunk of information (or new information unit, to use Halliday's term). Similarly, Halliday (1967: 200–1; 1985: 274) and Chafe (1984: 437) note an unmarked correlation between the clause and the information unit. Finally, they also note a general tendency for the last major constituent of the clause to receive a tonic accent. That is, there seems to be a general correlation between Rhematic status and the culmination of the New information. At the other end of the clause, most Themes are presented as Given information, and often contain presuming reference. It would be wrong, however, to assume that the correlations between these concepts are perfect. Many Themes (particularly marked Themes) are pronounced as separate tone groups and thus are presented as New information, and while most Themes do contain presuming reference, many do not. Similarly, while Rhemes usually are presented as containing New information, many are not so presented. (Indeed, Davies (1989) points out that the placement of Given information in the Rheme can function as a cohesive device.)

The role of information structure may be illustrated by a discussion of text 3:

Text 3

//4 ⌒ in / **this** job / Anne we're // 1 working with / **silver** / ⌒ //

(Halliday 1985: 283)

Text 3 is the initial sentence of a conversation in which a job trainee is being oriented to a new job. This is one of several jobs which the trainee has encountered or will encounter. Both participants know this fact. The sentence is divided into two tone groups (tone-group boundaries are marked by //).

Each tone group contains one tonic syllable (marked in bold). In this sentence the New information is restricted to the tonic syllables. In this context the listener can recover the notions of 'job', 'working', etc. The newsworthy part of the message lies in 'this' (in opposition to other jobs) and 'silver' (in opposition to other sorts of objects). The restriction of New to single words is merely an aspect of this example, and should not be interpreted as a general restriction on the occurrence of New. Indeed, later in this chapter, examples will be seen in which entire sentences will be considered to function as New. The example in text 3 illustrates a Theme being presented as a separate information unit and therefore containing New information. That information is presuming reference. Thus, the example shows that Thematic status and presuming reference are independent of status as Given information.

Two important points should be made about the definitions of Given and New. (1) Given and New are oriented toward the listener. They constitute instructions to the listener about how to interpret what is said and how it is to be related to what the listener already knows. (2) The decision of what to signal as Given or New rests with the speaker. It is a meaningful choice, and therefore it is not predictable. That is, even if we know that the listener knows some bit of information, and we know that the speaker knows that the listener knows that information, we still cannot predict with certainty that that information will be presented as Given.

DISCOURSE EFFECTS OF THEME AND RHEME

So far my presentation has followed the Hallidayan model fairly closely. There are several problems, however. One problem lies in the description of the meaning of Theme. The Hallidayan descriptions of 'the peg on which the message is hung' and the 'point of departure of the clause as message' are clearly metaphorical. Even my rephrasing of this notion 'providing a framework for interpretation', though less metaphorical, is still difficult to interpret in many examples. In my work on Theme, I have tried to provide a better 'fix' on the meaning of Theme by a three-pronged approach. (1) I have tried to describe strategies for the development of texts which would lead one to make certain items of information Thematic in specific contexts (see Fries forthcoming a). (2) I have tried to connect Thematic content with the perceived meanings of texts (see Fries 1981). (3) I have tried to contrast the effect of giving information the status of Theme with the effects of information which has been given other sorts of status (see Fries 1981).

Points (2) and (3) can be seen in the following hypotheses, which I made in Fries (1981).

(1) If a text segment is perceived as having a single method of development, then the words which contribute to the expression of that method of development will occur Thematically within the T-units of that text segment.
(2) If a text segment is perceived as expressing a single point, then the words

which contribute to the expression of that point will occur within the Rhemes of the component T-units of that text segment.

(3) The perception of a nominal item as topic of a text segment is unrelated to the Thematic or Rhematic placement of the references to that item.

The model used here is a correlational model.[3] No claim is intended that every text segment must have a single simple method of development or must express a single point, or must have a simple nominal topic. Indeed, many people object to using the notion of a single method of development or single point, since many text segments do not have such phenomena. Even in these more complicated text segments, however, the intent of my basic hypothesis remains: Themes and Rhemes of clauses and clause complexes are used for different purposes. As part of specifying the uses of Thematic information, it is useful to examine a longer text which is not so uniform as the ones I previously examined. I will use a written text because I suspect that the differences between the uses of Thematic and Rhematic information will be more prominent.[4]

First, let me explain why I believe that the differences between Thematic and Rhematic information will be most prominent in formal written English. We have already said that New information is that which is being presented as 'newsworthy', and that in the spoken language, the culmination of the New information is signalled by the location of the tonic accent. Of course, in the written language, there is no accent, and thus a major means of signalling New information is lost. What alternatives exist within the written language to signal 'newsworthiness'? Perhaps the most obvious means are graphic signals such as underlining, capitalization, the use of coloured ink or the use of different type faces or sizes. In addition there are considerations such as paragraphing and placement of information on the page. Most of these means are used with restraint in more formal writing. (Editors often do not approve of using capital letters or underlining for emphasis.) As a result, writers in these formal contexts are restricted to using other means to indicate what is 'newsworthy'. Two major resources come to mind: (1) writers sequence the information in their texts so that readers have the relevant background information in their attention as they read each new sentence; (2) writers tend to sequence the information presented in each sentence so that, where possible, the New information is placed where the unmarked tonic accent would be in the spoken sentence. That is, writers will tend to place New information towards the end of the clause, thus strengthening the correlation of New with Rheme.[5]

THEME, N-RHEME AND DISCOURSE GOALS

To summarize, we are assuming that there is a correlation between Thematic position and Given information on the one hand, and Rhematic position and New information on the other. My hypothesis is that writers use position at the end of the clause to indicate the newsworthy information to their readers, and that they use the beginnings of their clauses to orient their readers to the message which will come in the rest of the clause.

We already have a good term ('Theme') for the first clause-level constituent at the beginning of the clause. However, we need a term for the end of the clause. Rheme is too inclusive, since in Halliday's terminology it includes everything that is not Theme. Since we are interested in the unmarked association of Rheme with New, and since New typically is associated with the last constituent of the clause, we can coin the term N-Rheme to indicate the last constituent of the clause.

As we examine the text, we should keep in mind that the N-Rheme is the newsworthy part of the clause,[6] that is, the part of the clause that the writer wants the reader to remember. As a result we should expect the content of the N-Rheme to correlate with the goals of the text as a whole, the goals of the text segment within those larger goals, and the goals of the sentence and the clause as well. On the other hand, the Theme is the orienter to the message conveyed by the clause. It tells the reader how to understand the news conveyed by the clause. As a result, we should expect the choice of Thematic content usually to reflect local concerns. For example, if we are examining a text which has a problem–solution structure, we should expect the meanings to change as the text moves from the description of the problem to the description of the solution. Both the Thematic content and the N-Rhematic content should change. However, the content of the N-Rhemes should be more obviously connected with the goals of each text portion. For example, in the section which describes the problem, the N-Rhemes should have an obvious connection with what is wrong, while in the section which describes the solution, the N-Rhemes should have an obvious connection with what was done to solve the problem. The Themes of the problem section, on the other hand, might well concern different aspects of the item which is causing the problem (say an engine which is not functioning properly), while the themes of the solution section might concern notions such as the relative temporal order of the actions taken in solving the problem.

A SAMPLE ANALYSIS

I wish to take as my text a fund-raising letter sent out by the political action group Zero Population Growth (henceforth ZPG). The text of the letter is provided in Appendix I, while Appendix II contains the same letter with items labelled to facilitate reference. Each new paragraph has been assigned a capital letter and each punctuated sentence has been given a number. Each non-embedded clause in each sentence has been given a lower-case letter and placed on a separate line. The logo, the date and other information associated with the genre of letter writing have also been assigned capital letters and numbers even though they do not clearly constitute clauses, sentences or paragraphs. Since not every item that has been assigned a number is actually a sentence, I will refer to numbered items as segments. (Thus, 'segment 7' refers to clauses 7a and 7b.) The Theme of a clause is written in small capitals, while the N-Rheme of the clause is indicated by italics. All underlining is in the original.

The letter was written by an officer of ZPG to people who were on her mailing list, usually because they had already contributed money. That is, the audience was presumed to be already sympathetic. But sympathetic as the audience might have been, the author still needed to persuade her readers to contribute money to this particular project, and she chose to take an advertising approach to the task. This is not the only approach which might have been used, but it is not an unusual one. The approach she took is basically one of first motivating a request, and then expressing that request.[7] How can she motivate her request? Two points are obvious: (1) she must show a need for money; and (2) she must show the value of her project. Since the author is writing to an audience that she presumes is already sympathetic with the basic issue, she can assume that her readers agree that overpopulation is an issue. As a result, she does not emphasize that idea. Rather, she spends her effort on describing the value of this particular project. One way of showing the value of a political action project is to show the effects it has had. Relevant effects for a political action group are of two basic types: (1) getting the message heard (so that political forces can be brought to bear); and (2) influencing decisions made by political officials. Thus, the author should show the effects of ZPG on three audiences: public officials (who make decisions), members of the media (who can get information out to the public), and the public (who can affect decisions that the public officials make). The need can be demonstrated by showing (a) that harmful things are happening to the organization because of the lack of funds, or (b) the organization could be much more effective if it had more funds to take advantage of opportunities which are being presented at this time. This appeal can be made more dramatic by adding a note of urgency. (Indeed, in general, it would seem to be prudent when trying to raise funds to do one's best to get the audience to send the money *now*, or they may find other things to spend it on.)

A couple of other general factors in the situation also affect this letter. First, in our society requests are better received if they are personalized. That is, if they are seen as coming from some person (or group) and as showing that the person they are addressed to has some personal stake in the success of the group. As a result, we should expect that the author of this fund-raising letter will try to involve the reader, and will try to make the organization more obvious as a group of people. Finally, the request cannot be too direct. The author cannot merely say 'Send money!' From what has been said here, we may hypothesize that the letter will generally emphasize the following meanings:

(1) the value of the project;
(2) the reactions of non-ZPG people. This description will include the reaction of the three primary groups mentioned above:

(a) public officials;
(b) members of the media;
(c) the public;
(3) the need for help;
(4) the urgency of the need for help.

Since these meanings relate to the goals of the text, we predict that they will regularly be found in the N-Rhemes rather than the Themes of the component clauses.

The above list describes a number of meanings which can be seen to be important for the functioning of a fund-raising letter, particularly one which attempts to raise funds for a political action group. That is, the list applies to the purposes of the text as a whole. Since the goals of the various portions of the text may vary, we also need an interpretation of the text which describes the goals of each of its parts. Rhetorical Structure Theory (RST), as developed by William Mann and Sandra Thompson (see, for example, Mann and Thompson 1985, 1986), provides just such an interpretation. RST analysis describes a text as composed of a number of text portions. Each text portion (except the largest) is related to at least one other text portion by one of a small list of relations such as antithesis, concession, etc. The combination of the two is then seen as a larger text portion, which has a nucleus and satellite structure. Finally, each relation is seen as deriving from a goal which the author wishes to achieve by adding the satellite to the nucleus. Appendix III presents an analysis of the ZPG letter published in Mann, Matthiessen and Thompson (1992). It provides a detailed interpretation of certain aspects of the ZPG text, one which relates explicitly to the presumed goals that the author had in creating this text. Finally, I should note that it was done by others independently of my work, and without consideration of Thematic and N-Rhematic structures.

Since their analysis concerns relations between clauses and larger portions of the text, Mann, Matthiessen and Thompson have not treated those aspects of this letter which concern its structure as a letter. For example, segments 1–3 – the ZPG logo, the date and the address to the reader – are missing from their analysis. Rather they have focused on the body of the letter. They find that the body of the letter expresses two requests: the first is expressed in segments 4–23, and the second is expressed in segments 29–30. The nucleus of the first request is segment 22. Segments 4–21 and 23, then, constitute two motivations for the reader to comply with the request expressed in 22. Within the first motivation section (segments 4–21) there is again a nucleus–satellite structure, with segments 11–16 constituting the nucleus of the motivation, and groups 4–10 and 17–21 constituting the satellites. In this case, the two satellites each provide evidence to support the claims in 11–16. Within the group which includes segments 4–10, segments 4–6 provide a background for segments 7–10. Segments 4, 5 and 6 are in a sequence relation and in fact constitute a small narrative. But, of course this narrative is the beginning of a section intended to motivate the reader to comply with a request to send money. Let us examine what happens in that narrative.

4 AT 7.00 A.M. ON OCTOBER 25 our phones *started to ring.*
5 CALLS jammed our switchboard *all day.*
6a STAFFERS stayed *late into the night,*
6b answering *questions,*
6c AND talking *with reporters from newspapers, radio stations, wire services and TV stations in every part of the country.*

The information which is emphasized in this passage (see Appendix II for conventions) seems to begin with activity (*started to ring*) and then moves into the duration of that activity (*all day*) and the range of that activity (*with reporters from newspapers . . . in every part of the country*). One of the interesting aspects of this small narrative is the absence of action on the part of *we* (= ZPG). That is, while *started to ring* describes an activity, it is the phones, not the people, that engage in that activity. Further, we know that phones ring in response to someone else calling. Though *jamming* is a material process, it is the nominalized process *calls* that is the actor. To uncover the people involved in this process, one must infer something such as *people called us.* Again, the ZPG is the goal of the action and is seen to respond to the actions of others. Finally, *stayed* (in 6a) is not an activity but a relational process. It is only when one gets to clause 6b that one finds a human connected with ZPG actually doing something – answering questions – and even that activity is clearly done in response to some other person. In the light of all the reactive meanings in the previous clauses, one could very well interpret the last clause ((6c) *talking with reporters . . . country*) also as ZPG personnel reacting to others outside the organization.

Indeed, in segment 7, the author does refer to the previous narrative as a response.

7a WHEN WE released *the results of ZPG's <u>1985 Urban Stress Test</u>,*
7b WE had *no idea we'd get such an overwhelming response.*

In fact this reference is located at the very end of segment 7 (the N-Rheme of both the clause and the sentence), where it receives a natural prominence. Further, the term *overwhelming* is used to describe the response. What justification have we been given for this description? The reactive nature of ZPG in the narrative has already been pointed out. The author has prepared us for 'overwhelming' by consistently placing information which would lead to that judgement in the N-Rhemes of the component clauses.[8] In clauses 5 and 6a *all day* and *late into the night* indicate the (great) extent of the reaction. The N-Rheme of 6c details the wide range of the reaction. We are given a list of the major news media. Such a list has much the same effect as saying 'all the major news media'.

Segment 8 explicitly repeats the evaluation of the response described in segment 7.

8   MEDIA AND PUBLIC REACTION has been *nothing short of incredible.*

Mann, Matthiessen and Thompson describe the relation between segments 7 and 8 as one of Restatement. But there is a difference between the two segments. In segment 7 the grammar of the main clause focuses on the surprise the response caused. (*We'd get such an overwhelming response* is an embedded clause within the noun phrase *no idea we'd get such an overwhelming response.*) Clearly, the notion of surprise *had no idea* is grammatically prominent here. Segment 8 focuses exclusively on an evaluation of the response (*nothing short of incredible* is an attribute of *media and public reaction*). It is of interest to note that in this context, receiving an overwhelming reaction to an activity is good, since the goal of the organization is to affect people's lives. Doing something which people react to is therefore an indication of being effective.

Lest that message be lost on the reader, the author goes on in segments 9 and 10 to elaborate on the nature of that reaction:

9   AT FIRST, THE DELUGE OF CALLS came *mostly from reporters eager to tell the public about Urban Stress Test results and from outraged public officials who were furious that we had 'blown the whistle' on conditions in their cities.*

10   NOW, WE are hearing *from concerned citizens in all parts of the country who want to know what they can do to hold local officials accountable for tackling population-related problems that threaten public health and well-being.*

Again, the N-Rhemes are devoted to the elaboration of the range of response engendered by the report. Segments 9 and 10 consist of single clauses. Segment 9 is coded as a metaphorical motion, with the source of the calls coded as a directional source, while segment 10 is coded as a mental perception, again with the source being coded as a direction. In both cases, the N-Rhemes of the clauses are entirely devoted to an elaborate description of the sources of the calls – that is, the people who are doing the calling. Again we are given a list and it is seen to include the people whom ZPG might well consider it important to affect (i.e. reporters, public officials and concerned citizens).

Clearly, it is obvious from the content of the N-Rhemes of segments 4–10 that the author is emphasizing the great reaction engendered by the release of the ZPG Urban Stress Test. At this point, a large reaction is good. One would expect this from the general mode of argumentation used by other letters in similar situations, and one can see this value in the wording of this portion of the ZPG letter.

However, the letter undergoes a change at this point. Mann, Matthiessen and Thompson indicate this change by saying that segments 11–16 constitute the nucleus of the motivation of the request. Segments 11–12 form a background for segment 13. Segments 11–13 are in a concessive relation to segments 14–16 and, finally, segment 12 elaborates segment 11, while clause

11b elaborates 11a. How are these relations reflected in the Thematic and N-Rhematic structures of these segments?

We see that the Themes in segments 11–13 all refer to the Urban Stress Test. The Urban Stress Test is being elaborated in this passage, and this portion of the letter focuses on the various attributes of the Urban Stress Test. This effect is achieved by repeatedly placing references to the Urban Stress Test within the Themes of each clause, which has the effect of making the ZPG Urban Stress Test the method of development of this portion of the letter. The N-Rhemes, on the other hand, contain the new information about the elaborated item. In this case, the N-Rhematic information gives a general description of the nature of the test (in 11a), emphasizes the work that went into developing the test (in 11b), gives a more detailed description of the test (in 12) and describes who might use it (in 13). All these attributes are quite useful in helping the reader understand the nature of the test, and in pointing out the quality and usefulness of the test.

11a ZPG's 1985 URBAN STRESS TEST, «F11b», is *the nation's first survey of how population-linked pressures affect U.S. cities*
11b created *after months of persistent and exhaustive research.*
12 IT ranks 184 urban areas *on 11 different criteria ranging from crowding and birth rates to air quality and toxic wastes.*
13 THE URBAN STRESS TEST translates complex, technical data *into an easy-to-use action tool for concerned citizens, elected officials and opinion leaders.*

At this point in the letter, the author apparently feels that she has established the basic argument as to the effectiveness of the organization. She then turns to an argument to establish the need for further support. While she has to demonstrate that the organization is doing well, she cannot afford to imply that the organization is so effective that it no longer needs help. That is, she needs to prevent the response 'If the organization has done so well so far, why does it need my money right now?' She does so at this point by distinguishing between having a tool and using it well. Mann, Matthiessen and Thompson describe the relation between 11–13 and 14–16 as Concession. Thus this portion of the text has roughly the meaning of 'Though we have this marvellous tool [implying that we do not need help], we still need your help'. Certainly, the author emphasizes the truth of segment 14 and devotes segment 15 to supporting it. The author must emphasize the notion of need at this point, and it can be seen that the N-Rhemes of the various clauses do contain meanings which relate to that notion:

14a BUT TO USE it *well,*
14b WE urgently need *your help.*
15a OUR SMALL STAFF is being swamped *with requests for more information*
15b AND OUR MODEST RESOURCES are being stretched *to the limit.*
16 YOUR SUPPORT NOW is *critical.*

Clause 14a implies a distinction between having the test and using it well (with *well* receiving emphasis as the N-Rheme of the clause). Similarly, the N-Rheme of 14b contains *your help* as the object of *need*. Clauses 15a and 15b seem to provide evidence to support the statement in 14b. The N-Rheme of 15a (*with requests for more information*) encoded as the Actor of the process of *being swamped* links the great reaction described in segments 4–10 to the present problems of ZPG. The harmful aspect of the great reaction is also emphasized in 15b by placing *to the limit* in the N-Rheme of its clause as an adverbial of the verb *being stretched*. It is worth noting again that the N-Rhemes do not necessarily contain *all* the New information in the clause. Thus in segment 14b, the New information would probably include *urgently need* in addition to *your help*. Similarly, the New information in 15a would include *swamped*, and the New information in 15b would include *stretched* in addition to the italicized portions of those clauses. Thus, while the N-Rheme of these clauses does not exhaust the New information contained in the clause, each N-Rheme does contain at least a part of the New information.

The negative effects described in clauses 15a and 15b are applied directly to aspects of ZPG. (*Our small staff* is goal of *being swamped*, and *our modest resources* is goal of *being stretched*.) So, in this passage, we see that the good results of the reaction mentioned at the beginning of the letter have their bad aspects for ZPG.

Finally, in segment 16, *critical* is coded as an attribute of *your support now*, with *critical* emphasized by being made N-Rheme of the clause. As in the case of segments 7 and 8, Mann, Matthiessen and Thompson suggest that segments 14 and 16 are in a restatement relation, and indeed, these clauses provide very similar information. However, these segments have rather different information structures and emphasize different aspects of the message. *Your help* is N-Rheme in 14b, *your support* is Theme in 16. *Urgently* is neither Theme nor N-Rheme in 14b, but *critical* is N-Rheme in 16. The clause Theme of 14b is *we* (= ZPG). This sets up clauses 15a and b, which describe the reason why help is needed and continue the Thematic content of the Theme of 14b (14b . . . *we* . . . , 15a *Our small staff* . . . , 15b . . . *our modest resources* . . .). Clearly, all of the clauses in segments 14–16 emphasize meanings which can be seen to relate to the need of ZPG for funds by placing these meanings within the N-Rhemes of the component clauses.

SUMMARY

Rather than continue with a detailed analysis of each clause in context, let me turn now to general trends which are evident in the letter. Several bits of evidence point to the fact that N-Rhemes are being used as a position of emphasis, and that the information placed within the N-Rhemes relates to the general goals of the text.

First, the N-Rhemes regularly contain evaluative terms, and usually these terms involve extreme evaluations. That is, if we look at the placement of

words and phrases which indicate the author's involvement in the information
– phrases such as *all day*, *late into the night* or the use of extended lists (such
as the list of major news media in clause 6c) – we see that the N-Rhemes of
the various clauses of the text regularly contain such terms. The N-Rhemes of
twenty of the thirty-five clauses in this text contain such terms. This count
includes clauses 11a–13, where the author describes the characteristics of the
Urban Stress Test. (These are clauses which are supposedly completely
objective.) By contrast, only three Themes obviously contain such words
(*deluge* (segment 9), *now* (segment 16) and *every day* (segment 20)), and two
other themes might be regarded as containing such words (*small* (clause 15a)
and *modest* (clause 15b)). In other words, at most, only a total of five out of
twenty-six[9] clauses have Themes which contain such words. While N-Rhemes
contain a high concentration of evaluative terms, the Themes contain most of
the references to the ZPG organization, its members and the Urban Stress
Test. Nineteen of the thirty clause Themes contain such references, while
only six N-Rhemes refer to the ZPG organization, its members or the Urban
Stress Test. Clearly there is a major difference in the content between the
Themes and the N-Rhemes of this text.

Second, even where Themes and N-Rhemes contain similar information,
that information is being used in different ways. For example, temporal
adverbials appear both Thematically and N-Rhematically. However, these
adverbials have quite different effects in the two positions. Chart 1 lists the
clauses which contain Thematic temporal adverbials.

Chart 1: Thematic temporal adverbials

4　AT **7.00** AM ON OCTOBER **25**, our phones started to ring.

7a　WHEN we released the results of ZPG's 1985 Urban Stress Test,

9　AT FIRST, THE DELUGE OF CALLS came mostly from reporters eager to tell
the public about Urban Stress Test results and from outraged public
officials who were furious that we had 'blown the whistle' on conditions
in their cities.

10　NOW, WE are hearing from concerned citizens in all parts of the country who
want to know what they can do to hold local officials accountable for tackling population-related problems that threaten public health and well-being.

20　EVERY DAY decisions are being made by local officials in our communities
that could drastically affect the quality of our lives.

Chart 2 contains all the clauses of the ZPG text which contain temporal
adverbials in the N-Rhemes of the clauses.

Chart 2: N-Rhematic temporal adverbials

5　Calls jammed our switchboard *all day*.

6a　Staffers stayed *late into the night*,

11b　created *after months of persistent and exhaustive research*,

22　Please make a special contribution to Zero Population Growth *today*.

23　Whatever you give – . . . – will be used *immediately*.

In chart 1, with one exception (that in segment 20, which I wish to return to later) the adverbials are being used to locate the clause in time. One Theme, *when* in clause 7a, is a structural Theme and is required to be initial in its clause. As a result, I do not wish to lay great store on the fact that it is Thematic.[10] In the remainder of these examples, the temporal adverbial seems merely to locate the action described in the rest of the clause. It is not a major part of the news. This is true even in cases in which the initial adverbial is separated from the remainder of its clause by a comma (as in segments 4 and 9), and so can be seen to require a focus of information. (In fact, when I read segments 10 and 20 aloud, I also tend to emphasize the initial adverbials. As a result, these can be seen to convey important information. However, that information seems to be used to orient the reader to the message which follows – the function that we have been hypothesizing for the meaning of Theme.)

By contrast, the temporal adverbials in chart 2 seem to constitute an integral part of the message. One might say that this impression results from the different nature of the adverbials. For example, the first three clauses contain adverbials of extent (*all day*, *late into the night* and *after months of persistent and exhaustive research*). However, the other two adverbials (*today* and *immediately*) locate the action in time, and convey meanings similar to the ones expressed by the adverbials in chart 1. However, there is a great difference in the effect of the use of *today* and *immediately* in segments 22 and 23 from the use of *at 7.00AM on October 25* (in segment 4), *at first* (segment 9) or *now* (segment 10). In segments 22 and 23, the adverbials are much more an integral part of the message. There is an urgency about the use of these words in this context that the other examples do not convey. Note that the urgency is not merely conveyed by the nature of the words themselves. That is, the same words, used in a different way would not have the same effect. Note the difference between saying 23 and 23i:

23 Please make a special contribution to Zero Population Growth today.
23i Today, please make a special contribution to Zero Population Growth.

Example 23i simply does not have the same urgency as segment 23 has.[11]

Finally, as my third point, let me return to the five segments (mentioned above in point 1) which contain evaluative terms in their Themes. These are given in chart 3.

Chart 3: Evaluative terms in the Themes

 9 AT FIRST, THE DELUGE OF CALLS came *mostly from reporters eager to tell the public about Urban Stress Test results and from outraged public officials who were furious that we had 'blown the whistle' on conditions in their cities.*

15a OUR SMALL STAFF is being swamped *with requests for more information*
15b AND OUR MODEST RESOURCES are being stretched *to the limit.*
16 YOUR SUPPORT NOW is *critical.*

20 EVERY DAY decisions are being made by local officials in our communities
   that could drastically affect the quality of our lives.

The examples in chart 3 are exceptional in that the Themes contain words
which are evaluative. Do these examples constitute counterexamples to the
basic hypothesis that the N-Rheme of the clause generally contains evaluative terms while the Themes do not? The answer is 'no', for the N-Rhemes
of these clauses also contain evaluative material. Indeed, the N-Rhemes of
these clauses contain information which is much more relevant to the goal of
the clause in its context. For example, the purpose of segment 9 is to
elaborate on the nature of the public and media reaction mentioned in
segment 8. *The deluge of calls* is a cohesive phrase referring back to and
evaluating the reaction mentioned in segment 8, while the list of callers is
given in the N-Rheme of segment 9. Clauses 15a and 15b provide similar
examples. Segment 14 asserts that we need help, and segment 15 describes
why that help is needed. *Our small staff* and *our modest resources* (from
segment 15) again involve cohesive reference together with evaluation,
while the main point of the clauses is the swamping with requests and the
stretching to the limit – the information that is found within the Rhemes of
the two clauses.

Segment 16 is slightly different. Here *now* modifies *support*, and since
support has been made Theme, *now* is also included as part of the Theme. It
is worth noting, however, that segment 16 contains *critical* as N-Rheme, a
word which clearly contains an urgent evaluative meaning which is directly
relevant to the purpose of that clause.

Segment 20 is, perhaps, more interesting. In the discussion of the clauses in
chart 1, segment 20 was exceptional in that it contained a temporal Theme
which clearly communicated a sense of urgency. However, let us look at the
structure of that clause more closely. It is reproduced below:

20 EVERY DAY decisions are being made by local officials in our communities
   that could drastically affect the quality of our lives.

The double underlined portions constitute a single noun phrase that has been
separated by placing the relative clause at the end of the including clause. If
we examine this relative clause, we see that it contains the 'emotive' term
drastically. Further, it describes the practical effect of the decisions. That is,
the relative clause describes the urgent importance for us of the decisions
which are being mentioned. Thus, segment 20 fits into the pattern that we
have already seen in this letter: the N-Rhemes of the component clauses
express ideas that involve some emotive judgement, and show the importance
of what is being discussed for the reader. Segment 20, however, contains two
portions which convey that sort of information: the postposed relative clause,
and *every day*. Given the content of that segment, the author had to choose
which meaning was most important to emphasize, and chose to emphasize the
effect of the decisions on the lives of the readers. I believe that she could very

well have chosen to emphasize the urgency via the frequency. She could have chosen to write:

20i Decisions that could drastically affect the quality of our lives are being made by local officials in our communities every day.

But that wording would have had another effect. (Notice that although placing the relative clause at the beginning increases the 'weight' and complexity of the Subject and thus the flow of the resulting sentence is rather unusual, the resulting construction is far from ungrammatical. That is, we cannot explain the appropriateness of the actual wording of segment 20 merely by referring to sentence-internal concerns.)

In summary, then, all of the five clauses in chart 3 contain N-Rhemes which are directly relevant to the goals of their respective clauses. Indeed, most of those N-Rhemes contain strongly evaluative terms such as *to the limit*, *critical* and *drastically*. In other words, the importance to the goals of these clauses of the information in their N-Rhemes seems to outrank the evaluative meanings which appear in their Themes. Thus, there seems to be a hierarchy of relevance to the goals of these segments with the highest-ranking information appearing in the N-Rheme of the clause.[12]

In the interests of ease of investigation, I have taken a particularly rigid approach to the notion of information. Something either is or is not 'newsworthy', and I considered placement in the N-Rheme to be the indicator of 'newsworthiness' in writing. In spite of that rigid approach, there is a general correlation of newsworthiness and placement within the N-Rheme. In only one of thirty-six clauses was there a true exception to this tendency. One case was doubtful. In several other clauses the New information included more than merely the N-Rheme. This last situation is merely a complication of the picture, however. By contrast, information placed Thematically in the clauses was never informationally prominent in a way paralleling the role of the N-Rheme. In other words, the author of the ZPG letter clearly used Thematic and N-Rhematic position in the clause for different purposes. The content of the N-Rhemes regularly concerned information which related to the purposes of the text, of the text segment, and of the sentence and clause of which it was a part. On the other hand, the content of the Themes, even when they were separated from their main clauses by commas, regularly did not relate to the purposes of the text and text segments. Rather the content of the various Themes served as orienters to the information contained in the clauses. Comparing the information placed in the two positions helps us develop a better sense of the operation of each one separately.

APPENDIX I

[[ZPG LOGO]]

November 22, 1985

Dear Friend of ZPG:

At 7.00 a.m. on October 25, our phones started to ring. Calls jammed our switchboard all day. Staffers stayed late into the night, answering questions and talking with reporters from newspapers, radio stations, wire services and TV stations in every part of the country.

When we released the results of ZPG's 1985 Urban Stress Test we had no idea we'd get such an overwhelming response. Media and public reaction has been nothing short of incredible!

At first, the deluge of calls came mostly from reporters eager to tell the public about Urban Stress Test results and from outraged public officials who were furious that we had 'blown the whistle' on conditions in their cities.

Now we are hearing from concerned citizens in all parts of the country who want to know what they can do to hold local officials accountable for tackling population-related problems that threaten public health and well-being.

ZPG's 1985 Urban Stress Test, created after months of persistent and exhaustive research, is the nation's first survey of how population-linked pressures affect U.S. cities. It ranks 184 urban areas on 11 different criteria ranging from crowding and birth rates to air quality and toxic wastes.

The Urban Stress Test translates complex, technical data into an easy-to-use action tool for concerned citizens, elected officials and opinion leaders. But to use it well, we urgently need your help.

Our small staff is being swamped with requests for more information and our modest resources are being stretched to the limit.

Your support now is critical. ZPG's 1985 Urban Stress Test may be our best opportunity ever to get the population message heard.

With your contribution, ZPG can arm our growing network of local activists with the materials they need to warn community leaders about emerging population-linked stresses before they reach the crisis stage.

Even though our national government continues to ignore the consequences of uncontrolled population growth, we can act to take positive action at the local level.

Every day decisions are being made by local officials in our communities that could drastically affect the quality of our lives. To make sound choices in planning for people, both elected officials and the American public need the population-stress data revealed by our study.

Please make a special contribution to Zero Population Growth today. Whatever you give – $25, $50, $100 or as much as you can – will be used immediately to put the Urban Stress Test in the hands of those who need it most.

Sincerely

Susan Webster
Executive Director
P.S. The results of ZPG's 1985 Urban Stress Test were reported as a top news story by hundreds of newspapers and TV and radio stations from coast to coast. I hope you'll help us monitor this remarkable media coverage by completing the enclosed reply form.

APPENDIX II

ZPG test – Analysed by non-rankshifted clauses

Key

BOLD SMALL CAPS   indicate the Theme of the clause
Italics   indicate the N-Rheme of the clause
Underlining   as in the original
Numbering
Capital letters indicate paragraphs.
Arabic numbers indicate punctuated sentences or other segments.
Small letters indicate clauses within a sentence.

B4   **AT 7:00 A.M. ON OCTOBER 25**, our phones *started to ring*.
B5   **CALLS** jammed our switchboard *all day*.
B6a   **STAFFERS** stayed *late into the night*.
B6b   answering *questions*
B6c   **AND** talking *with reporters from newspapers, radio stations, wire services and TV stations in every part of the country.*
C7a   **WHEN WE** released <u>*the results of ZPG's 1985 Urban Stress Test*</u>,
C7b   **WE** had *no idea we'd get such an overwhelming response.*
C8   **MEDIA AND PUBLIC REACTION** has been *nothing short of incredible!*
D9   **AT FIRST, THE DELUGE OF CALLS** came *mostly from reporters eager to tell the public about Urban Stress Test results and from outraged public officials who were furious that we had 'blown the whistle' on conditions in their cities.*
E10   **NOW, WE** are hearing *from concerned citizens in all parts of the country who want to know what they can do to hold local officials accountable for tackling population-related problems that threaten public health and well-being.*
F11a **ZPG's 1985 URBAN STRESS TEST**, «F11b», is *the nation's first survey of how population-linked pressures affect U.S. cities.*
F11b created *after months of persistent and exhaustive research,*
F12   **IT** ranks 184 urban areas on *11 different criteria ranging from crowding and birth rates to air quality and toxic wastes.*
G13   **THE URBAN STRESS TEST** translates complex, technical data *into an easy-to-use* <u>*action tool*</u> *for concerned citizens, elected officials and opinion leaders.*
G14a **BUT** to use it *well,*
G14b **WE** urgently need *your help.*
H15a <u>**OUR SMALL STAFF** is being swamped *with requests for more information*</u>
H15b <u>**AND OUR MODEST RESOURCES** are being stretched *to the limit.*</u>
I16   **YOUR SUPPORT NOW** is *critical.*
I17   **ZPG's 1985 URBAN STRESS TEST** may be *our best opportunity ever to get the population message heard.*

J18   WITH YOUR CONTRIBUTION, ZPG can arm our growing network of local activists *with the materials they need to warn community leaders about emerging population-linked stresses before they reach the crisis stage.*

K19a EVEN THOUGH OUR NATIONAL GOVERNMENT continues to ignore *the consequences of uncontrolled population growth,*

K19b WE can *act*

K19c to take positive action *at the local level.*

L20   EVERY DAY decisions are being made by local officials in our communities *that could drastically affect the quality of our lives.*

L21a To make *sound choices in planning for people,*

L21c BOTH ELECTED OFFICIALS AND THE AMERICAN PUBLIC need *the population-stress data revealed by our study.*

M22 PLEASE MAKE a special contribution to Zero Population Growth *today.*

N23a WHATEVER YOU GIVE – «N23b» – will be used *immediately*

N23b $25, $50, $100 or *as much as you can*

N23c to put the Urban Stress Test *in the hands of those who need it most.*

O24 Sincerely

O25 [SIGNATURE]

O26 Susan Weber

O27 Executive Director

P28 P.S.

P29 THE RESULTS OF ZPG's 1995 URBAN STRESS TEST were reported as a top news story *by hundreds of newspapers and TV and radio stations from coast to coast.*

P30a I *hope*

P30b YOU'll help us monitor *this remarkable media coverage.*

P30c BY completing *the enclosed reply form.*

NOTES

1   This is a revised version of 'The flow of information in a written English text', published in Michael Cummings and Michael Gregory (eds), *Relations and Functions in Language.*

2   See also Winter (1977b: 475) for a similar wording when describing the meanings of Theme and Rheme.

3   A correlational model is actually too simple. For example, it is highly likely that Thematic status in particular structurally important sentences in a text segment will correlate with perception of a nominal constituent as a topic. I am using the simple correlational model first in order to get a rough approximation.

4   Certainly, such a study could be carried out on spoken text, but the results would probably differ. The interest in N-Rheme arose here from the limited tools available to writers to signal emphasis, and the hypothesis that one major tool which they use is word order. Since speakers have a number of additional tools available to them to signal their emphases, one would suspect that the correlation of N-Rheme and emphasis would not be as great in the spoken language.

5   Chafe (1984) provides figures comparing adverbial clauses in written and spoken English. These figures give rough evidence that something of this sort takes place.

6   Saying that the N-Rheme is the newsworthy part of the clause should not be taken to imply too close an association between the N-Rheme and the placement of the tonic accent. Though the initial reason for positing N-Rheme lay in the unmarked placement of the tonic on the last major constituent of the clause, there are a number of reasons for deviating from this pattern. The question is whether the N-Rheme can be seen to correlate with the goals of the text and the text segments, regardless of whether or not it would receive the tonic accent if read aloud. Thus, in segment 4 of the text that will be analysed here, the N-Rheme would probably not receive the accent, since the action of ringing is predictable from the fact that <I1>*our phones*<I2> is the Actor. In this particular case, however, since this segment constitutes the beginning of the letter, the entire clause is news and <I1>*started to ring*<I2> describes the first event of the narrative. As a result, this N-Rheme is considered to be closely related to the goals of the text and of the text segment of which it is a part.

7   Winter (1992: 147–8) points out the intimate relation between imperatives and motivations.

> We are, so to speak, linguistically free human beings; we have a very strong tendency to why-question any imperative. The rule runs something like this: if an imperative is *not* preceded by a reason, then this reason is predicted as the next clause. If, however, the reason *does* precede the imperative, then it is linguistically complete and no longer predicts the reason to come.
>
> (emphasis in the original)

8   It has already been pointed out that the New information in a clause may not be restricted to the content of the N-Rheme. The whole of segment 4 is clearly New information. Similarly, we can reasonably say that *jammed* in segment 5 and *stayed* in clause 6a would most likely form part of the New information in those clauses.

9   The difference in total numbers for the Theme and the N-Rheme counts arises because eight non-finite dependent clauses which begin with Predicators and segment 23b (which is not a clause) do not have Topical Themes according to Halliday's analysis.

10 While one cannot draw major conclusions on the basis of the placement of *when* within its clause, we can move up a level and examine the relative placement of the two clauses within the T-unit in segment 7. At the level of T-unit, the entire clause 7a serves as a temporal adverbial for segment 7. Further, it functions as Theme for the T-unit by setting the time-frame for the event depicted in that T-unit. In other words, when considered as a whole, Segment 7 fits the pattern of the effects of the Thematic placement of temporal adverbials established by the other clauses in chart 1.

11 It is worthy of note that most fund-raising letters contain some identifiable request such as this one, and the sentence which expresses that request will usually contain a temporal adverbial in the N-Rheme. A survey of 21 fund-raising letters shows that all letters contained at least one identifiable request. Some letters contained more than one request so that the corpus contained a total of 26 requests. Of these 26 requests, four made no mention of time. The remaining 22 made at least one reference to time. One contained two references to time. As a result, the corpus contained 23 references to time. *Today* (with 14 occurrences) and *now* (with six occurrences) were the most frequently used temporal adverbials in the data. Two temporal adverbials were neither Theme nor N-Rheme. Four temporal adverbials were placed within the Themes of their clauses, while 17 temporal adverbials occurred in the N-Rhemes of their clauses.

12 This approach is reminiscent of the notion of communicative dynamism discussed by Firbas (1982).

APPENDIX III: DIAGRAM FOR THE BODY OF THE ZPG LETTER
(Mann, Matthiessen and Thompson 1992: figure 6)

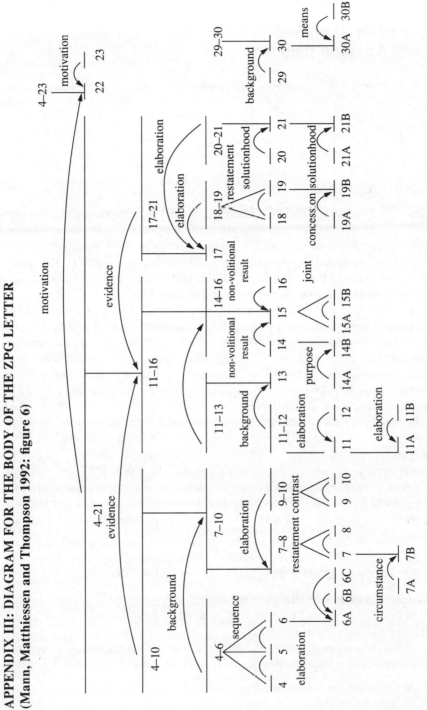

16 Negatives in written text

Adriana Pagano

INTRODUCTION

Studies of negation have traditionally focused on morphological, syntactic and logical aspects, without considering use or meaning in context. Indeed, there have been relatively few studies dealing with negatives from a pragmatic perspective, and still fewer attempting to systemize the uses of negation. Among the latter, Tottie (1982, 1987) has proposed a classification of the uses of negatives in both oral and written language.

I collected examples of negatives from written texts and approached my data from three different perspectives, corresponding to the three language functions pointed out by Halliday (see Pagano 1991). From an interpersonal perspective, I analysed the role of negatives in the interaction between writer and reader in order to see why negatives appear in texts. From a textual perspective, I looked at the role of negatives in both the micro- and the macrostructure of the texts. That is, I analysed how negatives relate to adjoining clauses and to the text as a whole. Finally, from an ideational perspective, I compared overt (i.e. negatives having a formal marker of negation such as *not*, *no*, *nowhere*, etc.) and covert negatives (i.e. propositions expressing a negative meaning but having a positive form, such as *I forgot*), in order to see whether equivalent forms of overt and covert negatives (e.g. *I did not remember – I forgot*) represented similar ways of expressing content in language. In the present chapter, I will concentrate on the first of these three perspectives: why do negatives appear in texts?

NEGATIVES FROM A PRAGMATIC PERSPECTIVE

Before discussing negatives in the interaction between writer and reader, I will first define the object of my study, which is *implicit negatives* or *denials*, as Tottie (1987) labels them.

What then are implicit negatives or denials? According to Tottie, negatives are used for two main purposes:

to reject suggestions (including refusals)
to deny assertions

from which she draws two categories:

Rejections (including Refusals)
Denials

The main difference between Rejections and Denials, Tottie claims, is that rejections express volition on the part of the sender, for example:

A: Would you care for a drink?
B: *No*, thanks.

whereas denials do not; they are concerned with facts; they just state that an assertion is not true, for instance:

A: So you are still living out there.
B: *No, I am not*. I have rented a flat near the bank.

This explanation, however, is not satisfactory in its differentiation of the two negative uses, since it might be argued that volition, a quality associated exclusively with rejections by Tottie, may also underlie denials. That is, there is also volition in expressing a denial.

The difference between rejections and denials may be better explained from a functional perspective, considering the function which is predominant in each situation.

If we regard rejections and denials from the perspective of language function (Halliday 1970, 1973), we note that the language component that predominates in each of these uses is different. In denials, the ideational component is predominant: when we deny something, we are concerned with expressing our view on a particular fact, that is, with whether things are one way or another, such as:

A: Then finally she got what she wanted.
B: Well, I wouldn't say that. *She never wanted to break with him*. Things just happened that way.

B's denial of A's assumption (the woman in question wanted to end her relationship with her boyfriend) has a strong ideational component: B wants to correct A's view of a fact; the truth or correctness of the fact is more relevant than the interpersonal element in the conversation. However, if the conversation went like this:

A: So the party is at 9. Shall I bring something to eat or . . . ?
B: *No*, thanks. Don't worry. We'll have pizza.

In saying 'no', B is assuming a role in the conversation; he is providing an answer to A's offer (interpersonal function). There is certainly an ideational component (A does not need to bring anything to the party), but the interactional function (a rejection) is the one that predominates. Thus, taking into account the predominant language component in a particular instance of language use, rather than the notion of volition, we can posit in agreement with Tottie that rejections and denials constitute two different categories of negative use.

What denials negate, Tottie further states, can be either an explicitly stated assertion, as in

> There are two kinds of waste producers: those that produce inorganic waste and *those that do not.*

or an assertion that is somehow implicit in the context of the interaction, generally an assumption by the producer of the denial with respect to his interlocutor's beliefs or expectations, for example:

> The most significant departure in the CEELT examination is that video recordings are used in the Oral and Listening Comprehension section. These are clips from actual lessons and *not specially scripted.* For the Oral test the clip acts only as a stimulus to interactive communication in groups of three.
>
> (*MET*, 15 March 1988: 43)

In this example, the denial 'not specially scripted' refers to a proposition which has not been explicitly asserted, as would be the case, for instance, if the paragraph had read:

> In previous tests, the clips were specially scripted by our language specialists; this time they are not.

where an assertion is first presented and then denied. In the example taken from *MET*, the denial refers to an expectation which the writer assumes his reader has concerning the scripts of the tests.

At this point, a brief explanatory note concerning Tottie's terminology is necessary. Her terms *explicit* and *implicit denials* are perhaps a bit misleading in that what is explicit or implicit is not, as might be expected, the denials themselves, but the propositions that are being denied. In other words, the explicitness/implicitness criterion used in her classification refers to the thing that is denied and not to the negative itself. Thus, in an exchange like:

> A: Has the garbage been emptied?
>
> B: You know bloody well I've been out all day, how could I have emptied the garbage can?

B certainly produces what is commonly called an implicit negative answer, meaning 'No, I haven't done it'; however, it is not what Tottie (1982) considers as *implicit denial.* Indeed, it is not a denial at all in Tottie's terms, since there is no formal marker of negation, such as *no, never, nothing,* etc. An implicit denial, according to Tottie, is a denial of a proposition which has not been explicitly formulated in the text. For example:

> WHY MOSQUITO REPELLENTS REPEL
> *They are not substances that a mosquito somehow finds distasteful.* They jam the mosquito's sensors so that it is not able to follow the warm and moist air currents given off by a warm-blooded animal.
>
> (Wright 1975: 104)

Here, the writer is denying what the reader might believe in relation to repellents: they are distasteful to the mosquito. This is an idea implicit in the text, inferable from the text. This is what Tottie calls *implicit denial.*

Implicit denials then are denials which originate as a product of an assumption by the producer in relation to his/her interlocutor's beliefs. Being denials of implicit assertions, they reveal aspects of discourse which are not explicit. In other words, they reveal the process going on in the producer's mind when constructing a communicative message.

Among all the uses of negatives, implicit denials seem particularly interesting, as they raise questions as to what the producer has in mind to cause him/her to produce a denial, why a particular assertion should be implicit in a particular situation, why a denial fits the context in which it appears.

In order to investigate these questions, I analysed examples of implicit denials taken from a wide range of written texts: text-books, magazines, journals, scientific papers and newspapers. The criterion used to select implicit denials in the written texts is in line with that adopted by Tottie, that is, negatives in which the proposition denied did not appear in the text. Since in this study I have concentrated on denials, the data chosen from the source texts are those falling within what Quirk *et al.* (1985) call 'clause negation', namely instances in which the whole clause is negated, either through the main verb, for example *he doesn't know any Russian*, or through means other than verb negation, such as *he knows no Russian*.

WHY DO DENIALS APPEAR IN TEXTS?

I have repeatedly mentioned the term 'interaction' between writer and reader. But what are the characteristics of this interaction? Unlike in spoken discourse, in written text there is no physical receiver of the producer's message at the moment of composition. Nevertheless, the writer replaces the absence of a physical interlocutor by a mental representation of the reader. That is, the writer creates a picture of the reader, who thus becomes an 'ideal reader', and attributes to this reader certain experience, knowledge, opinions and beliefs on the basis of which the writer builds his/her message. (See Coulthard, this volume, pp. 4–5.)

As Widdowson (1979) states, in writing texts 'the writer assumes the roles of both addressor and addressee' and thus, as s/he writes, the writer thinks of the reader's possible reactions, anticipates them and acts accordingly. Whenever the writer feels the text may raise a doubt or leave a question unanswered, s/he tries to provide the information s/he thinks the reader is expecting. As the writer somehow assumes what the reader's questions and expectations are, s/he tries to provide information about these.

Therefore, in cases where certain information is non-existent, the writer can report that by means of denials of what was expected, for example:

In Trankle & Markosian (1985), Expert System Adaptive Control (ESAC) is described. The system consists of a self-tuning regulator augmented with three different expert system modules: the system identifier, the control system designer and the control implementation supervisor. *A real time version of the system has not been implemented.*

(Automatica, 26 June 1989: 815)

In this piece of text, the writer talks about an expert system which has been developed by some researchers. The writer probably thought that the reader might be interested in knowing whether the system has been implemented. That is probably why he tries to satisfy the reader's question with the information expressed through the denial.

A writer is often aware that the message may contain parts which are dubious or likely to be misinterpreted. In order to be clear and not to mislead the reader, s/he will point to the ambiguous stretches and cancel the potentially wrong interpretations. This can also be done by means of denials, such as:

Anyone with a passion for hanging labels on people or things should have little difficulty in recognizing that an apt tag for our time is the Unkempt Generation. *I am not referring solely to college kids.* The sloppiness virus has spread to all sectors of American society. People go to all sorts of trouble and expense to look uncombed, unshaved, unpressed.

(TIME, 2 April 1990: 46)

Here, the writer denies what readers might have thought in connection with the expression 'unkempt generation', namely that he was referring to adolescents, an idea typically associated with the above-quoted expression.

Of course, for writers to deny certain ideas or expectations which they assume on the part of their readers, the propositions denied have to be somehow plausible or expected in the context of the text. As Miller and Johnson-Laird (1976: 262) state:

people do not ordinarily go about uttering such denials as 'George Washington is not a table' or 'Sealing wax is not a dog', even though they are perfectly true. . . . These denials seldom occur because their corresponding affirmations seldom occur.

That is to say, for a writer to deny a belief or an expectation, s/he has to have some reason to think that the reader(s) may hold that belief or expectation, as is the case of the idea of youngsters in connection with 'unkempt generation'.

EXISTENTIAL PARADIGM

According to Miller and Johnson-Laird's observation, then, a writer cannot deny just anything, but only assumptions which are plausible or acceptable in the context of interaction. Borrowing Brazil's (1985) terminology, we could say that all those assumptions that are plausible or probable in a particular context of interaction constitute *an existential paradigm*. Why paradigm? Paradigm implies a group or set of linguistic items that are related in such a way that they may substitute each other in a given context. What determines the inclusion of the items within a single set is a series of conditions that all the members have to fulfil. *Existential* implies that what determines the inclusion of items within a set is experiential factors such as shared experience or understanding in relation to a given environment.

Brazil establishes a difference between the *general* and *existential* paradigms. The former consists of the conditions in the language system that limit the number of elements that can fill a slot. For instance in

A: Which card did you play?
B: The *Queen of Hearts*.

in B's response, the slots filled by 'Queen' and 'Hearts' can be linguistically filled by many possibilities in the general paradigm of the language, for example the *Fourteen of Lions*. But, for these choices to be meaningful in this context, they have to be part of the existential paradigm, that is they have to be regarded as possibilities actually available in the given situation, which, in this particular case, they are not. Here, the limitation to the choices for these two slots is extralinguistic, imposed by the fact that in the real world, a pack of cards has four suits (none of them being 'Lions'), each of which has a determinate sequence of cards (in which 'fourteen' is non-existent).

If we take these two concepts (*general* and *existential paradigm*) and apply them to our study of denials, we can see that in a given situation, there are many linguistically possible denials that can be produced (certainly by linguists) and which make up the general paradigm, such as *colourless green ideas don't sleep furiously*, but as Miller and Johnson-Laird state, those denials are nonsensical, because those propositions could never take place in a real-world context. Thus, the set of propositions that could be denied in a given context is limited by the propositions which are experientially possible in that context (existential paradigm). We could then define *existential paradigm* as a set of assumptions which are experientially linked in a certain context. In order to clarify this, let us go back to the example on page 254, in which the writer writes about the 'unkempt generation'.

This expression is, in our culture, associated with ideas such as hippies and rebellious, long-haired adolescents. These ideas are part of an experience in our culture. If we hear or read 'unkempt generation', we expect the speaker/writer to be referring to youngsters. Thus, we could say that the existential paradigm of the idea of 'unkempt generation', that is, the assumptions experientially linked with that idea, are matters related to young people, adolescents. Therefore, the idea of referring to college kids can be plausibly denied in the context of 'unkempt generation', since 'college kids' is part of the existential paradigm of this context. Had the writer written *I am not referring solely to politicians* we, as readers, would have found this idea odd or incomprehensible, certainly unexpected, which would have made us read on to find out the link between 'unkempt generation' and 'politicians'. The denial would not be a plausible one in this context. For us, 'politicians' is not within the existential paradigm of 'unkempt generation'.

It is interesting to notice that when a denial is expressed, the producer is projecting a world in which what is denied is accepted, that is, in which there is an understanding that the producer and his/her readers accept the proposition being denied. For instance, when somebody, commenting upon a wedding, says *The bride was not wearing a white dress*, that person is projecting a world in which brides normally wear a white dress in contrast to the one he is talking about. Similarly, when he says *The bride was not wearing a blue dress*, he projects a world in which there was a reason to expect that she would wear blue, either because it is a custom in the group or because there was reason to believe that this particular bride would wear one. This has significant implications which are generally exploited in certain mass media. For example, if a bottle of juice is advertised as having *no sugar*, it is because producers assume people believe juices typically contain added sugar. If the label on the bottle read *no fish-bone*, people's first reaction would be one of surprise, because in our society nobody expects a juice to contain fish-bone. But then the very denial would project a world in which at least some other juices contain fish-bone. This can actually create an expectation in the consumer's mind, as they may start to wonder whether the juice they habitually buy contains fish-bone, a substance certainly undesirable and perhaps prejudicial to health, since nobody would advertise something as not having a healthy or positive thing.

On some occasions, the writer provides a denial or idea s/he wants to correct after an assertion stating what s/he considers to be the right choice. For example:

Menstrual changes were significantly related to the intensity, *not the activity*, of running.

(*Runner's World*, June 1985: 29)

Making friends with the neighbouring Indians, he argued that the land belonged to them and *not to the king or to the Massachusetts Bay Company*. The Massachusetts government decided to deport him as a dangerous character.

(Current and Goodwin 1975: 12)

In these cases the writers are making explicit the choices or existential paradigm from which they selected the option asserted. In so doing, they are making sure the reader learns about the other members of the existential paradigm which they consider wrong. For instance, in the example about the Indians, the set of possible owners of the land (that is, the existential paradigm in this context) includes the king, the Massachusetts government and the Indians. On stating that the land did not belong to the first two, the writers are adding after their assertion a piece of information to make sure these two options are known to the reader. If the writers did not do this, the reader would probably never learn about the discarded options. And, usually, these options are added to the text because they are significant to the discussion of the topic.

Compare these two alternatives of a magazine advertisement.

PCB CAD/CAE
TO MAKE YOU MONEY.

PCB CAD/CAE
TO MAKE YOU MONEY . . .
NOT TAKE YOUR MONEY.

(Computer Design, July 1983)

In this case, the second version (the authentic one) makes explicit the option or choice that is being rejected. This is important, because the option denied represents a disadvantage with which the advertisement's offer is contrasted.

SCHEMATA

Besides discussing the set of choices a speaker has in a given context in the form of paradigms (existential and general), we can also regard this set of choices in terms of schemata.

Schemata or schemas are 'packets of information stored in memory representing general knowledge about objects, situations, events or actions' (Cohen *et al.*, 1986: 27).

Why are schemas relevant to our discussion of denials? If, as has already been said, we can deny propositions which are plausible in a given context and if schemas determine our expectations in connection with a given situation, then when referring to a particular schema, we can only identify propositions which are assumed to be part of that schema. Let me clarify this with an example: a picnic schema.

If somebody comments after a picnic *The picnic was nice but **nobody took any food***, it is because they expected the people going picnicking to take food. 'Food' is a defining element in the schema of a picnic. If, on the other hand, somebody commented *The picnic was nice but **nobody watered the grass***, this would sound an odd comment on a picnic: when you go to a picnic, you do not normally water the grass of the place where you stay. This seems to indicate that the things we can plausibly deny concerning a schema have to be considered as likely to be part of that schema.

We should always bear in mind that even the more general schemas are culture-specific, which implies that the values which a culture considers part of a schema may be different from the ones considered by another culture. Let us take the wedding schema. For us, a traditional wedding involves the bride and bridegroom, a ceremony performer, etc. (fixed values) and also a white dress for the bride, throwing confetti, music, etc. (conventionally optional ones). So, if somebody remarked about a wedding:

the bride wasn't wearing a white dress

this denial would represent the expectations the producer had in connection with the bride. If, however, that person remarked the bride didn't turn over the cash gifts to her parents

this denial would sound odd to us, because giving the cash gifts to the bride's parents is not part of our schema of a wedding. But for a Korean, this denial is meaningful, because that practice is customary in his culture and constitutes an element in the schema of a wedding.

All this indicates that for people to deny something, they assume that they and their interlocutors share a common world in which certain beliefs and expectations are usual. Taking up the concept of ideal reader, all this implies that the writer attributes to his/her ideal reader certain knowledge (schemas) and beliefs or ideas specific to the topic being dealt with. Taking those attributes for granted, the writer can build a message aimed at a target reader.

DATA ANALYSIS

In order to see how denials appear in this process of text construction, I selected and considered a reasonable number of denials and tried to see which ideas or propositions were denied and whether there was any reason for the writer to deny them. Remember that implicit denials, as their name states, refer to propositions which are not explicit in the text. The fact that they make no reference to an explicit proposition, however, does not mean that they appear out of the blue, without any connection at all to the topic being developed. They occur because there must be some reason why the writer feels the need to use a negative.

From the analysis of the data, I extracted four reasons why the writer does this and I classified them into four categories:

(1) *Denials of background information*: that is, denials used when the writer assumes that the reader entertains certain mistaken ideas from his previous background knowledge.
(2) *Denials of text-processed information*: that is, denials used when the writer assumes that the reader could derive a wrong idea from the text.
　(a) Denials used to prevent an erroneous inference from text to come.
　(b) Denials used to correct an idea already processed in the text.
(3) *Unfulfilled expectations*: that is, denials used when the writer wants to express an unfulfilled expectation of which s/he makes the reader co-participant.
(4) *Contrasts*: that is, denials used to compare or contrast two or more items.

In order to clarify these categories, let us consider each of them with examples from my data.

Denials of background information

In this class, the propositions denied by the writer are ideas which s/he assumes the interlocutor may, irrespective or independent of the text itself, entertain in connection with some aspect of the topic being dealt with, for instance:

> Another important point to remember is that *sexual orientation is not completely permanent*. Especially in adolescence, but also throughout adulthood, sexual orientation can change.
>
> (Coleman 1981: 217)

The idea that sexual orientation is permanent is attributed to the reader. The writer, being familiar with the topic and with ideas generally held about it, such as the one denied in the example, feels the need to correct those wrong views through a denial and present his own view afterwards. Similarly in

> *Oat-bran muffins alone aren't going to save you.* Eat a high-fiber diet with a variety of foods. Emphasize vegetables, fruit and whole grains.
>
> (*Runner's World*, March 1990: 68)

The writer denies a view which gained popularity through mass-media publicity: the miraculous power of oat-bran to reduce cholesterol, and which he knows his audience is likely to entertain. As the wrong idea (from the writer's viewpoint) is a popular and widespread one, he assumes his reader believes or at least is familiar with it. Thus, he must explicitly correct it.

The idea denied can also be a specific one (e.g. in academic writing), which only those who are familiar with the basic assumptions and theories of the specific area can actually have, as they belong to the community which sustains those ideas. Hence in:

> *Design is not art. It is also not engineering, and it is not science.* It is time to recognize this and distinguish the differences. Design is not separative, it is integrative. One of the hallmarks of design is its penchant for integration.
>
> (Owen 1989: 4)

a number of misconceptions about design, which the writer knows his reader may entertain, are denied. For someone outside the field of design, the denials and/or the necessity for them may sometimes not be fully understood.

This category of denials is the commonest in the data. Here are some more examples.

> A text is a semantic unit, *not a grammatical one*. But meanings are realized through wordings . . .
>
> (Halliday 1985: xvii)

> Also to learn. Chamorro owes her election *not to any natural gift for leadership* but to her married name. Though graced with regal poise and an engaging personality, she has had little experience in public life.
>
> (*TIME*, 12 March 1990: 13)

> One reason is to help you learn new, permanent eating patterns. While restricting your calories certainly will help you lose body fat, *weight loss*

and dieting cannot go on forever. They're merely temporary therapeutic measures to help you attain a desirable body composition.

(*Runner's World*, January 1987: 36)

It must be remembered that, as I have already stated, what is denied must be within the range of possibilities that can be plausibly denied (existential paradigm). Thus in

He was carrying the .25 when the cops arrested him on the street the following day. *He wasn't wearing colors*; few members do any more, since gang emblems are as open an invitation to arrest as carrying a semi-automatic rifle. But just the fact that he was dressed in low-slung black trousers, Nikes and Pendleton shirt gave him away.

(*TIME*, 18 June 1990: 22)

the statement that the boy was not wearing colours is denying the idea that is generally assumed of a gang: they usually have special or distinctive clothes. In fact, the writer goes on to explain that wearing colours is a practice no longer followed by gang members. Wearing colours is an idea that is plausibly related to gangs. Had the writer said *he wasn't eating peanuts*, it would certainly have been unexpected, unless the writer later explained that eating peanuts is a usual practice among gangs, that is, unless it were part of the existential paradigm of gangs.

Denials of text-processed information

This class of denials involves propositions (i.e. the ideas or beliefs) which the writer thinks the reader could wrongly infer from the text. This implies an awareness by the producer of which points in the text will be dubious or ambiguous for the reader. Therefore, out of solidarity with the reader and because the writer is interested in the reader's understanding and eventually supporting his/her view, the writer detects those misleading parts in the text and through denials cancels the wrong inferences, for example:

If a male increases his chances of reproduction through this type of cooperation because the favor is returned later on, the behavior is referred to as reciprocal altruism. In many species reciprocal altruism appears to have evolved in response to situations where it is difficult, if not impossible, for a solitary male to successfully mate with a female. *This interpretation is not universally accepted.* Scott Kraus and John Prescott . . . suggest . . . that the males are not cooperating but rather are competing with one another for access to the female.

(Wursig 1988: 81)

In this example, the writer presents a theory accounting for the sexual behaviour of whales. The way in which Wursig presents the theory may lead the reader at that point in the text to think the theory is an accepted or probable one. As this is not the case, the writer points out the relativity of the view presented, denying what he thinks may be the reader's possible wrong inference: that the theory is generally accepted.

Within this kind of denial, we can distinguish between (a) and (b):

(a) Denials in which the ideas denied may actually be ideas or reactions which the writer anticipates or expects the reader to have in connection with what s/he is going to say in the text, for instance:

> '*I don't want to sound sentimental* but they've been saving up to come here to see me and they'd see me talk the songs . . .'
>
> (*The Sunday Times*, 22 April 1990: 1)

Here the speaker cited in the text anticipates the reaction that his words may produce in his interlocutor (the reporter that interviewed him); he denies what he believes the listener will think about him.

(b) Denials in which the proposition denied has been suggested by previous parts of the same text as in:

> 'Relatively few people have applied for studies in the exercise line', says Wood. '*The number's not negligible*, but proportionately it's rather small. Drugs are ridiculously over-represented, and that has to reflect the importance of the drug companies . . .'
>
> (*Runner's World*, May 1990: 1)

> It has been estimated that nearly 50% of recent marriage cohorts will experience marital dissolution . . . . However, *these figures do not necessarily mean a massive rejection of marriage and family life*, as most individuals who experience marital dissolution eventually remarry.
>
> (Teachman and Heckert, 1985: 185)

In these examples, there is some idea in the text which, the writer thinks, is likely to lead the reader to a wrong interpretation. That is why that idea has to be expanded or clarified; for example, if the writer states that graffiti became more elaborate and less vulgar, the reader may very well come to think that from that moment onwards all graffiti were elaborate and critical, which is not true. Hence the writer's clarificatory denial.

Unfulfilled expectations

Implicit denials can also represent unfulfilled expectations on the part of the writer and the reader, as the former assumes his/her expectations are also the latter's. Let us consider the following example:

> To control the development of a plant, light must have some effect on the developmental blueprints, the genes. Yet whereas the biochemical reactions involved in photosynthesis have been described at length, *it is not at all*

clear how light influences the expression of plant genes. Six years ago we set out to clarify the biochemical basis for photomorphogenesis by beginning with the light-responsive genes themselves.

(Moses and Chua 1988: 64)

The writers here acknowledge some information (the biochemical reactions in photosynthesis have been described at length) but then indicate that some information which for them is relevant and, they assume, for their reader too, is not clear. We could say that the writers have an expectation connected with something that is significant for the field of research and believe that their reader, being someone interested in that field of research, has the same expectation; therefore, they inform the reader about what they expected.

It could be claimed that some expectations seem to be the writer's, in which case the denials give the reader access to the writer's own thought processes. However, we must always bear in mind that the writer writes for an ideal reader and the very fact that s/he includes an expression of an unfulfilled expectation in the text may indicate that s/he thinks that information about that unfulfilled expectation (be this missing information or an excuse for not presenting or dealing with some aspect of the topic in question) is relevant for the ideal reader.

Similarly, in

Bowheads are also believed to feed at the bottom (usually at depths of less than 60 meters), *but it is not clear how, equipped with long and finely fringed baleen, they are able to do so.* We have seen bowheads surfacing with muddy water streaming from the sides of the mouth, a behavior that in gray whales is clearly associated with bottom feeding.

(Wursig 1988: 79)

But Bart doesn't illuminate why Kerkorian does what he does. He offers a few new anecdotes about Kerkorian's gambling habits, but *the financier never comes alive.* Bart seems content with his conviction that the MGM boss lives simply to be a trader and is not a manager.

(*Business Week International*, 23 July 1990: 8)

Generally, an unfulfilled expectation leaves implicit the idea that what is missing, absent, etc., should be otherwise.

Sometimes, the writer tries to respond to expectations which are only the reader's expectations. That is, the writer did not expect that but thinks the reader probably will. This is clearly seen in prefaces, introductory or aclaratory notes, in which the writer states his/her intention concerning the text and the scope of his/her work. Consider these examples:

This article attempts not grand solutions but rather a clarification of some of the theoretical differences between two major camps in the current debates, recognizing that in these debates political commitments often precede and determine theoretical positions.

(Valverde 1989: 237)

The purpose of this short section . . . is to explore a few points prompted by material in the main part of each chapter . . . *No attempt is made to be comprehensive* and some comments are concerned with areas marginal to the main themes.

(Pears 1985: 9)

Both writers exempt themselves from presenting information which their readers could otherwise have reasonably expected.

Contrasts

To this class belong those denials which appear as implicit contrasts between two or more things, for example:

For past generations, lifestyle was the leading pharmacopeia. *They had no antibiotics, no cures for infectious disease.* They had to rely on their manner of living to preserve their health.

(*Runner's World*, February 1990: 16)

Here, there is an implicit comparison between the past and the present, and the differences are pointed out. These are actually the denials indicating the absence of antibiotics and cures, which we now have. In

About three fourths of the U.S. population is concentrated in urban areas. People growing up in the inner city often have little exposure to or opportunity for leisure/recreation experiences in a natural environment. Adult urbanites, however, are more likely than rural residents to be recreation/leisure users of public outdoor areas. Yet, *they were not provided the opportunities during youth to learn the skills and knowledge which would allow them to understand the dynamics of the natural environment.*

(*Journal of Physical Education, Recreation and Dance*, April 1990: 49)

the comparison takes place between the people living in town and the people living in rural areas. In

At Sudbury Valley there is no curriculum. There are no academic requirements. There is no evaluation of students except when requested, no grades or other devices to rank them from best to worst. There is no school-imposed segregation of any kind – not by age, not by sex, not by ability. Students are free to move about at will, using the school's laboratories, workshops, library, playground, and other resources.

(*Phi Delta Kappa*, May 1984: 609)

the contrast is established between traditional schools and Sudbury school, which claims to be special.

Another category?

In a small number of cases in the data, denials apparently have a different purpose from those already analysed. These specific denials contain a modal verb meaning possibility and are followed by a restriction which actually opposes them, for instance:

> *Saabs may not look large.* Yet the Saab 9000 is the only imported car in the USA rated 'large' by the Environmental Protection Agency.
>
> *(Business Week International*, 12 March 1990: 1)

Through the denial the writer is actually admitting, or better, conceding the fact that Saabs do not look large. It is as though he were saying: 'O.K. I agree. Saabs may not look large. But . . .' And there comes a restriction implying some Saabs are large.

Another example is:

> *Solar technology may never eclipse conventional power sources.* But it already promises the children of Africa a brighter future.
>
> *(Business Week International*, 23 July 1990: 15)

The same process takes place here. The writer admits something but then presents an alternative which reduces the effect of the denial.

As the number of examples having similar features to these two examples above is very small, we cannot at the moment formulate or state any features of this category but just point to its potential existence.

CONCLUSIONS

In analysing the claim of the writer when producing a denial, we have so far dealt only with the interpersonal perspective of denials, that is, denials in the interaction between writer and reader. We can also approach negatives from a pragmatic perspective and see how denials relate with adjoining clauses. For instance, we can analyse the environments or clause relationships in which denials appear most frequently, as in Denial–Correction,

> *What Lithuania is experiencing, therefore, is not betrayal, nor is it appeasement.* It is tragedy.
>
> *(TIME*, 16 April 1990: 52)

and see whether the accompanying member of the denial is actually predicted or anticipated by the denial. That is, whether after the denial in the Denial–Correction pattern, we, as readers, expect a correction.

From an ideational perspective, we can also ask ourselves whether apparently equivalent forms such as

These two insects do not belong to the same species.
These two insects belong to different species.

represent the same way of expressing content in language and for what purposes would one be used instead of the other.

A final goal could be to integrate the three perspectives and see the three language components at work in negatives.

APPENDIX: TEXTS USED OR REFERRED TO

Journals

Automatica, 26 June 1989: 815.
Business Week International, 12 March 1990: 1; 23 July 1990: 8, 15.
Computer Design, July 1983.
Journal of Physical Education, Recreation and Dance, April 1990: 49.
MET, 15 March 1988: 43.
Phi Delta Kappa, May 1984: 609.
Runner's World, June 1985: 29; February 1990: 16; March 1990: 68; May 1990: 1.
The Sunday Times, 22 April 1990: 1.
TIME, 2 April 1990: 46; 16 April 1990: 52.

Articles and books

Brazil, D. (1985) *The Communicative Value of Intonation in English*, Discourse Monographs No. 8, Birmingham: University of Birmingham.
Cohen, G. *et al.* (1986) *Memory: A Cognitive Approach*, Philadelphia: Open University Press.
Coleman, E. (1981) 'Counselling adolescent males', *The Personnel and Guidance Journal* (December): 215–18.
Current, R. and G. Goodwin (1975) *A History of the United States to 1877*, New York: Alfred Knopf.
Halliday, M. A. K. (1970) 'Language structure and language function', in J. Lyons (ed.), *New Horizons in Linguistics*, Harmondsworth: Penguin Books, 140–65.
—— (1983) *Explorations in the Functions of Language*, London: Edward Arnold.
—— (1985) *An Introduction to Functional Grammar*, London: Edward Arnold.
Miller, G. and P. Johnson-Laird (1976) *Language and Perception*, Cambridge: Cambridge University Press.
Moses, P. H. and N. Chua (1988) 'Light switches for plant genes', *Scientific American* 258/4 (April): 64–9.
Owen, C. H. (1989) 'Design education in the information age', a speech given at Korea Institute of Technology's Exposition and Design, 20 November, Seoul.
Pagano, A. (1991) 'A pragmatic study of negatives in written text', unpublished MA diss., Florianópolis: Universidade Ferderal de Santa Catarina.
Pears, N. (1985) *Basic Biogeography*, London: Longman.
Quirk, R. *et al.* (1985) *A Comprehensive Grammar of the English Language*, London, Longman.
Teachman, J. and A. Heckert (1985) 'The impact of age and children on remarriage', *Journal of Family Issues* 6/2 (June): 185–203.
Tottie, G. (1982) 'Where do negatives come from?', *Studia Linguistica* 36/1: 88–105.
—— (1987) 'Rejections, denials and explanatory statements – a reply to Fretheim', *Studia Linguistica* 41/2: 154–63.
Valverde, M. (1989) 'Beyond gender dangers and private pleasures: theory and ethics in the sex debates', *Feminist Studies* 15/2: 237–54.
Widdowson, H. G. (1979) *Explorations in Applied Linguistics*, Oxford: Oxford University Press.
Wright, R. (1975) 'Why mosquito repellents repel', *Scientific American* 233/1 (July): 104–11.
Wursig, B. (1988) 'The behavior of Baleen whales', *Scientific American* 258/4 (April) 78–85.

17 *It*, *this* and *that*

Michael McCarthy

The zany American film *Airplane* contains the following dialogue:

> Stewardess: Excuse me, Sir, there's been a little problem in the cockpit.
> Passenger: The cockpit! What is it?
> Stewardess: It's a little room at the front of the plane where the pilot sits, but that's not important right now.

Humour frequently depends on the violation of linguistic rules and expectations, and this exchange is no exception. But the relevance of the comic extract to the present chapter is that it raises the question of what the norms of usage of the impersonal pronoun *it* and the demonstrative pronouns *this* and *that* are, and why the stewardess's response to the question 'What is it?' is absurd in this situation. If the passenger had not known what a cockpit was, he would probably have asked: 'The cockpit? What's *that*?', rather than 'What is *it*?' or 'What's *this*?'. Clearly, *it*, *this* and *that* occupy separate domains in the way they attach to items in discourse which should be amenable to description.

Descriptive linguists do not offer any adequate explanations of this particular usage. It is fair to say that linguists writing within the transformational-generative paradigm consider the problem of the *Airplane* text to be beyond the purview of sentence grammar and to belong to 'pragmatics' (see Evans 1980, who rehearses arguments put forward by Chomsky and others, but who still seems unhappy with the sharp line between grammar and pragmatics). But even those overtly engaged, from a discourse or pragmatic viewpoint, in describing intersentence relations do not do sufficient justice to *it*, *this* and *that* in the kind of function displayed and exploited for humour in the *Airplane* exchange.

Some studies touch on the problem indirectly. Crymes (1968: 64–70), looks at contrasts between *do so*, *do it*, *do this* and *do that* as substitutes but is only concerned with the relationship between the whole substitute clause and the clause it replaces, whereas the present chapter casts its net considerably wider. Bolinger (1972: 56), although solely considering relative *that*, does touch upon the significance of choosing a demonstrative rather than *it*, when he says that 'the demonstratives single out and set off their noun phrases', a theme we shall return to later. Halliday and Hasan's (1976) account of cohesion in English is helpful on the use of *it*, and does address the distinction between *this* and *that*, but does nothing to resolve the difference between *it* on the one hand and *this* and *that* on the other. Lyons (1977: 657–77) includes remarks on *this* and *that* in his examination of deixis and anaphora, but he too does nothing to resolve the distinction that interests us here. Quirk *et al.*'s (1985) grammar gives good examples of *it*, *this* and *that* as cross-referring to clauses, sentences and groups of sentences in texts (p. 868), and illustrates the difference between *it*, *this* and *that* on the one hand and *so* on the other in this kind of function (p. 881), but still does not resolve the internal distinction of *it*, *this* and *that*.

Lakoff (1974) is more helpful and has some interesting things to say on *this* and *that*, including their use in 'discourse deixis'; however, most of Lakoff's examples are of *this* and *that* as noun modifiers (whereas the present study is concerned with their use as pro-forms), and there is no attempt to investigate the potential contrast with *it*.

Thavenius (1983: 169) is even more helpful; she makes a direct attempt to summarize the difference in usage (in speech, at least):

A speaker's strategies when using *it* to refer are then as follows: first he has to make a choice between *it* on the one hand, and *this* or *that* on the other. He will decide on *this* and *that*, only if there are special reasons for doing so. His next step is to make a choice between *this* and *that*, and then the aspects of proximity and remoteness will often be involved, although they are not relevant in all cases.

But Thavenius' explanation (hedges and all) does not resolve the *Airplane* problem. Her statement lacks precision (what might constitute the 'special reasons' for choosing *this* and *that*?), and the final caveat concerning proximity and remoteness diffuses the matter further. What is more, her explanation does not account for many of the instances of *it*, *this* and *that* occurring in day-to-day data. It is to such data that we must turn both to establish the precise nature of the problem and to find possible solutions.

However, within the tradition of what might be called American College Composition studies, we do find an interesting paper on *this* (Geisler *et al.*, 1985), which in itself is a response to an earlier paper by Moskovit (1983). Both papers work within a strongly evaluative framework, concerned with what makes *good* writing and how items such as pronouns and demonstratives can be used clearly, efficiently and in a reader-friendly way by writers. Geisler *et al.* reject purely syntactic and semantic explanations of the use of 'unattended' (i.e. without an accompanying noun phrase) anaphoric *this*, and import the essentially pragmatic notions of topic and focus to explain the function of *this* as opposed to *it*. Their conclusions are in sympathy with those of the present study, but here we shall extend the discussion to cover the three-way, *it*, *this*, *that* choice.

The *Airplane* text with which we opened raises the question of what sorts of entities *it*, *this* and *that* may attach to in the 'world of discourse' created and elaborated in the mind of sender and receiver during any interaction through speech or writing. By 'world of discourse' is meant the accumulating shared and mutual knowledge that the text can refer to and add to as the discourse unfolds. The 'text' is but the verbal record of the interaction that creates that world. The term 'world of discourse' is also associated with the view that co-textual noun phrases and reference items *co-refer*, rather than the idea that reference items such as pronouns refer '*back*' (or 'forward') to noun phrases. Co-reference theory considers 'backward reference' to noun phrases as an inadequate explanation of how reference works, since noun phrases exist in the *text*, not in the discourse world or in the real world. Co-reference implies no distinction between anaphoric ('backward') and exophoric ('outward') refer-ence, but sees reference items instead as referring to entities in the discourse world, which noun phrases have originally created in that world (see Brown and Yule 1983: 201). Entities may be *retrievable* as noun phrases in the text, or indeed as clauses, sentences or whole paragraphs, but reference, as such, is to those entities in discourse and not to the linguistic forms that encode them.

The different types of retrievable entities in text may be illustrated by the following data extracts, which exemplify *it*, *this* and *that* in turn (portions of text encoding the entities referred to and the co-referring *it*, *this* or *that* are italicized):[1]

It

1   *The brain* is our most precious organ – the one above all which allows us to be human.
   The brain contains 10 billion nerve cells, making thousands of billions of connections with each other. *It* is the most powerful data processor we know, but at the same time, *it* is incredibly delicate.

   (*The Observer*, 16 October 1988)

2   According to the centre, the region's electricity network is falling apart. '*We are losing a third of our farming time and it's getting close to impossible to get any results*', says Bower. '*The top 10 centimetres of soil dries out completely in two days. It*'s very sad'. Given half a chance, these farmers could succeed.

   (*New Scientist*, 23 January 1986)

3   Egypt's three million farmers agree on only one thing *when choosing wheat seeds: white ones are the best. It* is a matter of tradition. But seed that produces a high yield of grain is not an automatic choice, because most farmers also want a high yield of straw for feeding animals.

   (*New Scientist* 23 January 1986)

This

4   Coming out from the base of the brain like a stalk is *the brain stem. This* is the swollen top of the spinal cord, which runs down to our 'tail'.

   (*The Observer*, 16 October 1988)

5   You may prefer *to vent your tumble-dryer permanently through a non opening window. This* isn't quite as neat, since the flexible hose remains visible, but it does save knocking a hole in the wall.

(*Which?*, October 1988)

6   Companies are tremendously profitable. They are investing at a very high rate. The problem is on the import side, where *the British consumer's appetite for imported goods is apparently insatiable. If we don't have the cash to buy, we borrow.* Why *this* should have happened is one of the great puzzles. Part of the answer is that the figures are wrong. What we do not know is by how much.

(*The Guardian*, 2 November 1988)

That

7   Enforcement of the Consumer Protection Act regarding toys should become much simpler – and the protection it offers more comprehensive – in *January 1990. That*'s when new regulations based on a new European Standard for toy safety, and legally enforceable in all EEC countries, are due to come into effect.

(*Which?*, December 1988)

8   So there will be a one-day conference in London some five or six weeks before a full conference begins, at which *final 'composite' motions are prepared.*

If *that* is done, say party managers, it will be possible to allocate more time to debates, and therefore to lengthen the time limit for speeches from the rostrum.

(*The Guardian*, 7 October 1986)

9   It is, of course, impossible *to analyse style. That* wouldn't be stylish, would it? And anyway, what is commendably stylish in one person is offensive in another.

(*Options*, October 1985)

In examples 1, 4 and 7, it is a relatively straightforward matter to retrieve the discourse entity referred to by *it*, *this* and *that* as being in each case the italicized noun phrase, which can directly substitute for the respective *it*, *this* or *that* in the surface structure. In examples 2, 5 and 8, the situation is less clear; 5 is amenable to direct substitution, but 2 and 8 are not, and in all three cases the entities can only be retrieved in terms of quite lengthy strings of text or paraphrase of some sort. Indeed, in 8, it is not at all obvious that the italicized words adequately retrieve the referent of *that*, though no competent reader would have any difficulty in following the text. Examples 3 and 6 are equally problematic in that the italicized words do not easily and directly substitute for *it*, *this* and *that*. Example 6 is perhaps the most difficult of all to paraphrase in this respect. In 9, *that* can be substituted by the non-finite clause 'to analyse style'.

In example 1, the *it*'s are not replaceable by *this* or *that*; in examples 2 and

3, there does seem to be the possibility of replacement of *it* by *this* or *that*. In example 4, replacement by *it* or *that* is not possible, but does seem possible in 5. In example 6, *that* but not *it* would seem to be acceptable. In 7, *this*, but not *it*, would seem to fit; the same goes for 8.[2] Example 9 seems to offer the possibility of using *it*, but *this* would hardly be acceptable. Substitutability, where it is possible, must be measured against the almost idiom-like nature of clauses such as *It's a matter of tradition* and *It's very sad*, but, there again, the most tantalizing aspect of the possibility of substitution in such phrases is that it is precisely the subject that is most flexible (e.g. ***That's** a matter of tradition* sounds perfectly normal, as does ***That's** very sad*). So while all three items seem to refer in similar ways to entities, there are restrictions which operate at the discourse level, and even where substitutable for one another, there appear to be subtle shifts in meaning.

How, then, can one disentangle this apparently complex set of choices? One useful notion which may help to throw light on the affair is that of discourse segmentation. Texts may indeed consist of sentences and orthographically marked paragraphs, but it is more illuminating to view discourse (i.e. the interaction occasioned by a textual artefact) as consisting of *segments* (see Fox 1987c). Segments are the functional units which create discourse structures, and their boundaries may be (but are not necessarily) overtly signalled in text. Fox looks at the rhetorical units of texts and labels each segment in terms of its function in the creation of a discourse structure. A typical unit in an argumentative text might be assigned a functional label such as *claim*, or *evidence*; these are semantico-textual units. *Within* such segments, Fox observes the progression from full noun phrase to co-referring pronouns. Pronouns continue as subsequent mentions of an introducing noun phrase until there is a shift to a new discourse segment, when the full noun phrase surfaces again (or is *re-entered* in Jordan's (1985) terms). Applied to one of our example texts (with sentences numbered), the observation seems valid:

10 (1) The brain is our most precious organ – the one above all which allows us to be human.
(2) The brain contains 10 billion nerve cells, making thousands of billions of connections with each other. (3) It is the most powerful data processor we know, but at the same time, it is incredibly delicate. (4) As soft as a ripe avocado, the brain has to be encased in the tough bones of the skull, and floats in its own waterbed of fluid. (5) An adult brain weighs over 3lb and fills the skull. (6) It receives one-fifth of the blood pumped out by the heart at each beat.
(7) The brain looks not unlike a huge walnut kernel: it is dome-shaped with a wrinkled surface, and is in two halves joined in the middle.

(*The Observer*, 16 October 1988)

There seems to be an intuitive functional segmentation which is paralleled by the choices of noun phrase and pronoun:

segment 1: abstract (S1)
segment 2: the brain as data processor (S2), (S3)
segment 3: the brain's physical environment (S4)
segment 4: the adult brain (S5), (S6)
segment 5: the brain in appearance (S7)

Textual segments of this kind are independent of sentence and orthographical paragraph; their boundaries may coincide with sentences or paragraphs, but not necessarily (segment 1 is one sentence and one paragraph; segment 2 is two sentences but only part of a paragraph). The noun and pronoun choices co-referring to 'the brain' as a discourse entity correlate with segments:

segment 1: the brain
segment 2: the brain, it, it
segment 3: the brain, its
segment 4: an adult brain, it
segment 5: the brain, it

Each new segment resurrects the full noun phrase, then subsequently refers with *it*. *It* functions as the unmarked reference item, referring to 'topical entity in current focus', identifiable within the discourse segment by the noun phrase that has raised it into focus. The allocation of 'unmarked' status to *it* accords with Thavenius' explanation (above). The pronoun *it* simply keeps going what it is we are talking about or focusing on; it does not itself perform the act of focusing. One study that does consider the orthographic paragraph in relation to discourse units, that of Hofmann (1989), also notes correlations between pronouns and topical entities. Hofmann observes that a pronoun is not normally used to refer to an entity in a previous paragraph except when its antecedent is the paragraph topic in the preceding paragraph. These correlations vary, according to Hofmann, from one text type to another, but, outside of narrative text, exceptions to this 'anaphor barrier' are rarer.

But what is a 'topical entity in current focus'? It seems that it is not sufficient just to name or mention something to make it the 'entity in current focus', but that it is necessary also to predicate something about the noun phrase that names it. Thus, in the following piece of non-native speaker data, *it* is misused to co-refer to *introduction* when *introduction* is only named, and is not yet *raised* to become an 'entity in focus'.

11 (the example comes from a dissertation synopsis)
    Introduction: it deals with the developments in dialectology over the last twenty years.

Normal usage here would demand 'Introduction: *this* deals with . . .', or else repetition of the full noun with: 'The introduction deals with . . .' Another example, this time consumer advice in English on a packet of German-produced biscuits, translates 'kuhl und trocken lagern' as 'store it cool and dry', which would normally be rendered as 'store this product in a cool and dry place' or else without any pronoun at all ('store in a cool and dry place'). This suggests that Givón's (1983) remarks concerning the 'preferred, even obligatory' use of pronouns where some referent has been recently mentioned, providing a unique referent can be selected, is only valid in the case of *it* when the referent has been raised to current focus in the discourse, rather than merely existing as a name or label, as it does in the sub-heading in the dissertation synopsis or in the brand name on the biscuit packet.

So far, then, it would seem that pronominalization with *it* is related to functional segments and is used to refer to an entity in current focus within the segment, which certainly accords with Hinds' (1977) view of pronominalization and paragraph structuring. On the other hand, *this* and *that* have quite a different function. Hawkins (1978: 151) has already pointed out that *this* and *that* do not normally introduce completely *new* referents, as shown by the unacceptability of:

12 *This/*That man you should talk to is Dan Smith.

What then is their function? What I have referred to as 'entity in current focus' is close to what Isard (1975) calls 'focus of attention' (see also Linde 1979), and is exemplified in sentences such as:

13 First square 19 and then cube it.
14 First square 19 and then cube that.

In 13, we are cubing 19, in 14 we are cubing the product of 19^2 (i.e. 361); the current focus has shifted from 19 to 361, and *that* functions to signal that we have, as it were, crossed a focus boundary and are referring back to a previous focus. When we look at *this*, the picture is slightly different, but not fundamentally. In an extract from our earlier, 'brain text' (4), *this* seems to have the function of signalling that the 'brain stem' is to take over as new focus of attention:

15 Coming out from the base of the brain like a stalk is the brain stem. *This* is the swollen top of the spinal cord, which runs down to our 'tail'.

This and *that* therefore seem to function in a similar way in that they operate to signal that focus is either shifting or has shifted. Further evidence comes from Linde's (1979) data, where people are describing their apartments. Although the data extract is spoken, unlike the written data concentrated upon here, it does seem to support the general hypothesis of shifting or shifted focus. Linde specifically addresses the *it/that* choice, and gives examples to underscore the contrasting usage:

16 And the living room was a very small room with two windows that wouldn't open and things like that. And *it* looked nice. *It* had a beautiful brick wall.

17 You entered into a tiny little hallway and the kitchen was off *that*.

Example 16 remains within one current entity or focus of attention (the living room) and therefore uses *it*, while 17 shifts from one entity (the hallway) to another (the kitchen), and uses *that* to refer across from the one focus of attention to the other. It is interesting to note that 17 does not seem to depend on the temporal framework: even if the utterance were in present tense instead of past, *that* would still be preferred to *this*.

Based on these examples, we may, at this point, make tentative hypotheses as to the different functions of *it, this* and *that*:

(1) *It* is the unmarked reference item and refers to current entities or foci of attention.
(2) *This* signals a shift of entity or focus of attention to a new focus.
(3) *That* signals reference *across* entities or foci of attention, that is, to a topical entity which is not the current one.

So, whereas *it* simply carries on a current focus, *this* and *that* highlight their antecedents in some way, for purposes of signalling discourse shifts. The idea that demonstratives perform this highlighting function was, it will be recalled, a point made by Bolinger (1972). However, a slight re-assessment needs to be made of hypothesis (3), to accommodate the kind of reference to preceding statements *qua statements* noted by Lakoff (1974) and by Linde (1979). Metalinguistic reference to a preceding statement is typically effected by *that*:

18 You walk into my apartment and you walk down a long thin hall full of garbage. Actually, *that*'s a lie. It's not full of garbage anymore.

(Linde 1979)

Such an example is only superficially special; *that* can be seen as the speaker stepping away from the current focus and referring across the boundary created by the metadiscursive side-sequence. A similar metadiscursive signal would have been given by the passenger in the *Airplane* sequence if he had said 'The cockpit! What's that?' (i.e. 'explain that word/ identify its referent').

Alternatively, the *that* hypothesis may be reworded to take into account reference to entities which are *given*, but not current in the sense of *salient* or 'activated for the main current purpose'. Contrasting uses of *this* and *that* in the present data support this view. *This* certainly seems regularly to function as a signal that an entity is to be understood as raised to current focus. Not infrequently, the pattern in the data is the raising of a focus for the purpose of making either a comparison or contrast with another, new, or re-activated focus, for the purpose of evaluation. Examples 19 and 20 (from a text on acid rain) are typical examples. Example 19 describes a situation (events in Galloway), then focuses on it as a plausible comparison with events in the Lake District. Example 20 is similarly concerned with comparison:

19 The sulphate anions are very mobile and move through the soil drag-
   ging cations such as the hydrogen ion with them, which then acidify
   surface waters.
      They believe that if *this* is what happened in Galloway, it could well be
   what happened in the Lake District.

                                             (*New Scientist*, 23 January 1986)

20 Explanations include the idea that trees 'scavenge' more acid from
   passing clouds or that drains dug to accompany the planting reduce the
   chance of soils to neutralise acid rain before it reaches streams or lakes.
      But in Galloway, *this* does not appear to be relevant.

                                                                     (*ibid.*)

Example 21 signals the discovery of the body of a young wolf as significant
and as the focus of attention for the subsequent text:

21 The mutilated body of a young wolf has been discovered by Swedish
   wildlife researchers. Illegal hunters had shot and scalped the animal, and
   cut off its ears and a hind leg. *This* is another grizzly reminder that the
   inhabitants of Wermland, where the wolf was found, are not happy to have
   the only pack of wolves in Sweden and Norway in their midst.

                                             (*New Scientist*, 23 January 1986)

As stated, an entity is often the focus of attention for the purpose of
evaluation, and, indeed, comparison is a form of evaluation. The evaluation
pattern is frequently in the form of a *this . . . but . . .* sentence structure, as it
was in example 5 above.

   Examples of *that* in the data confirm the view that it refers across to another
topical entity, often for the purpose of marginalizing it in the informational
structure, rejecting its validity or importance in an argument, or else doing
what Halliday and Hasan (1976: 60) talk of in terms of other-attribution, that
is, attributing an entity or proposition to a third party. In 22 the author is
referring to the economic goals of the British Chancellor of the Exchequer:

22 On the other hand, the current account gap has to be seen to be closing soon;
   and inflation has to come back toward the norm for industrial nations.
      That means continued restriction of growth of demand, which in turn
   means continued high interest rates.

                                             (*The Guardian*, 2 November 1988)

Example 8 above is a similar case. In 23, an exception to a general truth is
dealt with and signalled as marginal in the overall argument:

23 Only a handful of satellite orbits are known to be changing. Such changes
   are usually subtle and can be detected only by long-term observations. One
   exception is the orbit of Neptune's large moon Triton, which is shrinking
   quite rapidly. *That* is because it circles Neptune in the direction opposite to
   the planet's revolution, generating strong gravitational friction.

                                             (*New Scientist*, 23 January 1986)

From the brief illustrations of the present data and the arguments scattered here and there among the work of others, we may draw together the facts of the usage of *it*, *this* and *that* in a revised set of statements:

(1) *It* is used for unmarked reference within a current entity or focus of attention.

(2) *This* signals a shift of entity or focus of attention to a new focus.

(3) *That* refers across from the current focus to entities or foci that are non-current, non-central, marginalizable or other-attributed.

These statements must remain tentative until tested on a lot more data, but they do enable us to account for a wide range of uses of *it*, *this* and *that*, and dispense with the necessity of making special cases of metastatement, or of 'emotional deixis' (Lakoff 1974). The findings are based on a considerable body of written data only briefly exemplified here, and are supported by examples from the data of others; such data offer a more reliable basis for the description of discoursal phenomena than do concocted sentences.

In conclusion, it is worth noting that, although *it*, *this* and *that* may only play a relatively minor role in textual organization, close examination of their characteristic environments raises fundamental questions about the status of paragraphs and discourse segments, and about how writers (and speakers) structure their arguments, create foci of attention in texts and signal desired interpretations.

NOTES

1 The data for the present study were taken from British newspaper and magazine articles selected randomly over the period 1985–8. Fifty examples of *it*, *this* and *that* were analysed and a representative sample is cited in support of the present arguments. Much more speech data than are cited here would need to be studied before statements could be made as to any significant differences between speech and writing for the items in question, though casual observation would suggest no notable differences. Lakoff (1974) does, however, perceive differences in levels of formality in the usage of *this* and *that*.

2 I make these judgements on the basis of Standard British English (SBrE) usage. I am aware that dialectal differences exist, such as the East Anglian tendency to use *that* in many cases where SBrE uses *it* (as in *That's raining*), and the American English usage which renders the normal SBrE request for a telephone-caller to state their identity, *Who's that?*, as *Who's this?* (for bringing this latter piece of information to my notice, I am grateful to John Sinclair, personal communication).

18 The structure of newspaper editorials

Adriana Bolívar

INTRODUCTION

It seems to me that one of the most important contributions of discourse analysis to linguistics is the observation that spoken discourse, mainly conversation, can be subject to structural analysis (Sinclair and Coulthard 1975 and followers). It is very interesting to note that most linguists involved in this type of analysis agree on the fact that the **exchange** is 'the minimal interactive unit most amenable to linguistic structural analysis' (Stubbs 1981: 9) and the unit 'basically concerned with the transmission of information' (Coulthard and Brazil 1981: 99) and, in fact, 'the primary unit of language interaction' (Sinclair and Brazil 1982: 49). If this is the case, one can then assume that the exchange, or a similar unit, may be used in the analysis of written text. In this chapter I intend to show how newspaper editorials, taken as an instance of interaction through written text, can be analysed using a unit called the **triad** (Bolívar 1986). The triad shares similarities with the exchange in that it consists of up to three elements of structure and constitutes the minimal unit of interaction in written text. The difference lies in that we are not examining face-to-face interaction but interaction of another kind.

As is well known, Sinclair and Coulthard (1975) use the term 'exchange' to refer to structures that consist of up to three elements: an initiation (I), a response (R) and a follow-up (F). Each initiation consists of an initiating move, informing, eliciting or directing, followed by a second move which fits the initiation. The third follow-up move is seen as obligatory in some contexts but not in others. The two examples below, taken from the analysis of classroom interaction, illustrate this analysis.

1 I Can anyone have a guess, a shot at that one?
   R Cleopatra
   F Cleopatra. Good girl. She was the most famous queen, wasn't she, Cleopatra of the Nile.

(Sinclair and Coulthard 1975: 80)

2 I What kind of food would you cut with a knife?
   R Meat.

(ibid.: 95)

In example 1 the third element is seen as obligatory because the teacher evaluates the answer given by the student, while in example 2 the third element is missing, apparently because the teacher delays the evaluation to make it global and applicable to the answer of several students.

Although Sinclair and Coulthard's observation is very interesting, some linguists believe that the distinction between bipartite and tripartite structures was not properly formalized and the conditions for the third element not explicitly stated (Berry 1981). In fact, most of the later developments of Sinclair and Coulthard (1975) have something to say about the third element. Burton (1978) makes an attempt to expand the original model for the purpose of applying it to the description of any type of naturally occurring talk. She recognizes two types of exchanges, explicit boundary exchanges and conversational exchanges, but she seems to dispense with the third element altogether. In her view, 'one would expect features that are prominent in classroom interaction to be less prominent, or even not apparent at all, in other types of talk and vice-versa' (Burton 1981: 62).

Coulthard and Brazil (1979) define the elements of structure in terms of two features: ± predicting and ± predicted, and use two criteria for identifying the elements: '(1) does the given element generate constraints which amount to a prediction that a particular element will follow; and (2) has a preceding element predicted its occurrence?' (Coulthard and Brazil 1979: 39).

Coulthard and Brazil characterize follow-up as 'not predicting' and 'not predicted', which makes it optional. They see exchanges as consisting of two elements: I R (initiation, response) and maximally four: I (R/I) RF (*ibid.*: 40) and study the elements of structure only in relation to the immediately adjacent move. Stubbs (1981) distinguishes between obligatory and optional feedbacks, but he does not specify the circumstances under which each would occur.

Berry (1981) attempts to bring together the accounts given by Sinclair and Coulthard (1975), Coulthard and Brazil (1979), Burton (1978) and Stubbs (1979). She makes some very interesting observations. In the first place she believes that there are three part structures in discourse where the third element is predicted. Second, she points to the fact that in the accounts developed later, the relationship between elements of structure is shown between successive elements when, in her view, follow-up is predicted by the initiating move rather than by the immediately preceding move (Berry 1981: 123). Third, she observes that those who have continued with the study of exchange structure seem to lose sight of the fact that both obligatory and optional feedback typically occur in the third place. I believe that these statements are fundamental for examining discourse structures in either spoken or written language. In fact, in the analysis of editorials I have found evidence to sustain the claim that the third element of structure is obligatory in some contexts, and that this depends on the type of initiation. The third element seems to have a fundamental structural function in that it closes the minimal unit of interaction. In editorials this function is still more

278 Advances in written text analysis

important because the third element presents the evaluation of events as seen by the writer.

Initiations in spoken discourse are of the utmost importance because they impose constraints on what is to come next and so determine the structure of the discourse. This is not so obvious in written text, but it happens all the same. The importance of initiations is well explained by Sinclair and Brazil (1982: 38):

> The very name initiation, makes it clear that we are looking ahead – not at what actually follows, to begin with, but at what the initiation does to whatever follows. Then we can assign a value to the next utterance in the context of this particular initiation. Each successive utterance, then, has to fit into an existing framework. It is not just dropped into a pool, but meets a predetermined network of choices, many of which have just been set up by the utterance which has just finished. The notion of 'structure' is very much one of anticipation, and the prominence of structure in conversation helps to explain how we can work with such subtlety and complexity.

Initiations are particularly important in written text because they are responsible for introducing topics and modalities in the discourse. In editorials, initiations can be of at least three types, they **inform**, they **elicit information** or they **organize** the discourse (Bolívar 1986: 238), in a manner similar to spoken interaction. The interesting thing is that the third element is obligatory in triads that have informing and eliciting initiations but optional in triads that organize the discourse, as we shall see later.

Other studies of the structure of conversation reinforce the view that the basic unit of analysis consists of three parts: for example, Hinds (1982) believes that the primary unit is a 'triplet'. He identifies two basic units of this type: (1) question–answer(–acknowledgement) and (2) remark–reply (–acknowledgement). In his view, 'these formulae indicate that a structural unit consists of a question–answer sequence with an optional acknowledgment' (Hinds 1982: 302). Hinds also believes that these triplets are frequently units which are part of a larger conversational scheme, and says (Hinds 1983b: 304): 'If we think of conversations as consisting of a hierarchically ranged sequence of topics and subtopics, these triplets form the basic unit of structure at the lowest level in the hierarchy.'

Apparently, Hinds takes the notion 'topic' as the criterion for identifying units of different sizes, but not necessarily the interaction itself. This allows us to see that there are, in discourse analysis, different ways of approaching the hierarchical description of conversation. Something similar happens with respect to the analysis of written text.

Most of the problems related to the analysis of written text derive from the fact that linguists have different conceptions of what text is. This, in turn, leads to descriptions of text 'organization' or text 'structure', which is not just a simple matter of labels but rather implies two different conceptions of interaction and quite different processes. If the linguist is more concerned with the interaction between the reader and the text, s/he will focus on the patterns of organization likely to be discovered by the reader (Hoey 1983; Winter 1986); however, if the main concern is the interaction between writer and reader, the attention will focus on the structure of the text in terms of the sequence of speech acts assumed to be performed by the writer (Tadros 1981, 1985; Cooper 1983). I believe that we have to take both processes into account, that is, the retrospective and the prospective patterns of organization in the discourse.

In my own analysis I assume that the initial categories of discourse are (i) **social interaction**; (ii) **two participants**; and (iii) **a text** (Bolívar 1986: 119). The text can be described on two planes; one that relates the text to the participants, and the other that concerns autonomous text processes. Following Sinclair (1983), I call these planes **interactive** and **autonomous**. The distinction allows for the description of both prospective and retrospective discourse patterning in discourse. The difference is important because in the first case we refer to interaction between real (or imagined) participants, while in the second we mean interaction between the reader and the text. In this respect Sinclair claims that 'the forward or prospective control of discourse construction is by negotiation of participants, whereas each participant in a turn has an opportunity to develop his personal messages out of what has gone before, through the creation of retrospective patterns' (Sinclair 1980: 255). In fact, retrospective patterning is so different that 'it is misleading to call it structure at all' (*ibid*.: 256). I use the term **posture** to refer to the prospective changes in the discourse, and the term **recall** to refer to what is traditionally called the semantic content and, in this way, we can account for what the writer is 'doing' and 'saying'. While it is true that the two planes depend on each other, I assume that the interactive plane determines the eventual meaning of the linguistic choices made on the autonomous plane (Bolívar 1986: 132).

THE MODEL OF ANALYSIS

Coulthard and Brazil (1979) suggest that 'for any unit one must provide two kinds of information: what position or function it has in the structure of other larger units and what its own internal structure is' (1979: 7). With this in mind, I assume that the function of the triad is to negotiate the transmission of information and evaluation in written text. Its internal structure can be described in terms of three fundamental **turns** (Tn) called **lead** (L), **follow** (F) and **valuate** (V), which are realized by **sentences** (s) conceived as 'the product of ordinary language behaviour' and not as 'system sentences' (Lyons 1977: 30). The example below shows a complete triad:

Tn   s

L   1   Britain and Ireland are now trying, at long last, to work out a less artificial link between them than that which binds two foreign states.

F   2   This is the most hopeful departure of the past decade because it opens for inspection what had lain concealed for half a century and goes to the root of the anguish in Northern Ireland.

V   3   The two countries now recognise that though they are independent of one another they cannot be foreign.

. This triad is the first in an editorial entitled 'Behind closed Irish doors' (*The Guardian*, 3 March 1981), which forms part of a corpus of twenty-three editorials selected from *The Guardian* during the first three months of 1981.

The triad above represents a coherent piece of text used by the leader-writer not only to negotiate information but also to make evaluations. The first turn, the lead, has the function of introducing the 'aboutness' (Hutchins 1977b) of the triad and a posture or modality; the second turn, the follow, responds to this initiation, keeping the same topic and evaluating the preceding piece of information; and the third turn, the valuate, closes the unit with an evaluation of the preceding two turns. The valuate turn has the function of ending the aboutness of the triad and of closing a postural scheme, so it is the coincidence of a discourse function, termination, and a discourse form, an opinion. While all turns may make evaluations, a particular status attaches to the valuate: it ends the smallest communicative cycle with an evaluation. The difference from other turns is that while the lead presents new information and the follow refers to it, the valuate refers to **both** of them. I call this a **content** triad because its function as a whole is to refer to and evaluate an event or state of affairs, and it is thus different from a **boundary** triad, whose function is to deal with the discourse itself. In the content triad the valuate is obligatory. This does not mean, however, that all triads must have three turns; triads can exhibit more than three turns provided the sequence L F is repeated and V is final, that is, triads such as LFLFV or LFLFLFV can be found when the V turn is delayed by the writer.

In spoken interaction turn-change depends on speaker change, but in written discourse the equivalent to turn change is observed in changes that take place in the main clauses of the sentences, particularly in tense, mood and modality. I prefer not to look at sentences as realizing acts because 'in uttering a sentence one sometimes performs more than one illocutionary act, with different parts of the sentences involved in each of the acts' (McCawley 1981: 210). In the model of analysis I propose, the allocation of more than one sentence to a turn depends on whether subsequent sentences do or do not maintain the same posture, by using signals that indicate the same modality, tense or mood. The analysis of editorials has shown that it is possible to identify certain conditions for the allocation of more than one sentence to a turn, and we can talk about a general system for the maintenance and change of turns in written text (see below).

The triad may combine with other triads in order to make up a unit at a higher rank. I call this larger unit **movement** (Mv). The movement may combine with other movements to make up the largest unit at the highest rank, which I call **artefact**. Thus a hierarchical model is created, with artefact and sentence at opposite ends of the rank scale.

The triads can be classified according to position and function into **Situation** (S), **Development** (D) and **Recommendation** (R). S triads are presented in initial position and have the function of referring to an event and evaluating it. The first S triad in an editorial refers to the current event being evaluated, while the S triads that appear later refer back to the main event, although they may introduce other related events. D triads occur in medial position, after S types, and their function is to develop the reference to and the evaluation of the event considered in the immediately preceding S triad, either the first one in the text or others. R triads occupy final position in the sequence and their function is to close the reference and the evaluation of the event introduced by the S triad that initiates the sequence.

The initiating triad presented above is now shown below together with the triads that follow it. As can be seen, each triad has been assigned a function: the initiating triad is called S, for situation, the one that follows it is D, for development, and the third one is R, for recommendation. The three triads (Td) made up a movement which, in this case, forms the first major part of the artefact.

Td	Tn	s	
	L	1	Britain and Ireland are now trying, at long last, to work out a less artificial link between them than that which binds two foreign states.
S	F	2	This is the most hopeful departure of the past decade because it opens for inspection what had lain concealed for half a century and goes to the root of the anguish in Northern Ireland.
	V	3	The two countries now recognise that though they are independent of one another they cannot be foreign.
	L	4	It is a large task they have taken on, for each side has its privy jealousies and each is aware that a false step, or even a false reading of a right step, could bring out the worst of the Northern paramilitaries into communal war.
D	F	5	Someone in the Northern Ireland Office mentions defence and the Dail is in uproar.
		6	Someone in the Dail mentions federalism and Mr. Paisley stomps the mountains calling up the ghost of Carson to save the holy counties from Rome.
	V	7	But the process has begun of seeing where the islands went wrong in the first place and making whatever corrections are now feasible to a series of mistakes and misconceptions.
	L	8	Is Benelux a model?
		9	Is the Nordic Union?
R	F	10	Probably not, because nothing elsewhere quite simulates the petulance and lopsidedness of the partners in Iona, the islands of the North Atlantic.

V   11   Whatever emerges, though, has to make irrelevant for all
time both the ruthlessness of the Republicans, even when it
is directed against themselves, and the grand delusions of
embittered loyalists.

In this first movement there are three complete triads, each one with an
obligatory turn. The first triad in the movement has the function of presenting
the actual event. The event is stated in evaluative terms in the first turn, as
seen in the use of 'at long last' and 'a less artificial link', but the reader is
informed about what is happening in the world of phenomena. The whole
triad has an initiating function in that it gives the grounds for what follows in
the next segment of text. The second triad develops the statement of the event
and evaluates the preceding piece of discourse. The use of 'they' in turn L of
triad D refers back to 'Britain and Ireland' and continues with the main theme
of the movement but goes deeper into the problem. The whole triad has a
'response' function and as readers we expect more information or an
evaluation after it. The third triad performs the function of evaluator. It ends
the movement and evaluates the two preceding triads. This indicates that the
internal structure of each movement can be described in terms of triads which
follow the natural sequence S D R, similar in function to the turns within a
triad but at a higher rank.

The triads that make up a movement cannot be shuffled at will (nor the
turns within a triad) because if this is done the result is another text and not
the one intended by the writer for the reader he has in mind. In the text just
quoted the writer assumes a reader who is fairly well informed about what is
happening. I say 'fairly well informed' because the writer makes a semi-
explicit statement of the event. He assumes the reader knows about the kind
of 'link' that Britain and Ireland are working out.

If the ordering of the triads were changed we might still get a coherent
movement, but the meaning and the interaction between the writer and reader
would be different. For example, if we initiated the movement with triad D,
we would obtain an order that seems perfectly correct from a semantic point
of view because the reader could make sense of this new text and understand
its content. However, the new organization affects the discourse and a new
type of interaction has to be described. In the original text the writer's
assumption is that the reader is fairly well informed about the event, while in
the new order starting with 'It is a large task they have taken on . . .', the
writer's assumption is that the reader is very well informed. The triads in the
example above could still be shuffled into another order and efforts could be
made to understand and explain the new text. But in doing this we would be
showing our capacity to understand and make sense out of parts of text but we
would be saying nothing about the interaction between writer and reader in a
particular social context.

Movement is the second largest unit in the model. In an editorial a
movement may be the whole or part of an artefact; its size cannot be

determined in terms of the number of paragraphs that compose it because movements and paragraphs belong to two different types of organization. The size of a movement depends on the number of triads that relate the text to the world of events within the same modal perspective, and the only condition is that a movement must contain at least one content triad, which is the basic unit of interaction in written text.

The movement that refers to the actual world, a world *that is or was*, is called **type A**, and this can be followed by **type B** movement, which refers to the world of possibilities, or the world *that might be*. If the editorial contains yet another movement, this follows the type B movement. This last movement, **type C**, refers to the world *that should be* and, in fact constitutes a major evaluation that refers back to movements B and A. The three movements in the sequence A B C represent major modal changes in the artefact.

The artefact is analysed fully below so that we can see the sequence of triads and their function in each one of the movements:

Behind closed Irish doors

Mov	Td	Tn	s	
A	S	L	1	Britain and Ireland are now trying, at long last, to work out a less artificial link between them than that which binds two foreign states.
		F	2	This is the most hopeful departure of the past decade because it opens for inspection what had lain concealed for half a century and goes to the root of the anguish in Northern Ireland.
		V	3	The two countries now recognise that though they are independent of one another they cannot be foreign.
	D	L	4	It is a large task they have taken on, for each side has its privy jealousies and each is aware that a false step, or even a false reading of a right step, could bring out the worst of the Northern paramilitaries into communal war.
		F	5	Someone in the Northern Ireland Office mentions defence and the Dail is in uproar.
			6	Someone in the Dail mentions federalism and Mr Paisley stomps the mountains calling up the ghost of Carson to save the holy counties from Rome.
		V	7	But the process has begun of seeing where the islands went wrong in the first place and making whatever corrections are now feasible to a series of mistakes and misconceptions.
	R	L	8	Is Benelux a model?
			9	Is the Nordic Union?
		F	10	Probably not, because nothing elsewhere quite simulates the petulance and lopsidedness of the partners of Iona, the islands of the North Atlantic.

V   11   Whatever emerges, though, has to make irrelevant for all time both the ruthlessness of the Republicans, even when it is directed against themselves, and the grand delusions of embittered loyalists.

B   S   L   12   The end of the Republicans' dirty protest, which has kept them confined and surrounded by filth for years on end, probably has no part in the British–Irish reconciliation.

13   More likely it is designed to prevent it from taking a form which the IRA would not like.

F   14   By one means or another the Republicans want to focus on their demand for political status, which those who committed their offences before a certain date still enjoy.

V   15   They have had no success with the European Commission on Human Rights, or with the public generally in either country, yet there is just enough truth in their assertion to stimulate the Anglo-Irish negotiators to feats of invention.

D   L   16   In Sunday's communique announcing the fast of Bobby Sands, the Republicans described their crimes as 'selfless'.

F   17   In that they did not blow up innocent people entirely for personal gain there is a fragment of tortured reason there.

V   18   They oscillate between demands for political status and simpler requests about clothes and degrees of prison work.

R   L   19   At Christmas the authorities and the prisoners were within range of a settlement.

F   20   They could be again before Mr Sands comes to his crisis.

L   21   But if they are, what will Mr Paisley and the UDS say?

F   22   Treachery?

23   Connivance?

24   Capitulation?

V   25   Anything to keep hatred on the boil.

C   S   L   26   Mr Humphrey Atkins has said all he can to conciliate the Protestants, not all of whom in any case rise to Mr Paisley's heights of indignation.

27   Mr Haughey in Dublin has not contradicted him.

F   28   At the end of 11 years of almost unremitting bloodshed and disruption calls for patience sound limp.

V   29   Yet unless London and Dublin can work out a series of agreements – a bill of rights, a supervisory council of ministers or judges, a guarantee of traditions, an incentive towards mutual respect – perhaps a more formal association embracing all those things – the prospects for extremism seem bright.

     30   Patience in negotiation is the only way of rescuing Northern Ireland from the hell on which it so often seems bent.

D   L   31   Mr Paisley would not deny that he adjoins the Irish Republic or, as Mrs Thatcher puts it, Britain has a land frontier with a fellow-member of the EEC.

   F   32   That is a starting point from which the crooked triangle, Dublin–London–Belfast, can be straightened.

   V   33   Allow time.

This analysis enables us to see three-part structures of different sizes, such as the triad and the movement. We can also see that in all content triads there is an obligatory third element, the valuate turn, which closes a segment of text with an opinion about the topic introduced by the lead and developed by the follow. However, the third element seems to be optional in units of a larger size, as witnessed by the fact that, although the first and second movements consist of three triads each in the sequence S D R, this is not the case in movement C, which consists of only two triads in the sequence S D. In fact, this seems to be the situation in most editorials analysed in the original corpus. There are no boundary triads in this editorial, but we shall see some examples later.

We can also observe that the triads do not always consist of three turns. For example, triad R in movement B consists of five turns in the sequence LFLFV. This means that the model allows for the delay of turn V provided it is preceded by sequences of LF. This is so because, in these cases, there is more negotiation of information and evaluation. The explanation is that the writer delays the evaluation either to introduce more information or to make the reader wait for his opinion on a particular point. In the analysis of *The Guardian* 1981 corpus there was a total of 147 triads of which 124 (84.4 per cent) consisted of three turns (LFV). Only twenty-three exceptions were found, of which fourteen (60.9 per cent) were made of five turns (LFLFV), four (17.4 per cent) of seven turns (LFLFLFV), and five (21.7 per cent) of two turns (LV). In the case of deviant triads of two turns (LV), the explanation lay in the fact that the F turn was apparently skipped by the writer who jumped from the initiation to the conclusion, or perhaps due to problems of punctuation as in the example below, where a new orthographic sentence could have started with 'Yet':

L (F) s.11   In the year to September 1980, the Department of Employment estimates that the number of jobs lost in the economy amounted to 806,000, *yet* the number of people registering on the dole in the same period was only 522,000.

V   S.12   In other words, 283,500 people in one year failed to register either because they were not eligible for benefits or because they took early retirement.

(*The Guardian*, 'Another 103,000 on the dole', 28 January 1981)

The editorial 'Behind closed Irish doors' also shows that turns vary in size. For example, sentences 5 and 6 make up a turn F in triad D of movement A, sentences 8 and 9 make up turn L in triad R of the same movement, sentences 12 and 13 make up turn L in triad S of movement B; sentences 22, 23 and 24 form the second turn F of triad R in the same movement; and sentences 26 and 27 compose turn L in triad S of movement C; while sentences 29 and 30 make up turn V of the same triad. The 1981 corpus shows that turns consisting of one sentence are highly frequent (78.1 per cent) and that turns of two sentences are moderately frequent (15.3 per cent) but that turns consisting of more than two sentences are exceptions. It is interesting to note that turns consisting of more than two sentences are often found in follows and valuates but rarely in leads.

TURN-CHANGE AND TURN-MAINTENANCE IN TRIADS

Content triads can be classified into **informing** and **eliciting**, depending on the type of lead that initiates them. The informing triad typically contains a lead turn realized by a sentence in declarative syntax, while the eliciting triad is initiated with a lead in interrogative form. In order to explain turn-change and turn-maintenance in informing triads it is necessary to examine the forms used by the writer in the lead turns. The description must focus on (i) tense selection, (ii) modality selection, and (iii) lexical anticipation. Any choice made in the lead anticipates a particular type of selection in the follow and imposes constraints on the form of the valuate.

Tense selection

Tense selection in the lead is important because it indicates the time dimension, and editorials are very sensitive to time. Tense change can be accompanied by adverbials of time such as *last year*, *this year*, *next year*, etc. or by discourse adjuncts which indicate agreement or disagreement such as *In fact*, *Indeed*, *But*, *However*, etc. The example below shows the transition between turns by tense change:

L   s.1   'It is true that the block vote is suspect', Mr Sid Weighell, the railwaymen's leader, told Labour's constitutional conference.

     s.2   'I know because I have got one in my hand.'

F   s.3   In fact, the NUR makes more efforts than many to see that the 180,000 votes Mr Weighell casts for or against this, that or the other cause at party conferences represent the views of a majority of his members.

V   s.4   Even so, Mr Weighell demonstrates a certain unease as he holds up his card at conference after conference –

      s.5   as well he might.

      (*The Guardian*, 'Black marks for block votes', 28 January 1981)

Apparently, turn-maintenance with same tense tends to occur in all types of turns, while the use of sentences with different tense, particularly with quoted text, seems to be typical of leads and follows but not of valuates. This is explained mainly because the role of the valuate is fundamentally to evaluate information and only secondarily to give new information.

Although the transition between past and present is found, as in the example just given, this is not the most common type of transition since the predominant tense in an editorial is the present. The results obtained for triads of three turns only indicate that this tense is used in 74.5 per cent of the cases. It is also observed that the present tense occurs in a similar proportion in all types of turns, which suggests that the transition past to present is not the most frequently used by the writer, but rather present to present or present to past.

Modality selection

Modality selection is probably the most common way of indicating turn-change and turn-maintenance in an editorial. Modality is important because it belongs to 'a system derived from the interpersonal function of language, expressing the speaker's assessment of probabilities' (Halliday 1970 in Kress 1976: 204), which means that through signals such as modal verbs, modal adjuncts, special nouns, adjectives, verbs and others, the writer indicates his/her attitude towards his/her own speech in the role of declarer. The triad below exemplifies the case of a triad that has chosen an informing lead in the past which is also non-modal. As the information refers to the past, the lead anticipates more information from another point of view or evaluation of this information. What is expressed in the follow is evaluation in hypothetical terms by means of a change into modal verbs ('would') and a return to information about the real world in the valuate, as seen in the use of the present perfect tense 'has reached' and 'As it is', reinforced by the use of 'now':

L   s.12 As the CRE notes: 'Despite intervention from the local MP, the police never *took* any action against the culprits and no charges *were brought*'.

F   s.13 If the family had been white, the reaction *would* have been rather different.

s.14   There *would* have been outraged banner headlines;

s.15   MP's *would* have spoken sonorously of the racialist strains to society,

s.16   and the police *would* have wasted no time in bringing prosecutions and restoring law and order.

V   s.16   *As it is*, the intimidation of black people *has reached* such a pitch that even the cautious CRE and the still more cautious Home Office have *now* registered alarm.

(*The Guardian*, 'On the street where you live', 18 March 1981)

However, the selection of a modal verb or a modal adjunct does not necessarily imply that the lead anticipates a modality change in the same way that the selection of present or past tense does not inevitably anticipate a tense change. A whole triad may be written in modal verbs or in the present tense. What must be done then is to see how a triad in the same tense indicates modal changes and how one written in modals expresses changes in types of modality, tense and other signals such as lexical anticipation.

Lexical anticipation

Lexical anticipation can also serve as a signal of turn-change. This is defined as the phenomenon whereby a lexical item signals in advance a relation (Winter 1977a, 1979). According to Winter, the relation itself is a 'lexical realization' and allows for signals to indicate a prospective as well as a retrospective realization. I use the term only to refer to prospective realizations on the grounds that the writer has the commitment to clarify the signal in a linear progression and also because anticipation in itself is not enough to show the transition between turns but rather a complement to either tense or modality changes. The analysis of the 1981 corpus suggests that lexical anticipation in the lead can be expressed by means of a noun, an adjective or a prepositional phrase. These signals are typically evaluative and therefore anticipate information that must clarify the given information. The two triads below show cases of anticipation with a noun and with an adjective.

L   s.1   Between now and the end of the financial year on March 31, health authorities are likely to be casting around for *projects* on which they can spend money at speed.

F   s.2   Wards may have closed;

s.3   doctors may be trying to save their hospitals' money by shunting prescriptions into local chemists;

s.5   patients may be foregoing prescriptions because they can't afford the charges.

s.6   But *new wallpaper, fresh paint*, perhaps *the odd bit of new furniture*, are likely to grace many a hospital or administration office.

V   s.7   *The doctrine of annuality*, or *the bureaucrats' spring fever* is upon us once again.
           (*The Guardian*, 'Spend, spend, spend, think', 20 February 1981)

The relation between 'projects' in L and 'new wallpaper', 'fresh paint', 'the odd bit of new furniture' in F constitute the two parts of the lexical realization, while 'the doctrine of annuality, or the bureaucrats' spring fever' in V evaluate both.

L   s.1   Hollywood – the new Hollywood – where westerns are out of fashion – might have rejected it as *too corny*.
F   s.2   In Teheran with minutes to go, after innumerable twists, turns and desperations, the 52 take off for freedom.
        s.3   On the West side of the Capitol, looking steadfastly across the swathe of Washington, a rugged old actor exhorts Americans, 'you, the citizens of this blessed land', to dream 'heroic dreams'.
V   s.4   Distinctly *too corny*:
        s.5   far better something realistic, like Charlton Heston jumping between jets at 35,000 feet.
           (*The Guardian*, 'Exemplars of a true freedom', 21 January 1981)

This time, with the signal 'too corny', the writer commits himself to explaining his first evaluation. He does so in F (s.2 and s.3), but he makes the final evaluation in V repeating 'too corny' followed by an ironic comment.

Lexical anticipation must be distinguished from enumeration, which is a category of prediction (Tadros 1981) that commits the writer to perform an act of discourse. While anticipation commits the writer to give new information of some kind in another turn, enumeration implies a stronger commitment which forces the writer to keep the turn in order to complete the information in one turn. The difference between an anticipation and a prediction can be seen in that the first part of the prediction carries a signal that belongs to the class 'numeral' or 'enumerables', that is, exact numerals like *two*, *three*, *double*, etc. and sub-technical words such as *reasons*, *issues*, etc., which are inexact numerals (Tadros 1981: 143). Since enumeration by definition may include more than two sentences, this type of floor maintenance is the longest type found. However, even the longest turn in the 1981 corpus does not contain more than seven sentences. The important point is that the lead turn presents the enumerating and the enumerated parts of the prediction because these sentences are not evaluated individually but as a whole.

The lead turn that initiates an eliciting triad is typically realized by a sentence in interrogative syntax and has the function of asking a question in order to obtain an answer. The distinction between elicitations and rhetorical questions must be kept clear. In editorials, rhetorical questions are used to give information in evaluative terms or simply to evaluate information already given. The analysis of the 1981 corpus reveals that eliciting triads are not often used by the leader-writer of *The Guardian*. However, it is significant that most of them occur in type R triads, which could indicate a tendency to negotiate final evaluation in a dialogic manner.

THE FUNCTIONS OF BOUNDARY TRIADS

Boundary triads, those whose main function is to deal with the discourse and not necessarily with the content, are used before or between movements and very rarely between triads. They can be classified into at least three types, depending on the class of act they express or imply. The may indicate (i) *an act of identification*, which explicitly states or gives some orientation about the event to be dealt with, as in 'Let us spare a thought this weekend for the King of Spain' ('The disease of the kingdom', *The Guardian*, 20 February 1981); (ii) *an act of analysis or explanation*, as in 'So it is worth examining the "suspect" mechanism behind block vote' ('Black marks for block votes', *The Guardian*, 28 January 1981); (iii) *an act of conclusion and/or recommendation*, as in 'Bystanders (like this newspaper) who happen to share much of the diagnosis can hardly cavil over the ends and means. But there are no simplicities' ('A footnote, a chapter, a chance?', *The Guardian*, 3 March 1981).

Boundary triads can also act as *reminders*, with the purpose of guiding the reader, as in 'We are still in the world of ifs' ('A footnote, a chapter, a chance?', *The Guardian*, 3 March 1981) in the middle of a movement B to indicate that the world of possibilities is still being analysed. Most of these triads consist of only one obligatory turn. However, cases of triads consisting of two turns (LdFd) were found in the 1981 corpus. In these cases the writer mainly addresses the attention to his own text with some kind of evaluation, but it is a different kind of evaluation. See, for example, the first part of the editorial below in which the actual event is introduced in the second triad of the first movement, after a triad that presents a hypothetical situation:

L   s.1   Mr and Mrs N. are a white couple with three children who live on an almost all black council state.

F   s.2   As soon as they moved there, one of their windows was broken and their neighbours banged constantly on their front and back doors.

      s.3   A month later, a large stone was catapulted through the main bedroom window, narrowly missing Mr N. and the baby who was in his cot.

      s.4   A few days later, an air pellet was shot through the same window;

      s.5   almost every time the family left the house, black people shouted abuse and threw stones.

V   s.6   Within two months, the family were living under siege, too terrified to go to work or even open a window.

Ld   s.7 This *report* is, it must be admitted, not entirely accurate;
Fd   s.8 It is in fact the negative of a true photograph.
L   s.9 The events did indeed occur, and are recorded with other similarly distressing events in the *report* on racial harassment produced yesterday by the Commission for Racial Equality.
F   s.10 But the victims, of course, were black and their oppressors white.
V   s.11 Mr and Mrs N. are a Bengali couple who eventually had to move away to escape such harassment.

(*The Guardian*, 'On the street where you live', 18 March 1981)

This editorial allows us to see the difference between reference to the discourse ('report' in s.7) and reference to the world ('report' in s.9). In the first instance the writer names his own act of reporting; in the second he informs about something that happened in the world of phenomena.

As already seen, initiations are fundamental because they select the topic and a posture. They are particularly important in the first triads of movement A because the reference to the event is often made in the first and second turn of the first triad, although exceptions such as the above are also found when the writer takes more text to present the actual event, either because he assumes the reader needs to be reminded or told about what has happened, or for stylistic reasons. Follow turns seem to function mainly as a transition between the initial information (or evaluation) and the final evaluation. In fact, as observed in the 1981 corpus, apparently the topics most frequently developed derive from L and V turns but not from F.

THE FUNCTIONS OF VALUATE TURNS

We must now examine valuate turns in more detail, because they are responsible for closing the smallest unit of interaction with an opinion. On the basis of the evidence obtained, valuate turns can be classified into three main groups that I have called **concluders**, **prophecies** and **directives**. The function of concluders is to intimate that a conclusion has been reached, with reference to the present time, which in this case is the time of publication of the newspaper. Concluders can be further sub-classified into (i) **logical conclusion** or **result**, (ii) **temporal result**, and (iii) **informative comments**. The first two are indicated by signals such as *Therefore, Thus, Now, As a result, If . . . then, In general, At the moment*, etc., but the last one consists of sentences in the past or present tense used by the writer to offer new information that evaluates preceding turns and cannot be taken as an initial posture. Tadros had already noticed this phenomenon when she said that 'the position of the reporting clause in its sentence and paragraph must be taken into account. Where the report is the only one and it comes at the end, it is not predictive but interpreted as a comment' (Tadros 1981: 27). It is worth remembering though that, in our case, the discourse structure does not always overlap with the paragraph organization (Bolívar 1986: 209).

It is also worth noticing that the signals themselves can be misleading. It is the signal in the context of the sentence where it appears and in the context of the sentences that precede and follow which will indicate whether the signal must be interpreted as belonging to the valuate turn or to an initial posture or to a response in a follow.

Prophecies are valuate turns which consist of declarative sentences whose function is to predict future events in life. They must be distinguished from textual predictions, such as Tadros (1981), where the writer sets up a prediction which must be fulfilled in the discourse itself. The use of prophecies allows the writer to make an evaluation of the situations s/he presents and also to indicate the assessment of probabilities for future developments. These prophecies may be the writer's or may be assigned to others and are typically realized by verbs that indicate futurity.

Directives in editorials may be found in any type of turn, but only those directives in valuates have the function of proposing or suggesting 'desirable' courses of action. Directives in valuates can take different forms and can be found in various degrees of explicitness. The most explicit form is the imperative, but not the most frequent. Directives can be sub-classified into **direct** and **indirect**. Direct directives can be defined as declarative turns consisting of sentences which carry signals that indicate the agent, the kind of action to be performed and, optionally, the circumstances of the action, in the main clause of the sentence that makes up the valuate turn. If the turn consists of more than one sentence the signal will be found in the first sentence of the sequence and only exceptionally in the second. The directive is indirect when the suggestion for action has to be inferred from the context of the discourse. The use of *should* and *need* may be quite different in direct directives, and expressions such as *It is essential that*, and the construction *If . . . then*, as well as questions, are often found in indirect directives.

CONCLUDING REMARKS

The study of editorials from other British newspapers has confirmed the analysis and the existence of three-part structures. The difference between editorials seems to depend mainly on how each newspaper evaluates the world, and on the assumptions they make about the reader's knowledge of events and states of affairs but, above all, on their assumptions about sharing or not sharing the same system of evaluation. These differences are often expressed in the number of turns that triads may take, in the use of boundary triads, in the preference of some type of syntax over another, and in the manipulation of the paragraph organization, so that initiations of paragraphs overlap with leads, follows or valuates, depending on the particular interests of the newspapers (Bolívar 1986: 309).

The consistent use of three-part structures makes us wonder whether this only applies to editorials or whether this is a type of structure that exists in other types of discourse. One also wonders why three parts and not four or five. Is it, perhaps, that we are faced with a rhetorical convention that goes back to Plato and Aristotle or to Kant and Hegel? Or is it that the three parts are used in an editorial because there is a cultural constraint that forces the writer to do so? The analysis of *The Guardian* 1981 corpus, and also *The Times* for 1981, as well as other analyses I have done after these, suggest that the minimal unit of interaction, the triad, is made up of three turns with distinct functions in the discourse: the lead introduces the aboutness and a posture, the follow responds and the valuate closes the cycle with an evaluation. Both the lead and the valuate represent more definite attitudes, but the follow acts like a mediator, a sort of 'cushion' or transition towards the final evaluation.

Studies in contrastive rhetoric point to the fact that not all cultures seem to follow the same rhetorical conventions (Kaplan 1966, 1982; Kaplan and Ostler 1972; Hinds 1976, 1980, 1982, 1983a, b, c), but there is evidence that three-part structures are also found in other languages. For example, Hinds notes that in Japanese there is a style known as the *jo-ha-kyu*, or 'introduction', 'development' and 'climax', which, in his view, is 'similar to normal English rhetorical style' (Hinds 1983c: 80). In his comparison of English and Japanese paragraphs, Hinds also notes that Japanese paragraphs are structured in three parts, and says: 'The overall structure of a Japanese paragraph contains (1) an introduction, (2) directly or indirectly related comments, and (3) an optional generalization, summation or both' (Hinds 1980: 158).

However, he also brings to our attention a major rhetorical style which 'does not exist in English' (Hinds 1983a: 183). The style is termed *ki-shoo-ten-ketsu* and refers to a pattern originating in classical Chinese poetry. The four parts indicate a pattern of expository prose where *ki* introduces the topic, *shoo* develops it, *ten* forms an abrupt transition or a vaguely related point and *ketsu* concludes the topic (*ibid.*: 158). Hinds points out that this pattern represents potential problems for ESL learners since *ten* introduces information considered irrelevant by western audiences, and *ketsu* is defined differently in Japanese than conclusion is in English.

Hinds' remark is particularly relevant to the description of newspaper editorials and the existence of three-part structures in discourse because he takes the primary data from a Japanese daily newspaper called *Asahi Shimbum*, whose editorial comments are translated into English 'sentence by sentence' (*ibid.*: 187). According to Hinds' analysis, these comments are structured in four parts and follow the *ki-shoo-ten-ketsu* pattern. However, when we compare them with the English editorials, we realize that the difference derives from the form in which Japanese writers negotiate the evaluation. We note that the segments called *ten* and *ketsu* can easily be interpreted as only one part whose function is similar to that of movement C, but with a more complex internal structure where the *ten* is introduced as a preliminary to mitigate the conclusion or recommendation. Apparently, Japanese expository writers avoid reaching conclusions or making evaluations in an abrupt manner and they introduce this preliminary part in order to distract the reader's attention and so follow implicit rules of politeness. At this point, it might be argued that the discourse of Japanese editorials reflects tacit rules of interaction in the Japanese culture, but this can only be confirmed by studying how Japanese people interact in everyday life and how they negotiate evaluations. The three-part structures of English editorials, though, seem to indicate a similarity with English spoken interaction in that there are three-part structures in spoken discourse as well.

The comparison between Japanese and English rhetorical structures cannot be taken as sufficient evidence to claim that three-part structures are universal and that they occur in all types of discourse, but it is worth finding out what types of discourse they occur in and what forms these structures take in different cases. It would be interesting to start by examining a larger sample of British editorials and comparing them with editorials written in other languages, in other cultures.

19 On reporting reporting: the representation of speech in factual and factional narratives

Carmen Rosa Caldas-Coulthard

INTRODUCTION

The report of what people said is a major feature of many kinds of written texts: court proceedings, news in the press, police statements, fictional narratives, etc. The most extreme case of the representation of speech in written form is the dramatic text, where the story unfolds through talk. In all cases, there is a teller who either creates a conversation, in the case of fictional texts, or reports what somebody else supposedly said, in the case of a factual report. What is said can be either directly attributed to characters in a direct mode or presented by the teller indirectly. The teller is, therefore, in charge of selecting what to report and of organizing the way what has been selected is going to be reported. The same words, for example, can be interpreted and therefore retold differently according to different points of view and according to different social conventions and roles. If, for example, a reporter writes:

The director *claimed* that it was snowing

instead of

The director *said* that it was snowing

what s/he is doing in the first example is to detach him/herself from the responsibility of what is being reported by choosing the particular reporting verb *claim* to gloss the report ('the director *claims* something but I do not take responsibility for or necessarily agree with what he said'). In the second example, the reporter is apparently neutral in relation to the supposed saying, because s/he introduces it by using the verb *say*. Strategies of this kind can carry non-explicit meaning and it is important that readers become aware of them.

In this chapter, I will examine speech representation in factual and factional texts in order to discuss the following issues:

(a) the means and the implications of inserting one text into another;
(b) the question of veracity and truthfulness;
(c) the exclusion of women as speakers from the press.

QUOTATION AS INTERTEXTUALITY

In all written texts, any reported speech is a form of quotation. Linguistically, 'quote' is the final layer in a hierarchy of narrative levels, since it is the introduction of one text into another. For Halliday, speech representation is a manifestation of a logicosemantic system of projection, which is an inter-clausal relation or a relation between processes (1985: 193). There are, for him, two fundamental sub-types of projection:

(1) 'locution': one clause is projected through another as locution, a con-struction of wording (he said: *It is snowing*). Halliday describes this projection as a relation of interdependency between clauses, one initiating (primary) and the other continuing (secondary), both having equal status and he calls it 'parataxis'.
(2) 'idea': one clause is projected through another, as an idea, a construction of meaning (he said *it was snowing*) (p. 197). This is a relation of 'hypotaxis', where one element is dependent (the reported clause) on another dominant one (the reporting clause).

While 'wording' is presented at a lexicogrammatical level, since it implies a prior referent or some previous occasion of speaking that can then be referred back to, 'idea' is presented at a semantic level (there is nothing but the reported text) and is processed by the linguistic system only once and not twice as in the case of 'wording'. Halliday says that 'when something has the status of wording it lies not at one but at two removes from experience . . . . When something is projected as a meaning, we are not representing "the very words", because there are no words' (p. 230).

When a writer uses projection as 'locution', s/he is supposed to represent the actual wording, although, as I hope to demonstrate below, there are many exceptions to this rule; the idealized function of projection as meaning (indirect presentation), on the other hand, is to represent the sense or the gist of what was supposedly said. 'Quoting' and 'reporting', for Halliday, are therefore not simply formal variants, but they also differ in meaning. Halliday's distinctions, of course, are not absolutes, because the reporting verb in a 'wording' can also be an idea and it is also possible to 'report' a saying by representing it as a meaning, as in the following example:

Liberace *argued* that the article implied that he was homosexual, which he emphatically *denied*.

(*The Independent*, 5 February 1987)

All speech representation in written discourses falls basically into the two sub-types of projection. But as Fairclough (1988a, based upon Voloshinov 1973) suggests, there is a dynamic interrelationship between the 'primary discourse' (the reporting) and the 'secondary discourse' (the reported or represented discourse): 'in one major "style" of representation, primary and secondary discourse are clearly differentiated, in the other, they are merged . . . . The way in which secondary discourse is interpreted may be controlled by the way it is contextualized in primary discourse' (p. 2). There are therefore degrees of author's interference in 'quoting' and 'reporting' and the interesting aspect to be considered is how they are used to reproduce interaction, since the possible choices determine different meanings. Another interesting point is to investigate how the secondary discourse(s) relates to the primary one.

Structural simplification

Writers, when representing oral interaction, make use of their assumptions about real interactive strategies in order to create their intratextual interactions. A report of interaction (factual or fictional) is always a reduction of an initial communicative event, especially because the reported talk is embedded in a text which has a different purpose from an original communicative event.

Another important aspect is that, because text is linear, it forces tidiness on written conversation. Reported talk is therefore a cleaned-up version of real talk. The representation of speech is a simplification and a reduction of the organizational characteristics of real interaction. There is no place, for example, for the interpersonal features of conversations to be reported. **Openings**, **closings** (see Schegloff and Sacks 1973) or **phatic communion**, for example, are not present in reported interaction. Readers, however, use their interactional competence, and assume that some kind of beginning and end to the conversation reported took place.

In terms of structural organization, the *exchange structure* is also simplified. In naturally occurring interactions, the exchange is generally realized by three moves: initiation, response and follow-up (see Sinclair and Coulthard 1975). Fictional interaction, at exchange level, is characterized by chains of two moves (initiations and responses) and three-part exchanges are rarely found (see Caldas-Coulthard 1988 for a detailed discussion):

'What animals were they?'	I-elicit
'There were three animals altogether', he explained. 'There were two goats and a cat and then there were four pair of pigeons.'	R-reply
'And you had to leave them?'	I-elicit
'Yes, because of the artillery. The captain told me to go because of the artillery.'	R-reply
'And you have no family?'	I-elicit
'No', he said, 'only the animals.'	R-reply

(Hemingway, 'The old man at the bridge', p. 79)

In factual reports, exchanges are still more reduced and the vast majority of them are represented by just one move, generally an informing one, which is evaluatory in its function in the discourse. The shortened texts below exemplify this point:

Jail after horror accident
A pedestrian died from multiple injuries after being mown down by a van. He was then dragged for almost half a mile underneath it, Birmingham Court was told yesterday.

Behind the wheel was 30-year-old John Morahan who had been disqualified from driving and was three times over the legal alcohol limit, said Mr Richard Griffiths-Jones, prosecuting.

Morahan, of Tanhouse Farm Road, Solihull was jailed . . . .

Judge Richard Cole told him: 'It is very seldom that you can experience a more horrible case in these courts.'

Mr Griffiths-Jones said the accident happened after a Sunday lunch time drinking session.

(*Birmingham Daily News* 5 February 1987)

In this text we have a series of medial exchanges reported. The first one is an indirect report of an informing move, but the reporter is not identified. We assume, given the next paragraph, that Mr Richard Griffiths-Jones, prosecuting, 'tells the court' about the crime, since he is then given another turn indirectly. In paragraph 4, we have a report of a direct move 'It is very seldom . . .' by another voice, this time Judge Richard Cole, evaluating the crime. The verb of saying signals that an exchange has taken place, but again, just one move is reported. In some cases, however, although just one move is represented, the verb of saying, *admit* in the following example, makes explicit that there was a previous move that is not reported:

Top model Jerry Hall is in the clear, a vital witness told her drugs smuggling trial yesterday.
Airline employee Jane Branker admitted to the court: 'Don't blame Jerry – it was all my fault.'

(*Daily Mirror* 14 February 1987)

It seems that the main reason for speech representation, especially in factual reports, is 'significance'; in other words, the reporter only reports those parts of the exchange that are significant for him/her according to his/her view of the world. So exchanges are reduced to significant 'utterances'. Sometimes the reduction is even more severe and only fragments of an utterance are quoted, as in the example below:

Mr Gilbert Gray, QC, defending, claimed that prosecution witnesses had lied to '*send a man of God like a lamb to the slaughter*'.

(*Daily Telegraph* 13 February 1987)

Fairclough (1988a), in his discussion of reported representation in media discourse, suggests that one of the tendencies which emerges from the analysis of this discourse is that what is represented is to a large extent the ideational meanings of the words used, rather than their interpersonal meanings. Quoting Voloshinov (1973: 119), he goes on to say that it may be that ours is a highly ideational culture, that another's speech is received as one whole block of social behaviour, as the speaker's indivisible, conceptual position – in which case only the 'what' of speech is taken in and the 'how' is left outside reception.

Newspaper reports tend to exclude interpersonal and social features of interaction, and reduce structural features, because what is important is the informational and therefore again, the ideational meaning.

Although fictional and factual reports of saying basically share the characteristics pointed out above, they also differ in certain crucial ways.

Fictional and factual distinctions

The world of factions

Sinclair (1986) proposes two contrasting terms and one relationship in order to handle the distinction between *fact* and *fiction*. He defines as *fact* states of affairs in the real world which do not require verbalization. The verbal assertion of any fact he calls **averral** – 'an averral is an utterance; therefore it is said by someone on some occasion' (p. 44). **Correspondence** is the relationship between fact and averral, since participants 'devise or deduce that what is being averred corresponds to a state of affairs' (*ibid.*). If there is no correspondence between a state of affairs and an averral, 'the speaker or writer is seen to be either *misleading* or *misled*' (p. 48). A participant as a speaker in a discourse is misleading when s/he believes that there is no correspondence between the terms and still makes the averral, and misled, as a hearer, if s/he believes that there is such a correspondence.

The status of fiction, according to Sinclair, is reserved for utterances 'which are averred by a speaker without regard for their correspondence, and where this curious relationship is recognised by other participants, who are expecting that the correspondence will be irrelevant' (*ibid.*: 49). Sinclair (1981) suggests that this status is

> brought about by an author detaching himself from the responsibility of averring each successive utterance, but not attributing them to any other author in the real world – either no one at all, or a fictitious narrator. The utterances, therefore, lose their status as being identified with a participant in any real situation.
>
> (p. 11)

Factual status, by contrast, entails authorial averral. In a real oral conversation there are speakers who aver what they assert. However, when they report or write about another speaker speaking, they can only choose to aver that that speaker said something and not to aver the factuality of what has been said; that is, they detach themselves from the propositions. The following fabricated example illustrates this point:

Mary remarked that Peter complained that he was being misinterpreted. At least that's what she said he said.

The last part of the utterance makes it clear that the speaker (in the above quote) is saying: 'Don't take me as averring the truth of what was said, but only as averring that Mary said what I say she said about Peter.'

One point in common between a factual and a fictional representation of interaction, however, is that *sayings* are made reportable by reporters who choose to make them significant. In this sense, the two kinds of accounts are not different. There are people who interpret the world (or facts) according to their perceptions, ideology and situation as human beings living in a social context at a particular time (which may or may not be different from that of their subject-matter). Therefore, as Fowler (1981: 108) suggests, there is no text in which the context has not been filtered by an author who has selected the propositions and has a particular posture or point of view towards them. Even so, many people, according to Bird and Dardenne (1988), continue to think that factual reporting, because it has a basis in reality/factuality, is objective, fair, impartial, balanced and reflects reality and true representation. The authors quote a crime reporter who said:

When I needed quotes, I used to make them up, as did some of the others . . . for we knew what the 'bereaved mother' and the 'mourning father' should have said and possibly even heard them speak what was in our minds rather than what was in theirs.

(Bird and Dardenne 1988: 72)

The examples below are interesting cases. Because they are reports presented in a newspaper, we as readers take for granted that the averrals are based on fact. So we have two accounts of criminal offences reported on the same day (12 February 1987), by the same reporter (Pam Newbold), in the same newspaper (*Birmingham Daily News*).

The first narrative has the following title: *Mother is victim of sex attack* and is summarized as:

A young mother-of-two stood screaming in a city street after being attacked by a sex-fiend as passers-by turned a deaf-ear to her pleas for help, police revealed last night.

(*Birmingham Daily News*, 12 February 1987)

The headline of the second narrative is *Mates save stab victim from death*:

A man cheated death after a vicious mugger stabbed him in the neck, severing an artery.

The attacker plunged a five inch blade through 24-year-old Raymond Gee's cheek, mouth and throat, and left him bleeding in the street on Tuesday. Police said it was a miracle he survived.

(*Birmingham Daily News*, 12 February 1987)

In both cases, although there is an explicit reporter, Pam Newbold, we can see that what she recounts has in fact been taken from police reports: 'Police revealed last night' and 'Police said it was a miracle he survived'. This means, of course, that the reporter herself was not present and her reports are second-layer narrations. However, she also reports, in direct speech, the policemen's evaluation of the attacks and the reader assumes that she really had talked to the policemen:

First report:
> Digbeth-based Sgt Roger Billington *said*: '**It was a particularly nasty attack** because the woman was with her children.'

Second report:
> Det Con Alan Jones, of Dudley Road police station, *said* it was a miracle Mr Gee was alive. '**It was a particularly vicious attack**. He was in a very bad way for a while.'

We are given names and places in order to place the policemen in the real world and as proof of the veracity of the report. However, it is open to question whether two men, in different places, could produce almost exactly the same evaluation: 'It was a particularly nasty/vicious attack.' This suggests that the reporter, using direct speech as evaluation of the action and as evidence for her report, may have created, just like the crime reporter quoted by Bird and Dardenne, sayings that the two policemen did not actually produce.

The *correspondence* between averral and state of affairs, it could be suggested by a sophisticated reader, is a *misleading* one, although the reporter of the *Birmingham Daily News* could prove the contrary, if she had a recording of her conversation with the policemen, and she could show they really did use the same words.

Sinclair (1986) also suggests the notion of **verisimilitude**, which is 'the evaluation of an utterance as simultaneously fictional and factual' (p. 50). Usually we do know the stance of the writer with reference to actuality. Sinclair points out two important aspects:

(a) fiction and fact in relation to sentences are not in contrast with each other. If they were, they would be mutually exclusive. A writer of fiction would have to avoid anything he or she knows to be a fact;
(b) fictional status takes preference over factual, where both are relevant. That is to say, verisimilitude does not confer the status of factual averral on an utterance. Once a fiction, always a fiction.

(p. 50)

Sinclair points out that we can distinguish factual from fictional discourses by applying the 'accusation of untruth' criterion. A journalist would have to face up to such an accusation – is the text true or not? The fictional writer can dismiss this accusation as irrelevant. In some cases, however, the averral identification is not explicit and the reader may have problems in deciding what is fact and what is fiction.

If a journalist reports events which can be shown not to have happened, and a fictional writer reports with great accuracy events which did happen (Truman Capote, *In Cold Blood*, for example), we readers read and evaluate them differently, because the medium determines for the reader what sort of text s/he is exposed to. Newspapers and biographies, for instance, are supposed to inform about facts and most people believe what they read. If 'personas' are given a voice, readers tend to assume that the speech presented is a close approximation of what was actually said. However, as I have pointed out above, factual reports may not be 'true'. The fundamental difference between factual and fictional reports of speech is that in a factual report, the writer's averral depends on words produced elsewhere; in other words, there are two averrals, one depending on the other. In fiction, by contrast, a simulated conversation is created by only one averral, that of the author. Fictional writers, however, can base their report on factual reality while factual reporters, although having a previous referent, can distort what was said in the first place and, in this case, the distinction between a factual and a fictional saying can be blurred.

An interesting example of confusion in the distinction between what is fact and what is fiction is the representation of speech in the controversy about the Falklands film, *Tumbledown*, shown on British television in June 1988. The film is based on the book *When the Fighting is Over*, written by Scots Guards lieutenant Robert Lawrence about his experiences in the war and how he was seriously injured. At one point, Lawrence describes an incident in which a young officer said to him, while in a state of shock, after being caught in the back-blast of an anti-tank weapon:

> Don't go on. It's horrific. You'd be better off turning round, and shooting anyone who tried to stop you going back.
>
> (transcribed in *The Times*, 7 June 1988)

A 12-second sequence including the supposed words uttered by the officer had to be cut from the film, after Captain James Stuart, who felt that the reference in the play and the book pointed to him, took legal action against the BBC. Bloomsbury publishers were also asked to remove the 'saying' from the original book. The interesting fact is that Captain Stuart was not named either in the play or in the book. However, he issued a 'statement denying that he had ever spoken the words attributed to "a young officer"' (*The Times*, 8 June 1988). The authenticity of these specific words could be challenged on the grounds that the television drama at least was presented as fictional, but since the BBC did not make it clear that the statements were fictional and presented real facts in the retelling of the events, the controversy was established. After these events, the BBC decided 'to crack down on TV drama that mixes fact with fiction', according to R. Evans, the Media Editor of *The Guardian* (13 July 1988), because the issue of what he calls 'factional' drama needed to be re-evaluated and discussed. The BBC even ran a seminar called 'Representing reality' in November 1988!

The world of fact: news is what is said

Direct observation of facts or first-hand evidence is a basic condition sought by newsmakers. The immediacy of descriptions and the closeness of the reporter to the event in a sense guarantees the truthfulness of the news. However, news, most of the time, is about events that are not observed directly by media producers. News agencies and other media supply 'stories' to reporters. The initial sources can be **primary**, in other words, an immediate participant who describes facts *in loco* (an eyewitness or an opinion-giving person), or **secondary**, somebody who retells the report of a primary participant. However, in both cases, much of what is finally reported is filtered through the news process, in other words, through the re-interpretation and evaluation of many people – reporters, copy-writers, sub-editors and editors.

Sources are 'accepted' in a hierarchical order. People linked to power relations or institutions, in the main male, as I will demonstrate below, tend to be more 'reliable' and consequently more 'quoted' than others, so a lot of what is reported is associated with power structures. In all cases, what is seen as a direct quotation or even as a quasi-direct quotation is interpreted as being a direct link to a source.

Direct and indirect reporting of words in the news have the function of legitimizing what is reported. The representation of speech is thus one of the rhetorical strategies used by the media discourse to implicate reliability. Besides, this representation makes the narrative more lively: 'introducing participants as speakers conveys both the human and the dramatic dimension of news events', (Van Dijk 1988: 87), which is why much of what is reported has to do with 'saying'.

Writers who report speech in factual reports are extremely powerful because they can reproduce what is most convenient for them in terms of their aims and ideological point of view. So, if they witness a whole conversation, they can reproduce it in full (though this is unlikely due to space constraints), or reproduce the parts they think are important, allocating turns to people they also think are important and leaving aside all the contributions that might be relevant from a different point of view.

Words produced by a primary source are very rarely replicated verbatim in the final **copy**. Even a report of a live face-to-face interview can be altered, since reporters will cut and paste. Although in many cases we could arrive at an outside source who produced some 'saying' in the real world, the complicating situation of authorship in the discourse of the media makes the process of reporting factual speech very problematic. In some cases two explicit layers of narration could be arrived at – the primary source and the reporter – but both of them could be submitted to questions of truthfulness. However, because of the linguistic property of 'recursiveness' (*She said he said Mary said that. . .*), the quoted saying can be presented through many different voices and the 'real' words become as fictionalized as any dialogue created by a fictional narrator. The example from *The Times* (20 January 1992) illustrates this point:

BBC Television quoted Mr Nazarbayev as saying of his republic's nuclear weapons: 'We are prepared. We are ready to sign all of the treaties . . . .'

In this case, the reporter from *The Times*, Susan Viets, quotes the institutionalized voice (the BBC) as quoting Mr Nazarbayev! The multilayering of saying makes the direct quote very dubious.

The problem is that the words of a real person who takes part in a reportable event are already interpreted and represented according to the point of view of a first reporter, are re-interpreted (and probably changed) by a chain of people. In most cases, a direct attribution to characters in a direct mode,

Mary said: 'I will not go there'

or the averral by the teller in an indirect mode,

Mary refused to go there

have nothing to do with people speaking in the real world. The direct mode is as I mentioned previously, a textual strategy which dramatizes the narrative, legitimizes or evaluates the story being told. The indirect mode marks the explicit interference of the reporter in the report. In this mode, there is 'integration' of the secondary discourse into the discourse of the narrator: the primary discourse absorbs the secondary one. The author, therefore, is in complete control of the character's supposed talk, since a speech-act verb generally introduces reported utterances that are averred by the author. There is not even the pretence that the voice of the character is heard. In both cases, however, the recounter is always in control of what is being reported and faithfulness to the words originally produced can always be challenged.

The choice of who is given voice depends on the importance given to some people instead of others. But again here the selection of the speakers reflects cultural belief systems and power structures.

ACCESSED VOICE AND GENDER BIAS

I will not explore here the concept of **accessed voice** (Hartley 1982); in other words, who is given voice and how this voice is reported in factual reports, especially in the genre **news**. As I mentioned in the previous section, much of the time, 'news is what is said' and the values and words of a privileged body of people who have special roles in society are generally put forward. Women in general are part of the **unaccessed voice** group and the small quantity of female speech reported in the press, as I shall point out below, is sufficient to demonstrate that their social role has a special or deviant status. Unequal access is evident in what is reported and who speaks, and as a consequence the linguistic code imposes and reinforces attitudes and values on what it represents.

The discourse of the media is an instrument of cultural reproduction, highly implicated within the power structures and reflecting values about the world. One of them is male supremacy. Newspapers in general, both quality and the tabloids, are basically oriented to a male audience and exclude women from the speaking role.

Although women constitute 52 per cent of the population in Britain, they are misrepresented in the news as speaking participants, whereas men, in general, are represented speaking in their public or professional roles. Women, when speaking, are identified within their private sphere. They are the mothers, the daughters, the wives, the widows, the page 3 girls, the stars. The private/public distinction is a very important feature of social organization. If women are represented mostly speaking in their personal roles, they are marginalized in terms of public or ritual speech. If, in the media, women are less heard than men, and their contributions less reported, newspapers continue to encode bias and legitimate assumptions about linguistic behaviour and social asymmetries.

Where are all these 'talkative women'? Some figures

Since most news is about public issues, it is normal that voice is given to representative personalities. Typically, therefore, the exploitation of a topic includes the opinions and 'arguments' of a privileged body of powerful members of the society. As Fowler (1991) suggests, access is a reciprocal relationship between the powerful and the media:

> The political effect between the accessed and the unaccessed provokes an imbalance between the representation of the already privileged, on the one hand, and the already unprivileged, on the other, with the views of the official, the powerful and the rich being constantly invoked to legitimate the status quo.
>
> (p. 22)

To demonstrate the fact that women do not have a voice in the press, I made use of concordance lists of verbs of 'saying' from a 5 million word corpus of *The Times* and from a 20 million word corpus of the BBC World Service. Both corpora are part of the Bank of English at Cobuild – Collins Birmingham University International Language Database. I selected from *The Times* corpus one example (the most frequent one) of the subcategories of a general taxonomy of **verbs of saying** (Caldas-Coulthard 1987, 1988). I classified the verbs of saying according to their function in relation to the reported clause. **Neutral** and **structuring** 'glossing' verbs are the ones that introduce a 'saying' without explicitly evaluating it. So, verbs like *say, tell, ask, enquire* simply signal the illocutionary act – the saying.

By using these verbs, the author only gives the reader the 'literal meaning' (sense and reference in Austin's terms) of the speech. The intended meaning (illocutionary force) has to be derived from the saying itself. The **illocutionary glossing verbs** are the ones that convey the presence of the author in the text, and are highly interpretive. They name a supposed speech situation, they clarify and make explicit the illocutionary force of the quote they refer to. These verbs are not only **metalinguistic**, they are also **metapropositional**, since they label and categorize the contribution of a speaker. Verbs like *urge*, *declare* or *grumble* mark, for example, a directive, an assertive or an expressive proposition. Other verbs are **descriptive** in relation to the represented interaction. Verbs like *yell, shout, scream* or *whisper, murmur*, mark the **manner** and **attitude** of a speaker in relation to what is being said. Finally, **discourse-signalling verbs** are not speech-reporting verbs at all, but very often they accompany direct speech. They mark the relationship of the quote to other parts of the discourse, like *repeat, add*, or they mark the development of the discourse – *pause, continue, go on*.

Table 19.1 summarizes this taxonomy. The neutral verb *say* in its past-tense form *said* is the most frequent verb in the corpus, with a total occurrence of 14,154 instances. The present form *says* occurs 3,634 times. The verb *tell* also in its past form is the next most frequent neutral verb, occurring 1,445 times. The structuring verb *ask*, in its past form, appears in 1,050 instances. By contrast, all the other reporting verbs occur fewer than 500 times. The discourse-signalling verb *add* (*added*) occurs 1,023 times and metapropositional *agree* (*agreed*), 794.

I examined 250 occurrences of the more frequent verbs and 150 of the less frequent ones. I also looked at 100 occurrences of those verbs that appear

Table 19.1 Reporting verbs

Speech-reporting verbs		
Neutral structuring		say, tell
		ask, enquire
		reply, answer
Metapropositional	assertives	remark, explain
		agree, assent, accept
		correct, counter
	directives	urge, instruct, order
	expressives	accuse, grumble, lament
		confess, complain, swear
Metalinguistic		narrate, quote, recount
Descriptive verbs		
Prosodic		cry, intone, shout, yell, scream
Paralinguistic	voice qualifier (manner)	whisper, murmur, mutter
	voice qualification (attitude)	laugh, giggle,
		sign, gasp, groan
Transcript verbs		
Discourse signalling	relation to other parts of discourse	repeat, echo
		add, emend
	discourse progress	pause, go on, hesitate, continue

between 100 and 200 times. These were the metapropositional *suggest* (*suggested*) and the discourse-signalling *continue* (*continued*). All the other verbs that occur in the corpus fewer than 100 times were disregarded. The main thrust of this research was to verify whether the sayer was a woman or a man. The results are indicative: men are quoted 497 times, women 62 times.

As expected, the frequency of the descriptive verbs is naturally very low. However, these verbs point to a crucial linguistic assumption about gender relations. Men *shout* and *groan* while women (and children) *scream* and *yell*. Other verbs like *nag*, *gossip*, *chatter*, etc. are associated with beliefs which are accepted as common sense within a society and mark 'stereotypes' of particular groups. There is a vocabulary, according to Cameron (1985: 31), which denigrates the talk of women who do not conform to the male ideas of femininity. 'Screaming', 'yelling', 'nagging' mark the negative image of the 'housewife', the 'mother-in-law', the 'mother'.

In a corpus of 200 narratives from the English quality newspapers (*The Guardian*, *The Independent* and *The Times*, collected during a period of ten consecutive days (January 1992), I isolated 451 instances where men were given voice as compared with 76 times for women.

These figures show that there is a rhetoric of silencing and alienation at work in the way women are excluded from speaking in the news. In the context of the news, women are in statistical terms under-represented linguistically. When given voice, they are not given the same speaking space.

CONCLUDING REMARKS

By investigating the role and function of speech representation in the overall structure of factual and fictional narrative texts, I found that quoted material is either borrowed from another interactive situation and re-interpreted by a series of people, in the case of factual reports, or created by an author, in the case of fiction. Factional texts are a very interesting category because they pretend to be something they are not. In all cases, represented speech is a mediated and indirect text. By transferring averral to other people, reporters detach themselves from the responsibility of what is being reported in order either to distance themselves, or to evaluate or legitimize their own previous discourse. This is a very important strategy, used especially by factual reporters to pass their own judgement on the action.

At the stage of selecting and processing what to report, writers reveal their own stance towards what is represented. No speech representation is objective or simply neutral. 'Quoting' what people say is a very dangerous activity. Sayings are transformed through the perspective of a teller, who is an agent in a discursive practice. In this way, social identities and roles are created according to the values of who reports and the institution this person represents.

The press is thoroughly preoccupied with what *important* people say. The concept of *importance*, however, is directly linked to power and social structures. Only a number of institutionalized speech situations are regularly accessed and women, as I showed in the last part of this chapter, are silenced by the press. They are seen as a minority group that is marginalized by being denied the role of speakers. The linguistic differences in the way women are represented in 'hard news' are a reflection of women's lack of access to power, since language is located in a power structure which is, in its turn, reflected in the linguistic production. The male representatives of powerful institutions, frequently accessed, 'provide newspapers with the modes of discourse which already encode the attitudes of a powerful elite' (Fowler 1991: 23). And women, according to this research, are far from being in powerful positions. The striking disproportion between the two genders makes clear a disproportion which most people do not reflect upon.

By making explicit the strategies used by authors to represent what other people say, we can start to be aware of how language is used to manipulate and control information. By showing that specific textual features, like the representation of speech, may be understood to invoke extratextual social, cultural and ideological relations, I have tried to demonstrate that language continuously shapes the ideas presented, moulding them in the direction of established beliefs – authority is given prominence, social roles are created, gender values are assigned.

References

Alderson, C. and A. H. Urquhart (eds) (1984), *Reading in a Foreign Language*, London: Longman.

Arnaud, P. and R. Moon (forthcoming), 'Fréquence et emploi des proverbes anglais et français', in C. Plantin (ed.), *Lieux communs, topoi, stéréotypes, clichés*, Paris: Klimé.

Austin, J. L. (1962 [1972]), *How to do Things with Words*, Oxford: Oxford University Press; repr. Cambridge, MA: Harvard University Press.

Ballmer, T. T. (1981), 'Context change and its consequences for a theory of natural language', in H. Parrett (ed.), *Possibilities and Limitations in Pragmatics*, Amsterdam: Benjamins, 17–55.

Bartlett, F. C. (1932), *Remembering: A Study in Experimental and Social Psychology*, Cambridge: Cambridge University Press.

Bastide, F. (1992), 'A night with Saturn', *Science, Technology and Human Values*, 17: 259–81.

Bazerman, C. (1984), 'Modern evolution of the experimental report in physics: spectroscopic articles in *Physical Review*, 1883–1980', *Social Studies of Science*, 14: 163–96.

—— (1988), *Shaping Written Knowledge: Studies in the Genre and Activity of the Experimental Article in Science*, Madison: University of Wisconsin Press.

Beardsley, M. C. (1950), *Practical Logic*, Englewood Cliffs, NJ: Prentice-Hall.

de Beaugrande, R. (1980), *Text, Discourse and Process*, Norwood, NJ: Ablex.

Becker, A. L. (1965), 'A tagmemic approach to paragraph analysis', *College Composition and Communication*, 16: 237–42.

Beekman, J. and J. Callow (1974), *Translating the Word of God*, Grand Rapids, MI: Zondervan Press.

Bell, A. (1991), *The Language of the News Media*, Oxford: Blackwell.

Benson, J. D. and W. S. Greaves (1985), *Systemic Perspectives in Discourse*, vol. I: *Selected Theoretical Papers from the Ninth International Systemic Workshop*, Norwood, NJ: Ablex.

—— (1987), 'A comparison of process types in Poe and Melville', in R. Steele and T. Threadgold (eds), *Language Topics: Essays in Honour of Michael Halliday*, Amsterdam: John Benjamin, vol. II, 133–43.

Berry, M. (1981), 'Systemic linguistics and discourse analysis: a multilayered approach to exchange structure', in R. M. Coulthard and M. Montgomery (eds), *Studies in Discourse Analysis*, London: Routledge & Kegan Paul, 120–45.

Bird, S. E. and R. W. Dardenne (1988), 'Myth, chronicle and story – exploring the narrative qualities of news', in J. W. Carey (ed.), *Media, Myths and Narratives – Television and Press*, Newbury Park: Sage, 67–86.

Bolinger, D. (1972), *That's that* (Janua Linguarum, Series Minor 123), The Hague: Mouton.

—— (1980), *Language – the Loaded Weapon*, London: Longman.

Bolívar, A. C. (1986), 'Interaction through written text: a discourse analysis of newspaper editorials', PhD thesis, University of Birmingham.

Brazil, D. (1985), *The Communicative Value of Intonation in English*, Birmingham: University of Birmingham.

Brooks, P. (1984), *Reading for the Plot: Design and Intention in Narrative*, Oxford: Oxford University Press.

Brown, G. and G. Yule (1983), *Discourse Analysis*, Cambridge: Cambridge University Press.

Burton, D. (1978), 'Towards an analysis of casual conversation', *Nottingham Linguistic Circular*, 7, 2: 131–59.

—— (1980), *Dialogue and Discourse: The Sociolinguistics of Modern Drama Dialogue and Naturally Occurring Conversation*, London: Routledge & Kegan Paul.

—— (1981), 'Analysing spoken discourse', in R. M. Coulthard and M. Montgomery (eds), *Studies in Discourse Analysis*, London: Routledge & Kegan Paul, 61–81.

Caldas-Coulthard, C. R. (1987), 'Reported speech in written narrative texts', in R. M. Coulthard (ed.) *Discussing Discourse*, Birmingham: University of Birmingham, 149–67.

—— (1988), 'Reported interaction in narrative: a study of speech representation in written discourse', PhD thesis, University of Birmingham.

Cameron, D. (1985), *Feminism and Linguistic Theory*, London: Macmillan.

Candlin, C. N., J. M. Kirkwood and H. M. Moore (1978), 'Study skills in English: theoretical issues and practical problems', in R. Mackay and A. Mountford (eds), *English for Specific Purposes*, London: Longman, 190–219.

Carrell, P. L. (1983), 'Some issues in studying the role of schemata, or background knowledge in second language comprehension', *Reading in a Foreign Language*, 1, 81–92.

Chafe, W. L. (1980), 'The deployment of consciousness in the production of a narrative', in W. L. Chafe (ed.), *The Pear Stories: Cognitive, Cultural, and Linguistic Aspects of Narrative Production*, Norwood, NJ: Ablex, 9–50.

—— (1984), 'How people use adverbial clauses', in *Proceedings of the Tenth Annual Meeting of the Berkeley Linguistics Society*, Berkeley: Berkeley Linguistics Society, 437–49.

Chatman, S. (1978), *Story and Discourse: Narrative Structure in Fiction and Film*, Ithaca: Cornell University Press.

Chomsky, N. (1957), *Syntactic Structures*, The Hague: Mouton.

Chomsky, N. and M. Halle (1968), *The Sound Pattern of English*, New York: Harper & Row.

Clark, H. H. (1977), 'Bridging', in P. N. Johnson-Laird and P. C. Wason (eds), *Thinking: Readings in Cognitive Science*, Cambridge: Cambridge University Press, 411–42.

Cohen, A. (1987), 'Mentalistic measures in reading strategy research: some recent findings', *English for Specific Purposes*, 5, 2: 131–45.

Collins, H. M. (1985), *Changing Order: Replication and Induction in Scientific Practice*, London: Sage.

Collins, A., J. Brown and K. Larkin (1980), 'Inference in text understanding', in R. Spiro, B. Bruce and W. Brewer (eds), *Theoretical Issues in Reading Comprehension*, Hillsdale, NJ: Lawrence Erlbaum, 73–92.

Cooper, M. D. (1975), 'A report on the University of Malaya ESP project', 11th Regional Seminar, SEAMEO Regional English Language Centre (mimeo).

—— (1983), 'Textbook discourse structure: an investigation into the notion of predictability structuring in the discourse of scientific books', PhD thesis, University of Birmingham.

Coulthard, R. M. (1977, 1985), *An Introduction to Discourse Analysis*, London: Longman.

―― (ed.) (1986), *Talking about Text*, Birmingham: English Language Research.

―― (1987), *Discussing Discourse* (Discourse Analysis Monographs 14), Birmingham: English Language Research.

Coulthard, R. M. and D. Brazil (1979), *Exchange Structure*, Birmingham: English Language Research.

―― (1981), 'Exchange structure', in R. M. Coulthard and M. Montgomery (eds), *Studies in Discourse Analysis*, London: Routledge & Kegan Paul, 82–106.

Cowie, A. P. (1992), 'Multiword lexical units and communicative language teaching', in P. Arnaud and H. Béjoint (eds), *Vocabulary and Applied Linguistics*, London: Macmillan, 1–12.

Crombie, W. (1986), *Process and Relation in Discourse and Language Learning*, Oxford: Oxford University Press.

Crookes, G. (1986), 'Towards a validated analysis of scientific text structure', *Applied Linguistics*, 7, 1: 57–70.

Crymes, R. (1968), *Some Systems of Substitution Correlations in Modern American English* (Janua Linguarum, Series Minor 39), The Hague: Mouton.

Crystal, D. and D. Davy (1969), *Investigating English Style*, Harlow: Longman.

Dahan, H. M. (1991), 'The structure of conversations in the English of Malaysians', PhD thesis, University of Birmingham.

Darwin, Charles (1979), *The Origin of the Species by means of Natural Selection*, with a new foreword by Patricia Horan, New York: Avenel.

Davies, M. (1989), 'Prosodic and non-prosodic cohesion in English', *Word*, 40: 255–62.

Dehn, N. (1984), 'An AI perspective on reading comprehension', in J. Flood (ed.), *Understanding Reading Comprehension*, Newark: International Reading Association, 112–28.

Dudley-Evans, A. (1986), 'Genre analysis: an investigation of the introduction and discussion sections of MSc dissertations', in R. M. Coulthard (ed.), *Talking about Text*, University of Birmingham: English Language Research, 128–45.

Dudley-Evans, A. and W. Henderson (eds) (1990), *The Language of Economics: The Analysis of Economics Discourse* (ELT Documents 134), London: Macmillan in association with the British Council.

Emmott, C. (1985), 'Expanded nominals; a computer-assisted stylistic study with particular reference to D. H. Lawrence', MA thesis, University of Birmingham.

―― (1989), 'Reading between the lines: building a comprehensive model of participant reference in real narrative', PhD thesis, University of Birmingham.

―― (1992), 'Splitting the referent: an introduction to narrative enactors', in M. Davies and L. Ravelli (eds), *Advances in Systemic Linguistics: Recent Theory and Practice*, London: Pinter, 221–8.

―― (forthcoming), *Mind Reading: Cognitive Modelling and Narrative Discourse*.

Evans, G. (1980), 'Pronouns', *Linguistic Inquiry*, 11: 337–62.

Fahnestock, J. (1986), 'Accommodating science: the rhetorical life of scientific facts', *Written Communication*, 3: 275–96.

―― (1989), 'Arguing in different forums: the Bering Strait crossover controversy', *Science, Technology, and Human Values*, 14: 26–42.

Fairclough, N. (1988a), 'Discourse representation in media discourse', *Sociolinguistics*, 17: 125–39.

―― (1988b), 'Register, power and socio-semantic change', in D. Birch and M. O'Toole (eds), *Functions of Style*, London: Pinter, 98–111.

Farnes, N. C. (1973), *Reading Purposes: Comprehension and the Use of Context*, Milton Keynes: Open University Press.

Firbas, J. (1982), 'Has every sentence a theme and a rheme?', in J. Anderson (ed.), *Language Form and Linguistic Variation*, Amsterdam: John Benjamins, 97–115.

Fitzgerald, P. J. (1966), *Salmond on Jurisprudence*, London: Sweet & Maxwell.

Fleck, L. (1935 [1979]), *The Genesis and Development of a Scientific Fact*, Chicago: University of Chicago Press.

Flood, J. (ed.) (1984), *Understanding Reading Comprehension*, Newark: International Reading Association.

Fowler, H. W. (1926), *Fowler's Modern English Usage*, 2nd edn, Oxford: Oxford University Press.

Fowler, R. (1981), *Literature as Social Discourse*, London: Batsford Academic.

—— (1991), *Language in the News*, London: Routledge.

Fox, B. A. (1987a), *Discourse Structure and Anaphora: Written and Conversational English*, Cambridge: Cambridge University Press.

—— (1987b), 'Anaphora in popular written English narratives', in R. S. Tomlin (ed.), *Coherence and Grounding in Discourse*, Amsterdam: Benjamins, 157–74.

—— (1987c), 'Morpho-syntactic markedness and discourse structure', *Journal of Pragmatics*, 11: 359–75.

Francis, G. (1986), *Anaphoric Nouns*, University of Birmingham: English Language Research.

—— (1991), 'Nominal group heads and clause structure', *Word*, 14, 2.

Frederiksen, C. H. (1986), 'Cognitive models and discourse analysis', in C. R. Cooper and S. Greenbaum (eds), *Studying Writing: Linguistic Approaches*, London: Sage, 227–67.

Freedle, R. O. (ed.) (1977), *Discourse Production and Comprehension*, Norwood, NJ: Ablex.

—— (ed.) (1979), *New Directions in Discourse Processing*, Norwood, NJ: Ablex.

Fries, P. H. (1981), 'On the status of theme in English: arguments from discourse', *Forum Linguisticum*, 6, 1: 1–38.

—— (1982), 'On repetition and interpretation', *Forum Linguisticum*, 7, 1: 50–64.

—— (forthcoming a), 'Patterns of information in initial position in English', in P. H. Fries and M. Gregory (eds), *Discourse in Society: Functional Perspectives*, Norwood, NJ: Ablex.

—— (forthcoming b), 'Toward a discussion of the flow of information in a written English text', in M. Cummings and M. Gregory (eds), *Relations and Functions in Language*, Amsterdam: Benjamins.

Geisler, C., D. Kaufer and E. Steinberg (1985), 'The unattended anaphoric "this"', *Written Communication*, 2, 2: 129–55.

Gilbert, G. N. (1977), 'Referencing as persuasion', *Social Studies of Science*, 7: 113–22.

Gilbert, G. N. and M. Mulkay (1984), *Opening Pandora's Box: A Sociological Analysis of Scientists' Discourse*, Cambridge: Cambridge University Press.

Givón, T. (1983), *Topic Continuity in Discourse*, Amsterdam: Benjamins.

Gleason, H. A., Jr (1968), 'Contrastive analysis in discourse structure', *Georgetown University Monograph Series on Languages and Linguistics* 21: 39–64.

Goffman, E. (1975), *Frame Analysis: An Essay on the Organization of Experience*, Harmondsworth: Penguin.

Goodman, K. S. (1967), 'Reading: a psycholinguistic guessing game', *Journal of the Reading Specialist*, 4: 126–35.

Gopnik, M. (1972), *Linguistic Structures in Scientific Texts*, The Hague: Mouton.

Greenwell, G. (1988), 'A light matter', *Scientific American*, 258, 2: 22.

Gregg, J. Y. (1985), *Communication and Culture: A Reading Writing Text*, Belmont, CA: Wadsworth.

Gregory, M. (1967), 'Aspects of varieties differentiation', *Journal of Linguistics*, 3: 177–98.

—— (1985): 'Towards "communication" linguistics: a framework', in J. Benson and W. Greaves (eds), *Systemic Perspectives on Discourse*, vol. I: *Selected Theoretical Papers from the Ninth International Systemic Workshop (1982)*, 119–34.

Grice, H. P. (1975), 'Logic and conversation', in P. Cole and J. L. Morgan (eds), *Syntax and Semantics*, vol. III: *Speech Acts*, New York: Academic Press, 41–58.

Grimes, J. E. (1975), *The Thread of Discourse*, The Hague: Mouton.

Halliday, M. A. K. (1961), 'Categories of the theory of grammar', *Word*, 17, 3: 241–92.

—— (1967), 'Notes on transitivity and theme in English', part 2, *Journal of Linguistics*, 3: 177–274.

—— (1970), 'Language structure and language function', in J. Lyons (ed.), *New Horizons in Linguistics*, Harmondsworth: Penguin, 140–64.

—— (1973), *Explorations in the Functions of Language*, London: Edward Arnold.

—— (1977), 'Text as semantic choice in social contexts', in T. A. van Dijk and J. Petöfi (eds), *Grammars and Descriptions*, Berlin: Walter de Gruyter, 176–225.

—— (1978), *Language as Social Semiotic*, London: Edward Arnold.

—— (1982), 'How is a text like a clause?', in S. Allen (ed.), *Text Processing: Proceedings of Nobel Symposium 51*, Stockholm: Almquist & Wiksell International, 209–39.

—— (1985), *An Introduction to Functional Grammar*, London: Edward Arnold.

—— (1987), 'Language and the order of nature', in N. Fabb, D. Attridge, A. Durant and C. McCabe (eds), *The Linguistics of Writing*, Manchester: Manchester University Press, 135–54.

—— (1988a), 'Poetry as scientific discourse: the nuclear sections of Tennyson's "In memoriam"', in D. Birch and M. O'Toole (eds), *Functions of Style*, London: Pinter, 31–44.

—— (1988b), 'On the language of physical science', in M. Ghaddessy (ed.), *Written Language: Register and Style*, London: Pinter, 17–31.

Halliday, M. A. K. and R. Hasan (1976), *Cohesion in English*, London: Longman.

—— (1985 [1989]), *Language, Context and Text: Aspects of Language in a Social-Semiotic Perspective*, Victoria: Deakin University Press; repr. Oxford: Oxford University Press, 1989.

Halliday, M. A. K., A. McIntosh and P. Strevens (1964), *The Linguistic Sciences and Language Teaching*, London: Longman.

Hanson, J. L. (1953 [1972]), *A Textbook of Economics*, London: Macdonald & Evans.

Harris, J. B. N. (1980), 'Suprasentential organisation in written discourse with particular reference to writing by children in the lower secondary school', MA thesis, University of Birmingham.

Harris, Z. (1952), 'Discourse analysis', *Language*, 28: 1–30.

Hartley, J. (1982), *Understanding News*, London: Methuen.

Hawkins, J. A. (1978), *Definiteness and Indefiniteness: A Study of Reference and Grammaticality Prediction*, London: Croom Helm.

Henderson, W. and A. Hewings (1990), 'Language and model building?', in A. Dudley-Evans and W. Henderson (eds), *The Language of Economics: The Analysis of Economics Discourse* (ELT Documents 134), London: Macmillan in association with the British Council, 43–54.

—— and E. Rado (1980), 'Case studies in the teaching of development', *Institute of Development Studies Bulletin: Teaching Development at Graduate Level*, 11, iii, 34–44.

Hinds, J. (1976), *Aspects of Japanese Discourse Structure*, Tokyo: Kaitakusha.

—— (1977), 'Paragraph structure and pronominalisation', *Papers in Linguistics*, 10: 77–97.

—— (1980), 'Japanese expository prose', *Papers in Linguistics: International Journal of Human Communication*, 13, 1: 117–58.

314   *References*

‐‐‐‐ (1982), 'Japanese conversational structure', *Lingua*, 57: 301–26.
‐‐‐‐ (1983a), 'Contrastive rhetoric; Japanese and English', *Text*, 3, 2: 183–95.
‐‐‐‐ (1983b), 'Japanese conversational narrative', *Descriptive and Applied Linguistics*, 17: 124–41.
‐‐‐‐ (1983c), 'Linguistics and written discourse in English and Japanese: a contrastive study (1978–1982), *Annual Review of Applied Linguistics*, 3: 78–84.
Hoey, Michael (1979), *Signalling in Discourse* Birmingham: University of Birmingham.
‐‐‐‐ (1983), *On the Surface of Discourse*, London: Allen & Unwin, reprinted (1991) by Department of English Studies, University of Nottingham.
‐‐‐‐ (1986), 'The discourse colony: a preliminary study of a neglected discourse type', in R. M. Coulthard (ed.), *Talking about Text*, Birmingham: University of Birmingham, 1–26.
Hofman, T. R. (1989), 'Paragraphs, and anaphora', *Journal of Pragmatics*, 13: 239–50.
Hopkins, A. and A. Dudley-Evans (1988), 'A genre-based investigation of discussion sections in articles and dissertations', *English for Specific Purposes*, 7: 113–22.
Hosenfeld, C. (1977), 'A preliminary investigation of the reading strategies of successful and nonsuccessful second language learners', *System*, 5, 2: 110–23.
House, J. A. (1977), *A Model for Translation Quality Assessment*, Tübingen: Narr.
Hozayen, G. (work in progress), 'A study of the discussion sections in medical journal articles', University of Birmingham.
Huckin, T. (1987), 'Surprise value in scientific discourse', paper given at CCCC Convention, Atlanta, GA.
Huddleston, Rodney (1971), *The Syntax of English Sentences*, Cambridge: Cambridge University Press.
Hunston, S. (1985), 'Text in world and world in text: goals and models of scientific writing', *Nottingham Linguistic Circular*, 14: 25–40.
‐‐‐‐ (1989), 'Evaluation in experimental research articles', PhD thesis, University of Birmingham.
‐‐‐‐ (1993a), 'Evaluation and ideology in scientific discourse', in M. Ghadessy (ed.), *Register Analysis: Theory and Practice*, London: Pinter, 57–73.
‐‐‐‐ (1993b), 'Projecting a sub-culture: the construction of shared worlds by projecting clauses in two registers', in D. Graddol *et al.* (eds), *Language and Culture*, Clevedon: BAAL/Multilingual Matters, 98–112.
Hunt, K. 1965), *Grammatical Structures Written at Three Grade-Levels*, Champaign, IL: NCTE.
Hutchins, W. J. (1977a), 'On the problem of "aboutness" in document analysis', *Journal of Informatics*, 1, 1: 17–35.
‐‐‐‐ (1977b), 'On the structure of scientific texts', *UEA Papers in Linguistics*, 5: 18–39.
Isard, S. (1975), 'Changing the context', in E. K. Keenan (ed.), *Formal Semantics of Natural Language*, Cambridge: Cambridge University Press, 287–96.
Iser, W. (1978), *The Act of Reading*, Baltimore, MD: Johns Hopkins University Press.
Ivanic, R. (1991), 'Nouns in search of a context: a study of nouns with both open- and closed-system characteristics', *International Review of Applied Linguistics in Language Teaching*, 2: 93–114.
Jameson, Frederick (1971), *The Prison-House of Language*, Princeton: Princeton University Press.
Johns, A. and A. Dudley-Evans (1991), 'English for specific purposes: international in scope, specific in purpose', *TESOL Quarterly*, 25, 2: 297–314.
Johns, T. F. (1975), 'The communicative approach to language teaching in the framework of a programme of English for academic purposes', in E. Roulet and H. Holec (eds), *L'Enseignement de la compétence de communication en langues secondes*, Neuchatel: CILA, 35–47.

Johns, T. F. and T. Dudley-Evans (1980), 'An experiment in team teaching of overseas students of transportation and plant biology', *Team Teaching in ESP*, British Council, ELT Docs, No. 106, 6–23.

Johnson-Laird, P. N. (1983), *Mental Models*, Cambridge, MA: Harvard University Press.

Johnson-Laird, P. N. and P. C. Wason (eds) (1977), *Thinking: Readings in Cognitive Science*, Cambridge: Cambridge University Press.

Jordan, M. P. (1978), 'The principal semantics of the nominals "this" and "that" in contemporary English writing', PhD thesis, CNAA, UK.

—— (1980), 'Short texts to explain Problem–Solution – and vice versa', *Instructional Science*, 9: 221–52.

—— (1981), 'Structure, meaning and information signals of some very short texts', *Lacus Forum*, 410–17.

—— (1984), *Rhetoric of Everyday English Texts*, London and New York: George Allen & Unwin.

— (1985), 'Non-thematic re-entry: an introduction to and an extension of the system of nominal group reference/substitution in everyday English use', in J. D. Benson and W. S. Greaves (eds), *Systemic Perspectives on Discourse*, vol. I, Norwood, NJ: Ablex, 322–32.

Just, M. and P. Carpenter (1980), 'A theory of reading: from eye fixation to comprehension', *Pyschological Review*, 87: 87–103.

—— (1987), *The Psychology of Reading and Language Comprehension*, Boston, MA: Allyn & Bacon.

Kaplan, R. B. (1966), 'Cultural thought patterns in intercultural education', *Language Learning*, 16: 1–20.

—— (1972), *The Anatomy of Rhetoric: Prolegomena to a Functional Theory of Rhetoric*, Philadelphia: Center of Curriculum Development.

Kaplan, R. and S. Ostler (1982), 'Contrastive rhetoric revisited', paper given at the 1982 TESOL Conference, Honolulu, May.

Kelly, L. G. (1969), *Twenty-five Centuries of Language Teaching*, Rowley, MA: Newbury House.

Kempson, R. (1975), *Presupposition and the Delimitation of Semantics*, Cambridge: Cambridge University Press.

Kress, G. (ed.) (1976), *Halliday: System and Function in Language*, Oxford: Oxford University Press.

—— (1988), 'Textual matters: the social effectiveness of style', in D. Birch and M. O'Toole (eds), *Functions of Style*, London: Pinter, 112–29.

Labov, W. (1972), *Language in the Inner City*, Philadelphia: University of Pennsylvania Press.

Labov, W. and D. Fanshel (1977), *Therapeutic Discourse*, New York: Academic Press.

Labov, W. and J. Waletzky (1967), 'Narrative analysis: oral versions of personal experiences', in *Essays on the Verbal and Visual Arts: Proceedings of the 1966 Annual Spring Meeting of the American Ethnological Society*, Seattle: University of Washington Press, 12–44.

La Follette, M. (1990), *Making Science our Own: Public Images of Science 1910–1955*, Chicago: University of Chicago Press.

Lakoff, R. (1974), 'Remarks on this and that', *Papers from the Regional Meeting: Chicago Linguistic Society*, 10, 345–56.

Latour, B. (1987), *Science in Action*, Milton Keynes: Open University Press.

Latour, B. and S. Woolgar (1979), *Laboratory Life: The Social Construction of Scientific Facts*, Beverley Hills, CA: Sage.

Leech, G. (1983), *Principles of Pragmatics*, London: Longman.

Lemke, J. L. (1984), *Semiotics and Education* (Toronto Semiotic Circle, Monographs, Working Papers and Prepublications), Toronto: Victoria University.

Levinson, S. C. (1983), *Pragmatics*, Cambridge: Cambridge University Press.

Linde, C. (1979), 'Focus of attention and the choice of pronouns in discourse', in T. Givón (ed.), *Syntax and Semantics*, vol. 12: *Discourse and Syntax*, New York: Academic Press, 337–54.

Lipsey, R. G. (1963), *An Introduction to Positive Economics*, London: Weidenfeld & Nicolson.

Longacre, R. E. (1972), *Hierarchy and Universality of Discourse Constituents in New Guinea Language*, Washington, DC: Georgetown University Press.

—— (1974), 'Narrative versus other discourse genres', in R. Brend (ed.), *Advances in Tagmemics*, Amsterdam: North-Holland, 357–76.

—— (1976), *An Anatomy of Speech Notions* (Publications in Tagmemics 3), Lisse: Peter Ridder Press.

Lyons, J. (1977), *Semantics*, 2 vols, Cambridge: Cambridge University Press.

MacCawley, J. D. (1981), *Everything that Linguists always Wanted to Know about Logic (but Were Ashamed to Ask)*, Oxford: Basil Blackwell.

McKinlay, J. (1982), 'An analysis of discussion sections in medical journal articles', MA thesis, University of Birmingham.

Malcolm, L. (1987), 'What rules govern tense usage in scientific articles', *English for Specific Purposes*, 6: 31–44.

Mandler, J. M. and N. S. Johnson (1977), 'Remembrance of things parsed: story structure and recall', *Cognitive Psychology*, 9: 111–51.

Mann, W. C. and S. A. Thompson (1985), 'Assertions from discourse structure', *Proceedings from the Eleventh Annual Meeting of the Berkeley Linguistics Society*, Berkeley, CA: Berkeley Linguistics Society, 245–58.

—— (1986), 'Relational propositions in discourse', *Discourse Processes*, 9, 1: 57–90.

Mann, W. C., C. M. I. M. Matthiessen and S. A. Thompson (1992), 'Rhetorical structure theory and text analysis', in W. C. Mann and S. A. Thompson (eds), *Discourse Descriptions: Diverse Analyses of a Fund-Raising Text*, Amsterdam: Benjamins, 39–78.

Martin, J. R. (1985), 'Process and text: two aspects of human semiosis', in J. D. Benson and W. S. Greaves (eds), *Systemic Perspectives on Discourse*, vol. I, Norwood, NJ: Ablex, 67–83.

—— (1989), *Factual Writing: Exploring and Challenging Social Reality*, Oxford: Oxford University Press.

—— (1992), *English Text*, Amsterdam: Benjamins.

Mauranen, A. (1993), 'Cultural differences in academic rhetoric: a text linguistic study', PhD thesis, University of Birmingham.

Miller, C. (1984), 'Genre as social action', *Quarterly Journal of Speech*, 70: 151–67.

Miller, G. and P. Johnson-Laird (1976), *Language and Perception*, Cambridge: Cambridge University Press.

Minsky, M. (1977), 'Frame-system theory', in P. N. Johnson-Laird and P. C. Wason (eds), *Thinking: Readings in Cognitive Science*, Cambridge: Cambridge University Press, 355–76.

Morgan, J. L. and Sellner, M. (1980), 'Discourse and linguistic theory', in R. J. Spiro, B. Bruce and W. Brewer (eds), *Theoretical Issues in Reading Comprehension*, Hillsdale, NJ: Lawrence Erlbaum, 165–200.

Moskovit, L. (1983), 'When is broad reference clear?', *College Composition and Communication*, 34: 454–69.

Munby, J. (1978), *Communicative Syllabus Design*, Cambridge: Cambridge University Press.

Myers, G. (1988), 'Every picture tells a story: illustrations in E. O. Wilson's *Sociobiology, Human Studies*, 11: 235–69; repr. in M. Lynch and S. Woolgar (eds), *Representation in Scientific Practice*, Cambridge, MA: MIT Press, 1990, 231–66.

—— (1989), 'The pragmatics of politeness in scientific articles', *Applied Linguistics*, 10: 1–35.

—— (1990a), *Writing Biology: Texts in the Social Construction of Scientific Knowledge*, Madison: University of Wisconsin Press.

—— (1990b), 'The double helix as an icon', *Science as Culture*, 9: 49–72.

Myers, T., K. Brown and B. McGonigle (1986), *Reasoning and Discourse Processes*, New York: Academic Press.

Nakhimovsky, A. and W. J. Rapaport (1989), 'Discontinuities in narrative', *COLING Budapest: Proceedings of the Twelfth International Conference on Computational Linguistics (11–27 August 1988)*, 2: 465–70.

Nelkin, Dorothy (1988), *Selling Science*, New York: Freeman.

Olshavsky, J. (1976), 'Reading as problem solving: an investigation of strategies', *Reading Research Quarterly*, 12, 4: 654–74.

Ortony, A. (ed.) (1979), *Metaphor and Thought*, Cambridge: Cambridge University Press.

Oster, S. (1981), 'The use of tenses in reporting past literature', in L. Selinker, E. Tarone and V. Hanzell (eds), *English for Academic and Technical Purposes: Studies in Honour of Louis Trimble*, Rowley, MA: Newbury House, 76–90.

Pagano, A. (1991), 'A pragmatic study of negatives in written text', MA thesis, Universidade Federal de Santa Catarina.

Palek, B. (1968), 'Cross-reference: a contribution to hypersyntax', *Travaux Linguistiques de Prague*, 3: 17–35.

Peng, B. (1987), 'Organisational features in chemical engineering', in A. Dudley-Evans (ed.), *Genre Analysis and ESP (ELR Journal* vol. 1), 79–116.

Peters, P. (1985), *Strategies for Student Writers*, Queensland: Wiley.

Pike, K. L. (1959), 'Language as particle, wave and field', *The Texas Quarterly*, 2: 37–54.

Pinch, T. (1985), 'Towards an analysis of scientific observation: the externality and evidential significance of observational reports in physics', *Social Studies of Science*, 15: 3–36.

Polanyi, L. (1979), 'So what's the point?', *Semiotica*, 25: 207–41.

Poutsma, H. (1926–9), *A Grammar of Late Modern English*, 2nd edn, Groningen: Nordhoff.

Quirk, R. (1954), *The Concessive Relation in Old English Poetry*, New Haven, CT: Yale University Press.

Quirk, R., S. Greenbaum, G. Leech and J. Svartvik (1985), *A Comprehensive Grammar of the English Language*, London: Longman.

Ravelli, L. J. (1991), 'Language from a dynamic perspective: models in general and grammar in particular', PhD thesis, University of Birmingham.

Reid, T. B. W. (1956), 'Linguistics, structuralism, philology', *Archivum Linguisticum*, 8: 23–38.

Renouf, A. J. and J. M. Sinclair (in preparation), *Collocational Frameworks in English*.

Rumelhart, D.E. (1975), 'Notes on a schema for stories', in D. G. Bobrow and A. Collins (eds), *Representation and Understanding: Studies in Cognitive Science*, New York: Academic Press, 211–36.

Samuelson, P. A. (1948 [1964]), *Economics: an Introductory Analysis*, New York: McGraw-Hill.

Sanford, J. and C. Garrod (1981), *Understanding Written Language*, Chichester: Wiley.

Schank, R. C. and R. P. Abelson (1977), 'Scripts, plans, and knowledge', in P. N. Johnson-Laird and P. C. Wason (eds), *Thinking: Readings in Cognitive Science*, Cambridge: Cambridge University Press, 421–32.

Schegloff, E. A. and H. Sacks (1973), 'Opening up closings', *Semiotica*, 8, 4: 289–327.

Schiffrin, D. (1984), 'How a story says what it means and does', *Text*, 4: 313–46.

Searle, J. R. (1969), *Speech Acts: An Essay in the Philosophy of Language*, Cambridge: Cambridge University Press.

Shiro, M. (1988), 'A study on inferencing in written texts', MA thesis, University of Birmingham.

Sidner, C. L. (1983a), 'Focusing in the comprehension of definite anaphora', in M. Brady (ed.), *Computational Models of Discourse*, Cambridge, MA: MIT Press, 267–328.

—— (1983b), 'Focusing and discourse', *Discourse Processes*, 6: 107–30.

Silverstone, R. (1985), *Framing Science: The Making of a BBC Documentary*, London: British Film Institute.

Sinclair, J. McH. (1966), 'Beginning the study of lexis', in C. E. Bazell, J. C. Catford, M. A. K. Halliday and R. H. Robins (eds), *In Memory of J. R. Firth*, London: Longman, 410–30.

—— (1972), *A Course in Spoken English: Grammar*, London: Oxford University Press.

—— (1980), 'Some implications of discourse analysis for ESP methodology', *Applied Linguistics*, 1, 3: 253–61.

—— (1981), 'Planes of discourse', in S. N. A. Rizvi (ed.), *The Two-fold Voice: Essays in Honour of Ramesh Mohan*, Saltzburg: University of Saltzburg, 70–89.

—— (1986), 'Fictional worlds', in R. M. Coulthard (ed.), *Talking about Text*, University of Birmingham: English Language Research, 43–60.

—— (1987a), 'Mirror for a text', ms., University of Birmingham.

—— (1987b), 'Collocation: a progress report', in R. Steele and T. Threadgold (eds), *Language Topics: Essays in Honour of Michael Halliday*, vol. II, Amsterdam: Benjamins, 319–31.

—— (1989), 'Uncommonly common words', in M. L. Tickoo (ed.), *Learners' Dictionaries: State of the Art* (Anthology Series 23), Singapore: SEAMEO Regional Language Centre.

—— (1991), *Corpus Concordance Collocation*, Oxford: Oxford University Press.

—— (1992), 'Trust the text', in M. Davies and L. J. Ravelli (eds), *Advances in Systemic Linguistics: Recent Theory and Practice*, London: Pinter, 5–19.

Sinclair, J. McH. and D. Brazil (1982), *Teacher Talk*, Oxford; Oxford University Press.

Sinclair, J. McH. and R. M. Coulthard (1975), *Towards an Analysis of Discourse: The English Used by Teachers and Pupils*, Oxford: Oxford University Press.

Sinclair, J. McH., I. J. Forsyth, R. M. Coulthard and M. C. Ashby (1972), 'The English used by teachers and pupils', report submitted to the Social Science Research Council.

Sinclair, J. McH., S. Jones and R. Daley (1972), 'English lexical studies', report to OSTI.

Sinclair, J. McH., R. E. Moon, *et al.* (1989), *Collins Cobuild Dictionary of Phrasal Verbs*, London: Collins.

Sinclair, J. McH. *et al.* (1987), *Collins Cobuild English Language Dictionary*, London: Collins.

Smith, F. (1971), *Understanding Reading*, New York: Holt, Rinehart & Winston.

Sperber, D. and D. Wilson (1986), *Relevance*, Oxford: Blackwell.

Spiro, R. J., B. Bruce and W. Brewer (eds) (1980), *Theoretical Issues in Reading Comprehension*, Hillsdale, NJ: Lawrence Erlbaum.

Strässler, J. (1982), *Idioms in English: A Pragmatic Approach*, Tübingen: Narr.

Stubbs, M. (1979), Review of Coulthard and Brazil, *Exchange Structure*, in *Nottingham Linguistic Circular*, 8, 2: 17–31.

—— (1981), 'Motivating analyses of exchange structure', in R. M. Coulthard and M. Montgomery (eds), *Studies in Discourse Analysis*, London: Routledge & Kegan Paul, 107–19.

—— (1983), *Discourse Analysis*, Oxford: Basil Blackwell.

Swales, J.M. (1981), *Aspects of Article Introductions* (Aston ESP Monographs 1), Birmingham: Aston University.

—— (1986), 'A genre-based approach to language across the curriculum', in L. Tickoo Makhan (ed.), *Language Across the Curriculum*, RELC, 10–22.

—— (1990), *Genre Analysis: English in Academic and Research Settings*, Cambridge: Cambridge University Press.

Tadros, A. A. (1978), 'The notion of predictive structure and its pedagogical implications', *MALS Journal*, Summer: 33–48.

—— (1980), 'Prediction in economics text', *ELR Journal*, 1: 42–59.

—— (1981), 'Linguistic prediction in economics text', PhD thesis, University of Birmingham.

—— (1985), *Prediction in Text*, University of Birmingham: English Language Research.

Tarone, E., S. Dwyer, S. Gillette and V. Icke (1981), 'On the use of the passive in two astrophysics journal papers', *ESP Journal*, 1: 123–40; repr. in J. Swales (ed.), *Episodes in ESP*, Oxford: Pergamon, 1985.

Thavenius, C. (1983), *Referential Pronouns in English Conversation*, Lund: Gleerup.

Thomas, S. (1991), 'A merging of voices: an investigation of the way discourse is reported in medical research articles', PhD thesis, University of Birmingham.

Thompson, G. and Ye, Y. Y. (1991), 'Evaluation in the reporting verbs used in academic papers', *Applied Linguistics*, 12: 365–82.

Thompson, S. A. (1985), 'Initial vs final purpose clauses in written English discourse', *Text*, 5, 1–2: 55–84.

Thorndyke, P. W. (1977), 'Cognitive studies in comprehension and memory of narrative discourse', *Cognitive Psychology*, 9: 77–110.

Toolan, M. (1988), *Narrative: A Critical Linguistic Introduction*, London: Routledge.

Tottie, G. (1982), 'Where do negative sentences come from?', *Studia Linguistica*, 36, 1: 88–105.

—— (1987), 'Rejections, denials and explanatory statements – a reply to Fretheim', *Studia Linguistica*, 41, 2: 154–63.

Tsui, B. M. (1986), 'A linguistic description of utterances in conversation', PhD thesis, University of Birmingham.

Ure, J. (1969), 'Lexical density and register differentiation', in *The International Congress of Applied Linguistics*, Cambridge: Cambridge University Press, 443–52.

Urquhart, A. (1975), *King Abdul Aziz University Project Report*.

—— (1981), 'Operating in learning texts', in L. Selinker *et al.* (eds), *English for Academic and Technical Purposes*, Rowley, MA: Newbury House, 87–98.

Van Dijk, T. A. (1977), *Text and Context: Explorations in the Semantics and Pragmatics of Discourse*, London: Longman.

—— (ed.) (1988), *News as Discourse*, Hillsdale, NJ: Lawrence Erlbaum.

Voloshinov, V. I. (1973), *Marxism and the Philosophy of Language*, New York: Seminar Press.

Warren, W., D. Nicholas and T. Trabasso (1979), 'Events, chains and inferences in understanding narratives', in R. Freedle (ed.), *New Directions in Discourse Processing*, Norwood, NJ: Ablex, 133–5.

Weissberg, R. and S. Buker (1990), *Writing up Research*, Englewood Cliffs, NJ: Prentice Hall Regents.

Widdowson, H. G. (1973), 'An applied linguistic approach to discourse analysis', PhD thesis, University of Edinburgh.

—— (1975), *Stylistics and the Teaching of Literature*, London: Longman.

—— (1978a), 'The realization of rules in written discourse', *Pariser Werkstatt, gesprach*, 1980.

—— (1978b), *Teaching Language as Communication*, Oxford: Oxford University Press.

—— (1979), *Explorations in Applied Linguistics*, Oxford: Oxford University Press.

—— (1983), *Learning Purpose and Language Use*, Oxford: Oxford University Press.

Winter, E. O. (1969), 'Grammatical question technique as a way of teaching science students to write progress reports: the use of the short text in teaching', mimeo, The English Institute, University of Trondheim.

—— (1970), 'Connection in science material: a proposition about the semantics of clause relations', in *Science and Technology as a Second Language* (CILT Reports and Papers 7), London: Centre for Information on Language Teaching and Research, 41–52.

—— (1974), 'Replacement as a function of repetition: a study of some of its principal features in the clause relations of contemporary English', PhD thesis, University of London.

—— (1976), 'Fundamentals of information structure: a pilot manual for further development according to student need', mimeo, Hatfield Polytechnic.

—— (1977a), 'A clause-relational approach to English texts: a study of some predictive lexical items in written discourse', *Instructional Science* (special issue) 6, 1: 1–92.

—— (1977b), *Replacement as a Function of Repetition: A Study of Some of its Principal Features in the Clause Relations of Contemporary English*, Ann Arbor, MI: University Microfilms, no. 77–70,036.

—— (1979), 'Replacement as a fundamental function of the sentence in context', *Forum Linguisticum*, 4, 2: 95–133.

—— (1982), *Towards a Contextual Grammar of English: The Clause and its Place in the Definition of Sentence*, London: Allen & Unwin.

—— (1986), 'Clause relations as information structure: two basic text structures in English', in R. M. Coulthard (ed.), *Talking about Text*, Birmingham: English Language Research, 88–108.

—— (1992), 'The notion of unspecific versus specific as one way of analysing the information of a fund-raising letter', in W. C. Mann and S. A. Thompson (eds), *Discourse Descriptions: Diverse Analyses of a Fund-Raising Text*, Amsterdam: Benjamins, 131–70.

Young, R. E. and A. L. Becker (1965), 'Towards a modern theory of rhetoric: a tagmemic contribution', *Harvard Educational Review*, 35: 450–68.

Young, R. E., A. L. Becker and K. L. Pike (1970), *Rhetoric: Discovery and Change*, New York: Harcourt, Brace & World.